Officially Endorsed by
The Congressional Medal of Honor Society

THE SPIRIT OF AMERICA

The Biographies of Forty Living
Congressional Medal of Honor Recipients

by Hugh Kayser

"I would rather have the right to wear this medal,
than be President of the United States."
                    Dwight D. Eisenhower

An ✺ ETC Publication

```
Library of Congress Cataloging in Publication Data

Kayser, Hugh,        1926-
     Spirit of America.

     "Officially endorsed by the Congressional Medal of
Honor Society."
     Includes appendices.
     1. Medal of Honor.      2. United States—History,
Military—20th century—Biography.      3. United States—
Armed Forces—Biography.      I. Title.

UB433.K38            355.1'342'0922 [B]            81-12533
ISBN 0-88280-087-6                                  AACR2
```

Published by ETC Publications
Palm Springs
California, 92263-1608

Printed in the United States of America.

CONTENTS

THE MEDAL OF HONOR

The Medal of Honor, sometimes called the Congressional Medal of Honor, was created in the name of the Congress of the United States of America during the Civil War of 1861-1865 to be awarded to members of our Armed Forces for extraordinary courage and conspicuous gallantry at the risk of life above and beyond the call of duty while engaged in action with an enemy of the United States. It is the highest honor our country can bestow on its greatest heroes.

Since inception only 3,411 Medals of Honor have been awarded to America's fighting men although more than thirty million military personnel have served during wartimes from 1861 until the present. "The first Medals of Honor awarded following enactment of the law which established the decoration went to 19 Union Army volunteers of the raiding party sent by General Mitchell in April 1862, to sabotage the vital Confederate rail link between Atlanta and Chattanooga. Disguised as civilians, the raiders captured the locomotive 'General' at Big Shanty, Ga., 200 miles deep in enemy territory. Under close pursuit by the Confederates, the party fled north, attempting to burn bridges and destroy track along the way, but after 90 miles, the 'Great Locomotive Chase' came to an end. In a few days, all of the raiders were captured and eight were tried and executed. On March 25, 1863, six of the party arrived in Washington after parole from a Confederate prison, and these six men were the first to be presented with Medals of Honor by Secretary of War Stanton. Medals were subsequently awarded to 13 other members of the raiding party, some posthumously."*

Medals of Honor have been awarded during the following wars and campaigns—Civil War, 1861-1865—The Indian Campaigns, 1863-1898—The Korean Campaign, 1871—The Spanish-American War, 1898—The Philippine Insurrection, 1899-1913—The Boxer Rebellion, 1900—the Action Against Philippine Outlaws, 1911—The Mexican Campaign (Vera Cruz), 1911—The Haitian Campaign, 1915—The Dominican Campaign, 1916—World War I, 1917-1918—The Haitian Campaign, 1919-1920—The Second Nicaraguan Campaign, 1925—World War II, 1941-1945—the Korean Conflict, 1950-1953 and The Vietnam War, 1963-1973. Also Medals of Honor have been awarded during interim periods and to certain individuals in peacetime and to Unknown Soldiers of the United States, Belgium, Great Britain, France, Italy and Rumania.

In the past there have been eight Medals of Honor awarded by special legislation to individuals for peacetime heroism. However, the stringent requirements currently needed to even be recommended for the Medal of Honor preclude an individual being awarded the CMH unless that person has been a member of our Armed Forces engaged in action against an enemy of the United States. For example, Charles A. Lindbergh was a recipient of the Medal of Honor for his historic flight from New York to Paris in 1927, but none of our gallant spacemen have thusly been honored in current times. During the period of World War I through Vietnam more than half of the Medal of Honor recipients received their award posthumously. The late President and General of the Army, Dwight D. Eisenhower, refused to allow Congress to recommend him for the Medal of Honor since he had not been in actual close combat with the enemy during World War II.

*Medal of Honor Recipients, 1863-1978, U.S. Government Printing Office, Washington, D.C., 1979.

It has been the policy of the Armed Forces to restrict women to non-combatant roles during wars while serving on active duty. This would normally preclude a woman from receiving or being recommended for the Medal of Honor. However, Dr. Mary Edwards Walker was awarded the Medal of Honor for services during the Civil War.

A complete listing of America's Medal of Honor Recipients is reproduced as an appendix to this book from "Medal of Honor Recipients, 1863-1978," Senate Committee Print Number 3, as prepared by the Committee On Veterans' Affairs, United States Senate, February 14th, 1979, and printed by the United States Printing Office, Washington, D.C. In 1980 two men, Matt Urban of Holland, Michigan and Tony Casamento of West Islip, Long Island were presented with Medals of Honor by president Carter for their actions above and beyond the call of duty during World War II. Matt Urban's life sketch is presented in this book. On February 24, 1981, Master Sgt. Roy P. Benavidez of El Campo, Texas was awarded the Medal of Honor by President Reagan in a ceremony at the Pentagon, Washington, D.C.

"The modern hero, the modern individual who dares to heed the call and seek the mansion of that presence with whom it is our whole destiny to be atoned, cannot, indeed must not, wait for his community to cast off its slough of pride, fear, rationalized avarice, and sanctified misunderstanding. 'Live', Nietzsche says, 'as though the day were here.' It is not society that is to guide and save the creative hero, but precisely the reverse. And so, every one of us shares the supreme ordeal— carries his tribe's victories, but in the silence of his personal despair."*

*Joseph Campbell, *The Hero with a Thousand Faces,* The Bollinger Series, Pathenon Books, New York, 1949, XVII, p. 391.

"The Congressional Medal of Honor Society of the United States, was chartered by the 85th Congress under a legislative act signed into law by President Eisenhower on August 14, 1958. The purposes of the society are—

'To form a bond of friendship and comradeship among all holders of the Medal of Honor.

'To protect, uphold, and preserve the dignity and honor of the Medal at all times and on all occasions.

'To protect the name of the Medal, and individual holders of the Medal from exploitation.

'To provide appropriate aid to all persons to whom the Medal has been awarded, and their widows or their children.

'To serve our country in peace as we did in war.

'To inspire and stimulate our youth to become worthy citizens of our country.

'To foster and perpetuate Americanism.' "*

"Ask not what your country can do for you; ask what you can do for your country."**

---

*Page 6, "Medal of Honor Recipients, 1863-1978", Senate Committee Print No. 3, February 14, 1979, U.S. Government Printing Office, Washington, D.C.

**From the inaugural address of John F. Kennedy.

FOREWORD

Oh, America, you melting pot of the world, you brotherhood of people, you most beloved of countries with your Red, White and Blue Flag of Freedom, there are those people and evil forces who wish to tear you down, to destroy your soul, and to send you crashing into oblivion.

Therefore, your brave humanitarian and gallant heritage must now be narrated through the lives and deeds, thoughts and aspirations of those heroic men whose souls are portrayed in this book as living testimony of your greatness so that all Americans will rededicate themselves to the immortal words of Emma Lazarus which are inscribed on the Statue of Libery in New York harbor:

"Not like the brazen giant of Greek fame,
　　With conquering limbs astride from land to land;
Here at our sea-washed, sunset gates shall stand
　　A mighty woman with a torch, whose flame
　　Is the imprisoned lightening, and her name
　　Mother of Exiles.
From her beacon-hand glows world-wide welcome;
　　Her mild eyes command
　　The air-bridged harbor that twin cities fame.
'Keep ancient lands, your storied pomp!' cries she
　　With silent lips. 'Give me your tired, your poor,
　　Your huddled masses yearning to breathe free,
The wretched refuse of your teeming shore,
　　Send these, the homeless, tempest-tost to me,
　　I lift my lamp beside the golden door!' "

DEDICATION

This book is dedicated to the 273 living members of the Congressional Medal of Honor Society, who, in the immortal words of John F. Kennedy, are "the watchmen on the walls of world freedom."

ACKNOWLEDGEMENT

A deep debt of gratitude is hereby acknowledged to Colonel Charles W. Davis, USA (Ret), President of The Congressional Medal of Honor Society, without whose great enthusiasm and kind assistance this book could never have been created. Colonel Davis, a member of the 25th Infantry Division during World War II, was awarded the Medal of Honor for supreme gallantry above and beyond the call of duty while in combat on Guadalcanal Island in 1943.

"While the storm clouds gather
Far across the sea,
Let us swear allegiance
To a land that's free;
Let us all be grateful
For a land so fair,
As we raise our voices
In a solemn prayer."*

*First stanza of "God Bless America" written by Irving Berlin, 1938.

PART I
THE VERA CRUZ INCIDENT
1914

A navy crew from the U.S.S. Dolphin went ashore at Tampico, Mexico on April 6, 1914 to purchase supplies. They were arrested by Mexican soldiers and marched through the streets of Tampico under armed guard. After the refusal of Mexican authorities to apologize and to salute the American flag, President Woodrow Wilson, at a joint session of Congress on April 20th, requested approval for use of the armed forces of the United States to obtain recognition of the rights and dignity of the United States from the President of Mexico, General Victoriano Hueta.

In part, President Wilson stated, "There can in what we do be no thought of aggression or of selfish aggrandizement. We seek to maintain the dignity and authority of the United States only because we wish to always keep our great influence unimpaired for the uses of liberty, both in the United States and wherever else it may be employed for the benefit of mankind."

Congress approved his request for a show of force in Mexico and disclaimed any hostility to the Mexican people or any purpose to make war upon Mexico. A task force was dispatched to Vera Cruz.

"Accordingly, Adm. Fletcher landed with a regiment of marines from the Prairie, Utah, and Florida together with a

1

seaman battalion from the latter ship. These forces, augmented by seamen from the Utah as the engagement developed, seized the customhouse and other vital facilities near the waterfront. Marines and bluejackets advanced into the city despite street fighting and sniper fire.

"Mexican troops firing from the naval school near the pier were taken under fire by naval vessels. The end of the first day found only about one-half of the city cleared of the Mexican forces.

"During the night Adm. Fletcher took personal command ashore with additional forces landed, and Marine regiments under Lt. Col. Wendell C. Neville and Maj. Albertus W. Catlin resumed the difficult work of clearing their sector of snipers shooting from windows and the tops of buildings.

"By noon of the third day, buildings had been searched, firearms confiscated and strong outposts established around the sandhills to the sea. Before Army detachments were sent to Vera Cruz to take over occupation of the city, 15 Americans had been killed and 56 wounded."*

Fifty-six gallant American military men earned the Medal of Honor during the Vera Cruz incident. They all survived. The brave actions of the only living Medal of Honor survivor of Vera Cruz is related on the following pages.

*pgs. 407 & 408, *Medal of Honor Recipients, 1863-1978*, U.S. Government Printing Office, Washington, February 14, 1979.

GEORGE M. LOWRY

George M. Lowry is a retired Rear Admiral of the U.S. Navy. He currently lives in Carmel, California. Born to Ricardo St. Phillip Lowry and Annie Maus Lowry in Erie, Pennsylvania on October 27, 1889, Admiral Lowry is of Scotch-Irish and German ancestry. His father was a newspaper editor in Erie. His grandfather, Commodore Reigert B. Lowry, for whom the missile destroyer U.S.S. LOWRY was named, served in the U.S. Navy during the Civil War, and his great-grandfather was Robert K. Lowry, the first diplomatic representative to Venezuela, appointed by President James Monroe.

Rear Admiral Lowry was married in 1920 to the former Caroline Coleman of Burlingame, California. She died in 1979. Their son, Dr. Ritchie P. Lowry, is a professor at Boston College and the author of many books. Mrs. Ann Lowry Brawner of Atherton, California is the daughter of Admiral Lowry. He also has six grandchildren and four great-grandchildren.

After attending Erie High School, Admiral Lowry graduated from the U.S. Naval Academy in 1911. He served in the U.S. Navy from 1912 until 1927, at which time he became a General Partner in the Investment Banking Firm of Sutro & Company in San Francisco, California. In 1940 he was recalled to active duty with the rank of Lieutenant Commander and retired from the U.S. Navy in 1947 as a Rear Admiral. Upon his retirement, Admiral Lowry returned to Sutro & Company in San Francisco as a General Partner. He served in that capacity until 1956, at which time he became a Special Partner.

Standing five feet, eight inches in height, Admiral Lowry weighs 150 pounds. At his current age of 91, Admiral Lowry is in good health, although he was wounded in the leg at Vera Cruz in 1914.

Early in his naval career, Admiral Lowry commanded the historic U.S.S. Niagra, original flagship of Commodore Perry, on the memorable cruise through the Great Lakes in 1913, commemorating the 100th anniversary of the Battle of Lake Erie, War of 1812. He served for many years on the Armed Forces Committee of the San Francisco Chamber of Commerce, as Vice President of the San Francisco Council and Northern California Chairman of the Navy League of the United States, as regional Vice President and Director of the Defense Orientation Conference Association of Washington, D.C., and as a member of the Board of Directors of the Carmel Foundation. In 1979, Admiral Lowry gifted securities to the Naval War College in Newport, Rhode Island, to establish the RADM George M. Lowry Professorship.

On December 4, 1915, the then LTJG George M. Lowry was awarded the Congressional Medal of Honor for leading his men, as head of the First Company, U.S.S. FLORIDA Battalion, with "skill, courage, and extraordinary heroism" in both day's fighting in the engagement of Vera Cruz, April 21 and 22, 1914. Ensign Lowry's company was the first to land at Vera Cruz on the morning of April 21, with orders to capture the Customs House to prevent a foreign merchant ship from landing arms and ammunition for President Herta of Mexico. His citation for the Medal of Honor reads:

> LOWRY, GEORGE MAUS
> Rank and organization: Ensign, U.S. Navy. Place and date: Vera Cruz, Mexico, 21-22 April 1914. Entered service at Pennsylvania. Birth: Erie, Pa. G. O. No: 177, 4

December 1915. Citation: For distinguished conduct in battle, engagements of Vera Cruz, 21-22 April 1914. Ens. Lowry was in both days' fighting at the head of his company, and was eminent and conspicuous in his conduct, leading his men with skill and courage.

A more comprehensive description of Admiral Lowry's role in the engagement at Vera Cruz is found in Jack Sweetman's THE LANDING AT VERA CRUZ: 1914 (Annapolis, Maryland: United States Naval Institute, 1968):

As the First Company marched down Morales Street toward the Customs House across the city, heavy fire was encountered from rooftops, houses, and buildings. Since the Company could not continue without heavy casualties, Ensign Lowry called for five volunteers to go with him down an alley and along an open warehouse to the Customs House. Advancing against enemy machine gun fire from the warehouse and a cross-fire from a hotel on the other side of the street, the group dislodged the enemy. One volunteer was killed and two were wounded. Under fire, Ensign Lowry, with a leg wound, and the two remaining volunteers scaled a side wall and balustrade of the Customs House, broke through a window, and overpowered the armed Mexican Customs' personnel.

Admiral Lowry feels that, "In a world full of tension, distrust, and hatred there is a grave responsibility for Americans to maintain the freedom of the seas and resist aggression."

His advice to the youth of America and to all Americans is "Be willing to engage in unostentatious hard work and do the best you can. Do everything well, not slighting chores, commitments, or duties which may seem to you to be unimportant or frivolous. Everything has a meaning and a place, even seemingly routine activities. Also, perform everything the very best way you can and don't worry about whether that way is great or small. There is a place and need for all kinds of talents and abilities in our country and the world. Small tasks are often as honorable as large ones. If you serve others well, they will admire you, and the admiration of colleagues, friends, citizens, and co-workers is the highest reward one can receive."

PART II
WORLD WAR I
1914-1918

The assassination of Archduke Francis Ferdinand, heir to the throne of Austria-Hungary, and his wife Sophie, on June 28, 1914, on a bridge in an open carriage in Sarajevo (now a part of Yugoslavia) was the overt act which began World War I. Austria-Hungary believed that Serbia had planned the death of Ferdinand and a month later declared war on Serbia. However, there were underlying reasons of greater significance which actually caused World War I: the growth of nationalism, the competition for colonies and land, and the use of secret diplomatic and military alliances which began in the latter part of the nineteenth century.

On August 1, 1914 Germany declared war on Russia. When Germany invaded Belgium three days later, Great Britain entered the war. Germany then declared war on France on August 14. By October of 1914, the Central Powers of Austria-Hungary, Germany, the Ottoman Empire and Bulgaria were at war with the Allies, comprised of Belgium, France, Great Britain, Russia and Serbia. Ultimately, Brazil, China, Costa Rica, Cuba, Greece, Guatemala, Haiti, Honduras, Italy, Japan, Liberia, Montenegro, Nicaragua, Panama, Portugal, Romania, San Marino, Siam, and the United States joined the Allies in the war against the Central Powers.

The United States attempted for three years to stay neutral. However, the indiscriminate sinking of both American and Allied ships with the loss of American lives by the German submarines, plus the proposal of Germany to assist Mexico in reconquering the land which she lost in the Southwestern United States in 1836 at the Battle of San Jacinto, forced the United States to declare war on Germany on April 6, 1917.

More than 22,800,000 military personnel fought on the side of the Central Powers while the Allies mobilized over 42,000,000 men and women. For the first time in the history of warfare, tanks were introduced into the conflict. Basically WWI was a war of the trenches; grenades, mortars, and heavy artillery were developed. The airplane and the submarine became death dealing weapons and poison gas was first used by the Germans.

The Allies suffered over 19,000,000 casualties while the Central Powers losses were approximately 13,000,000. Also civilian deaths attributed directly to the war totaled about 5,000,000. The total cost of the war was 337 billions of dollars. The casualties of the United States were 320,518. Of that number, 116,516 Americans lost their lives, 204,002 were wounded and 4,500 either became prisoners or were listed as missing in action.

World War I officially ended on November 11, 1918 but the overly punitive peace treaties which were signed after the cessation of hostilities paved the way for World War II, some twenty-one years later. The irony of WWI was that it was commonly referred to "as the war to end all wars."

In 1920 the League of Nations was created by the Allies for the purpose of maintaining peace throughout the world. However, it failed to prevent the attack by Italy against Ethiopia in 1935 and the second World War which began with the invasion of Poland by Germany in 1939. When the United

Nations was formed after the end of the second World War, the League of Nations was disbanded.

One hundred twenty-seven gallant Americans earned the Medal of Honor during World War I. Only 94 survived. The personal accounts of two of the living Medal of Honor recipients of World War I follows.

PHIL C. KATZ

Phil C. Katz, who was born in San Francisco, California, is the oldest living recipient of The Medal of Honor. He was born on December 12, 1887. During a typical week, at age 93, he swims three-eights of a mile four or five times a week and walks a mile at least twice a week. In addition to his regular exercise, he goes deep-sea fishing six to eight times a year and spends one month each year on his favorite stream in northern California, fly-fishing for trout and steelheads. He is five feet, nine inches tall and weighs 150 pounds. He has no physical impairments.

His father's parents came to America from Germany. His mother's forbearers were Scotch and English. He was born and raised in the Protestant religion. He had a year and one half of high school and is the retired Public Administrator of the city of San Francisco.

General "Black Jack" Pershing, the commander of the American Expeditionary Forces in Europe during World War I, personally presented Phil Katz with The Medal of Honor. In Phil Katz's words, "I was proud when General Pershing pinned on the Medal but I did not realize at the time what the Medal really meant." His citation for the Medal of Honor reads:

KATZ, PHILLIP C.
Rank and organization: Sergeant, U.S. Army, Company C, 363d Infantry, 91st Division. Entered service at San Francisco, Calif. Birth: San Francisco, Calif. G. O. No: 16, W.D., 1919. Citation: After his

13

company had withdrawn for a distance of 200 yards on a line with the units on its flanks, Sgt. Katz learned that one of his comrades had been left wounded in an exposed position at the point from which the withdrawal had taken place. Voluntarily crossing an area swept by heavy machine-gun fire, he advanced to where the wounded soldier lay and carried him to a place of safety.

Phil Katz quite modestly describes his most courageous and unselfish action that saved his friend's life—"When I heard that my friend was left wounded in an exposed position, I said to our Lieutenant, I was going out for him so that he would know where I was if I did not come back.'

"The Lieutenant said it was very risky and I replied 'That Page would come for me' so the Lieutenant said go ahead and I went.

"Being an American means everything to me," affirms Phil Katz. "I have been around the world twice and have been to many foreign countries but would not trade all of them for my home in San Francisco."

His advice to the youth of America is—"Get an education and do not be afraid of hard work or self denial. Live each day so that you can look anyone in the eye and when you go to bed at night be able to say to yourself 'I have done my best.'

"We have the greatest country in the world and have more freedom in ten minutes than some people have in two years. It's up to you to preserve this freedom. At times it may seem like a struggle but if you could only see the way many people have to live, you would know it was worth while, so keep America forever free."

LOUIS M. VAN IERSEL

An article, titled "The Greatest Living Hero of the World War," written by H.W. Scott after World War I for the American Legion Navy Post 278 in California, relates the incredible saga of Louis M. Van Iersel.

"Louis M. Van Iersel was born in Holland in 1895. He worked in Krupp's Ammunition factory in Germany in 1914. Torpedoed in English Channel in 1915. As a sailor on a Norwegian ship, he saved the crew of 27 on the British Schooner, 'Little Secret,' in Feb., 1917, on a stormy, cold sea, by the breach buoy method.

"Landed in Jersey and drove a coal cart until he learned enough English to join the American Army, as he only spoke Dutch, French, German and Belgium (sic). In June, 1918, he joined our army and for the first six months he did K.P. duty as he was looked upon as a spy. He has four battle clasps.

"On July 18th, at Soissons, during a retreat with 80 percent casualty, he and another comrade carried seventeen wounded men from no-man's land in the trenches. He was wounded three times and gassed twice, but spent only ten days in the hospital. Walked six days to get back into action with his old outfit after leaving hospital. Received Croix de Guerre with Silver Star, as per French Order No. 14599 below.

"French Citation No. 11728, Croix de Guerre with Palm received for capturing five officers and 60 men by telling them he was a German spy in an American uniform. In gaining this trench position, he had his shoes shot off in a shell hole and he clubbed the German machine-gunner before entering the trench. (With the loss of his shoes he lost his temper.)

"November 9th, 1918, U.S. Order No. 16043, Croix de Guerre with Palm: At Mouzon on the Seine river. Was ordered by Major Janda to cross the river and find out what he could. He did so and talked to the German machine-gunner, found out their position and that a terrible barrage would be put over before daylight. Swimming back, he gave this information to his superiors, saving in excess of 1,000 American casualties. This engagement won him the Congressional Medal of Honor from the United States, Medal Militaire of France, Italian War Cross, the highest award of Montenegro, and about ten more of lesser value.

"Was in the Army of Occupation. Smuggled himself back into Holland after the war. Married the girl of his choice and two years later he returned for her. He weighs 118 pounds, is five foot three inches tall and works for the City of Los Angeles, Calif., off and on at common laborer's wages. Receives $39.00 per month compensation for bronchitis received from a gas attack. Has three children of school age and is so nervous he cannot even drive a car."

The citation for Sergeant Van Iersel's Medal of Honor reads:

VAN IERSEL, LUDOVICUS M. M.
Rank and organization: Sergeant, U.S. Army, Company M, 9th Infantry, 2nd Division. Place and date: At Mouzon, France, 9 November 1918. Entered service at: Glen Rock, N.J. Birth: Holland. G. O. No: 34, W.D., 1919. Citation: While a member of the reconnaissance patrol, sent out at night to ascertain the condition of a damaged bridge in the face of heavy machine-gun and rifle fire from a range of only 75 yards. Crawling alone along the debris of the ruined bridge he came upon a trap, which gave way and precipitated him into the water. In spite of the swift current he succeeded in swimming across the stream and found a lodging place among the

timbers on the opposite bank. Disregarding the enemy fire, he made a careful investigation of the hostile position by which the bridge was defended and then returned to the other bank of the river, reporting this valuable information to the battalion commander."

General "Black Jack" Pershing, Commander-in-Chief of the American Expeditionary Forces, personally presented Louis Van Iersel with the Medal of Honor on March 18, 1919 at a 2nd Division review in Vallendar, Germany.

When Sgt. Van Iersel's Commanding Officer informed him that he was going to do his utmost to get him the Medal of Honor, Louis said, "that's nice." His Commanding Officer just shook his head in vexation.

Although Louis Van Iersel took out his citizenship papers the same day he enlisted in the U.S. Army on June 5, 1917, he did not become an American citizen until after the war. His wife died on April 23, 1979. They were married for over 58 years. He has three sons, eight grandchildren, and 14 great-grandchildren. Louis Van Iersel is a Catholic and belongs to St. Rita's Parish in Sierra Madre, California, where he has been an usher for 25 years.

After his discharge from the Army in September of 1919 at Fort Dix, New Jersey, Louis Van Iersel worked on a coal wagon. From February of 1920 until March of 1921, he operated an ice cream and candy store in Passau, New Jersey. Then he and his wife moved to Los Angeles, California where he attended a Federal Class at UCLA to become a powerhouse operator. However his lungs were so fragile from being gassed in France that he couldn't work inside. He then took a position with the Los Angeles Survey Division where he worked until his retirement in 1954. He presently is 100 percent disabled due to his military injuries.

Louis Van Iersel deeply believes in America and is concerned about "the way some of the lawmakers are trying to mess us up."

As for the youth of America, "I hope they will feel this country is worth fighting for any and all times."

PART III
WORLD WAR II
1939-1945

Germany's invasion of Poland on September 1, 1939 began World War II. It was truly a global war with major battlefields and engagements in Asia, Europe, North Africa, the Atlantic and Pacific Oceans, the islands of the Pacific and on the Mediterranean Sea. Fighting occurred on the land, on the sea, and in the air in almost every part of the world. Over fifty countries participated in WWII.

On the Allies side Argentina, Australia, Belgium, Bolivia, Brazil, Canada, Chile, China, Columbia, Costa Rica, Cuba, Czechoslovakia, Denmark, the Dominican Republic, Ecuador, Egypt, El Salvador, Ethiopia, France, Great Britain, Greece, Guatemala, Haiti, Honduras, India, Iran, Iraq, Lebanon, Liberia, Luxembourg, Mexico, the Netherlands, New Zealand, Nicaragua, Norway, Panama, Paraguay, Peru, Poland, Russia, San Marino, Saudi Arabia, South Africa, Syria, Turkey, the United States, Uruguay, Venezuela, and Yugoslavia opposed the Axis which was composed of Bulgaria, Finland, Germany, Hungary, Italy, Japan, and Rumania.

The basic reasons for World War II were the rise of dictatorships in Germany, Italy and Japan, the unsolved problems left from WWI, and the craving of Germany, Italy and Japan for more land.

In terms of casualties, World War II was mind boggling. About 55,000,000 civilian and military personnel were killed during the years of 1939-45. Over 10,000,000 Allied servicemen died while the Axis suffered almost 6,000,000 deaths. The total estimated cost of World War II was $1,150,000,000,000. The entire world felt the effects of the war.

The atomic age began in World War II. Ballistic missiles were introduced as well as jet aircraft, huge tanks plus great fleets of bombers. Airborne troops were deployed, jumping from planes and landing in gliders.

During World War I, the United States had 2,800,000 men in service. In the last year of World War II, 1945, the strength of the U.S. Army was approximately 6,000,000. The U.S. Navy had 3,400,000 in uniform, the Army Air Corps personnel was 2,400,000 while the U.S. Marines totaled 484,000 on duty and the U.S. Coast Guard's complement of personnel was 170,000.

On December 7, 1941, without warning or declaration of war, Japan attacked Pearl Harbor in Hawaii. Up to that time the United States was not directly involved in the war, although we were supplying war materials to the Allies. The day after Pearl Harbor the United States declared war on Japan. On December 11, 1941, Germany and Italy declared war on the United States. Congress then declared war on Germany and Italy.

The total casualties suffered by the United States during the four years of World War II in which our nation was involved were 1,215,954, including 405,399 killed, 227,815 wounded and 139,709 servicemen either taken prisoner or missing in action. In terms of dollars expended during World War II, the United States spent approximately ten times more than she spent in all of her previous wars combined.

Germany surrendered on May 7, 1945 at Reims, France. After the United States dropped an atomic bomb on Hiroshima, Japan on August 6, 1945 and a second atomic bomb on Nagasaki three days later, Japan quickly capitulated. On September 2, 1945 the Allies and Japan signed the surrender agreement aboard the U.S. battleship, Missouri, in Tokyo Bay, officially ending World War II.

On October 24, 1945, shortly after cessation of hostilities, the United Nations was established with headquarters in New York City. The basic purposes of the United Nations are to maintain international peace and security, to develop friendly relations among nations, to achieve international cooperation in solving problems, and to serve as a center for attaining these ends.

The United Nations, even though having many failures, has been much more effective in the years since WWII than the League of Nations was after World War I. This fact is evident in the significant achievements of the United Nations in halting the Arab-Israel war of 1949, the Korean war in 1953, and the Suez Canal dispute in 1956. Of far greater consequence is the salient fact that after 35 years existence of the United Nations there has been no World War III.

Four hundred seventy gallant American military men earned the Medal of Honor during World War II. Only 225 survived. On the following pages the personal, heart-rending accounts of 21 of these living Medal of Honor recipients are reported.

LUCIAN ADAMS

On April 22, 1945, a slender Staff/Sergeant, Lucian Adams, a member of the 30th Infantry Regiment of the 3rd Infantry Division, received the Medal of Honor from Lt. General Alexander Patch, 7th Army Commander, while standing at attention in the Adolph Hitler Plaza in Nurenberg, Germany. As General Patch hung our nation's highest award around the neck of the 22 year old native Texan of Hispanic ancestry, Lucian Adams thought of his eight brothers who also were serving in the armed forces of his beloved country. Then he thanked God, his mother and all who had prayed for him.

Lucian Adams was born on October 26, 1922 in Port Arthur, Texas. Prior to entering service four days before Christmas in 1943, Lucian Adams had completed the ninth grade of school at Woodrow Wilson Junior High. Subsequent to being honorably discharged he received his high school diploma via the GED program. He has two daughters, Herlinda Adams, age 25, Grace Adams, age 24, and a son, Lucian Adams Jr., age 19. In January of 1946, he accepted employment with the Veterans Administration as a Contact Representative. Lucian Adams is currently working as a Veterans Benefit Counselor for the VA in San Antonio, Texas. Both of his parents were native Texans of Hispanic origin.

An article, entitled "Tornado From Texas," written by Herbert L. Schon, date and publication unknown, vividly describes the heroic actions of Lucian Adams in Germany on

October 28, 1944 which resulted in General Patch presenting the Medal of Honor to the 22 year old Staff Sergeant . . . "Diminutive, 22-year-old Staff Sergeant Adams was no novice at this game of fighting Germans. From the time he left his home at Port Arthur, Texas, to enter the Army in 1943, the sturdy-looking doughboy had done everything possible to master those tricks of the soldier trade which paid off in combat.

"During the campaign in Italy, Adams had won a name for his whirlwind tactics in slam-banging a way through enemy defensive positions. Recognition in the form of a Bronze Star Medal had come to him for numerous exploits as the Fifth Army pushed its way up the Italian boot. Enemy recognition had come, too, in the form of a wound which failed to slow the Texan up for any appreciable length of time.

"Thoughts of what had happened in Italy were far behind Adams now, however. His company, a unit of the 30th Infantry Regiment and part of the history-making, crack 3rd Infantry Division, had been told hours before of stubborn resistance nearby which was holding up the sweep of American arms across France toward the inevitable breaching of German border defense.

"In the Mortagne Forest, just beyond St. Die, a specialized enemy force had taken up positions, armed with automatic weapons, grenade launchers and machine pistols. These men of the widely-touted German 201st Mountain Infantry had been able to block off a supply line to assault companies of Sergeant Adams' battalion. Now his outfit had been given the perilous mission of unloosing that stranglehold on the vital supply line.

"This, Adams thought, was the sort of die-hard resistance that could make a great military sweep grind to a halt. These were the day-to-day events that often bogged troops down and made his native Texan landscape seem even more remote than the 3,000 miles which actually separated St. Die and Port Arthur.

"If only there were some way of speeding things up.

" 'All right men. Let's get moving.'

"The command interrupted any idle reflections on the situation which may have been going through Adams' mind. Slowly and cautiously his company moved forward into the cover of the cold, dark forest.

"Care was essential, but the Germans were not to be caught napping. The men had not moved many yards before the enemy opened up a deadly fire. Three men were killed by the initial blast from the strongly-entrenched German troops. The company commander, executive officer and four enlisted men lay wounded.

"Now the enemy fire started with intensive fury. Adams' platoon seemed deluged by the fatal fireworks. One German climbed into a knocked-out reconnaissance car and was operating a machine gun against the Texan's unit. Three others with machine pistols were raking the platoon front. It didn't take a military expert to see that the attack had been stopped cold, almost before it started.

"Then something happened.

"Like a tornado whipping across the Texas plains, the Port Arthur soldier grabbed a BAR and started off on what his platoon leader, Lieutenant Frank H. Harrell of Orlando, Florida, later called 'a one man wave of destruction.'

"Firing from the hip, Sergeant Adams dashed from tree to tree, blasting away at the well-entrenched Germans. The Krauts saw him coming and seemed to concentrate every bit of their fire power on Adams. Rifle grenades shattered the stately trees of the forest and sent down a shower of burned branches and twigs on him. Bursts from machine guns followed the veteran campaigner's steps as he dodged from one position to another. But nothing in the world seemed to be able to stop the advance of this solitary, khaki-clad figure moving swiftly through the green forest.

"Within ten yards of the first machine gun nest, and with the weapon firing straight at him, the soldier from the Lone Star State calmly pulled the pin of a hand grenade and, with all the nonchalance of a World Series pitcher, lobbed it into the gun's position. It was silenced immediately.

"Seemingly stunned by the fury of his attack, Sergeant Adams' platoon looked on in what amounted to open-mouthed amazement. Every second of his solo drive against the enemy photographed itself on the memory of his comrades, so that later Lieutenant Harrel was able to tell with graphic detail what happened then.

" 'Just as Adams' grenade killed the gunner of the first machine gun,' he said, 'the Kraut who had been manning the gun in the old reconnaissance car climbed out and threw several hand grenades at Sergeant Adams. He was only ten yards away at the time, and the Sergeant had moved outside the traversing area of the machine gun. While these grenades were exploding around him, Adams killed this German with only a short burst from his BAR.' "

"Bullets clipped branches off the evergreen trees. They fell within a few inches of his body. Rifle grenades exploded as they struck limbs of trees around him. Still Adams refused to seek cover, rejecting the thought that the 3rd Infantry Division punch wasn't strong enough to lay any resistance low.

"A second machine gun, about fifteen yards to his right, was Adams' next objective. The gun began opening up in earnest on the cool-headed sergeant. Deliberately he walked in the direction of the fire, threw a hand grenade, and silenced the emplacement. Two Germans who had been serving the gun saw the handwriting on the wall. They came out of foxholes alongside the gun, trembling, their hands held high.

"Now the tide was beginning to turn. Texas spunk was beginning to tell. Why stop?

"Later Lieutenant Harrell would speak of what happened.

" 'Adams continued into the thickest of the fire directed on him. All the time his BAR was spraying fire. Nothing seemed to stop him. He went on to kill five more of the enemy in their protected positions.

" 'I saw him go up to within fifty yards of a third machine gun emplacement. The Germans were still firing directly on him. Up came Adams' automatic rifle again. There was a long burst. The emplacement was out of action.' "

"That was enough for the German mountaineers. Destruction of the third machine gun shattered their last hope of stopping the seemingly invincible American. They took off in complete rout and the line of supply was quickly cleared.

"Army reports assayed the damage inflicted by the Texan in a more statistical manner: nine Germans killed, three enemy machine guns knocked out, dispersal of a specialized enemy force armed with automatic weapons and grenade launches. Result: reopening of a blocked supply route and advance toward the Third Reich.

"In a little more than an hour Staff Sergeant Lucian Adams had won a place for himself among the small and distinguished group whom men have judged to be the nations' outstanding warriors: the winners of the Medal of Honor."

"Being an American means to me, a free person, to do what one wishes with his or her future," affirms Lucian Adams.

His advice to the youth of America is: "Love and respect your country. Remember many Americans have fought and died for it. Be good citizens."

STANLEY BENDER

Staff Sergeant Stanley Bender was born in the coal mining town of Carlisle, West Virginia on Halloween, 1909. His parents, now deceased, immigrated to the United States of America from Lithuania. They Americanized their Lithuanian name of Benderous to Bender. The Bender family moved to another coal mining camp, Scarbro, West Virginia while Stanley was very young. Scarbro is approximately five miles from Stanley's present home in Fayetteville, West Virginia. He has fond childhood memories of growing up in Scarbro. However, when he was fourteen, his father died and young Stanley was sent to Chicago to live with a married sister. As Stanley remembers his father, he was a frail, sickly man, who had lost his sight in one eye.

Chicago was not the best of places for this young coal-miner's son to mature. He completed the seventh grade and went to work. By 1939 Stanley Bender had a series of jobs—working in the stock yards, driving a taxi, and as a helper on a delivery truck. Completely frustrated, at age 31, he enlisted in the Army on December 12, 1939 and requested to be stationed as far away from Chicago as possible.

Shortly before his discharge from the Army after World War II Stanley was married. He has one daughter, Evelyn Marie, age 34. He completed his high school requirements after the war, via GED, and became a Contact Representative for the Veterans Administration from which he is now retired. Stanley Bender is a Catholic. He is five feet, eight inches tall and weighs 160 pounds.

On January 21, 1945 Staff Sergeant Stanley Bender received the Medal of Honor in southern France from General Patch. His citation for our Country's highest military award reads:

BENDER, STANLEY

Rank and organization: Staff Sergeant, U.S. Army, Company E, 7th Infantry, 3rd Infantry Division. Place and date: Near La Lande, France, 17 August 1944. Entered service at: Chicago, Ill. Born: 31 October 1910, Carlisle, W. Va. G. O. No: 7, 1 February 1945. Citation: For conspicuous gallantry and intrepidity at risk of life above and beyond the call of duty. On 17 August 1944, near La Lande, France, he climbed on top of a knocked-out tank, in the face of withering machine-gun fire which had halted the advance of his company, in an effort to locate the source of this fire. Although bullets ricocheted off the turret at his feet, he nevertheless remained standing in full view of the enemy for over two minutes. Locating the enemy machine-guns on a knoll 200 yards away, he ordered two squads to cover him and led his men down an irrigation ditch, running a gauntlet of intense machine-gun fire, which completely blanketed 50 yards of his advance and wounded four of his men. While the Germans hurled hand grenades at the ditch, he stood his ground until his squad caught up with him, then advanced alone, in a wide flanking approach, to the rear of the knoll. He walked deliberately a distance of 40 yards, without cover, in full view of the Germans and under a hail of both enemy and friendly fire, to the first machine-gun and knocked it out with a single short burst. Then he made his way through the strongpoint, despite bursting hand grenades, toward the second machine-gun, 25 yards distant, whose two-man crew swung the machine-gun around and fired two bursts at him, but he walked calmly through the fire and, reaching the edge of the emplacement, dispatched the crew. Signaling his men to rush the rifle pits, he then walked 35 yards further to kill an enemy rifleman and returned to lead his squad in the destruction of the eight remaining Germans in the strongpoint. His audacity so inspired the remainder of the assault company that the men charged out of their positions, shouting and yelling, to overpower the enemy roadblock and sweep into town, knocking out two antitank guns, killing 37 Germans and capturing 26 others. He had sparked and led the assault company in an attack which overwhelmed the enemy, destroying a roadblock, taking a town, seizing intact three bridges over the Maravenne River, and capturing commanding terrain which dominated the area.

To Stanley Bender, "Being an American is something that I am very proud of. It is difficult to explain in words the pride I have inside of me for being an American. I have never been asked to spell it out in words before, and it takes a lot of thought to put on paper what you feel in your heart. Being an American means freedom and peace for everyone, the right to choose what you want to do with your own life . . . and the luxuries that we have in our homes that most foreigners may never know. I fought in World War II because I was proud to be an American and wanted to stand up for my country. And, even though age has mellowed me, if it became necessary, I would be proud to do so again."

His advice to the youth of America is, "Be sober, be strong, avoid bad habits and bad company, and learn a trade or a profession."

ORVILLE E. BLOCH

Colonel Orville E. Bloch is a retired professional soldier living in Seattle, Washington. He was born in Big Falls, Wisconsin. His father immigrated to the United States at the age of sixteen in the late 19th century, having fled the rule of the Czar in Eastern Russia. Originally the Blochs were from Germany but they ventured to Russia where a land grant was offered to the family.

Since his retirement in 1970, Colonel Bloch has been engaged in real estate development and apple production. He was married in 1945 to Beverly M. Asplured in Streeter, North Dakota. They have four children, the oldest is 33 and the youngest is 17. Colonel Bloch is a college graduate from North Dakota State. He is of the Lutheran faith.

Enlisting in the Army in February of 1942, he was sent to Officers' Candidate School at Fort Benning, Georgia and was shipped overseas in February of 1944. Orville E. Bloch is a slightly built man, being only five feet, four inches tall and weighs less than 150 pounds.

An article written in the Pittsburg Press, on February 16, 1945 by Lt. Cmdr. Michael A. Musmanno vividly describes the superhuman exploit of this great Infantry officer, then, Lt. Orville E. Bloch.

"When the history of the war in Italy is written, the battle of Firenzuola will make a very interesting chapter.

"In the broad plan of movement, Company E was charged with the taking of Hill 711 northeast of the town.

"Although encountering heavy artillery and mortar

opposition, the company kept pushing ahead until on the morning of Sept. 21 it reached a certain point where it was stopped in its tracks by murderous automatic fire emerging from three houses on the right forward flank.

"These old stone buildings, in an irregular file with their sides facing the Americans, produced a broadside of fire impossible to cope with. Platoons 1 and 2 were pinned down by the swords of lead stabbing from Hill 733 where the grim dwellings stood.

"At right angles to the file of houses, like the arm of a gigantic T on the ground, stretched the German line with riflemen established in foxholes which commanded the American position. Anywhere that a GI showed his head a German bullet came zipping toward it.

"On the following morning Lt. Orville Bloch decided to investigate the Heinie position by circling round its left flank. To reach the desired reconnoitering spot it would be necessary to snake off to the right a couple of hundred yards and then climb Hill 733, which lifted some 700 feet above the embattled plain beneath.

"Asking for and obtaining three volunteers, Lt. Bloch lay on his stomach and crawled the distance which took him to the foot of the hill, on the crest of which stood the first house, its rear window gaping out on the precipitous declivity below.

"It was so unlikely that anyone would dare to approach this building from that suicidal angle that Jerry would not even bother to place a sentinel here. In this assumption he was correct.

"Crawling and digging, Lt. Bloch and his men worked their way to a point directly beneath the strategic window, through which they now heard German voices in conversation.

"There are a hundred different ways of looking over an enemy-controlled wall, of which any one of 99 methods can only result in getting one's head shot off. But there is one way to accomplish the view without detection. Bloch was familiar with this method and, putting it to use, he beheld five Heinies shepherding a machine gun, which was now chattering its song of death into the valley where his comrades waited.

"The North Dakotan felt for his grenades and checked his carbine, the only weapons he carried. Poising for an instant he sprang over the wall into the very faces of the astounded Nazis, his carbine spitting fire in the semicircle before him.

"Reaching the machine gun he swung his leg in a vicious kick, upsetting the weapon and scattering its parts. The principal gunner fell, the others lunged at the young American who continued snapping the trigger of his carbine, and then, bewildered and frightened at this wrathful apparition, the Germans fled into the house and took up a position in the corner of the room. The 'apparition' dashed in after them brandishing a grenade above his head and calling out: 'Aufgaben!'

"Scared to the marrow, the cornered Germans flung their hands ceilingwards and chorused: 'Kamerad!'

"Pushing the prisoners out of the house at the point of his carbine, Lt. Bloch directed them to the edge of the hill and ordered them to slide. One by one they went over the embankment, rolling to the bottom in clouds of dust, glad to be out of the war.

"Twenty feet in front of the first house, the second began its long rambling spread. Hugging the west wall of the ancient building, which had numerous projections and coves like the jagged outline of some rocky coast, the lieutenant continuously advanced toward the forward left hand corner, where a second machine gun bounced in its rat-a-tat-tat-tat concerto.

"Arriving within pitching distance of the gunner who was

squinting over the barrel stuttering out its music of flames and lead, Lt. Bloch whipped out a grenade, tore off its clip, and hurled it.

"The grenade failed to explode, but its flight revealed the presence of the American, and in an instant the stammering barrel was speaking its staccato phrases of fire all around him. In the storm of projectiles, Bloch flung himself to the ground and into a fortunate indentation of the crazily-shaped house.

"While the bullets spat up dust and raised showers of splintered stone about him, Lt. Bloch manipulated his carbine into position so he could aim without exposing himself, and he brought down the enemy gunner.

"Correctly guaging that the other members of the crew would now storm his cover of concealment, Lt. Bloch withdrew to the rear of the building and over to the other side But there he walked into the direct fire of still another machine gun stationed at the rear of the third house, which was not on the same alignment as the other two and in this way commanded the entire right wall of the second house.

"This rambling habitation was one evidently intended for the accommodation of many families, as the largest rooms on the right side did not communicate with one another, each having its own entrances. The third enemy machine gunner, who was about 200 feet away, had Lt. Bloch in his vision constantly and he swung the nozzle of his gun like a garden hose.

"As one ducks through a sudden shower, the lieutenant dashed in the first doorway, held that spot for an instant, and then madly sprinted to the second door, in the attempt to narrow the distance between him and his opponent.

"By this time pandemonium reigned in the German position. The sudden appearances and disappearances of the deadly invader, the shouts of terror and screams of pain of those who had come into immediate contact with him, the inexorable pinging of his lethally accurate carbine, all combined in an agonizing wail for reinforcements. From the reserve line another machine gun crew with weapon was rushed forward to the defense.

"As Bloch sent his runner back to bring up five riflemen, he looked up to the mule trail which led down to the cluster of houses and espied what he later described to me as a 'picnic.' A German sergeant was hurrying down the trail leading a squad of men carrying another machine gun. Bloch and Serge Sherwood, who had joined him, leaned against a stone step and proceeded calmly to pick off these hurrying Germans like clay pigeons.

"In the meantime the crew of the second machine gun had taken refuge in a room on the left side of the house where their forces were increased by several who had dashed into it from the group which had come down the mule trail. As these demoralized men were collecting their wits, their Nemesis charged in on them firing from the hip and calling angrily for their surrender.

"One of the Nazis made an effort to resist, throwing his gun to his shoulder. The others yelled at him that it was useless to resist and cried to him to put up his hands. But Lt. Bloch had already spoken and the recalcitrant enemy stretched his length on the floor while his more reasoning comrades stumbled out of the room.

"There was one more machine gun throbbing its solo above the accompaniment of the mortar shells which were exploding in the area. It was in place at the forward end of the third house, and was manned by six Germans who now spotted Bloch at the same time he saw them.

"Allowing not a split second for deliberation, Lt. Bloch tore forward to this position, hurling a grenade and snapping the trigger of his carbine as rapidly as his finger joint could hinge and unhinge.

"Knowing they could not swing its muzzle about soon enough to stop the onrushing tornado, the men abandoned the machine gun and drew pistols which they fired point-blank at the yelling American, who kept demanding: 'Aufgaben! Aufgaben!'

"Two fell before his fire and the others raced into the house with the American at their heels. At the far end of the room they went to their knees, cowering before the unbelievable force which was wiping out the consolidated force singlehanded.

"They not only surrendered, but called out to the Germans in the nearby foxholes to give up also, not knowing what to expect from this incredible man.

"When the latter straightened up in their foxholes, some Americans, not knowing what had happened, fired. The five riflemen that Lt. Bloch had called forward were now with him and he directed them to acquaint the remainder of the company with the fact that all resistance had ceased.

"When the final count was taken, 74 Germans had surrendered, 12 were wounded and 10 were dead."

His official citation for the Medal of Honor reads:

BLOCH, ORVILLE EMIL
Rank and organization: First Lieutenant, U.S. Army, Company E, 338th Infantry, 85th Division. Place and date: Near Firenzuola, Italy, 22 September 1944. Entered service at: Streeter, N. Dak. Birth: Big Falls, Wis. G.O. No: 9, 10 February 1945. Citation: For conspicuous gallantry and intrepidity at risk of life above and beyond the call of duty. 1st Lt. Bloch undertook the task of wiping out five enemy machine gun nests that had held up the advance in that particular sector for one day. Gathering three volunteers from his platoon, the patrol snaked their way to a big rock, behind which a group of

the three buildings and five machine gun nests were located. Leaving the three men behind the rock, he attacked the first machine gun nest alone charging into furious automatic fire, kicking over the machine gun, and capturing the machine gun crew of five. Pulling the pin from a grenade, he held it ready in his hand and dashed into the face of withering automatic fire toward this second enemy machine gun nest located at the corner of an adjacent building 15 yards distant. When within 20 feet of the machine gun he hurled the grenade, wounding the machine gunner, the other two members of the crew fleeing into a door of the house. Calling one of his volunteer group to accompany him, they advanced to the opposite end of the house, there contacting a machine crew of five running toward the house. 1st Lt. Bloch and his men opened fire on the enemy crew, forcing them to abandon this machine gun and ammunition and flee into the same house. Without a moment's hesitation, 1st Lt. Bloch, unassisted, rushed through the door into a hail of small-arms fire, firing his carbine from the hip, and captured the seven occupants, wounding three of them. 1st Lt. Bloch with his men then proceeded to a third house where they discovered an abandoned enemy machine gun and detected another enemy machine gun nest at the next corner of the building. The crew of six spotted 1st Lt. Bloch the instant he saw them. Without a moment's hesitation he dashed toward them. The enemy fired pistols wildly in his direction and vanished through a door of the house. 1st Lt. Bloch followed them through the door, capturing six. Altogether 1st Lt. Bloch had singlehandedly captured 19 prisoners, wounding six of them and eliminating a total of five enemy machine gun nests. His gallant and heroic actions saved his company many casualties and permitted them to continue the attack with new inspiration and vigor.

On the 6th of February, 1945 Lt. Orville E. Bloch was presented with the Medal of Honor by General Lucian K. Truscott, 5th Army Commander, during a ceremony at 5th

Army Headquarters front. And on the 9th of February, 1945, he was flown back to the United States.

In an interview after his most heroic and gallant action, Lt. Bloch, who by now was called "Blockbuster" Bloch, stated, "I don't think I would have tried it if the Nazis hadn't been picking off our men so fast." He modestly explained, "I got so riled up I guess I just didn't realize what I was doing!"

Concerning his faith in the United States of America, Colonel Orville E. Bloch states, "I have seen much of this world, have served and visited in many countries, but nowhere is there anything comparable to our nation. We have so much to be grateful for. We veterans have had the good life, we have received what we deserved and above all, freedom. I am certain that those who failed to come back wanted it this way."

To the youth of America he emplores—"Be a good citizen, protect our heritage, life and freedom. The pursuit of happiness is not free. When called, one must stand ready to do his part in preserving our way of life."

ROBERT E. BUSH

On October 2, 1945, two days before his nineteenth birthday, while on his honeymoon, Robert E. Bush was presented with the Medal of Honor on the White House lawn by President Harry Truman. After receiving his honorable discharge from the U.S. Navy, Robert Bush completed high school in 1946. He then attended specialized college classes on the G.I. Bill, and in 1951 became a partner in a lumber business. Today he owns and manages three lumber yards in the state of Washington, plus a Redi-Mix Concrete plant. He and his wife, Wanda, have four children—three sons and a daughter. All three sons are in business with him. Robert and Wanda Bush recently celebrated their 35th wedding anniversary.

Robert Bush is six feet tall, weighs 209 pounds. He lost one eye in combat while on Okinawa and has shrapnel in his back and in one lung. When he was nine months of age, his mother and father divorced. He is Catholic and the Bush family regularly attends church. He is a Past President of The Congressional Medal of Honor Society. Robert Bush is of Irish and German-Irish extraction.

His citation for the Medal of Honor reads:

BUSH, ROBERT EUGENE
Rank and organization: Hospital Apprentice First Class, U.S. Naval Reserve, serving as Medical Corpsman with a rifle company, 2nd Battalion, 5th Marines, 1st Marine Division. Place and date: Okinawa Jima, Ryukyu Islands, 2 May 1945. Entered service at:

Washington. Born: 4 October 1926, Tacoma, Wash. Citation: For conspicuous gallantry and intrepidity at the risk of his life above and beyond the call of duty while serving as Medical Corpsman with a rifle company, in action against Japanese forces on Okinawa Jima, Ryukyu Islands, 2 May 1945. Fearlessly braving the fury of artillery, mortar and machine gun fire from strongly entrenched hostile positions, Bush constantly and unhesitatingly moved from one casuality to another to attend the wounded falling under the enemy's murderous barrages. As the attack passed over a ridge top, Bush was advancing to administer blood plasma to a marine officer lying wounded on the skyline when the Japanese launched a savage counterattack. In this perilously exposed position, he resolutely maintained the flow of lifegiving plasma. With the bottle held high in one hand, Bush drew his pistol with the other and fired into the enemy's ranks until his ammunition was expended. Quickly seizing a discarded carbine, he trained his fire on the Japanese charging point-blank over the hill, accounting for six of the enemy despite his own serious wounds and the loss of one eye suffered during his desperate battle in defense of the helpless man. With the hostile forces finally routed, he calmly disregarded his own critical condition to complete his mission, valiantly refusing medical treatment for himself until his officer patient had been evacuated, and collapsing only after attempting to walk to the battle aid station. His daring initiative, great personal valor, and heroic spirit of self-sacrifice in service of others reflect great credit upon Bush and enhance the finest traditions of the U.S. Naval Service.

It is of interest that Robert Bush's mother was a registered nurse during his formative years. He believes receiving the Medal of Honor has changed his life ... "I left home a boy and came back a man with some understanding of the cost paid by our forefathers for the precious Freedom we enjoy.

"The American way of life affords an opportunity to each

citizen to grow to whatever goal he or she sets. We are a free nation of free people. This, however, does not mean the price is free. I experienced the tail-end of the depression years and made up my mind that my family would not live in poverty. With this interest and high goal, and some financial help, I have attained those goals (35 years later), and am enjoying my work each day," so testifies Robert E. Bush, CMH, of Aberdeen, Washington.

His personal advice to the youth of America: "Freedom was not guaranteed by our forefathers, as we are not given the right to happiness, but, the right to pursue happiness. Our youth should accept their responsibility to do whatever is necessary to continue our land of the free and the home of the brave."

JOSE CALUGAS

On January 16, 1942 a mess Sergeant of Battery B, 88th Field Artillery, Jose Calugas, left his assigned duty on Bataan Island in the Philippines to determine why the American guns on the front lines had stopped firing. This is his description of the situation 38 years later: "The gun duel started early, about six in the morning, while we were fetching water along the creek. We had just finished our breakfast. The Japanese opened fire on our place at Culis, Bataan, Philippines. At about two in the afternoon our guns were silent. It was only the Japanese guns that we heard bombarding us. I was very much amazed so I went looking for my comrades. I was able to find 16 men along the creek and I asked them to go with me to the front lines. The 16 men were willing to follow me, so we organized ourselves to be five yards apart so the Japanese could not readily spot us. From our kitchen we went toward the front but a Japanese airplane bombed us and two were hit. The others ran to the rear echelon except for Lt. Garcia, a Philippine Army officer, and myself.

"The two of us proceeded to the front line and reached our gun position. Two officers were there, Lt. Chua and Major Beefsala (our Battalion Commander). The four of us decided to fight the Japanese. Major Beefsala delegated me to operate the cannon because I was the only one who could handle all the firing mechanisms of the cannon. Major Beefsala was the observer. We fired one shot for observation and it landed on the Japanese gun position. We continued firing and consumed around 72 rounds. At about four in the afternoon Major

Beefsala asked if I wanted to stay with the gun or to go with them to the rear echelon.

"I responded that I had to stay with my kitchen because it was my most important duty for without the kitchen the soldiers would starve. So I stayed and fired the gun again by myself. Upon sighting Japanese soldiers marching in columns at the Denalopihan bridge I caused a direct hit. I do not know how many Japanese soldiers were killed but I saw from the cannon telescope that many rounds fell on them.

"At about dark, I ran back to the rear echelon to pick up two trucks and drivers to go with me to the front to get my kitchen. We drove without lights and reached the place where our battalion had retreated at about eleven at night. The soldiers were very happy for they had not eaten for quite some time."

On April 30, 1945, after the Philippines had been liberated, General George C. Marshall, Chief of Staff, U.S. Army, personally presented Jose Calagas with the Medal of Honor at Camp Olivas, Pampanga, the Philippines. His family and parents were present for this unique ceremony. The citation of Jose Calugas reads:

CALUGAS, JOSE

Rank and organization: Sergeant, U.S. Army, Battery B, 88th Field Artillery, Philippine Scouts. Place and date: At Culis, Bataan Province, Philippine Islands, 16 January 1942. Entered service at: Fort Stotsenburg, Philippine Islands. Born: 29 December 1907, Barrio Tagsing, Leon, Iloilo, Philippine Islands. G.O. No: 10, 24 February 1942. Citation: The action for which the award was made took place near Culis, Bataan Province, Philippine Islands, on 16 January 1942. A battery gun position was bombed and shelled by the enemy until one gun was put out of commission and all the cannoneers were killed or wounded. Sgt. Calugas, a mess sergeant of another battery, voluntarily and without orders ran 1000 yards across the shell-swept area to the gun position. There he organized a volunteer squad which placed the gun back in commission and fired effectively against the enemy, although the position remained under constant and heavy Japanese artillery fire.

Jose Calugas remained in the Army after WWII was over and retired with the rank of Captain in April of 1957. At that time he was employed by Boeing Aircraft in Seattle, Washington. Having completed his high school education while on active duty in the Army, Boeing agreed to allow him to leave their employment in September of 1957 to enter college with the understanding that he would return to work after receiving his degree. In June of 1961 he was reemployed by the Boeing Company after completing his Bachelors in Business Administration at the University of Puget Sound. He retired from Boeing in January of 1972.

Captain Jose Calugas, Sr., is married with four children, Noel, age 43, Jose, Jr., age 40, Minerva, age 38, and Jorge, 35 years of age. His parents were born in the Philippines. He is of the Catholic faith. Standing five feet, four inches, he weighs 138 pounds. Captain Calugas suffered a severe stroke in 1978 and is partially disabled but walks with a cane. He attends church as his condition permits.

Concerning his most unselfish and courageous actions at Bataan, during the early days of WWII, Captain Calugas stated, "When the situation confronted me, I did not have any hesitation to fight and give my life for the cause of freedom and my country. It was not my assigned duty to go to the front line for I was a mess Sergeant but when our guns were silenced, I was determined and ready to give my life for my country. I feel great being an American. I am proud to be such and I humbly say, thank you and thank you."

His advice to the youth of America is, "Be a man and fight for America and protect America as much as you can whether at war or in peace time."

JUSTICE MARION CHAMBERS

In a feature article of The Washington Post by Thomas Whinship, dated November 2, 1950, titled "Twin Babies Spar with Truman As Father Gets Medal of Honor," the presentation of the Medal of Honor to Colonel Justice Marion Chambers, who currently resides in Rockville, Maryland is vividly described:

Twins Peter and Paul Chambers, aged 7 months, sparred with President Truman in the White House rose garden yesterday.

The playful scene completely stole the show from the boys' Marine hero father.

Col. Justice Marion Chambers, U.S.M.C.R. (Ret) of Rockville, Md., had come to the White House to receive the country's highest award—the Medal of Honor—for conspicuous gallantry at Iwo Jima.

Peter tried to cop the citation from the President's hands. Paul tried to swipe the President's handkerchief.

Colonel Chambers brought the twins, two other sons and a daughter, his wife and a dozen relatives to the ceremony.

"For conspicuous gallantry . . . above and beyond the call of duty at Iwo Jima", the President began solemnly. Peter reached from the arms of his 17-year-old sister, Patricia, and grabbed one of the sheets of the citation. He shook it violently.

Mr. Truman read on haltingly, as he gently fended off the chubby little hand. The twins were shifted. Peter to his mother's arms and Paul to Patricia who was at the President's shoulder.

"The photographers went wild. And Paul didn't disappoint them. He had an act, too.

"Paul lunged for Mr. Truman's handkerchief, managing to pull it partly from the President's breast pocket. Mr. Truman held the would-be hijacker's hand until the ceremony was over.

"Later in a picture-posing session, Mr. Truman balked at photographers' repeated requests for him to hold the twins' hands.

"They don't seem to like too much of this", said the President. "I don't want to make them cry."

Secretary of Defense George C. Marshall—looking on with Navy Secretary Francis Matthews and Gen. C.B. Cates, Marine Corps commandant—was concerned about the colonel's 8-year-old son, Justice, Jr.

Twice during the picture taking, Justice seemed to become hidden behind the grownups.

"Get that young man out where he can be seen. Those pants are too nice to hide," Marshall commented quietly. Justice wore a freshly pressed long pants, blue suit.

"Colonel Chambers 42, and now staff adviser for the Senate Armed Services Committee, is a product of Washington's Fifth Battalion of Marine Reserves.

"He commanded the Third Battalion, Twenty-third Marine regiment, in the Iwo Jima landing. He won the Silver Star at Tulagi where he was wounded. He was again wounded at Saipan but returned to command his unit in Tinian. He earned a Legion of Merit there. Chambers is a native of Huntington, W. Va."

Ironically, the day that Colonel Chambers received the Medal of Honor from President Truman an attempted assassination of the President occurred. In recalling

November 1, 1950 Col. Chambers states, "I believe my decoration would have appeared as a one-paragraph item below the obituary column had it not been for the presence of my twin infant sons. This was the same day of the attempted assassination of President Truman, and certainly that was the major story of the day."

Justice Marion Chambers was born in Cabell County, West Virginia on February 2, 1908. His parents, Arthur Faye Chambers and Dixie Maryland Chambers, were of Scotch-Irish ancestry. both of his grandfathers served in the Civil War and one of his mother's ancestors served in the Revolutionary War and was captured by the British.

He has been listed in *Who's Who in America* since 1951. Since Col. Chambers was a Reserve Officer in the U.S. Marine Corps, his military and civilian experiences in many instances ran concurrently. He has had 30 years experience as a civilian employee of the Federal government. His last position was that of Deputy Director of the Office of Emergency Planning in the Executive Offices of the President. When he left the government in 1954 he established a company in Washington to represent various companies engaged in the field of international trade. However, Justice Chambers was personally requested by President Kennedy to serve in the Office of Emergency Planning in 1962. He remained there until the year following President Kennedy's assassination at which time he retired from the government and again formed a small corporation to represent companies in international trade. He retired from that position at age 65 in 1973. From time to time since his retirement, Justice Chambers has been retained as a consultant by various firms and is an active member of the Federal Executive Reserve program.

Colonel Chambers was raised in a protestant family; however he married a Catholic girl and during the war he

THE SPIRIT OF AMERICA

converted to the Catholic faith. In addition to the twins, Peter and Paul, who were born in 1950, the Chambers have a daughter, Patricia, born in 1933, a son, John A., born in 1937, and Justice Jr., born in 1942.

After completing high school, Justice Chambers was a student at Marshall College in 1925-1927 and received his J.D. degree at George Washington University in 1933. He also was awarded the L.L.D. in Law from Marshall College in 1954.

Colonel Chambers' citation for the Medal of Honor reads:

CHAMBERS, JUSTICE M.

Rank and organization: Colonel, U.S. Marine Corps Reserve, 3d Assault Battalion Landing Team, 25th Marines, 4th Marine Division. Place and date: On Iwo Jima, Volcano Islands, from 19 to 22 February 1945. Entered service at: Washington, D.C. Born 2 February 1908, Huntington, W.Va. Citation: For conspicuous gallantry and intrepidity at the risk of his life above and beyond the call of duty as commanding officer of the 3rd Assault Battalion Landing Team, 25th Marines, 4th Marine Division, in action against enemy Japanese forces on Iwo Jima, Volcano Islands, from 19 to 22 February 1945. Under a furious barrage of enemy machine gun and small-arms fire from the commanding cliffs on the right, Col. Chambers (then Lt. Col.) landed immediately after the initial assault waves of his battalion on D-day to find the momentum of the assault threatened by heavy casualties from withering Japanese artillery, mortar rocket, machine gun, and rifle fire. Exposed to relentless hostile fire, he cooly reorganized his battle-weary men, inspiring them to heroic efforts by his own valor and leading them in an attack on the critical, impregnable high ground from which the enemy was pouring an increasing volume of fire directly onto troops ashore as well as an amphibious craft in succeeding waves. Constantly in the front lines encouraging his men to push forward against the enemy's savage resistance, Col. Chambers led the 8-hour battle to carry the flanking ridge top and reduce the enemy's fields of aimed fire, thus protecting the vital foothold gained. In constant defiance of hostile fire while reconnoitering the entire regimental combat team zone of action, he maintained contact with adjacent units and forwarded vital information to his regimental commander. His zealous fighting spirit undimished despite terrific casualties and the loss of most of his key officers, he again reorganized his troops for renewed attack against the enemy's main line of resistance and was directing the fire of the rocket platoon when he fell, critically wounded. Evacuated under heavy Japanese fire, Col. Chambers, by forceful leadership, courage, and fortitude in the face of staggering odds, was directly instrumental in insuring the success of subsequent operations of the 5th Amphibious Corps on Iwo Jima, thereby sustaining and enhancing the finest traditions of the U.S. Naval Service.

Colonel Chambers states that there were other men who should have been awarded the Medal of Honor "I have known many men who not only had the courage but demonstrated that frequently at the cost of their lives. I believe that most people, when faced with an enemy with the power to kill, have a legitimate fear or concern, but to me the true hero is the man who goes ahead and gets his job done no matter how frightened he might be. I have seen many such. In my opinion, James Headley, who as a Captain, took command of my landing team because casualties had taken everyone senior to him and led it for the remaining 16 days on Iwo Jima, fully deserved the Medal of Honor. On Tinian I recommended a machine gunner by the name of Daigle for the Medal of Honor because he and his assistant gunner fought for several hours the first night against a Japanese counter-attack. There was a cone of dead and wounded Japanese totaling approximately 80 in number that led right down to their gun, in which both marines were dead and on top of Daigle's body was a Japanese whom Daigle had killed while being killed himself. There were others but these two are extremes. Neither received the Medal of Honor. Headley received his second Navy Cross and Daigle was posthumously awarded the Silver Star. The assistant gunner got nothing.

"I do not believe the receipt of the Medal caused any reaffirmation of the love and respect I have for my country. From the time I was born I was raised in the belief that in spite of some thinking to the contrary, 'My country—may she be always right, but right or wrong, my country.'

"To me, being an American demands a willingness to serve our country in any way possible against any threat that might arise. This carries with it a recognition that our way of life and our form of government is by far the best that can be found in the world.

"My advice to my own children and to anyone else's children is to recognize that with all of its faults, they are living in a country where human rights, religious rights, and civil rights are respected and protected. In the implementation of these rights throughout our history there have been many mistakes and abuses. Time has cured many of these and hopefully someday they will all be cured. The young of our country must have the patience and understanding to work with those changes within the system to improve their own lives and the lives of those to come."

WILLIAM J. CRAWFORD

On May 11, 1944 at Camp Carson, Colorado, General Terry Allen, the Commanding General of the 104th Infantry Division, presented the Medal of Honor to the father of Master Sergeant William J. Crawford in posthumous recognition of his son's gallant deeds in Italy during World War II. He had been listed as missing in action since September of 1943 shortly after the Salerno landing but was actually a prisoner of war until liberated by an American armored unit near Hanover, Germany on April 13, 1945. When the war was over, Sergeant Crawford "returned from the dead," and in 1946 married Virginia Eileen Bruce from Drennen, Colorado.

William Crawford was born in Pueblo, Colorado, May 19, 1918. He graduated from Pueblo Central High in 1936 and previous to joining the army in 1942, he was employed as a carpenter's helper. He also excelled as an amateur boxer. He weighs 155 pounds and is five feet, 11 inches tall. Since retiring from the army in 1967, with over 23 years active duty, Sergeant Crawford has operated a mini-farm at Palmer Lake, Colorado, while also being quite active in community affairs. Once a year he travels to Colorado Springs, Colorado to present the outstanding Engineering Science graduate of the Air Force Academy with the Wright Brothers award. The Crawfords have two children, a daughter, Beverly, age 34 and a son, Danny, 31, both of whom have their own families and live in close proximity to their parents.

In quiet modesty, that is so typical of the American foot-soldier of WWII, William Crawford relates his heroic action which resulted in his father being presented with his son's Medal of Honor—"I was awarded the CMH for knocking out two machine gun nests and routing another with rifle and grenades. This was while serving with Company I, 142nd Infantry, 36th Division (Texas National Guard). I was a Private at that time serving as a scout. Since I was agile, I was fortunate to get behind the gunners undetected. This allowed the company, which was pinned down by them, to advance and complete their objective. This was on the 13th of September 1943, five days after the Salerno landing and was during a flank attack on the mountain city of Altavilla, controlled by the Germans.

"As far as others getting the CMH, all of the men in my unit fought hard and deserved some type of recognition. I always felt that I was just lucky to be in the right position to do something extra. The real heroes are those who lost their lives for our country."

William Crawford's citation for the Medal of Honor reads:

CRAWFORD, WILLIAM J.
    Rank and organization: Private, U.S. Army, 36th Infantry Division. Place and date: Altavilla, Italy, 13 September 1943. Entered service at: Pueblo, Colo. Birth: Pueblo, Colo. G.O. No: 57, 10 July 1944. Citation: For conspicuous gallantry and intrepidity at risk of life above and beyond the call of duty in action with the enemy near Altavilla, Italy, 13 September 1943. When Company I attacked an enemy held position on Hill 424, the 3rd Platoon, in which Pvt. Crawford was a squad scout, attacked as base platoon for the company. After reaching the crest of the hill, the platoon was pinned down by intense enemy machine gun and small-arms fire. Locating one of these guns, which was dug in on a terrace on his immediate front, Pvt. Crawford, without orders and on his own initiative, moved over the hill under

enemy fire to a point within a few yards of the gun emplacement and single-handedly destroyed the machine gun and killed three of the crew with a hand grenade, thus enabling his platoon to continue the advance. When the platoon, after reaching the crest, was once more delayed by enemy fire, Pvt. Crawford again, in the face of intense fire, advanced directly to the front midway between two hostile machine gun nests located on a higher terrace and emplaced in a small ravine. Moving first to the left, with a hand grenade he destroyed one gun emplacement and killed the crew; he then worked his way, under continuous fire, to the other and with one grenade and the use of his rifle, killed one enemy and forced the remaining to flee. Seizing the enemy machine gun, he fired on the withdrawing Germans and facilitated his company's advance.

Sergeant Crawford describes his capture and subsequent life as a prisoner of war. . . . "I was captured in Italy shortly after I had eliminated the three machine gun nests which were holding up the company's advance. The majority of the Company moved on but I stopped to help a buddy who was shot through the stomach. While assisting him, we were surrounded (he, two others and myself). We tried to hide but were discovered and made prisoners along with about 200 others, who were victims of this huge counterattack. We lived on grapes for two weeks before getting soup in Germany.

"In Germany, the enlisted men were sent out on work projects. My first job was ox couchen. I had six oxen to care for, plus working on a farm. The farm was not owned by the farmer. He merely managed it for the state, as no one owned anything in Germany. I heard one of the large farm managers ask if he could have a piece of his cow which we were butchering on orders of the German Officer in charge. He said that he hadn't had a piece of meat in four years although there were some 60 odd cows in his yard. We gave him a piece of meat.

"I was a very unruly prisoner and made things exciting. On one occasion, I instigated a work strike (unheard of in Nazi Germany). On another occasion I beat up a guard quite severely and escaped with little punishment. Twice I attempted to escape but was returned harmlessly. The Germans tried to abide by the Geneva rules for treatment of POWs and did for the most part. I have never felt any bitterness toward them.

"During the closing months of the European conflict all prisoners in eastern Germany were placed in a transient status to avoid the Russian invasion. We marched over 500 miles with only a boiled potato or a half cup of soup per day for 52 days. The human body is a tough piece of mechanism. We were liberated by an American armored unit near Hanover, Germany on the 13th of April 1945.

"The Statue of Liberty looked mighty good to me as the ship pulled into the harbor. I am quite proud to wear the CMH as it gives one the inward feeling that he has served his country well. It has a stimulating effect on me and makes me feel as though I should do more for my country.

"Concerning religion, I became quite religious during the tour of duty in the POW camp. Having only one Bible to read, we organized our own church services and they were well attended. I still believe that the Lord was for me throughout the war or I would have never made it through unhurt and in fair health. My family has always attended church regularly and I have always looked upon my military service as serving God and country.

"At that time America meant to me the land of the plentiful, the land of milk and honey. America still means that but most important, it is the freedom of every major aspect in living a happy life.

"I had a great career in the service and my advice to the

youth today would be to take on a military career. It provides financial security as well as the rewarding satisfaction of knowing that one is serving the greatest nation in the world. Money isn't everything in life, in fact, it is nothing if you lose your country."

CHARLES W. DAVIS

Colonel Charles W. Davis was born in Gordo, Alabama, population 850, on February 2, 1917. In his words, "Being blessed with good health, I led the simple and active life of a southern boy growing into manhood. I could fish, hunt, play football and baseball acceptably. My grades in school were good, and I attended Sunday school and church regularly. We were a close family; a happy family, and even through the great Depression we fared well.

"I suppose my great love for country and my respect for those senior and in authority started as a child. I was taught that way. We kept a bust of General John J. Pershing on the mantel in our parlor. Fourth of July celebrations were memorable events—great wooden tubs filled with ice cold orange, grape, and strawberry drinks; ear-ringing speeches in the shade of the great oak grove near the school house, and a baseball game in the afternoon. Simple pleasures and experiences from which character could be molded. Looking back, I appreciate more and more the good fortune I had in being taught fairness, right from wrong, love of our flag, and love of God—taught by parents, teachers, and the church."

Charles W. Davis attributes the values and deep respect for people, God and Country to the influence of his parents, Gilbert E. and Leona Belle Davis, during his formative years. Following his father's term in the State Legislature of Alabama, the family moved to Montgomery in 1934 where he graduated from Sidney Lanier High School. He attended the University of Alabama from 1936 to 1940 with a major in

Political Science. After completing the first year of Law School and having been in the ROTC program at the University, he accepted a commission and reported for active duty at Ft. Benning, Georgia on July 5, 1940. On February 1, 1972, at the age of 54, he retired with the rank of Colonel after over 31 years of continuous service. Colonel Davis met his charming wife, the former Joan Kirk of St. Louis, Missouri, at Ft. Sam Houston in San Antonio, Texas, his first duty station. They have a daughter, Carol, born on December 8, 1941 and twin sons, Joseph Kirk and John Broderick Davis, born on December 21, 1945. It is of interest that Carol was born at Pearl Harbor, one day after the Japanese attack. Colonel Davis was a member of the 27th Infantry Regiment of the 25th Division which was stationed in Hawaii when Japan bombed Pearl Harbor.

The 25th Division had been organized in October of 1941 in Hawaii. It has remained a Hawaiian Division and is stationed there now after valiant service in WWII, Korea, and Vietnam. One of its Commanding Officers during World War II was General J. Lawton "Lightning Joe" Collins, who was later destined to become U.S. Army Chief of Staff during the Korean Conflict. In Colonel Davis's words, "General Collins, through his brilliant leadership, placed an indelible mark on this unit, and it was destined for a high standing in the Army's long line of magnificent forces."

After extensive training the 25th Division was ordered to reinforce the U.S. forces on Guadalcanal and then to relieve them. The Marines had been there since August of 1942 and had performed magnificently in the operation that first blunted the Japanese invasion forces.

Colonel Davis briefly describes the actions which led to his receiving of the Medal of Honor—"We had attacked on a broad front early on the morning of January 12 (1943). We followed an intense artillery barrage and Navy dive bombing; nervousness gave way to attention to the job at hand. The coolness of the early morning gave way later to the blistering tropical heat. After the attack of the 2nd battalion had bogged down, I told Col. Herbert Mitchell, Battalion Commander, that I would go forward to check on the units held up. The battalion communications officer, Lt. Weldon Sims of Georgia, and General Collins' aide, Capt. Paul Mellichamp, went with me. As we crawled forward across the draw between two coral ridges, Lt. Sims was shot in the chest, and I held him as he died. I cut his radio strap and took it with me as I continued forward. I reached the forward company; shortly afterward I called in mortar fire on the Japanese positions. It was so close that fragments and coral chips were falling on us. We spent the cold and miserable night huddled under a small ridge. I knew where the enemy positions were: further, I knew I wasn't going to spend another day on that particular part of 'Galloping Horse' hill (called that because of the shape of the series of ridges as seen on an aerial mosaic). I told Col. Mitchell, who had joined us late on the day of 12 January, that I would take a group of volunteers and move to dislodge the machine gun and mortar positions to our immediate front. Pvts. Ward, Woodard, Stec, and Sgt. 'Chubby' Curran went with me. As we inched forward we were sighted by the Japanese. A grenade hit five yards above me, took a couple of bounces, and stopped between Curran and myself. It didn't go off, but we did! Bolting from the prone to a running position, following our grenades that did go off, we made a charge much like those pictured during the Civil War. The position we neutralized was a key one for the Japanese; its loss seemed to provide a key to the collapse of their entire defense."

General "Lightning Joe" Collins witnessed the courageous charge led by Charlie Davis from an observation post overlooking the battle field through his field glasses. He asked an aide to find out who led the charge while waving his rifle in the air. The rest is history.

Charlie Davis describes his presentation of the Medal of Honor—"It is generally accepted that the Medal of Honor is presented by the President in the name of the Congress. My Medal of Honor was presented to me by General Millard Harmon, Commander of all forces in the South Pacific. The presentation was a most memorable event. Its setting was the 'Coconut Grove Theater' at the Division Headquarters. Representation from all units of the Division was present. It meant a great deal to me to receive this wonderful award in front of the men of the Tropic Lighting (25th Division). General Collins later took me to his quarters; gave me some 'refreshments'; some advice, and a warm feeling of respect and admiration for this great man, who later became a Corps Commander in Europe and Chief of Staff of the U.S. Army during the period of the Korean Conflict."

Colonel Davis' citation for the Medal of Honor reads:

DAVIS, CHARLES W.
Rank and organization: Major, U.S. Army, 25th Infantry Division. Place and date: Guadalcanal Island, 12 January 1943, Entered service at: Montogomery, Ala. Birth: Gordo, Ala. G.O. No: 40, 17 July 1943. Citation: For distinguishing himself conspicuously by gallantry and intrepidity at the risk of his life above and beyond the call of duty in action with the enemy on Guadalcanal Island. On 12 January 1943, Maj. Davis (then Capt.), executive officer of an infantry battalion, volunteered to carry instructions to the leading companies of his battalion which had been caught in crossfire from Japanese machine guns. With complete disregard for his own safety, he made his way to the trapped units, delivered the instructions, supervised their execution, and remained overnight in this exposed position. On the following day, Maj. Davis again volunteered to lead an assault on the Japanese position which was holding up

the advance. When his rifle jammed at its first shot, he drew his pistol and, waving his men on, led the assault over the top of the hill. Electrified by this action, another body of soldiers followed and seized the hill. The capture of this position broke Japanese resistance and the battalion was then able to proceed and secure the corps objective. The courage and leadership displayed by Maj. Davis inspired the entire battalion and unquestionably led to the success of its attack.

Concerning his personal feelings of those brave comrades of his during World War II, Colonel Charles Davis states the following: "What a great bunch of men America poured forth from its homes to defend its freedom. Honest, dependable, young, scared, brave, lonely, but friendly. Love of fellow man and the knowledge that other lives depended on his playing his part to the hilt made him a great soldier. The basic stock from which he came, which had been spawned in the Old World and cultivated in this sparkling, shining new world of America, served him in good stead. Generally, he believed in God and the fellow G.I. on his right and left. Hot and blistering during the day and bone-chilling cold at night contributed to a misery that was overcome only by a belief—a belief in his cause; a cause that was right for him, America, and the world. The big heart that is America drew its life blood from the men who sacrificed their life's blood that it could be sustained and grow to continue to offer hope to the world."

On religion Colonel Davis comments, "I am not an overly pious man, but have always believed in God. I have felt the need for a religion and the comfort that comes from the church. I was raised to respect the church and to believe in God, and I have retained those beliefs. I was a member of the Methodist Church in my early days; in 1951 I joined the Catholic Church and attend Mass regularly. The same God I knew as a boy is the same one I know now."

After the New Georgia Campaign, Colonel Davis was returned to Washington, D.C. He describes meeting General George C. Marshall and Secretary of War, Henry Stimson— "I remember the tension I felt as I entered the room to speak with each of them. It was soon dispelled. Mr. Stimson complimented me on the fact that my action leading to the award of the Medal of Honor was over a period of two days and not just a brief burst. He further remarked on the qualities of leadership exhibited.

"General Marshall related to me his concern for the infantry soldier and indicated the possiblity of an award of recognition solely for the infantryman. From this concern and as a symbol of courage came the coveted Combat Infantry Badge."

After a highly interesting and distinguished career which included being the American Liaison Officer to the British School of Infantry, the Commanding Officer of the elite 503rd Airborne Infantry Regiment of the 11th Airborne Division, and Deputy Senior Advisor, IV Corps Area in Vietnam, Colonel Charles W. Davis, retired in 1972. He and his beloved wife of forty years of marriage, Joan Kirk Davis, reside in San Francisco where he is the current President of the Congressional Medal of Honor Society. He and Mrs. Davis plan to visit Guadalcanal in the future.

Concerning his personal feelings of being a citizen of the United States of America, Colonel Davis has the following to say, "My love of country and my faith in her and the principles of freedom and justice for all might have been reconfirmed by the award of the Medal of Honor but, if so, I am not conscious of it. Our freedom is so precious that action to preserve it when it's threatened should be considered by each citizen as the natural and right thing to do. Thank God we still believe that Peace at *any* price is not the answer to the preservation of liberty and the opportunity to pursue happiness. The privilege of serving one's country should also be recognized as an obligation of citizenship.

"In a letter signed by President George Washington to the Congress from the Constitutional Convention, forwarding the Constitution, he said in part: 'It is obviously impractical in the federal government of these States, to secure all rights of independent sovereignty to each, and yet provide for the interest and safety of all—Individuals entering into society, must give up a share of liberty to preserve the rest. The magnitude of the sacrifice must depend as well on situation and circumstances as on the object to be obtained.' Later, when speaking of the Constitution, he added 'that it may promote the lasting welfare of that country so dear to us all, and secure her freedom and happiness, is our most ardent wish.'

"The greatest protection for individual rights existing anywhere exists in this, our country, the United States of America. That protection is guaranteed in the Bill of Rights. It protects our individual rights, and recognizes the need for a well regulated militia, implying the requirement to support it.

"The foregoing leaves no doubt in my mind that service to our country is an inherent obligation to citizenship. Military service is the highest form of performance to meet that obligation as the occasion for the supreme sacrifice is more apt to be encountered.

"This *is* my country—sweet land of Liberty. I can't envision being a citizen of any other land. We elect our leaders and influence decisions affecting the way we live. We are a compassionate, tender, and forgiving nation—perhaps to a fault, but better that way than not. I can worship or not; reap the fruits of another's labor at little cost! I have plenty to eat, a good family, good neighbors, and a good life. Americans are blessed by conditions under which they can produce enough to sustain their lives and live in reasonable comfort. I have my

Liberty and Freedom.

"My advice to the young of America is simple—never forget your obligation to serve your country; to give up a part of your liberty in so doing is to protect it, the country and your freedom as a whole."

Col. Davis who is now serving as President of the Congressional Medal of Honor Society for the second successive term, also is a member of the Board of Directors of the Retired Officers Association. In addition to the Medal of Honor, during his service he was awarded the Legion of Merit with two Oak Leaf Clusters; the Bronze Star with "V" for Valor and one Cluster; the Air Medal with three Clusters; the Army Commendatum medal; the Republic of Vietnam Gallantry Cross with Gold Star; the Vietnam Staff Service Medal and eight other Campaign medals. He wears the Combat Infantry Badge, the Glider Badge and is a Senior Parachutist.

"All Americans should be more aware of their heroes. From time to time, I will pick up my copy of Medal of Honor Recipients 1963-1978 to read copies of citations at random. It's an inspirational exercise. Great men! Great deeds!"

JAMES H. DOOLITTLE

On April 18, 1942, during the very early days of World War II, when the morale of the United States was at its lowest ebb, a 45 year old daredevil flyer, with a Doctor of Aeronautical Science Degree from M.I.T., led a group of 16 B-25 bombers off the deck of America's newest aircraft carrier, the U.S.S. Hornet, on a bombing raid of the mainland of Japan. This was the first offensive action of the United States in the Pacific theater in the second World War, only four short months after Japan bombed Pearl Harbor on the 7th of December in 1941. Never before in the history of aviation had a flyer attempted to take a bomber off the deck of a ship. Doubt existed that the heavily loaded bombers could even become airborne off the extremely short runway of the Hornet. The successful results of that raid are part of the great saga of American aviation. The man who personally hand picked, trained and led the crews of those 16 B-25's is Jimmy Doolittle. His name, "Doolittle," is one of the greatest misnomers of all time.

Jimmy Doolittle was born in Alameda, California on December 14, 1896 to Frank and Rosa Doolittle. In 1897, Frank Doolittle joined the Gold Rush in the Klondike River area of Northwest Canada, leaving his wife and infant son in Alameda. Although Frank Doolittle was not successful in his search for gold, he worked his way to Nome, Alaska, and in May of 1900 his wife and son, Jimmy, joined him there to live in a primitive, frontier type environment. Being a skilled carpenter, Frank Doolittles' services were in great demand. In addition to building houses for the homesteaders in Nome, he also constructed a wooden home for his young family.

Because of the rough and tumble life, harsh living conditions and limited educational facilities in Nome, Rosa Doolittle decided to return to California so that Jimmy could have the advantage of a better education than Alaska offered. She also desired to remove her son from the street fighting ambiance of Nome where he was fast becoming the toughest kid on the block. In the spring of 1908, Frank and Rosa Doolittle returned to California with Jimmy, settling in Los Angeles, where he was enrolled in the public school system. His father, still enamored by the lure of gold and the wanderlust of the Alaskan territory, soon left his family to return to the call of the frontier life. On occasions he sent money to Rosa and Jimmy; ultimately Frank Doolittle died in Alaska in 1917.

After completing his grade school education, Jimmy entered the Los Angeles Manuel Arts High School in 1910. During his high school years Jimmy Doolittle became interested in aviation as well as becoming a boxer. Using the plans from a *Popular Mechanics* magazine, he built a glider with an 18 foot wingspan. Unfortunately, it crashed when he jumped it off a 30 foot cliff. Undaunted by his first failure and bruises, he rebuilt the damaged plane and talked a friend into towing him behind a car in another attempt to become airborne. The resulting crash demolished the glider as well as roughing up the potential flyer.

Still not discouraged, he again turned to *Popular Mechanics* to study the drawings of a monoplane, powered by a gasoline engine. Jimmy built another plane and using the money he'd won from prize fighting, he purchased a used motorcycle engine which he installed in his newest flying machine. Before he had a chance to fly it, a storm lifted his aircraft from its resting place in the Doolittle yard and smashed it beyond repair.

During his high school years, Jimmy Doolittle met a pretty, genteel girl, Josephine Daniels, who would become his partner for life. Jo Daniels' good influence on Jimmy resulted in his decision to attend the Junior College of Los Angeles upon graduation from high school in 1914, where he studied engineering. In 1916 he enrolled at the University of California to major in mining engineering. Although he only weighed 130 pounds, the five foot, six inch athlete became the middleweight boxing champion of the University of California. On Christmas Eve in 1917 Jo Daniels and Jimmy Doolittle were married in the Los Angeles City Hall. This marriage so far has endured four wars and sixty three years of fantastic achievment for Jo and Jimmy Doolittle. Two sons, James H. and John P. Doolittle, both of whom served valiantly in the armed forces of the United States, were born to them.

In the spring of 1917, during his junior year at the University of California, the United States declared war on Germany. That summer Jimmy Doolittle enlisted in the Aviation Section of the Signal Corps Reserve so that he could qualify for pilot training. This began one of, if not, the greatest career in the history of aviation: First to fly across the United States in less than 24 hours: First to fly the outside loop: First to take off, fly a set course, and land without seeing the ground—thus pioneering the science of "blind flying": Winner of the Schneider Trophy Race in 1925: Winner of the Bendix Trophy Race in 1931: Pioneered the development, use and sales of 100 octane aviation fuel without which our aircraft could not be competitive in combat in wartime: Established the new transcontinental record in 1931: Winner of the Thompson Trophy Race in 1932: Established the World's land plane speed record in 1932: Awarded the Mackay Trophy in 1926: Awarded the Spirit of St. Louis Award in 1929: Awarded the Harmon Trophy of the Ligue

International des Aviateurs in 1930 and 1950: Won the Guggenheim Trophy in 1942: Won the International Harmon Trophy in 1940 and 1949: Was recipient of our nation's highest military award, the Medal of Honor, for his famous Tokyo Raid in 1942: Awarded the Wright Brothers Trophy in 1953: Awarded the F.A.I. Gold Medal in 1954: Awarded the Silver Quill Award for 1959: And was awarded the Thomas D. White National Defense Award for 1967.

In addition to the A.B. Degree Jimmy Doolittle received from the University of California in 1922, he earned an M.S. at the Massachusetts Institute of Technology in 1924 and his D.Sc. from the same school in 1925. Seven universities and colleges have bestowed honorary degrees in the diciplines of Doctor of Science, Laws, Engineering and Military Science to this pioneer of aviation.

Upon return to the United States from his famous raid on Tokyo, the then Brigadier General James H. Doolittle, who gave our country its greatest morale lift of the early days of World War II, in addition to successfully destroying the assigned targets in Japan, was awarded the Medal of Honor. Very reluctant to accept our nation's highest military honor, he simply said, "I'll spend the rest of my life trying to earn it."

DOOLITTLE, JAMES H. (Air Mission)

Rank and organization: Brigadier General, U.S. Army. Air Corps. Place and date: Over Japan. Entered service at: Berkeley, Calif. Birth: Alameda, Calif. G.O. No.: 29, 9 June 1942. Citation: For conspicuous leadership above the call of duty, involving personal valor and intrepidity at an extreme hazard to life. With the apparent certainty of being forced to land in enemy territory or to perish at sea, Gen. Doolittle personally led a squadron of Army bombers, manned by volunteer crews, in a highly destructive raid on the Japanese mainland.

Jimmy Doolittle then became the Commanding General of the 12th Air Force in North Africa in 1942: The Commanding General of the 15th Air Force in Italy in 1943: The Commanding General of the 8th Air Force in England in 1944 and at the wars end, the now Lieutenant General Doolittle was stationed on Okinawa, commanding the 8th Air Force for the final showdown with the Japanese which he had bombed way back in 1942.

After the end of World War II, Jimmy Doolittle's civilian careers were multidimensional and his advancement in professional capacities meteoric: Vice President and Director of Shell Oil Company, 1946-1967: Board Chairman, Space Technology Laboratories, Inc., 1959-1962; Director, 1959-1963: Director, Thompson Ramo Wooldridge Inc., 1961-1969: Consultant, TRW Systems, 1962-1966: Director, Mutual of Omaha Insurance Company, 1961- : Trustee, Aerospace Corporation, 1963-1969; Vice Chairman, Board of Trustees and Chairman, Executive Committee, 1965-1969: Director, United Benefit Life Insurance Company of Omaha, 1964- : Director, Tele-Trip Company, Inc., 1966- : Director, Companion Life Insurance Company, 1968- : And, Director, Mutual of Omaha Growth and Income Funds, 1968- .

His appointments are as impressive as his career positions: Member, Army Air Corps Investigating Committee (Baker Board), 1934: Chairman, Secretary of War's Board on Officer/Enlisted Men Relationships, 1946: Member, Joint Congressional Aviation Policy Board, 1948: Advisor, Committee on National Security Organization, 1948: Chairman, President's Airport Commission, 1952: Chairman, President's Task Group on Air Inspection-Stassen Disarmament Committee, 1955: Member, Air Force Scientific Advisory Board, 1951-1958; Vice Chairman, 1951-1955; Chairman, 1955-1958: Member, President's Foreign Intelligence Advisory Board, 1955-1965: Member, National

Advisory Committee for Aeronautics, 1948-1958; Chairman, 1956-1958: Member, Advisory Board National Air Museum-Smithsonian Institution, 1956-1965: Member, Defense Science Board, 1957-1958: Member, President's Science Advisory Committee, 1957-1958: Member, National Aeronautics and Space Council, 1958: Member, Plowshare Committee of the Atomic Energy Commission, 1959-1971: Member, National Institute of Health Studies, 1963-1965: And Member, Air Force Space and Missile Systems Organization Advisory Board, 1963- . At his current age of 84, Jimmy Doolittle is still very active in many areas of endeavor. He has been described as "the world's greatest aviator."

Concerning his attitude and feelings for America, he states: "Obviously, we are the greatest and the finest nation in the world and the leader of the free world.

"Great changes have taken place in the last 200 years and the rate of change is increasing.

"Some of the changes in our environment are obvious.

"We have gone from a few people to many. Our population is still more than doubling every 50 years. In the year 1800, it was just over 5 million. In 1900, it was almost 76 million. In the year 2000 it is anticipated that there will be over 300 million people in the United States.

"We have gone from a largely agricultural society to a largely industrialized society. This has caused a movement of workers to the industrial centers and has resulted in crowded metropolises. Those metropolitan centers were not properly planned for continuing growth, thus adding to the ensuing congestion.

"In a word, our environment has changed from one of freedom to one of restriction.

"The word 'freedom' epitomized our great Nation. We must continue to espouse freedom—and everything it represents—but we must not forget the obligation to protect the rights of others. We must protect the rights of the individual but, at the same time, must also protect the rights and the security of the body politic.

"With it all has come prosperity and, for a majority of our people, the highest standard of living the world has ever known.

"Unfortunately, some of our people have not participated, to the full, in this prosperity.

"This environmental change, naturally, has caused some change in our people.

"Changes in the natural animal instinct of man take place very slowly—over a long evolutionary period of time—but his outlook, his sense of values change, to some considerable degree, with his environment.

"I am afraid most of us in America have had it good, too good, for too long and have gotten soft.

"I do not think we, on the average, are as courageous, as ambitious or as moral as our founding fathers. Of course, there are many people today who will dare, will work and have integrity like our forebears. On the average, however, we are, in the words of a very wise friend of mine, 'suffering from the ravages of prosperity.' We, as a nation, incline to laziness and immorality.

"Certainly our environment will continue to change. Certainly our values will change.

"There will continue to be conflict between the haves and the have-nots.

"There will continue to be a tendency on the part of the older generation to resist change—to maintain the status quo—and a tendency on the part of the younger generation to demand change. The proper route is probably some place between no change and change for the sake of change without due consideration to the effects of change—whether it will improve or impair.

"I should like to suggest—well realizing that I am of the older generation and therefore out of touch with the times—that we consider a few values which, to me, are basic. I'd like to recommend that we don't change those until or unless something definitely better has been found or proposed.

"They are:

- Courage; physical and moral.
- Integrity; a man's word is his bond.
- Intelligence; a knowledge of things and people.
- Ambition; a willingness to strive mightly to attain our ends. A determination to progress—but not at the expense of others.
- Patriotism; to put Country above self.
- Humanity; love of people; Living by the Golden Rule.
- Spiritually; a realization that a universe as orderly as it is must be ruled by a Divine Purpose and not by the mind of man."*

Jimmy Doolittle's advice to the youth of America is profoundly simple—"STRIVE FOR EXCELLENCE."

Carroll V. Glines. *Jimmy Doolittle,* The MacMillian Company, New York: 1972. Pages 176, 177.

LEONARD A. FUNK

A newspaper article written by Vicki Jarmulowski, April 17, 1980, in the Pittsburg Post-Gazette, vividly tells the story and credo of Leonard Funk, American patriot and combat paratrooper of World War II—"Leonard Funk is happy to give his opinion on any subject you ask him about. Have him talk about World War II, or ask him about foreign affairs or politics, and he has a response ready.

"But ask him if it's true that he killed 21 Germans single-handedly, and he looks at the floor.

" 'I never really counted,' he says.

"Leonard Funk has been a marked man ever since he won the Congressional Medal of Honor. That's the way the lifelong Braddock Hills resident describes himself.

" 'Winning it affects your life alright. It changes it, too. You get all kinds of invitations to go places and speak. And you always have to watch yourself: no bad publicity to dishonor the medal,' he says.

"Funk earned the honor that changed his life in January 1945 at Holzhelm, Belgium. His men had rounded up 80 prisoners when they were tricked by a group of English-speaking Germans disguised in American uniforms.

"When one of the Germans shoved his rifle into Funk's stomach and demanded he surrender, Funk answered, 'Surrender, hell!' turned on his would-be-captor, and opened fire with his Tommy gun.

"His action resulted in the death of the 21 masquerading Germans and the recapture of the 80 prisoners.

"In August 1945, his bravery was rewarded when President Truman presented him with this country's highest honor.

"Funk's 15 months duty overseas earned him a number of other honors, including the Distinguished Service Cross, the Silver Star, a Certificate of Merit, a Bronze Star, the Purple Heart with two clusters and the Croix de Guerre from Belgium.

"While winning the Congressional Medal of Honor may have disrupted what might otherwise have been a quiet life, Funk doesn't regret it.

" 'It was the greatest thing I ever received,' he says. 'I probably would still be just a clerk with the Edmund L. Wiegand Co. if I hadn't won it.'

"The medal, and the notoriety that went with it, led to a post with the Veterans Administration in Pittsburg. Funk became division chief before he retired at age 55.

"Since then he has divided his time between such leisure pursuits as gardening and hunting and fishing on the 25 acres he owns in Elk County near Emporium, Cameron County.

"Considering his long association with the military and the government, it's not surprising that Funk, now 63, speaks like a partiot—a very traditional one—about such issues as the draft and Iran.

" 'There ought to be a draft,' says Funk, who was drafted. 'We're not getting the qualified men we need to protect our country with the volunteer army. I think everyone should be drafted for two years right out of high school.'

" 'It would be good training for them, and if anything ever came up, the country would have men to call upon who had the training. This country is in awful shape: we have to keep our defense up.'

"Shaking his head, he says, 'There's no respect for this country anymore. My hair stands up on end when I see them burning an American flag. When you let a little country like

Iran do things like that. . . .'

"Funk knows how he would have responded to the hostage situation.

" 'I said it right from the first: We should have moved them in then and there. Paratroopers, like my old division, could have gone in there, taken them completely by surprise and gotten those people out. Negotiating won't help: How do you negotiate with a mob? If we had taken care of it right away, Russia would never have had the nerve to do what they did in Afghanistan.'

"In Funk's opinion, it all comes down to poor leadership. 'Nowadays,' he says, 'there isn't a decent candidate in sight.'

" 'All the ones running put together don't make one decent candidate. Politicians are too concerned with getting reelected. They have no guts and no nerve.'

"The last President who had that combination in Funk's opinion was Dwight D. Eisenhower. The only time Funk became involved in politics was when he introduced Ike at the 82nd Airborne's annual convention in 1952.

"That convention, which will be held this year in Indianapolis, is an event Funk never misses. It is a chance to see old buddies and to relive the war.

" 'In combat you get close to each other. And when you remember you forget the bad things. You only remember the good things,' he says.

"For that occasion, and for the biennial banquet for Medal of Honor winners, Funk takes out his military decoration—or at least the major one. The rest of the time, they remain in the bottom of a closet, in a Gimbels box tied with a string.

" 'I always intended to get a nice box for them,' Funk says. 'But I never did.' "

Leonard A. Funk was born in Braddock Hills, Pennsylvania of French and German ancestry. He is five feet, five inches in height and weighs 175 pounds. Although he was wounded three times during World War II, he has no physical impairments. He was 28 years old at the time his fantastic actions resulted in his being awarded the Medal of Honor. He has never married and is a Presbyterian. Eight years ago, he retired as a Division Chief of the Veterans Administration Regional Office in Pittsburg, Pennsylvania.

His citation for the Medal of Honor reads:

FUNK, LEONARD A., JR.

Rank and organization: First Sergeant, U.S. Army, Company C, 508th Parachute Infantry, 82nd Airborne Division. Place and date: Holzheim, Belgium, 29 January 1945. Entered service at Wilkinsburg, Pa. Birth: Braddock Township, Pa. G.O. No: 75, 5 September 1945. Citation: He distinguished himself by gallant, intrepid actions against the enemy. After advancing 15 miles in a driving snowstorm, the American force prepared to attack through waist-deep drifts. The company executive officer became a casualty, and 1st Sgt. Funk immediately assumed his duties, forming headquarters soldiers into a combat unit for an assault in the face of direct artillery shelling and harassing fire from the right flank. Under his skillful and courageous leadership, this miscellaneous group and the 3rd Platoon attacked 15 houses, cleared them, and took 30 prisoners without suffering a casualty. The fierce drive of Company C quickly overran Holzheim, netting some 80 prisoners, who were placed under a four man guard, all that could be spared, while the rest of the understrength unit went about mopping up isolated points of resistance. An enemy patrol, by means of a ruse, succeeded in capturing the guards and freeing the prisoners, and had begun preparations to attack Company C from the rear when 1st Sgt. Funk walked around the building and into their midst. He was ordered to surrender by a German officer who pushed a machine pistol into his stomach. Although overwhelmingly outnumbered and facing almost certain death, 1st Sgt.

Funk, pretending to comply with the order, began to slowly unsling his submachine gun from his shoulder and then, with lightning motion, brought the muzzle into line and riddled the German officer. He turned upon the other Germans, firing and shouting to the other Americans to seize the enemy's weapons. In the ensuing fight 21 Germans were killed, many wounded, and the remainder captured. 1st Sgt. Funk's bold action and heroic disregard for his own safety was directly responsible for the recapture of a vastly superior enemy force, which, if allowed to remain free, could have taken the widespread units of Company C by surprise and endangered the entire attack plan.

"It's sure great to be an American," Sgt. Funk affirms.

His advice to the youth of America is, "Always be ready to defend your country which is the greatest country in the world."

DOUGLAS THOMAS JACOBSON

On October 5, 1945 a 19 year old Marine from Rochester, New York, in the company of his parents, stood before President Harry Truman in the White House at Washington, D.C. to receive our country's greatest military award, The Medal of Honor. When asked to state, in his own words, what he did to be awarded the CMH, he tersely stated to this writer, "There were 19 wounded Marines and 20 other Marines cut off on hill 382 on Iwo (Jima). I was one of them. We each grabbed a wounded man and started our retrograde movement. The other 19 (not wounded) were busy with the wounded. I took care of the enemy."

Douglas Jacobson's citation for the Medal of Honor elaborates on his modestly described action:

> For conspicuous gallantry and intrepidity at the risk of his life above and beyond the call of duty while serving with the 3rd Battalion, 23rd Marines, 4th Marine Division, in combat against enemy Japanese forces during the seizure of Iwo Jima in the Volcano Island, 26 February 1945. Promptly destroying a stubborn 20-mm. antiaircraft gun and its crew after assuming the duties of a bazooka man who had bee killed, Pfc. Jacobson waged a relentless battle as his unit fought desperately toward the summit of Hill 382 in an effort to penetrate the heart of Japanese cross-island defense. Employing his weapon with ready accuracy when his platoon was halted by overwhelming enemy fire on February 26, he first destroyed two hostile machine gun positions, then attacked a large blockhouse, completely neutralizing the

SOF

fortification before dispatching the five man crew of a second pillbox and exploding the installation with a terrific demolitions blast. Moving steadily forward, he wiped out an earth-covered rifle emplacement and, confronted by a cluster of similar emplacements which constituted the perimeter of enemy defenses in his assigned sector, fearlessly advanced, quickly reduced all six positions to shambles, killed ten of the enemy, and enabled our forces to occupy the strong point. Determined to widen the breach thus forced, he volunteered his services to an adjacent company, neutralized a pillbox holding up its advance, opened fire on a Japanese tank pouring a steady stream of bullets on one of our supporting tanks, and smashed the enemy tank's guns turret in a brief but furious action culminating in a singlehanded assault against still another blockhouse and the subsequent neutralization of its firepower. By his dauntless skill and valor, Pfc. Jacobson destroyed a total of 16 enemy positions and annihilated approximately 75 Japanese, thereby contributing essentially to the success of his division's operations against this fanatically defended outpost of the Japanese Empire. His gallant conduct in the face of tremendous odds enhanced and sustained the highest traditions of the U.S. Naval Service.

Douglas Jacobson retired from the Marines with the rank of Major after 25 years of active duty in the Corps. He is five feet, 11 inches, weighs 220 pounds, and is 70 percent disabled. He is married and the father of three girls. He knows several other Marines whom he believes should have received the Medal of Honor. Since retirement he has managed a family owned Real Estate Investment Corporation.

What does America mean to this great Marine? "Freedom, the right to a job of my choice, the right to own a home of my choice, the right to look out the window at fields, streams, neighbors over a small lake and say, I helped."

His advice to the Youth of America is to "Apply yourselves as best you can—get the most from our educational system because it helps—be true to thine self—work hard, and above all, remember, 'winners never quit; quitters never win.' "

ROBERT E. LAWS

Robert E. Laws of Altoona, Pennsylvania is the kind of person you always hoped would be your next door neighbor. Perhaps this is reflected in his profession as letter carrier for the Altoona Post Office for the past 26 years. He is married to Virginia Murray Laws and they have three children, Robert E., Jr., 19, Edward A., 17 and Sharon L., 16.

He was born in Altoona on January 18, 1921, is a high school graduate with two years of college. Previous to his employment with the Post Office, he had been with the Pennsylvania Railroad. Both of his parents are deceased.

There is no vain-glory in the make-up of this true American hero. He still lives the philosophy his father instilled in him during his youth—"Don't ask others to do something you wouldn't do yourself."

"When President Truman placed the Medal around my neck, I was a little stunned by his statement. He said that I was a real tall one. He wanted me to bend over.

"It was one of the moments of my life that I was humbled and very proud. When Truman presented it, I accepted it for the men who served under me.

"The Medal hasn't changed my life much," Sgt. Laws confides. "I'm still the same old fellow, perhaps a little older, a little wiser, and somewhat grayer. I still try to be the gentleman that I always was. I take things as they come. Because of the Medal, I ask no favors be done for me."

Robert Laws is six feet, three inches in height and weighs 175 pounds. He has a metal plate in his forehead and pieces of bullets and shrapnel in both arms and legs. "Otherwise, I'm in fine shape. I do have my bad days, mostly when the damp weather comes and when it gets too hot or too cold," he confides. "That plate in my head acts similar to a radiator in a car, absorbing the warmth and the cold."

His citation for the Medal of Honor reads:

LAWS, ROBERT E.

Rank and organization: Staff Sergeant, U.S. Army, Company G, 169th Infantry, 43rd Infantry Division. Place and date: Pangasinan Province, Luzon, Philippine Islands, 12 January 1945. Entered service at: Altoona, Pa. Birth: Altoona, Pa. G.O. No: 77, 10 September 1945. Citation: He led the assault squad when Company G attacked enemy hill positions. The enemy force, estimated to be a reinforced infantry company, was well supplied with machine guns, ammunition, grenades, and blocks of TNT and could be attacked only across a narrow ridge 70 yards long. At the end of this ridge an enemy pillbox and rifle position were set in rising ground. Covered by his squad, S/Sgt. Laws traversed the hogback through vicious enemy fire until close to the pillbox, where he hurled grenades at the fortification. Enemy grenades wounded him, but he persisted in his assault until one of his missiles found its mark and knocked out the pillbox. With more grenades, passed to him by members of his squad who had joined him, he led the attack on the entrenched riflemen. In the advance up the hill, he suffered additional wounds in both arms and legs, about the body and in the head, as grenades and TNT charges exploded near him. Three Japanese rushed him with fixed bayonets, and he emptied the magazine of his machine pistol at them, killing two. He closed in hand-to-hand combat with the third, seizing the Japanese's rifle as he met the onslaught. The two fell to the ground and rolled some 50 to 60 feet down a bank. When the dust cleared the Japanese lay dead and the valiant American was climbing up the hill with a large gash across the head. He was given first aid and evacuated from the area while his squad completed the destruction of the enemy position. S/Sgt. Laws' heroic actions provided great inspiration to his comrades, and his courageous determination, in the face of formidiable odds while suffering from multiple wounds, enabled them to secure an important objective with minimum casualties."

"A young doctor came up to the Laws family at the ceremony where President Harry Truman placed the Medal around each soldier's neck. The doctor introduced himself but the Laws were too excited about the event to remember the young man's name.

"He told about being on the field in Luzon where Sgt. Laws was hit. An older field doctor had given Bob up for dead since his *brain* was exposed, but the young doctor said he had seen the soldier's heroic actions and felt he must try to save him.

"He patched up Laws the best he could on the field and then lost track of him. When the doctor returned to Washington and heard Bob Laws was to receive the Medal of Honor, he asked special permission to attend the ceremony."*

"I've never had any doubt about America," states Robert Laws, "I believe highly in America. There are a few things that the President, Congress and the Supreme Court does that I disagree with, but that's government.

"America has a lot of faults from top to bottom but its the only 'free' country in the world where a person can speak his mind and not be put in prison or to death."

His advice to the Youth of America is:
1. Get a good education (all the education you can).
2. Do the very best job you can.
3. Fight, and fight hard, for your rights.
4. Be sincere.

*Article from The Shoppers Guide, Duncanville, Pa., November 8, 1978, by Linda Vance

JAKE W. LINDSEY

Jake Lindsey has never doubted his country's ability to defend itself. He states: "I would die for my country today if I were needed." During his military career, Lieutenant Lindsey spent 42 months in two wars in actual combat with the enemy.

He was born in Isney, Alabama on May 1, 1921. His parents, both deceased, were born in Mississippi. He is retired from the U.S. Army, having served from February 1940 until September 1963. Since retirement from the military he has been employed by the U.S. Forest Service as a forest ranger with headquarters in Hattiesburg, Mississippi and resides in Waynesboro, Mississippi. During his military career, he spent 15 years in the paratroopers, attaining the rank of Master Sergeant and then accepted a battlefield commission during the Korean Conflict. He is Methodist by religious preference, is married and has four sons. Lieutenant Lindsey is a high school graduate and attended college for one year. He is five feet, nine inches in height and weighs 180 pounds.

Included in his military awards are: The Medal of Honor, Silver Star, the Bronze Star, the Purple Heart, Good Conduct Medal, the American Defense Service Medal, the American Campaign Medal, the European-African-Middle Eastern Campaign Medal with one silver star and three bronze stars, World War II Victory Medal, the National Defense Service Medal, the Korean Service Medal with four bronze stars, the United Nations Service Medal, the Combat Infantryman Badge with one star, and the Parachute Badge.

He attributes his success in life and his love of his country to the influence of his mother, Ruby Mae Gandy Lindsey, during his formative years. She died in May of 1965.

In a precedent setting ceremony, Jake W. Lindsey, the 100th serviceman to receive the Medal of Honor during World War II, received our nation's highest award on May 21, 1945 at a joint session of Congress in Washington, D.C. As President Truman placed the Medal of Honor around his neck, the then T/Sgt. Jake W. Lindsey's reaction was "one of humbleness and gratitude to a wonderful Nation."

> His citation for the Medal of Honor reads: "Technical Sergeant Jake W. Lindsey, Company C, 16th Infantry, First Infantry Division, led a platoon reduced to six of its original strength of 40, in an attack on an enemy position near Hamich, Germany, 16 November 1944. His men captured their objective and were digging in when counterattacked by a German Infantry company and five tanks. Armed with a rifle and grenades, Sergeant Lindsey took position on the left and in advance of the remnant of his platoon, and though exposed to heavy fire, machine-gun and tank fire, beat off repeated enemy attacks. Tanks moved to within 50 yards of him but were forced to withdraw because of his accurate grenade fire. After driving off the tanks he knocked out two machine-guns to his front. Though painfully wounded Sergeant Lindsey continued firing and throwing grenades until his ammunition was expended. An enemy squad attempted to set up a machine gun 50 yards from him. Unmindful of his wounds and enemy fire, he rushed these eight German soldiers, single-handedly closed with them, killed three with his bayonet and captured three; the two other escaped. In his fearlessness, inspiring courage, and superb leadership, Sergeant Lindsey carried on a brilliant defense of his platoon's hard-won ground, securing the position and inflicting heavy casualties on the numerically superior enemy."

He had lost 34 men from his platoon during the attack in the Huertgen Forest in Germany in 1944 and yet he had only one thought in mind—"To kill every German I could before they got me." During the Korean Conflict Lieutenant Lindsey was a member of the only American Airborne unit committed to that war, the 187th Regimental Combat Team. He participated in both combat jumps of the 187th RCT and was wounded again at Pyongyang-hi in North Korea during March of 1951. He has always felt that the American paratrooper was the greatest combat soldier in the world.

To this gallant soldier and patriot being an American means "that I am free to say or do as I like; one of the greatest freedoms a person can have."

His advice to the youth of America is "to love their Country and be prepared to defend it with their life if it becomes necessary."

CHARLES A. MACGILLIVARY

During the action for which Charles MacGillivary received his Medal of Honor his left arm was shot off and he was also wounded in the left side by German machine gun fire. Serving as his own medic, Sergeant MacGillivary jabbed the stump of his arm into the deep snow until it froze, thereby saving his own life by preventing terminal bleeding!

Charles A. MacGillivary was born in Charlottetown, Prince Edward Island, Canada on January 7, 1917. In 1933, at the age of 16, he entered the Merchant Marine Service. He served as a fireman and a deck engineer on American, Panamanian, Canadian and Norwegian ships until 1941. In January of that year he joined the United States Army as a Private. He was honorably discharged (medical) on June 30, 1945 with the rank of Technical Sergeant. In 1975 Charles retired from the U.S. Customs Service after having been employed as a Criminal Investigator for 25 years.

Both of Sergeant MacGillivary's parents were born in Canada. His father was of Scotch descent. His mother was Irish. He is six feet tall, weighs 200 pounds and is a typical handsome Scotch-Irishman. In his words, "I was born a Roman Catholic and will die a Roman Catholic." He lives with his wife, Esther, in Braintree, Massachusetts. They have three married daughters, all college graduates, and eight grandchildren.

Before he went overseas during World War II, he became an American citizen. Charles holds the unique distinction of being the only living Canadian of World War II who is a recipient of the Medal of Honor. His decorations include: The Medal of Honor, The Distinguished Service Cross, June 6, 1944 at the Invasion of Omaha Beach in France, The Bronze Star with three Clusters in North Africa, The Soldiers Medal in Italy, The Purple Heart with three Clusters, and The French Crois de Guerre.

Charles A. MacGillivary is a life member of the following organizations: AMVETS, V.F.W., American Legion, Canadian Legion, Disabled American Veterans, and **Congressional Medal of Honor Society. He also is a past president of the CMH Society and one of its founders. His** civilian awards are numerous, but among the many he has received is The Gallantry Award from the United States Bureau of Customs. This is the highest honor the Customs Bureau can bestow on their civilian employees. His Veteran Citations and Awards again are so multitudinous as to preclude listing them all but it is of interest that he formed the Allied War Veterans Council of South Boston and was elected the First Chief Marshall from the Allied War Veterans Council for St. Patrick's Day Parade on March 17, 1948. Also, Sergeant MacGillivary was placed in The Hall of Fame of the 71st Infantry Regiment in the 71st Armory in New York as an outstanding combat soldier of WWII in Europe.

On the 23rd of August, 1945, in the accompanyment of his wife and two sisters, Sergeant Charles A. MacGillivary was awarded the Medal of Honor by President Harry S. Truman in the White House at Washington, D.C. As President Truman placed the Medal of Honor around Sergeant MacGillivary's neck he said, "I would rather have the Medal of Honor than be President of the United States."

The citation for Charles A. MacGillivary's Medal of Honor reads:

MACGILLIVARY, CHARLES A.

Rank and organization: Sergeant, U.S. Army, Company I, 71st Infantry, 44th Infantry Division. Place and date: Near Woelfling, France, 1 January 1945. Entered service at: Boston, Mass. Birth: Charlottetown, Prince Edward Island, Canada. G.O. No: 77, 10 September 1945, Citation: He led a squad when his unit moved forward in darkness to meet the threat of a breakthrough by elements of the 17th German Panzer Grenadier Division. Assigned to protect the left flank, he discovered hostile troops digging in. As he reported this information, several German machine guns opened fire, stopping the American advance. knowing the position of the enemy, Sgt. MacGillivary volunteered to knock out one of the guns while another company closed in from the right to assault the remaining strong points. He circled from the left through woods and snow, carefully worked his way to the emplacement and shot the two camouflaged gunners at a range of three feet as other enemy forces withdrew. Early in the afternoon of the same day, Sgt. MacGillivary was dispatched on reconnaissance and found that Company I was being opposed by about six machine guns reinforcing a company of fanatically fighting Germans. His unit began an attack but was pinned down by furious automatic and small-arms fire. With a clear idea of where the enemy guns were placed, he voluntarily embarked on a lone combat patrol. Skillfully taking advantage of all available cover, he stalked the enemy, reached a hostile machine gun and blasted its crew with a grenade. He picked up a submachine gun from the battlefield and pressed on to within ten yards of another machine gun, where the enemy crew discovered him and feverishly tried to swing their weapon into line to cut him down. He charged ahead, jumped into the midst of the Germans and killed them with several bursts. Without hesitation, he moved on to still another machine gun, creeping, crawling, and rushing from tree to tree, until close enough to toss a grenade into the emplacement and close with its defenders. He dispatched this crew also, but was himself seriously wounded. Through his indomitable fighting spirit, great initiative, and utter disregard for personal safety in the face of powerful enemy resistance, Sgt. MacGillivary destroyed four hostile machine guns and immeasurably helped his company to continue on its mission with minimum casualties."

When the Medal of Honor was placed around his neck by President Harry S. Truman, Sgt. MacGillivary felt "that I was being honored by the greatest nation in the world and it was a badge of honor I highly respect from a grateful nation.

"I always had strong beliefs in this great nation of ours," he states, "after all, I came from a foreign country and adopted this great nation. America is a free nation with freely given opportunities and a nation of people that are always willing to help people in distress in other countries. All you have to do is look at the history of this great nation.

"My advice to the youth of America is that a nation is only as good as what you put into it and the politicians that you elect to lead it. You can not have a nation without an army or navy. It is like having a city without a police force. You have to respect one another and what you put into this nation I can assure you, you will get dividends in return."

GINO J. MERLI

One of the most fantastic, incredible and ingenious feats of courage during World War II is described in terse sentences by the comrades of Pfc. Gino Merli, Medal of Honor recipient of Peckville, Pennsylvania. To visualize the situation under which Gino Merli performed his multi-splendoured achievement his citation for the Medal of Honor is presented:

MERLI, GINO J.

Rank and organization: Private First Class, U.S. Army, 18th Infantry, 1st Infantry Divison. Place and date: Near Sars la Bruyere, Belgium, 4-5 September 1944. Entered service at: Peckville, Pa. Birth: Scranton, Pa. G.O. No: 64, 4 August 1945. Citation: He was serving as a machine gunner in the vicinity of Sars la Bruyere, Belgium, on the night of 4-5 September 1944, when his company was attacked by a superior German force. Its position was overrun and he was surrounded when our troops were driven back by overwhelming numbers and firepower. Disregarding the fury of the enemy fire concentrated on him he maintained his position, covering the withdrawal of our riflemen and breaking the force of the enemy pressure. His assistant machine gunner was killed and the position captured; the other eight members of the section were forced to surrender. Pfc. Merli slumped down beside the dead assistant gunner and feigned death. No sooner had the enemy group withdrawn than he was up and firing in all directions. Once more his position was taken and the captors found two apparently lifeless bodies. Throughout the night Pfc. Merli stayed at his weapon. By daybreak the enemy had suffered heavy losses, and as our troops launched an assault, asked for a truce. Our negotiating party, who had accepted the German surrender, found Pfc. Merli at his gun. On the battlefield lay 52 enemy dead, 19 of whom were directly in front of the gun. Pfc. Merli's gallantry and courage, and the losses and confusion that he caused the enemy, contributed materially to our victory.

First Lieutenant Albert C. Packwood, Jr., of Dallas, Texas, executive officer of Pfc. Merli's company, reported that the determined stand by Pfc. Merli took the heart out of the Germans.

"The following day 700 Germans surrendered, 85 other enemy infantrymen came in from patrols and surrendered, and 100 wounded were captured," Lt. Packwood stated.

As the Germans swept forward in full fury of their attack, members of Pfc. Merli's machine gun section were taken prisoner, then released the following day by the counter attacking doughboys. Among these was Corporal Lyle E. Kuenzer of Bear Lake, Michigan, who related:

"As the enemy riflemen overran Pfc. Merli's position, he slumped to the ground and lay beside his dead assistant gunner. The troops entered the emplacement and prodded Pfc. Merli and his dead comrade with their bayonets.

"Assuming both were dead they continued their assault on our withdrawing troops. As they left he jumped to the machine gun and opened fire on them. He continued to deliver effective fire which enabled the withdrawal of our men with a minimum of casualties.

"They hadn't gone ten yards when Pfc. Merli opened up on them with the machine gun. As each attacking wave rushed the emplacement, he played dead and then kept up the fire. Pfc. Merli stayed at his weapon and broke up each assault wave all through the night."

When it was apparent the German attack would carry through the American lines, members of Pfc. Merli's section discussed withdrawing, but realized the weapon would have to be abandoned. Sergeant Milton V. Kokoszka of Chester, Pennsylvania, reported:

"We knew the enemy would have us surrounded very quickly. Pfc. Merli said, 'I'm staying' and the rest of us stayed, too. Just back of the position I saw two of the enemy get to within five yards of the gun and kill his assistant gunner with a bullet. Their fire damaged the water jacket of the gun. He swung around and killed these two.

"The enemy passed on both sides and we realized we were surrounded. They came in from all sides and I realized Pfc. Merli couldn't fire in all directions at once. The rest of us had to surrender.

"I noticed he had not been taken prisoner and after we'd moved some distance I heard our machine gun open up. He had pretended to be dead to escape capture. I saw different enemy groups move into the emplacement and the gun would stop firing but start up again as soon as they left. Next morning, when we were recaptured, I saw Pfc. Merli.

"He was covered with the blood of the dead assistant gunner. His clothing was tattered and cut where they'd probed at him with bayonets."

Second Lieutenant Harry Kelly of Brooklyn, New York, described the fury of the fighting thus:

"The enemy pushed through from sheer weight of numbers and overpowering fire. Only Pfc. Merli's gun remained to cover the withdrawal of our troops. All the fury of the enemy centered on this lone gun. The area was criss-crossed by tracer bullets and lighted by shell bursts. It was Pfc. Merli's last chance to withdraw and he knew it. But he stayed on.

"The bayonet assault on our line swept past his position and engulfed it. But in spite of the large number of grenades that were exploding, his gun continued to fire. I saw the fire of the gun swing in a complete circle and for short periods it would stop, then start up again.

"By day break the enemy was tired and frustrated. They had suffered heavy losses. when they saw that our assault was coming, they surrendered."

Gino Merli was born in Scranton, Pennsylvania on May 13, 1924. He entered the Army on July 22, 1943. In addition to the Medal of Honor, Gino was awarded the Bronze Star, the Purple Heart with Cluster, the Presidential Unit Citation, the Combat Infantry Badge, the ETO Ribbon with three battle stars and the Good Conduct Medal. He was honorably discharged from the Army on December 8, 1945 with the rank of Sergeant.

Both of Gino Merli's parents were born in northern Italy. They immigrated to the United States in 1921, leaving a baby daughter, Emma, in Italy, to be taken care of by Gino's great grandmother. On December 24, 1921 Gino's older brother, Nicholas, was born in Scranton, Pennsylvania. In January of 1928, after the Merli family had moved to Peckville, a third son, Chester, was born. And finally, on December 3, 1932 Gino's youngest brother, Joseph, arrived. His sister, Emma, who was left in Italy, joined the family in October of 1938.

Since Gino Merli was inducted into the Army at age 19, while still in high school, he returned to Blakely High School and graduated in 1946, becoming one of the only two Medal of Honor recipients known who formally completed high school after having received our Nation's highest honor. He is married to the former Mary Lemoncelli of Eynon, Pennsylvania. They have three children—Gino Merli Jr., who is a doctor, Maria, a registered nurse, and Phillip, who is a college student.

For the last 36 years, Gino Merli has been employed at the Veterans Administration Medical Center in Wilkes-Barre, Pennsylvania as a Veterans Benefits Counselor with outstanding performance. Also he has served in many civic organizations and has made hundreds of speeches of a patriotic nature for many of the Veteran and Civic organizations in the country. He is a deeply religous man of the Catholic faith.

Being an American for Gino Merli means, "Freedom, liberty, justice, love, opportunity, vastness, dedication, education, security, simplicity, progress, unity, forefathers and lastly, but foremost, God . . . for He must love America. He and He alone gave our forefathers this vast land, free and unencumbered, with opportunity and liberty—through education to simplify progress . . . toward unity, security and justice for all people so dedicated . . . this is America."

His advice to the youth of America is . . . "As you can see, not everyone can be a CMH . . . but everyone can have pride in himself—have pride in his heritage. This great land of ours—America—it takes every single person to make our nation operate. No matter how small a part you think you play, always remember that it is necessary—from your first cry, you were important to your parents; as a student, you were important to your teachers; as an adult, you were important to your community . . . and during this entire period you were important to your nation. What you must never forget . . . in each phase, you must do your very best . . . you must excel— again each one cannot be a genius, just your very best and the very best will return to you . . . because if everyone pulls his weight, the job will become lighter and easier. We must keep the wheels of progress turning. We must keep our ship of State afloat. We must always keep trying to better ourselves—our surroundings—our country, and we must never quit. A chain is only as strong as its weakest link. Keep that link strong and we, as Americans, can never lose. America, the beautiful! America, the free! But, always remember America is you and me!"

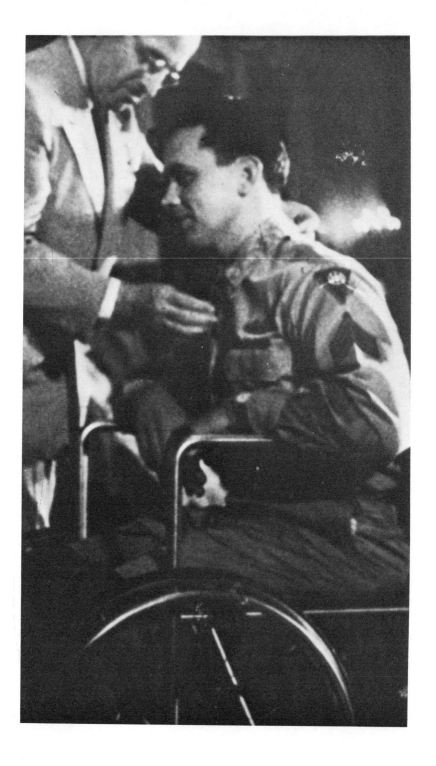

RALPH G. NEPPEL

Although he lost both of his legs defending an approach to the village of Birgel, Germany, as the leader of his machine gun squad, on December 14, 1944, Ralph Neppel has never lost his infectious sense of humor. If you met him in his home, he might shock you. For Ralph has three sets of artificial limbs. On special occasions he will leave a room full of people, wearing his normal set of legs. In a few moments he will return with his extra set of giant legs on, and then again will leave the party to return a second time wearing his midget sized legs. Always with a big grin on his countenance!

Ralph G. Neppel was born in Wiley, Iowa on October 31, 1923. His father Max Neppel and his mother Rose Neppel farmed in Carroll county, Iowa all of their adult lives. There were seven children in the Neppel family, including Ralph. They were a typical hard working, close-knit farming family of German ancestry. Then in 1932 tragedy struck the Neppels; Mr. Max Neppel died of diabetes and they lost their farm in the depths of the great depression. Mrs. Rose Neppel kept her children together and they became tenant farmers. In Ralph's words, "my widowed mother managed us well, raising the seven of us from age 14 to my youngest sister, who was only one. We always had plenty to eat and all of us were happy with simple things in life." However, Ralph had to quit school after the eighth grade in order to help support his brothers and sisters.

In March of 1943 Ralph Neppel was inducted into the Army. After completing basic training at Camp Butner in

Durham, North Carolina and advanced training at Ft. Meade, Maryland, Ralph went home to Iowa on furlough. During his leave Ralph became engaged to Miss Jean Moore, the beautiful girl he had met at the dance hall at McNabbs Roof Garden in Carrol, Iowa before he was inducted into military service. They mutually decided to wait until he came home for good before getting married. Ralph was shipped out to England.

He joined M Company of the 329th Infantry Regiment of the 83rd Division at the invasion of Normandy in June of 1944. Because he was strong, Pvt. Neppel was able to hold his .30-caliber machine gun in his hands without having to rest it on a tripod while firing this deadly weapon. While fighting through the terrible hedgerows of France, he became a battle-seasoned veteran and was promoted to lead his machine gun squad with the rank of Sergeant. In a letter to his sweetheart Jean, back home in Iowa, Ralph wrote—"I'm getting to be an old veteran already. And I have more guts than I thought I had . . . P.S. If you can pray, hon, it sure helps up here."

By December of 1944 the 83rd Division had fought its way across France into the terrible Hurtgen Forest in the heartland of Germany. On the 14th of December, Sergeant Neppel's machine gun squad moved through the tree bursts and booby traps of the Hurtgen Forest to the crossroads of the first German village on the other side of the forest—Birgel, Germany. He was ordered to set up his machine gun at this crossroad in order to repulse a possible German counter-attack.

It came just as night enveloped the village. After a mortar barrage shelled the area, a German tank roared over a ridge and fired directly at Ralph. The first shell smashed into him before he could open up with his 50-caliber. He was blown into the air and knew he had been frightfully wounded. As he smashed back onto the German earth he saw his bloody

118

combat boot lying in the snow. How he hurt! Now looking at his legs, he saw that his right leg was missing and the other one was a bloody mess. His machine gun was lying in the snow, some ten yards away. Pulling himself toward his weapon on his elbows through the red stained snow, he clawed the machine gun into his arms.

By now the German tank was only forty yards away. Ralph pulled his weapon to his chest and waited and waited and waited! Then the tank was only a scant twenty yards from his mangled body. Twenty Wermacht riflemen surrounded the massive tank protecting it from the lone farm-boy-soldier from Iowa. They came closer and Ralph fired and fired and fired until he lost consciousness, thinking "I'm bleeding out." His last remembrance was the sight of the tank as it stopped and a German Officer approaching him, pointing his Lüger pistol at Ralph's head.

The bullet smashed into Ralph's helmet and spun off in an oblique flight. The tank, minus its protective cover of German infantrymen, who were all dead from Ralph's deadly fire, reversed its direction and Birget belonged to Ralph's outfit.

The Iowa farm boy was evacuated to Belgium. In a hospital, his left leg was amputated as the remains of his other leg was repaired. Now he was in England, in a general hospital. Because of his infectious sense of humor, the other wounded soldiers epitomized his lust for life as one of them said—"That guy doesn't give the rest of us a chance to feel sorry for ourselves."

"He goes to bed smiling and wakes up laughing."

But under this facade of boosting the morale of his wounded brothers-in-war, Ralph Neppel hid his own concern for his greviously wounded body until he quietly confided to another casuality of war, Buck Walden, a fellow soldier from Iowa. Handing Buck his most treasured possesion, a photo of

Jean, Sergeant Neppel asked—"Do you think she'll still want to marry me, Buck? Do you think I should even ask her, Buck? One leg wouldn't be too bad, but two . . ."

This is what happened—As he was carried off the Queen Mary, Paulette Goddard was throwing kisses and when he was carried from the train at Temple, Texas for treatment at McCloskey General Hospital, a military band played "Deep in the Heart of Texas."

The bottom line. Driving non-stop from Carroll, Iowa to Temple, Texas was Ralph's immediate family and his sweetheart, Jean Moore. As his family entered his hospital room, Jean stood outside, fully aware that Ralph had put the stopper on the German counter-attack all by himself and had forced the Wermacht to withdraw but had lost both of his legs in his super-human effort. She was most concerned that Ralph would still be the big happy guy she remembered back in Iowa before he became an American soldier.

When she opened the door and went in, he was sitting on the edge of his hospital bed with his intact arms reaching out to her! And a big Iowa farm-boy-soldier grin on his face!

They now have four wonderful children and Ralph used the GI bill to obtain his first degree at Buena Vista College in Storm Lake, Iowa.

In his own words, Ralph has stated—"As a simple town farm boy, I was more than shaking (sitting in a wheel chair in the East Room of the White House) when President Harry Truman placed the Medal of Honor around my neck. I believe the wheel chair was also shaking. This was the biggest day of my life, being invited to our Nation's Capital at government expense; getting a commercial airplane ride, seeing the Pentagon and all the big government buildings."

He has always known that the examples that his beloved mother, still living at age 87, instilled in him during his formative years have been the motivating spirit of his life.

Ralph G. Neppel's official citation for the Medal of Honor reads:

NEPPEL, RALPH G.

Rank and organization: Sergeant, U.S. Army, Company M, 329th Infantry, 83rd Infantry Division. Place and date: Birgel, Germany, 14 December 1944. Entered service at: Glidden, Iowa. Birth: Willey, Iowa. G.O. No. 77, September 1945. Citation: He was leader of a machine gun squad defending an approach to the village of Birgel, Germany, on 14 December 1944, when an enemy tank, supported by 20 infantrymen, counter-attacked. He held his fire until the Germans were within 100 yards and then raked the foot soldiers beside the tank, killing several of them. The enemy armor continued to press forward, and at a pointblank range of 30 yards, fired a high-velocity shell into the American emplacement, wounding the entire squad. Sgt. Neppel, blown ten yards from his gun, had one leg severed below the knee and suffered other wounds. Despite his injuries and the danger from the onrushing tank and infantry, he dragged himself back to his position on his elbows, remounted his gun and killed the remaining riflemen. Stripped of its infantry protection, the tank was forced to withdraw. By his superb courage and indomitable fighting spirit, Sgt. Neppel inflicted heavy casualties on the enemy and broke a determined counter-attack.

After completing his first degree, Ralph Neppel continued his education and did graduate work at Drake University in Des Moines, Iowa. He was then employed by the Veterans Administration as a contact representative in Iowa. Since his retirement from the V.A., he has sold real estate in Iowa City, has purchased a four-plex apartment house, is active in several veteran organizations and the Iowa Government Committee on employment of the handicapped. He stays very active by mowing his lawns, painting, and also does the work on his properties. Most of all, he has never lost his great sense of humor and his love of life.

In response to the question, 'What does it mean to him to be an American,' he replies—"To me, it is freedom. The privilege of choosing a mate, to raise a family, to attend a church of my choice, to work for the employer of my choice, to feel content. To be able to sleep at night, to breathe the clean fresh air and to see the American Flag flying all over our land. To observe and witness the young and the old, the black and the white and all races working and praying for a better America, and a better tomorrow. To see smiles on the handicapped, the ill, the aged, day and night—this is America at its best!

"One can travel to and from, far and beyond, however a true American cannot wait to return to his secure and peaceful home! In a nutshell—no better place on God's earth! One can be thankful forever that he or she was born in America!"

To the youth of America—"Start the day by rising early in the morning to see the sun coming up, to hear the sweet singing of birds. To smile and to take in the clean, fresh, free air that was given to you by the big man in the sky. Many a veteran has spilled blood, fought in wars to pass on to you young Americans the freedoms that you and the average American citizen takes for granted almost all of your lives. It is not free! It is your responsibility, your job to work, donate, preserve, vote, serve in the military cheerfully, perform civic duties for your community. No, young Americans, it is not all free! It is up to you to carry on, to do something for our country. It is yours now and your turn to make a contribution to the greatest country in the world. Please don't let America down!"

So prays Ralph G. Neppel, CMH, All American Farm Boy, Soldier, Adult Citizen of Iowa.

MITCHELL PAIGE

Mitch Paige enlisted in the U.S. Marine Corps at the age of eighteen in 1936. In 1964, he retired with the rank of Colonel, having served in the field since 1942 at Guadalcanal, New Guinea, Cape Gloucester, New Britain Island, Pavuvu, the Russell Islands, Japan, China, Korea and Vietnam. In addition to being the author of *A Marine Named Mitch,* the true story of his combat experiences, since his retirement he has worked in the research and development of miniature rockets, miniature rocket weapons systems, penetration aids, and hypervelocity acceleration. Also he has invented the Universal Paige Inflatable Tent which he gave to the Army Natick Laboratories in Natick, Massachusetts.

Born to a hard working railroad construction family of Serbian ancestry on August 31, 1918, in the small town of Charleroi, Pennsylvania, Mitch Paige was the youngest of three children. He is a high school graduate and has completed the equivalency of four years of college while on active duty in the Marines. He considers himself to be a "Christian." His first wife, Jan, died on March 23, 1979. Col. Paige remarried on January 22, 1981 to Marilyn R. Bollman in Washington, D.C. following the inaugural of President Reagan. His two children, Mitchell John and his daughter, Janis Darlene are married and live in the Bay area of California.

Through the years, Colonel Paige has made thousands of speeches to the young people of our country, to State and National Conventions of Veterans and other organizations, both here and abroad, the subject usually being Americanism or Anti-Communism. He is the recipient of numerous awards and letters of commendation from government, civic and fraternal organizations. Colonel Paige is the Past President of the 1st Marine Division Association and the former 6th District Director of the Congressional Medal of Honor Society as well as being a Life Member of The Congressional Medal of Honor Society, The Army and Navy Legion of Valor, The Military Order of the Purple Heart, The Regular Veterans Association, The 1st Marine Division Association, The Marine Corps League, The American Legion, and a Life Member of The British Royal Marines. Also he is a Member of The Military Order of The World Wars, The Fleet Reserve Association, The National Rifle Club Association, The American Police Academy, The Commonwealth Club of California, and The International Optimists. He currently resides in Redwood City, California but travels extensively.

The Medal of Honor was awarded to Mitch Paige for his extraordinary heroism on Guadalcanal on October 26, 1942. His citation for the Congressional Medal of Honor reads:

"The President of the United States takes pleasure in presenting the CONGRESSIONAL MEDAL OF HONOR to PLATOON SERGEANT MITCHELL PAIGE, U.S.M.C., for service as set forth in the following:

CITATION: For extraordinary heroism and conspicuous gallantry in action above and beyond the call of duty while serving with the Second Battalion, Seventh Marines, First Marine Division, in combat against enemy Japanese forces in the Solomon Islands Area on October 26, 1942. When the enemy broke through the line directly in front of his position, Platoon Sergeant Paige, commanding a machine gun section with fearless determination, continued to direct the fire of his gunners until all his men were either killed or wounded. Alone, against the deadly hail of Japanese shells, he manned his gun, and when it was destroyed, took over

126

another, moving from gun to gun, never ceasing his withering fire against the advancing hordes until reinforcements finally arrived. Then, forming a new line, he dauntlessly and aggressively led a bayonet charge, driving the enemy back and preventing a breakthrough in our lines. His great personal valor and unyielding devotion to duty were in keeping with the highest traditions of the United States Naval Service."

Mitch Paige's heroic actions that early morning and day are so utterly fantastic and incredible that the following description is quoted from his book:

"About 0200, in a silence so pervasive that men many yards apart could hear each other breathing, I began to sense movement all along the front and deep in the jungle below us and to our left. We could hear the muffled clanking of equipment and periodically, voices hissing in Japanese. These were undoubtly squad leaders giving their instructions. At the same time, small colored lights began flicking on and off throughout the jungle. I could hear Price whispering for me to come to his foxhole. I quietly crawled over to him and he had an excellent view of someone flicking a light on and off. Price said, 'I thought I was cracking up seeing all those fireflies.' I assured him he was not cracking up because those were lights handled by Japanese soldiers. As I crawled around telling the men to glue their eyes and ears to anything and reminded them that the small lights we were seeing were assembly signals for the enemy squads. I again instructed everyone not to fire their guns as the muzzle flash would give away our positions and that we would be raked with fire and smothered with grenades. We had to let them get closer as we were outnumbered, but when things started popping I urged each man to just hang on. Earlier Jonjock, Swanek and I stretched a piece of wire out in front of our position and hung several empty blackened ration cans on it. We put an empty cartridge case in each can which would rattle if hit by someone's foot. I had previously requested an artillery and mortar concentration. This was, however, denied because the enemy was still in the jungle where the effect would almost be nil. I then returned to my foxhole. Manning my number two gun was Corporal Raymond 'Big Stoop' Gaston and Private Samuel 'Muscles' Leiphart. Their gun was at the part of our line which bordered on the side where the jungle came up to meet the ridge. They both whispered to me that there was considerable rustling very near to the undergrowth. I said, 'Hold your fire.' Corporal Richard 'Moose' Stansberry arranged several grenades in a neat row in front of him, then nervously rearranged them. He was fond of his Thompson sub-machine gun and I never worried about him as he was well-trained, a perfectly disciplined marine who could handle himself in any situation. Now everyone was straining to hear and see.

"The bushes rustled and the maddening voices continued their soft sibilant mutterings, but still nothing could be seen. Then I dimly sensed a dark figure lurking near Gaston's position. I grabbed a grenade, pulled the pin and held the lever ready to throw it. Around me I could hear the others also pulling pins as we did the night before. We heard the ration cans rattle and then somebody let out a shriek and instantaneously the battle erupted. Grenades were exploding all over the ridge nose. Japanese rifles and machine guns fired blindly in the night and the first wave of enemy troops swarmed into our positions from the jungle flanking Gaston's gun.

"Stansberry was pulling the pins out of his grenades with his teeth and lobbing them down the slope into the jungle. Leiphart was skying them overhead like a baseball pitcher. The tension burst like a balloon and many men found themselves cursing, growling, screaming like banshees. The Japanese were yelling Banzai! and 'Blood for the Emperor!'

Stansberry, in a spontaneous tribute to President Roosevelt's wife, shouted back, 'Blood for Eleanor!'

"The battleground was lit by flashes of machine-gun fire, pierced by the arching red patterns of tracer bullets, shaken by the blast of shells laid down no more than 30 yards in front of the ridge by Captain Louis Ditta's 60mm Mortars. It was a confusing maelstrom, with dark shapes crawling across the ground or swirling in clumped knots; struggling men falling on each other with bayonets, swords and violent oaths. After the first volley of American grenades exploded the wave of Japanese crowding onto the knoll thickened. Pfc. Charles H. Lock was killed from a burst of enemy machine-gun fire.

"I screamed, 'Fire machine guns! Fire!' and with that all the machine guns opened up with all the rifles and tommy guns. In the flickering light, I saw a fierce struggle taking place for the number two gun. Several Japanese soldiers were racing toward Leiphart, who was kneeling, apparently already hit. I managed to shoot two of them while the third lowered his bayonet and lunged. Leiphart was the smallest man in the platoon, weighing barely 125 pounds. The Japanese soldier ran him through, the force of the thrust lifting him high in the air. I took careful aim and shot Leiphart's killer. Gaston was flat on his back, scrambling away from a Japanese officer who was hacking at him with a two-handed Samurai sword and grunting with the exertion. Gaston tried desperately to block the Samurai sword with a Springfield he had picked up off the ground, apparently Leiphart's. One of his legs was badly cut from the blows. The rifle soon splintered. The Japanese officer raised his sword for the killing thrust and Gaston, with maniac strength, snaked his good leg up and caught his man under the chin with his boon docker, a violent blow that broke the Japaneses' neck. The attackers ran past Gaston's gun and spread out, concentrating their fire on the left flank gun, manned by Corporal John Grant, Pfc. Sam H. Scott and Willis A. Hinson. Within minutes, Scott was killed and Hinson was wounded in the head. Then Joseph A. Pawlowski was killed. Stansberry, who had been near me was hit in the shoulder, but the last time I saw him he was still firing his tommy gun with ferocity and shouting, 'Charge! Charge! Blood for Eleanor!'

"Corporal Pettyjohn on the right, cried out in anguish, 'My gun's jammed!' I was too busy to answer his call for help. At the center, we were beating back the seemingly endless wall of Japanese coming up the gentle slope at the front of the position. There were at that point approximately seventy-five enemy soldiers crashing through the platoon, most of them on the left flank, but the main force of the attack had already begun to ebb. The ridge was crowded with fighting men it seemed. Somehow I vividly recall putting up my left hand just as an enemy soldier lunged at me with a fixed bayonet. He must have been off balance as the point of the bayonet hit between my little finger and the ring finger, enough to let me parry it off, and as he went by me he dropped dead on the ground.

"The enemy started to melt back down the slope, and almost before they were out of sight, Navy Corpsmen began moving forward to treat the wounded. At Pettyjohn's gun, James 'Knobby' McNabb and Mitchel F. 'Pat' Swanek were badly wounded and had to be moved off the line. Stansberry was still around and didn't want to leave. I crawled over to Pettyjohn's gun. 'What's wrong with it?' Pettyjohn said 'a ruptured cartridge which refused to budge'. I said, 'Move over,' and fumbled with stiff fingers, broke a nail completely off, but somehow pried the slug out with a combination tool, which I found in the spare parts kit under the tripod. I also changed the belt feed pawl, which had been damaged in the rough slamming trying to get the round out. Pettyjohn and

Faust covered me. Though the first assault had flopped, a number of enemy soldiers had shinnied to the top of the tall hardwood trees growing up from the jungle between the platoon and Fox Company's position. From this vantage point, they could direct a punishing, plunging fire down in two directions. The men in the foxholes along the crest were especially vulnerable; Bob G. Jonjock and John W. Price were wounded and helped back of the line by corpsmen.

"I was getting ready to feed a new belt of ammunition into Pettyjohn's gun, my left hand felt very slippery so I rubbed it in the dirt under the tripod of the gun, then as I reached up to hold the belt again, I felt a sharp vibration and a jab of hot pain in my hand. I fell back momentarily and flapped my arm and stared angrily at the gun, which had been wrecked by a burst of fire from a Japanese Nambu light machine gun.

"Almost immediately, a second assault wave came washing over our positions. This attack was more successful than the first. Oliver Hinkley and William R. Dudly were wounded. Hinson, over on the left gun, already wounded, continued to fire until all his supporting rifles were silenced. He then withdrew down around the hill in the rear of George Company, putting the gun out of action before he left as I had instructed. That section had been hit hard with mortars and grenades, causing severe shock to all the men. One of the first being August P. Marquez. All the men on the spur had been literally blasted off, including Lieutenant Phillips, Bill Payne and John Grant.

"In the Fox Company area back toward my left rear, I saw Fox Company men pulling out and disappearing over the crest. I picked up a Springfield and fired a shot at them, yelling for them to hold the line. The Japanese swarmed up that seventy foot cliff in great numbers, armed with three heavy and six light machine guns, a number of tommy guns and several knee mortars. I thought, dear God, Major Conoley and his small command post are just over the crest, but here was the only grazing fire I had with my machine gun, so I quickly found Gaston's gun and swung it around toward our own lines as there was nothing between my gun and the crest but enemy soldiers. I fired a full belt of ammunition into the backs of those crouching enemy, praying that they could not get over the crest to the command post. I learned later from Captain Farrell, who was with Colonel Hanneken's command post, that the word was that the enemy had one of Paige's fast firing machine guns and the rounds were ricocheting over the line over Major Conoley's position. He had also heard reports that all my men had been killed and in fact some had seen me sprawled out dead on the ground before they left the ridge. I learned later, too, that this information had gotten back to the Division Command Post. By 0500 the enemy was all over the spur and it appeared they were going to roll up the entire battalion front. A second prong of the attack, aimed at our front had not fared as well, but my platoon was being decimated. A hail of shrapnel killed Daniel R. Cashman. Stansberry had been pulled back over the hill, after being hit again.

"I continued to trigger bursts until the barrel began to steam. In front of me was a large pile of dead bodies. I ran around the ridge from gun to gun trying to keep them firing, but at each emplacement I found only dead bodies. I knew then I must be all alone. As I ran back and forth, I bumped into enemy soldiers who were seemingly dashing about aimlessly in the dark. Apparently they weren't yet aware they had almost complete possession of the knoll. As I scampered around the knoll, I fired someone's Springfield that I happened to pick up. Then somehow, I stumbled over into the right flank into George Company. There I found a couple of men I knew named Kelly and Totman. They had a water-cooled machine gun. I told them I needed their gun. At the same time, I grabbed it and they took off with me. I said, 'Follow me!' and ordered several riflemen to fix bayonets and to follow us to form a skirmish line back across the ridge. I told the riflemen not to be afraid to use the bayonet. We still had the 1905, 16-inch bayonets with the front end sharpened throughout its length and the back edge five inches from the point. It was by then not quite as dark as it had been. Soon dawn would break. I knew that once the Japanese realized how much progress they had made, a third wave of attackers would come up the slope to solidify their hold on the hill.

"On the way back, I noticed some movement of Japanese on the ridge just above Major Conoley's position and which I had raked with grazing fire earlier. I fired Kelly's and Totman's full belt of 250 rounds into that area and once again the rounds were ricocheting over Conoley's head, but he had no way of knowing that I was doing the firing. He could only surmise that the enemy was now using our machine guns. As we advanced back across the ridge, some of the Japanese began falling back. Several of them, however, began crawling awkwardly across the knoll with their rifles cradled in the crooks of their arms and then I saw with horror that they were headed toward one of my guns, which was now out in the open and unmanned. Galvanized by the threat, I ran for the gun. From the gully area, several Japanese guns spotted me and swiveled to rake me with enfilading fire. The snipers in the trees also tried to bring me down with grenades and mortars burst all around me as I ran to that gun. One of the crawling enemy soldiers saw me coming and he jumped up to race me to the prize. I got there first and jumped into a hole behind the gun. The enemy soldier, less than 25 yards away, dropped to the ground and started to open up on me. I turned the gun on the enemy and immediately realized it was not loaded. I quickly scooped up a partially loaded belt lying on the ground and with fumbling fingers, started to load it.

133

"Suddenly a very strange feeling came over me. I tried desperately to reach forward to pull the bolt handle back to load the gun, but I felt as though I was in a vise. Even so, I was completely relaxed and felt as though I was sitting peacefully in a park. I could feel a warm sensation between my chin and my Adam's apple. Then all of a sudden I fell forward over the gun, loaded the gun, and swung it at the enemy gunner, the precise moment he had fired his full thirty-round magazine at me and stopped firing. For days later I thought about the mystery and somehow I knew that the 'Man Above' also knew what had happened. I never wanted to relate this experience to anyone, as I did not want to ever have anyone question it. I found three more belts of ammunition and quickly fired them in the trees and all along the ridge. I sprayed the terrain with the remaining rounds clearing everything in sight. All the Japanese fire in the area was being aimed at me apparently, as this was the only automatic weapon firing from a forward position. The barrage, concentrated on the ridge nose, made me feel as if the whole Japanese Army was firing at me. I was getting some help from our mortars control led by battalion with the George Company Commander, Captain L.W. Martin, observing. These rounds laid on the spur and prevented the enemy to move up which would have probably enveloped me from the rear. Other than this, I was still alone as my George Company friends were still behind me some distance. In addition to being in this position, I had an immediate need of more ammunition and I couldn't see anymore lying around anywhere. Just at that time, aid came that made me glow with pride. Three men of my platoon voluntarily crossed the field of fire to resupply me. The first one came up and just as he reached me he fell with a bullet in the stomach. Another one then rushed in and was hit in the groin just as he reached me too. He fell against me, knocking me away from the gun. Seconds later, Bob Jonjock who had also been wounded earlier, came from somewhere with more ammunition. Just as he jumped down beside me to help load the gun, I saw a piece of flesh fly off his neck. He had been hit by an enemy bullet. I told him to get back while I sprayed the area. He refused to leave. I said, 'Get the hell back, Jonjock!' and he again said, 'No, I'm staying with you.' I hated to do it, but I punched him on the chin hard enough to bowl him over and convinced him finally that I wanted my order obeyed. He somehow made his way back as I was afraid he would bleed to death.

"Meanwhile, Major Conoley, at the forward command post, was rounding up a ragtag force with which to retake the Fox Company spur. There were bandsmen serving as stretcher bearers, wiremen, runners, cooks, even mess boys, who had brought some hot food up to the front lines during the night and stayed just in case. Those men, numbering no more than twenty-four, mounted a counterattack up over the crest line that I fired some 500 rounds at. They found the Japanese machine guns and several of Fox Company's weapons, including three light machine guns, all in good working order. That counterattack found ninety-eight dead on the spur by actual count.

"That was about 0530 or so. Dawn was already breaking. I was able to observe the progress of that charge from my position as I was directly out in their front. I also watched quite a few enemy soldiers scrambling back into the jungle, but I couldn't fire in that direction. As I watched that beautiful charge, it gave me the inspiration to get up and yell to my George Company fighters with their fixed bayonets to stand by to charge. I yelled out in Japanese to stand up: 'Tate!—tah-teh, tah-teh!'; hurry: 'Isoge!'—ee-soh-geh, ee-soh-geh!' Immediately a large group of Japanese soldiers, about thirty in all, popped up into view. One of them looked quizzically at me through field glasses. I triggered a long burst and they just peeled off like grass under a mowing machine. At that point, I turned around to tell my friends I was going to charge over the knoll and I said, 'I want everyone of you to be right behind me,' and they were. I threw the two remaining belts of ammunition that my men had brought me over my shoulder, unclamped the heavy machine gun from the tripod and cradled it in my arms. I really didn't notice the weight which was about a total of eighty pounds, and was no more aware that the water jacket of the gun was red hot. I fed one of the belts into the gun and started forward, down the slope, scrambling to keep my feet, spraying a raking fire all about me. There were still a number of live enemy soldiers on the hillside in the tall grass, pressed against the slope. I must have taken them by surprise, as the gun cut them all down. One of them I noticed was a field grade officer who had just expended the rounds in his revolver and was reaching for his two-handed sword. He was no more than four or five feet from me when I ran into him head on.

"The skirmishers followed me over the rim of the knoll and they, too, were all fired up and were giving the rebel yell, shrieking and cat-calling like little boys imitating marines, sounding like there were a thousand rather than a mere handfull. They followed me all the way across the draw with fixed bayonets, to the end of the jungle, where long hours before, the Japanese attacks had started. There we found nothing left to shoot at. The battle was over. The jungle was once again so still, that if it weren't for the evidence of dead bodies, the agony and torment of the previous hours, the bursting terror of the artillery and mortars rounds and the many thousands of rounds of ammunition fired, it might only have been a bad dream of awful death.

"It was a really strange sort of quietness. As I sat down soaked with perspiration and steam still rising from my hot gun, Captain Louis Ditta, another wonderful officer who had joined the riflemen in the skirmish line and had earlier been firing his 60mm mortars to help me, slapped me on the back and as he handed me his canteen of water he kept saying, 'tremendous, tremendous!' He then looked down at his legs. We could see blood coming through his dungarees. He had a neat bullet hole in his right leg.

"There were hundreds of enemy dead in the grass, on the ridge, in the draw, and in the edge of the jungle. We dragged as many as we could into the jungle, out of the sun. We buried many and even blasted some of the ridge over them to prevent the smell that only a dead body can expell in heat. A corpsman sent by Capt. Ditta smeared my whole left arm with a tube of salve of some kind. He cleaned off the bayonet gash, since filled with dirt, and the bullet nicks on my hands also filled with dirt and coagulated blood. He stuck a patch on my back just below the shoulder blade. (In 1955, I felt something irritating in my back, and then had a piece of metal about 3/4 of an inch long removed from my back; right where the corpsman had placed that patch.) As the corpsman left he said, 'You know, you have some pretty neat creases in your steel helmet.' I replied, yes, thank God—Made in America."*

In response to the question, "What it means to be an American," Colonel Paige states—"At a very early age I was imbued with the spirit of Americanism and in particular the three basic principles of our American way of life—the Holy Bible, the Flag and our free enterprise system. All through the years I was reminded that we must constantly be aware of and reaffirm our convictions of morality as defined in the Holy Bible. I was reminded that we must constantly be aware of and reaffirm our convictions of government as defined in our

---

*From the book, *A Marine Named Mitch*, by Col. Mitchell Paige, published in 1975 by Vantage Press (after many years of urging by Colonel Paige's good friend, the actor, Lee Marvin.)

sacred Constitution of the United States. I was reminded that we must be constantly aware of and reaffirm our convictions in the rights of free men to work in callings and locality of their choice. I earnestly believe this.

"When I was about six or seven years old, I can vividly recall my Mother telling us that the American flag must never touch the ground, nor must it ever be defaced in any way. In fact, from those days until the "violence of the 60s" I was always under the impression that it was a federal offense with a $10,000 fine and ten years in prison for desecrating the American flag. But, like so many other sacred American traditions and beliefs, that too, unfortunately had disappeared from our American scene.

"It has always been a great inspiration to recall our cherished heritage. I will never cease to be thrilled with the stories of our great Americans—our Founding Fathers. George Washington, the father of our country who set the example for future generations and gave Americans the inspiration to make the United States of America the greatest nation on earth. I admired and worshipped all those gallant leaders who laid the foundation for our glorious nation—the fifty-six Signers of the Declaration of Independence: John Adams and Thomas Jefferson, two of the architects of the Declaration; Francis Marion, "The Swamp Fox"; Nathaniel Greene and Ethan Allen and his "Green Mountain Boys"; John Paul Jones, who captured more than 300 British ships; Nathan Hale, the 21 year old school teacher who volunteered his services to George Washington to go behind the enemy lines and when captured he was hanged with these words on his lips, "I only regret I have but one life to give for my country." And Patrick Henry and his immortal address of "Give me liberty or give me death."

"Our young nation was born in battle and our glorious history is the envy of peoples everywhere. We are akin by blood and descent to most of the nations of Europe. In the early days of our country many foreigners offered their assistance to us. Marquis De Lafayette, born in France, volunteered his services to help American colonies in their struggle for independence. Major General Baron Von Steuben, born in Germany, helped train George Washington's army at Valley Forge. Count Casimir Pulaski, born in Poland, volunteered to fight for America during the Revolutionary War and died fighting for that cause. Major General Baron Johann DeKalb, born in Bavaria, distinguished himself in battle for America's cause and also paid the supreme sacrifice.

"It is with great pride to read about the 'Great Emancipator,'Abraham Lincoln, who led our nation through an historic crisis when brother fought brother on our land during the Civil War. It is with great pride to know that our great nation saved the world in World War I, 1917-1918. It is with great pride to know that our great nation again saved the free world from dastardly Nazism in World War II, 1941-1945. From that time forward Americans have fought and died to save the free world from its greatest menace and enemy—atheistic Communism, in Korea, Vietnam and elsewhere.

"I am proud to be a citizen of a nation whose objective is peace and goodwill for all mankind. A nation which has contributed so much for the benefit of peoples all over the world. A nation, under God, with liberty and justice for all. I am proud to be an American. I can never believe it is old fashioned to love your Flag and Country nor can I ever believe it is being square to stand in readiness behind our flag to defend those ideals for which it stands against all enemies, foreign or domestic.

"In the fourth century B.C., Aristotle, the Greek philosopher said, 'All who have meditated on the art of governing mankind have been convinced that the fate of empires depends upon the education of youth. It is on the sound education of the people that the security and destiny of every nation chiefly rests.'

"In this connection, our American youth are the future leaders of a free America and it is imperative that they be educated in the history of our great country and to understand our Constitution. Patriotism, loyalty and fair play is part of our inheritance. It has always been the policy of atheistic Communism in its quest for world domination to try to capture the minds and hearts of the youth in the countries it seeks to subjugate. It is the responsibility of all Americans, young and old, to abide by the laws of our land with unwavering devotion and dedication to our Flag and Constitution. We witnessed the world-wide Communist stratagem in the 1960s in the agitating and mobilization of college students for demonstrations and violence against our government and it's Armed Forces.

"If we are to survive, the spirit of '76 must be rekindled in the hearts and minds of the youth of America. No nation had a better example than that set by our Founding Fathers who gave their all to preserve our freedom. This was epitomized in the words written by Thomas Jefferson in the last sentence of the Declaration of Independence where he wrote, "And for the support of the Declaration with a firm reliance on the protection of Divine Providence, we mutually pledge to each other, our lives, our fortunes and our sacred honor." It is the moral obligation of every American to always give his wholehearted and undivided loyalty to our flag. It is the moral obligation of every American to encourage our youth to hold high the torch of freedom and justice. We must not only live our lives according to the principle that freedom under God is man's destiny, but it is every American's obligation to defend that freedom unto death with the courage of free men. This is every American's responsibility—man, woman, and child.

LAWSON PATERSON RAMAGE

Vice Admiral L.P. (Red) Ramage, U.S. Navy (ret), the Commander of a submarine, the U.S.S. Parche, sank five Japanese ships on 31 July 1944 just north of the Phillippines in 46 minutes of violent action! The creative tactics and fantastic results of activities on that memorable night 36 years ago are vividly described by Admiral Ramage:

"Prior to being ordered to new construction, I had made five successful submarine war patrols and had been gunned, bombed and depth charged in good measure. So when I returned to Pearl Harbor and found that they had developed a most effective camouflage for submarines, I decided that henceforth, given the choice, I would try to make the night surface attacks thereby maintaining the initiative and avoiding the counterattacks. Such an oppurtunity presented itself during our first patrol with a wolf-pack. After an 18 hour chase we finally gained a position ahead of an enemy convoy from which we closed at full speed for the attack. We commenced firing at short range, aiming all torpedoes to hit (no spreads as was the usual custom). Got six hits, sank the two leading ships—having expended all forward torpedoes. It then became necessary to maneuver in such a manner as to bring the stern tubes to bear on the remaining wildly zig-zaging targets and at the same time having to avoid the escorts. The problem was further complicated by the fact that we had only the slow running electric torpedoes loaded aft. After about three attempts to reach a favorable firing position it became apparent that the enemy gunfire would not permit us to close sufficiently to insure hits with the slow torpedoes. About that time my torpedo officer came to the bridge and requested permission to reload the forward torpedo tubes. Such a thought was pure heresay—torpedoes were always reloaded when the submarine was at periscope depth or below, going dead slow on an even keel with no motion on the boat which might result in the torpedo getting out of control when it was broken out of the racks. And here we were zigging and zagging among several enemy ships at 20 knots on the surface with the very distinct possibility of having to dive suddenly without warning; certainly the most inconceivable conditions for a reload. However, the torpedo officer convinced me that he had made all preparations and that he was certain he could handle the situation safely—so permission was granted to proceed. In a short time two torpedoes had been reloaded and we drove straight on in and sank the last large ship. Our two other companions had taken their share but had expended all their torpedoes in doing so. Whereupon they departed the area and left us (with ten torpedoes—one in each tube) to remain on station by ourselves for another ten days to finish out our normal patrol and at the same time to absorb the wrath of the badly wounded enemy. Obviously we were not going to see any more ships in that area for sometime. Such was the reward for husbanding my torpedoes and making every one count.

"Having learned a great deal from that experience, I announced to my fellow wolf-pack companions prior to setting out on our next patrol that, given the opportunity, I was going to move right in and get my bag and that they need not worry about stray shots for all of mine were going to be aimed to hit. So, after a long, uneventful patrol without any targets for any of us, our wolf-pack commander asked for an extension of time on station. One of our group departed soon after, leaving just two of us. Then about three days later, the other submarine made contact with a convoy about sundown and relayed his position upon surfacing after sunset, giving the convoy course and speed. We immediately set course at full speed to intercept. However, after four hours we had heard nor seen nothing, so we opened up on the radio and asked for further information. In response we found that the convoy had changed course right after dark and that we had actually been running away from it.

"It then took another four hours to catch up. As we closed from astern we spotted three escorts between us and our quarry. After reaching a position abeam of the convoy, I decided to make a reverse spinner in order to get inside of all the escorts. This maneuver worked fine and just as we were plunging out of it, we discovered that the convoy had changed course 90 degrees toward us, putting us dead ahead of them and closing fast. In fact, we were abeam of the leading ship before we were ready to fire. So we sped past and gave him two shots out of the stern tubes as we closed on the next target. In the meantime, the torpedo rooms had been stripped of all extraneous gear and the reload crews went to work with a vengeance. This was opportunity that we had hoped and planned for. The citation pretty well describes the action that followed. The torpedomen were reloading the tubes fore and aft just as fast as we could fire them and we got 17 hits out of 19 shots—having only missed the first two stern shots fired at the initial target which was in a tight turn. As morning light came on we pulled clear leaving the scene in a shambles with no major targets afloat and only the escort picking up the survivors. Our other pack-mate watched from the sidelines as did the Army search planes from Chungking from overhead.

"We were the first U.S. submarine to combine such tactics: the series of night surface attacks while simultaneously reloading torpedoes. But we were ready and it was long overdue but best of all, it paid off handsomely."

For his extremely daring and dangerous innovation in submarine combat tactics, Vice Admiral Lawson Ramage was awarded the Medal of Honor by President Roosevelt on January 12, 1945 at the White House. His family was present at the ceremony. His offical citation for our nation's highest honor reads:

RAMAGE, LAWSON PATERSON

Rank and organization: Commander, U.S. Navy, U.S.S. Parche. Place and date: Pacific, 31 July 1944. Entered service at: Vermont. Born: 19 January 1909, Monroe Bridge, Mass. Citation: For conspicuous gallantry and intrepidity at the risk of his life above and beyond the call of duty as commanding officer of the U.S.S. Parche in a predawn attack on a Japanese convoy, 31 July 1944. Boldly penetrating the screen of a heavily escorted convoy, Comdr. Ramage launched a perilous surface attack by delivering a crippling stern shot into a freighter and quickly followed up with a series of bow and stern torpedoes to sink the leading tanker and damage the second one. Exposed by the light of bursting flares and bravely defiant of terrific shellfire passing close overhead, he struck again, sinking a transport by two forward reloads. In the mounting fury of fire from the damaged and sinking tanker, he calmly ordered his men below, remaining on the bridge to fight it out with an enemy now disorganized and confused. Swift to act as a fast transport closed in to ram, Comdr. Ramage daringly swung the stern of the speeding Parche as she crossed the bow of the onrushing ship, clearing by less than 50 feet but placing his submarine in a deadly crossfire from escorts on all sides and with the transport dead ahead. Undaunted, he sent three smashing 'down the throat' bow shots to stop the target, then scored a killing hit as a climax to 46 mintues of violent action with the Parche and her valiant fighting company retiring victorious and unscathed.

Lawson Ramage was born at Monroe Bridge, Massachusetts, on January 19, 1909, the son of Scottish parents. Upon the death of his mother, at age ten, he, together with his four younger brothers, was raised by a maiden aunt in Beaver Falls, New York. He describes the mode of growing up in a small eastern town during the early part of this century . . . "At the time we moved to Beaver Falls very few homes had electricity or running water and they were either heated by coal or wood furnaces. The winters were long, cold and bitter. Fresh milk was delivered to the door by a farmer who dipped it out of a milk can on his rig into a bucket each family provided. We raised all our own vegetables and pigs. We smoked all our own hams and bacon. Each household canned their own fruits, vegetables, jams and jellies—eggs were preserved in large crocks, submerged in water glasses. We filled our ice houses each winter with ice cut from the river. Only a few homes had a telephone and radio did not make its appearance until after World War I. I had the first crystal set in town but we were too far from Schenectady, the nearest broadcast station, to receive anything. We all had many chores to do daily and we had to make our own fun but we learned to appreciate everything we had that much more."

Vice Admiral Ramage completed high school at the age of 15, attended a prep-school for 18 months, decided to go to the Naval Academy, came home and spent the winter prepping himself for the entrance exams. He entered the Academy in June of 1927. During World War II, three of his brothers also saw service in the U.S. Navy. He was brought up in the Methodist church, and since his Academy days has been a practicing Espiscopalian. He is married and has four children, two boys and two girls.

Describing his feelings when President Roosevelt placed the Medal of Honor around his neck, Vice Admiral Ramage stated—"It was a very emotional situation, coming face to face with that great man and having my family present to share that moment was beyond my wildest dreams.

"Being an American means everything to me," affirms Lawson Ramage, CMH. "You have unlimited opportunities to take responsibility, exert your own initiative and achieve your fondest goals. In no other country in the world is there anywhere near the same personal freedom that we enjoy. Everyone who claims to be an American should be frequently reminded that: 'To be born free is merely a happenstance. To live free is one of God's greatest blessings. But to die free is everyone's personal responsibility.'

"Today many of the younger as well as the older generation seems to take the attitude that they are entitled to everything they need or want simply for the asking. Most of them have no sense of their responsibilities, they produce nothing and are content to let someone else do everything for them. The old spirit that made this country great is not what it used to be.

"I am greatly concerned about the direction in which this country is now going. I am concerned about the lack of purpose and moral courage exemplified by former President Carter, the Supreme Court, the Congress right on down through our whole political hierarchy. It is incredible that thousands of Iranian bums were not only allowed but also given police protection to conduct a series of protest marches in front of the White House in honor of the Ayotolla Komeni, who held 52 Americans as hostages for well-nign a year. What next can we expect? Hopefully, things will be different under President Reagan.

"I fought in two wars we were not allowed to win—all decisions on what to do and how to do it were taken completely out of the hands of those who had to do the fighting. As a result all our present youth holds the military services in very low repute and understandably so.

"It's high time that the youth of today take a good look at recent history and begin to turn things around before it's too late."

HENRY SCHAUER

Technical Sergeant Henry Schauer was born in Clinton, Oklahoma on October 9, 1918. His father, Jacob Peter Schauer of German ancestry was born in Neidorf, Russia on September 10, 1895. As an infant, he came to the United States where he married Pauline Radke, who was born in Germany in 1897. Henry's father was employed by the Santa Fe railroad. In 1928, upon the death of his mother, Henry Schauer left school in the eighth grade to help support his family. His father died in 1972.

On December 29, 1964 Henry Schauer was married to the former Ellen Duggan of Abernathy, Texas. He has four step-children, all girls. Henry Schauer, who stands six feet, and weighs 204 pounds, is retired from the Oregon State Highway Department. Also he is 100 percent disabled due to many service connected wounds. He was baptized a Lutheran.

Enlisting in the Army on February 14, 1941, his first action was in French Morocco where he served as Number 1 scout in the three day battle that ended with Casablanca falling to American troops. After the victory at Casablanca, his outfit moved to Rabat for further training in anticipation of the landing in Sicily. At that time he joined the 15th Infantry combat patrol for specialized training in hand to hand combat, removal of beach obstacles, and pillbox demolition.

On May 7, 1942 he went into action serving under General Truscott as part of Patton's 3rd Army. After extensive combat in Tunisia, he participated in the Sicily landing near Lacata, in the predawn of July 10, 1943. He was wounded in the left shoulder by a mortar fragment near Corina, Sicily. After a short stay in the hospital he was again wounded in both thighs and the left hand. This necessitated a stay of 97 days in a Casablanca hospital. He then rejoined his outfit in Southern Italy in time to participate in the crossing of the Volturno River. After 103 days of combat with no relief he was evacuated to a Naples hospital with sever frostbite in both feet. He again rejoined his unit in time for the Anzio beach head landing and fought on that beach head all winter. On May 23, 1944, while spearheading the drive to Rome on Highway 7, near Cisterna di Littoria, he was cited for the Medal of Honor as follows:

SCHAUER, HENRY

Rank and organization: Private First Class, U.S. Army, 3rd Infantry Division. Place and date: Near Cisterna di Littoria, Italy. 23-24 May 1944. Entered service at: Scoby, Mont. Born: 9 October 1918, Clinton, Okla. G.O. No. 83, 27 October 1944. Citation: For conspicuous gallantry and intrepidity at the risk of his life above and beyond the call of duty. On 23 May 1944, at 12 noon, Pfc. (now T/Sgt.) Schauer left the cover of a ditch to engage four German snipers who opened fire on the patrol from its rear. Standing erect he walked deliberately 30 yards toward the enemy, stopped amid the fire from four rifles centered on him, and with 4 bursts from his BAR, each at a different range, killed all of the snipers. Catching sight of a fifth sniper waiting for the patrol behind a house chimney, Pfc. Schauer brought him down with another burst. Shortly after, when a heavy enemy artillery concentration and two machine guns temporarily halted the patrol, Pfc. Schauer again left cover to engage the enemy weapons singlehanded. While shells exploded within 15 yards, showering dirt over him, and strings of grazing German tracer bullets whipped past him at chest level, Pfc. Schauer knelt, killed the two gunners of the machine gun only 60 yards from him with a single burst from his BAR, and crumpled two other enemy soldiers who ran to man the gun. Inserting a fresh magazine in his BAR, Pfc. Schauer shifted his body to fire at the other weapon 500 yards distant and emptied his weapon into the enemy crew, killing all four Germans. Next morning, when shells from a German Mark VI tank and a machine gun only 100 yards distant again forced the patrol to seek cover, Pfc. Schauer crawled toward the enemy machine gun, stood upright only 80 yards from the weapon as its bullets cut the surrounding ground, and four tank shells fired directly at him burst within 20 yards. Raising his BAR to his shoulder, Pfc. Schauer killed the four members of the German machine gun crew with one burst of fire.

On October 27, 1944, in a courtyard of a home for crippled children near Besancon, France, Henry Schauer was awarded the Medal of Honor by General Alexander Patch, who was appointed by President Roosevelt to make the award.

Reminiscing about his wartime combat experiences, Henry Schauer, who now lives in Salem, Oregon, has the following to say—"There were many, many other men whom I believe should have been awarded the Medal of Honor. The problem with it is that their acts were not witnessed by at least two persons. One that stands out in my mind is a sixteen year old rifle grenade launcher. The two of us were trying to knock out a machine gun nest. He advanced to a position which once he fired his weapon, gave his position away. Before his grenade exploded, he was killed by a burst of fire from the machine gun. When his grenade burst, it illuminated the area and I was able to kill the Germans manning the gun. He had to have known that his position would have been known once he fired, but he did it anyway.

"My feelings when I was awarded the Medal are hard to explain. It was strange having a three star General put a medal around my neck and then salute me. I didn't have much time to think about it beforehand, as I was told only about three days earlier that I was getting it, and I was pulled out of combat for the award ceremony. I thought I was getting the Silver Star. I felt numb when I learned I was getting the Medal of Honor.

"My personal beliefs in America never had to be reaffirmed as I have always had strong feelings about my country.

"Being an American means being part of the greatest nation the world has ever seen. It means being able to live where and how I wish to, without having to worry about unjust actions by the Government.

"My advice to today's youth is to keep an open mind about the possibility of war. Sometimes it is inevitable and when it comes, we need to be ready to defend ourselves. It is impossible to describe the horror of the war I and millions of others experienced. We need to stay in a good state of readiness to insure there is never that kind of fighting in our own land."

MAYNARD H. SMITH, JR.
"SNUFFY"

One of the greatest disappointments in "Snuffy" Smith's life was that his father did not live long enough to know that his son became the first enlisted man in the U.S. Army Air Corps in World War II to receive the Medal of Honor. Staff Sergeant Smith was born in Caro, Michigan, on May 19, 1911. His father was half Irish and half American Indian. Maynard H. Smith, Sr. became a very successful criminal lawyer and was a personal consultant to Henry Ford and also to the General Motors Corporation in Detroit. "Snuffy" Smith remembers one of the favorite quotations of his father—"A man should be so rich he could go fishing all the time or so poor he had to." Mrs. Smith, "Snuffy's" mother, was of German extraction and taught all eight grades of a country school.

Maynard H. Smith, Jr., is now 69 years old, is five feet, six inches in height and weighs 135 pounds. This is the same weight he carried when he was 18. In his own words, "my skin and muscle tone together with eyesight and coordination are about the same as when I was 30.

His great, great grandfather, Henry Harrison Smith, was a Major in the Northern Army during the Civil War. He was a prisoner of war in the South and starved to death in a Confederate PW camp. To this day, Maynard has the silver sheathed sword which Major Henry Harrison Smith wore during the Civil War.

As a child, "Snuffy" Smith was of the Methodist faith.

When he was six years old, his father "got into a political hassle with the Methodist minister. That ended religion for me," confides Maynard H. Smith, Jr. "Since that time I have been pretty much on the agnostic side. Man's inhumanity to man, to animals and to the environment just does not fit in with any religion," he feels.

"Snuffy" Smith is highly educated in several disciplines including psychology, English, chemistry, salesmanship, ancient and modern history, criminal evidence and procedure and in the field of accounting. He married an English girl he met during World War II. They were divorced fifteen years ago. He has four children ranging in age from twenty-eight to thirty-six, three boys and one girl.

Staff Sergeant Maynard H. "Snuffy" Smith was a member of the 8th Air Force's 306th Bomb Group as a B-17 Flying fortress ball turret gunner. In an article which appeared in the February, 1979 issue of *Sergeants* he describes his first combat mission, flying out of England to bomb the German submarine pens at St. Nazaire, France.

"It was my first trip out. In those days the saying went 'the first time out, you were due back, the second time out you're not coming back.' Why? Well, we were running about 50 percent losses then. It was May 1, 1943 and our mission was to bomb St. Nazaire, France. Thirty-six B-17's went out. This was a major effort at the time.

"We were hit by FW-190's prior to target. Eighty-eight-mm flak hit our left wing. It cut the wing tank off. Gasoline poured into the airplane and caught fire. I was in the ball turret. At this point I had lost my electrical controls and I knew something was wrong.

"I manually cranked the thing around, opened the armored hatch and got back in the airplane when I saw it was on fire. The radioman became excited and jumped out the window without a parachute. At this point we dropped our bombs. It was minus 50 degrees outside.

"After we made the drop, the pilot took the plane down real fast. They shot down probably eight or nine of our planes on the first attack. We lost our formation.

"We got down to 2,000 feet when one of the waist gunners panicked and tried to bail out but got caught on a .50 calibre gun. I unhooked him so he could jump. He jumped high, the stabilizer hit him and he must have broken into a dozen pieces.

"I took my oxygen mask off as the system was knocked out. All the radio equipment was on fire, wires were burning everywhere. I proceeded to put the fire out with fire extinguishers and water bottles. I did the best I could while being shot at. They were coming in at us from both sides. While not fighting the fire, I manned the workable waist guns.

"Everytime they would make a swoop one or more planes would go down. Eventually the fighters ran out of gas. In those days pursuit planes were limited to something like 25 minutes. We wound up with four B-17's.

"The tailgunner came crawling out of the back. He was all shot up real bad. Blood was coming out of his mouth. He had been shot real bad on the left side of the back. I remember very distinctly from my classes how to handle a situation like this. I laid him down, gave him a couple shots of morphine which put him to sleep immediately. By doing this, he lived. I am very thankful for that.

"In the meantime, the plane started to go down and up. I went forward to find the pilot and co-pilot pretty well shot up. I put some tourniquets on them so they could maintain control of the plane. I then went back to put the control cables together as we had no tail control. I think I remember I repaired the six wires. I then threw all the ammunition out.

"We got the plane back."*

*"IT WAS MY FIRST TRIP OUT" by Edwin J. Kosier, *Sergeants*, February, 1979. Pg. 10.

Maynard H. Smith's citation for the Medal of Honor states the following:

SMITH, MAYNARD H.

Rank and organization: Sergeant, U.S. Army Air Corps, 423d Bombardment Squadron, 306th Bomber Group. Place and date: Over Europe, 1 May 1943. Entered service at: Cairo, Mich. Born: 1911, Cairo, Mich. G.O. No.: 38, 12 July 1943. Citation: For conspicuous gallantry and intrepidity in action above and beyond the call of duty. The aircraft of which Sgt. Smith was a gunner was subjected to intense enemy antiaircraft fire and determined fighter airplane attacks while returning from a mission over enemy-occupied continental Europe on 1 May 1943. The airplane was hit several times by antiaircraft fire and cannon shells of the fighter airplanes, 2 of the crew were seriously wounded, the aircraft's oxygen system shot out, and several vital control cables severed when intense fires were ignited simultaneously in the radio compartment and waist sections. The situation became so acute that 3 of the crew bailed out into the comparative safety of the sea. Sgt. Smith, then on his first combat mission, elected to fight the fire by himself, administered first aid to the wounded tail gunner, manned the waist guns, and fought the intense flames alternately. The escaping oxygen fanned the fire to such intense heat that the ammunition in the radio compartment began to explode, the radio, gun mount, and camera were melted, and the compartment completely gutted. Sgt. Smith threw the exploding ammunition overboard, fought the fire until the enemy fighters were driven away, further administered first aid to his wounded comrade, and then by wrapping himself in protecting cloth, completely extinguished the fire by hand. This soldier's gallantry in action, undaunted bravery, and loyalty to his aircraft and fellow crewmembers, without regard for his own personal safety, is an inspiration to the U.S. Armed Forces.

"Snuffy" Smith flew a total of 13 air combat missions from

England with the 8th Air Force before he was reassigned to ground operations. President Roosevelt sent Secretary of War Stimson to England to present Staff Sergeant Maynard H. Smith, Jr. with The Medal of Honor on July 15, 1943. Ranking Generals from all combat areas were present. In "Snuffy" Smith's words, "to me it was a dream. I had just done what I had been trained to do. I didn't know what the hell it was all about. I wasn't there to get a medal. Like millions of others, I just wanted to get it over with and get home."

After the war was over "Snuffy" Smith owned and published THE POLICE OFFICERS JOURNAL in New York. He is now semi-retired, living in St. Petersburg, Florida. However, he is active in many areas of endeavor.

In his words, "I don't need anything to reaffirm my belief in America. With all our trials, troubles and tribulations, the USA is still the greatest in the world, bar none.

"Being an American means freedom of speech, of choice, unlimited opportunity and the protection of my person and property.

"My advice to American youth: Get your hair cut, look like a human being instead of some kind of animal. Get off the pills, the pot and the hippie scene. Go to work or join some branch of military service. And get over the idea your country owes you a living."

HERSHEL WOODROW WILLIAMS

In four terrible hours during February 23 of 1945, a five foot, six inch, 160 pound Marine Corporal, barely 21, from West Virginia, accomplished what other men, tanks, and air strikes had been unable to effectuate on the island of Iwo Jima in mortal combat with the fanatical Japanese during the last year of World War II.

Hershel Williams was born October 2, 1923 in Quiet Dell, West Virginia. He came from a family of dairy farmers. However, his father had died in 1934, leaving a great void in the family. Prior to joining the Marines, Hershel completed the ninth grade of high school. After the end of World War II, he completed his high school education. Until 1961, he had no religious background. At that time he became converted to Christianity, joined the Methodist Church, became a lay speaker and has been quite active since his conversion.

His parents, as farmers, were hard working, devoted to their tasks, honest, law-abiding and deeply believed in helping their neighbors and friends. They were devoted to their country and the democratic process. He was taught at home that America is the very best country and that the flag should always be honored. His parents also taught Hershel that when one has something to do, to give it his very best.

In modest terms, Hershel Williams describes the situation that day of February 23, 1945 on Iwo Jima—"Our unit, 1st Battalion, 21st Regiment, 3rd Marine Division had been on the Island for two days, We had reached the main line of resistance of reinforced concrete pillboxes. Our unit had lost a lot of men trying to break through the pillboxes. Tanks had been called in to try to knock them out but they could not get into position because of the volcanic sand. The tanks were being knocked out as fast as they arrived. Air strikes were not effective since the emplacements were buried under several feet of sand and ash.

"I was the NCO in charge of a flamethrower and demolition team. The flamethrower operators had been wounded or killed attempting to penetrate the enemy defense. After many attempts to break through with many casualties, the Commanding Officer of C company, Captain Beck, asked me if I thought I could do anything.

"My response was, 'I'll see what I can do.'

"I strapped on a flamethrower, asked for some men with rifles and automatic weapons. I began crawling toward the pillboxes. In a period of four hours I was able to knock out seven of them, utilizing six flamethrowers. The unit was able to break through the line and approach the other emplacements from the rear. The advance continued. I could not have achieved what I did without those riflemen. Several of them were killed or wounded during the time involved."

The citation for Hershel Williams' Medal of Honor reads:

WILLIAMS, HERSHEL WOODROW

Rank and organization: Corporal, U.S. Marine Corps Reserve, 21st Marines, 3rd Marine Division. Place and date: Iwo Jima, Volcano Islands, 23 February 1945. Entered service at: West Virginia. Born: 2 October 1923, Quiet Dell, W. Va. Citation: For conspicuous gallantry and intrepidity at the risk of his life above and beyond the call of duty as demolition sergeant serving with the 21st Marines, 3rd Marine Division, in action against enemy Japanese forces on Iwo Jima, Volcano Islands, 23 February 1945. Quick to volunteer his services when our tanks were maneuvering vainly to open a lane for the infantry through the network of reinforced concrete pillboxes, buried mines, and black volcanic sands, Cpl. Williams daringly went forward alone to attempt the reduction of devastating machine gun fire from the unyielding positions. Covered by four riflemen, he fought desperately for four hours under terrific enemy small-arms fire and repeatedly returned to his own lines to prepare demolition charges and obtain serviced flamethrowers, struggling back, frequently to the rear of hostile emplacements, to wipe out one position after another. On one occasion, he daringly mounted a pillbox to insert the nozzle of his flamethrower through the air vent, killing the occupants and silencing the gun; on another he grimly charged enemy riflemen who attempted to stop him with bayonets and destroyed them with a brust of flame from his weapon. His unyielding determination and extraordinary heroism in the face of ruthless enemy resistance were directly instrumental in neutralizing one of the most fanatically defended Japanese strongpoints encountered by his regiment and aided vitally in enabling his company to reach its objective. Cpl. Williams' aggressive fighting spirit and valiant devotion to duty throughout this fiercely contested action sustain and enhance the highest traditions of the U.S. Naval Service.

On November 5, 1945, in the presence of his mother, Lurenna Williams, and his fiancee, Ruby, who is now his wife, Hershel Williams was presented the Medal of Honor at the White House in Washington, D.C. by President Harry S. Truman. "I was very frightened at the time," Hershel admits. "It was difficult to believe this was happening to me. The President, aware of my shaking from head to feet, placed his hand on my shoulder and said, 'I would rather have this medal than to be president."

"Having the Medal of Honor caused me to know a new life, one that would not have been possible without it. I had a career with the Veterans Administration, became a Chief Warrant Officer in the Marine Corps and have received many other honors that would not have come my way otherwise. The Medal gave me a better reason and purpose in my life; to be respectful in the eyes of my fellow man and to have great pride in my country and family."

Hershel Williams retired from the Veterans Administration with the position of Contact Officer in charge of 14 field offices, after 33 years of outstanding service, in January of 1979. He, together with his wife, Ruby, is raising and training Morgan horses, the only breed of horses started in America. Morgan horses were used extensively in war and in the winning of the West. Today, according to Hershel Williams, they are utilized as show horses, riding horses, and police horses. Morgan horses can be seen pulling the caissons at Arlington National Cemetery.

Hershel Williams and his wife live on their horse farm at Ona, West Virginia. They have two daughters, both married, and five grandsons.

"Being an American is so important to me," affirms Hershel Williams. "I can't think of not being an American. It means that I live in the best country in the world. It means that I enjoy freedoms that do not exist anywhere else in the world. It means a spirit that abides in me that makes me care for others, even those who would do me in. It means a spirit that causes men to give of their bodies and lives and health to help another person. It means a safe haven for my children and my grandchildren."

His advice to the youth of America is—"Many fathers, mothers, sons, brothers, and sisters have given their lives to obtain and preserve the freedoms we enjoy daily. Freedom is not free. It has been earned by others for the benefit of others. Every citizen has inherited these freedoms, along with the responsibilities of keeping them for future generations. Be prepared to serve America in whatever form you are best suited. Be proud of the heritage others have given. Enjoy all of

our freedoms but be an example to the following generation
for in that way the American Spirit is kept alive and real."

MATT URBAN

In the annals of America's fighting men, Matt Urban is considered by many to have been the greatest combat soldier in the long and valorous history of the U.S. Army. He was born in Buffalo, New York on August 25, 1919. His parents, Stanley and Helen Urban are both deceased. Upon completion of high school, Matt enrolled at Cornell University where he graduated in 1941 with a major in history and government and a minor in community recreation. After graduation from Cornell he was commissioned a 2nd Lieutenant and went on active duty in July of 1941 at Ft. Bragg, North Carolina with the 60th Infantry Regiment of the 9th Infantry Division.

During his formative years, Matt Urban credits Bob Kane, his boxing coach at Cornell, as being the most influential person in his life relative to character development and the fighting spirit and iron will to go on during the most trying circumstances he faced as a combat soldier during World War II. Matt is married to Jennie G. Rockwell of Port Huron, Michigan. They have one daughter, Jennifer, age ten.

He was medically retired in 1946 due to a hideous wound he received in his last combat engagement with the rank of Lt. Colonel. In total, Colonel Urban was wounded seven times during the twenty months he was in combat.

Although Matt Urban became the most decorated American soldier in the history of World War II, his Infantry Division was not noted for being generous in awarding medals and commendations to its officers and enlisted men. Due to an administrative "foul-up," he didn't receive the Medal of Honor until July of 1980—35 years late! His many assignments with the 60th Infantry Regiment were: platoon leader, morale officer, special services officer, company executive officer, company commander, battalion executive officer, and battalion commander.

In a precedent setting ceremony long overdue, President Jimmy Carter placed the Medal of Honor around Matt Urban's neck at Washington, D.C. on July 19, 1980. Stepping back from this great American soldier after he embraced him President Carter wiped a tear from his eye. Matt was crying, too.

Matt Urban was awarded 29 medals for bravery in his 20 months as a front line combat soldier during World War II. He was wounded seven times during the six major battles he fought in Tunisia, Sicily, France, and Belgium. Many Congressional Medal of Honor recipients were awarded our Nation's highest honor for one action, sometimes of a few minutes duration. Matt Urban's gallantry and awe inspiring leadership was a long sustained ordeal from the 14th of June to September 3, 1944. Not only did he personally kill and rout the enemy, he saved countless American lives by his valorous actions.

From the time of his medical retirement in 1946, Matt Urban has been deeply involved in working with and for the young people of Michigan. Currently he is the Recreation Director, Civic Center Manager, and Riverside Stadium Manager for the city of Holland, Michigan. Previously, he was the City Recreation Superintendent with duties of establishing, administrating and maintaining social, leisure, and recreational programs and facilities for people of all ages. His intense interest and great work for the youth of Michigan are too numerous to list. For 16 years he was a Camp Director for underprivileged children. He was also a coach for the

Golden Gloves for 16 years and on the Committe at the finals of the Golden Gloves in Chicago for the same period of time. He has been the General Chairman for the State of Michigan funding organization for the U.S. Boxing Olympics. His activities for the young people of Michigan go on and on— National Vice-President of the Amateur Softball Association, chairman of the State UFW Marble Tournaments, Red Cross Board of Directors, Boy Scout Council and Cub Master. Matt Urban's civilian honors and awards even outstrip his military recognitions. He has been described as—"You are not just a leader—but, a leader of leaders." "You are the Youth's Pied Piper." and, "No more time—ever—had but one man."

In his own modest words, Matt Urban's actions which resulted in his greatest military achievements are—"With a torn-up left leg I maneuvered my way out of the hospital in England trying to get back to my front line troops because I was the only volunteer available and willing to lead. Actually, 'hand-carry'—not the 'Dirty Dozen'—but—the 'Dirty Forty' across the English Channel into the War Zone . . . The pin-point action in my Medal of Honor actually begins . . . when— limping with a homemade cane and a ".45" in my other hand . . . I hitch-hiked my way into our front lines, just in the nick of time as the grandeur of American warfare was about to erupt . . . The famous St. Lo Breakthrough!

"As far as I know this was the biggest U.S. frontal land as well as frontal air maneuver of the war. Operation Cobra. Twenty five hundred bombers paved the way as the assault, miles long, simultaneously was about to be off: But, as I shuttled myself into the front line troops, I found myself amidst not an attack but a deadlocked catastrophe. Men were frozen, cringing in the roadside ditches. Their tanks up front were going up in smoke, the road was heavily mined and enemy artillery zeroed in on the roadside. Fully realizing that these trapped soldiers had to be saved I, quickly yelling and screaming, was able to stimulate the troops to leave their shelled positions and to follow me into the right flank hedgerow country. As one soldier reported, 'one of the craziest officers suddenly appeared before us, yelling like a mad man and waving a gun in his hands! He got us on our feet though . . . gave us back our confidence, and well . . . he actually saved our lives for us.'

"We moved zig-zagging, crouching, running about one-half mile to the right . . . a mile forward and joined with the adjoining rifle company and found one of their two support tanks in flames. The other seemed intact, but had no turret gunner and was unable to move. The troops were stalemated under heavy fire!

"Time was of the essence . . . I had no wire, no radio to call for artillery support . . . My mortars were not near enough around. Every minute counted. The enemy I was sure was still regrouping, digging out of basements, shelters and other dug-outs still shaking off the cobwebs and debris caused by the aerial bombardment.

"The enemy was not yet at full strength. Yet, what they had quickly salvaged and brought forward, up to the front, did enable them to have the controlling, observing and dominating hill top. Our men were being picked off and especially so if we were to dig in for any amount of time. We had to move but quick. The immediate advantage was still ours. So act I did. Move the tank, attack! Our supporting tank lieutenant was to get in, as the attack was to be syncronized with the necessary movement and firing of the tank. He was shot down! I yelled for a volunteer to get up there . . . to man the tank's machine gun. A sergeant undertook the mission and was also machine-gunned down! I was not going to send any more of my men to likely, certain death! Only one thing left to do, and it was for me . . . myself . . . crawling up into the turret! The enemy guns opened fire at me. No one knows why, but I was in the tank . . . alive.

"I was convinced that my death was yet to come.

"As the tank had to ascend a slowly inclining hillside, I would have to get my head and shoulders far enough above the turret to aim my machine-gun fire at both opposing enemy gun crews. In that awful moment I scanned over a hundred prayers! Thoughts of my loved one, and heavy tears rolled down my face. God! help me, Goodby world, were my only other thoughts.

"Then, all hell broke loose! The tank was in high gear . . . my gun was thundering what seemed like thousands of shots directly at the enemy crews. My soldiers . . . leaping out . . . forward . . . others following the tank also picked up the tempo . . . spitting out tremendous fire power. Yelling with vengeance in a mission *ACCOMPLISHED!*

"If anyone was to ask me, how? Then I would have to refer them to the 'Guy' upstairs."

Matt Urbans' official citation for the Medal of Honor reads:

> The President of the United States of America, authorized by Act of Congress, March 8, 1863, has awarded in the name of The Congress the Medal of Honor to
>
> LIEUTENANT COLONEL MATT URBAN
> UNITED STATES ARMY, RETIRED
>
> for conspicuous gallantry and intrepidity in action at the risk of his life above and beyond the call of duty:
>
> During the period 14 June to 3 September 1944, Lieutenant Colonel (then Captain) Matt Urban distinguished himself by a series of bold, heroic actions, exemplified by singularly outstanding combat leadership, personal bravery, and a tenacious devotion to duty, while assigned to the 2nd Battalion, 60th Infantry Regiment, 9th Infantry Division. On 14 June, Captain Urban's company, attacking at Renouf, France, encountered heavy enemy small arms and tank fire. The

enemy tanks were unmercifully raking his unit's positions and inflicting heavy casualties. Captain Urban, realizing that his company was in imminent danger of being decimated, armed himself with a bazooka. He worked his way with an ammo carrier through hedgerows, under a continuing barrage of fire, to a point near the tanks. He brazenly exposed himself to the enemy fire and, firing the bazooka, destroyed both tanks. Responding to Captain Urban's actions, his company moved forward and routed the enemy. Later that same day, still in the attack near Orglandes, Captain Urban was wounded in the leg by direct fire from a 37mm tank-gun. He refused evacuation and continued to lead his company until they moved into defensive positions for the night. At 0500 hours the next day, Captain Urban, though badly wounded, directed his company in another attack. One hour later he was again wounded. Suffering from two wounds, one serious, he was evacuated to England. In mid-July, while recovering from his wounds, he learned of his unit's severe losses in the hedgerows of Normandy. Realizing his unit's need for battle-tested leaders, he voluntarily left the hospital and hitchhiked his way back to his unit near St. Loo, France. Arriving at the 2nd Battalion Command Post at 1130 hours, 25 July, he found that his unit had jumped-off at 1100 hours in the first attack of "Operation Cobra." Still limping from his leg wound, Captain Urban made his way forward to retake command of his company. He found his company held up by strong enemy opposition. Two supporting tanks had been destroyed and another, intact but with no tank commander or gunner, was not moving. He located a lieutenant in charge of the support tanks and directed a plan of attack to eliminate the enemy strong-point. The lieutenant and a sergeant were immediately killed by heavy enemy fire when they tried to mount the tank. Captain Urban, though physically hampered by his leg wound and knowing quick action had be be taken, dashed through the scathing fire and mounted the tank. With enemy bullets ricocheting from the tank, Captain Urban ordered the tank forward and, completely exposed to the enemy fire, manned the machine gun and placed a devastating fire on the enemy. His actions, in the face of the enemy fire, galvanized the battalion into action and they attacked and destroyed the enemy position. On 2 August, Captain Urban was wounded in the chest by shell fragments and, disregarding the recommendation of the Battalion Surgeon, again refused evacuation. On 6 August, Captain Urban became the commander of the 2nd Battalion. On 15 August, he was again wounded but remained with his unit. On 3 September, the 2nd Battalion was given the mission of establishing a crossing-point on the Meuse River near Heer, Belgium. The enemy planned to stop the advance of the allied Army by concentrating heavy forces at the Meuse. The 2nd Battalion, attacking toward the crossing-point, encountered fierce enemy artillery, small arms and mortar fire which stopped the attack. Captain Urban quickly moved from his command post to the lead position of the battalion. Reorganizing the attacking elements, he personally led a charge toward the enemy's strong-point. As the charge moved across the open terrain, Captain Urban was seriously wounded in the neck. Although unable to talk above a whisper from the paralyzing neck wound, and in danger of losing his life, he refused to be evacuated until the enemy was routed and his battalion had secured the crossing-point on the Muese River. Captain Urban's personal leadership, limitless bravery, and repeated extraordinary exposure to enemy fire served as in inspiration to his entire battalion. His valorous and intrepid actions reflect the utmost credit on him and uphold the noble traditions of the United States Army.

A few statements by his men reflect the love and admiration the entire Battalion felt for Matt Urban, "The man never asked anyone to do what he wouldn't do himself."

"Matt Urban moved forward, and damned if the U.S. Army didn't move forward also. He got us on our feet . . . Gave us back our confidence, and well . . . He actually saved our lives."

"Matt Urban is an outstanding example of what a National Hero should be. One who placed his life and well-being second to his duty as a soldier. One whose actions were not paralled by any other for such a prolonged period. A person who never lost his perspective even while in combat."

"He always gave us his best, and was never too busy or disinterested to personally listen to any of our problems or gripes. Soldiers admire that in an Officer, and respect the character of the actual man behind the rank."

"And, without exception, non-coms and men had the greatest affection for him that men can have for one another."

"He owes his life to one of the many GI's who would have risked anything for him . . . The kind of Commanding Officer Ernie Pyle writes about . . . A hero of his own men."

"There wasn't another leader more highly respected and admired as an Officer: Nor another soldier more liked as a man."

"The fact that Matt Urban . . . is an inspirational character . . . an idol to his GI's and still their champion. The kind of Officer that GI's worshipped."

"He was saved by a couple of GI's who loved him more than any kid ever loved his father."

A few statements by Matt Urban reflect his love and admiration for his men and his hatred of war. . . . "Kill or be killed, that's the mentality needed to survive. Despair, anger, remorse were part of it. Seeing, being right alongside your buddies as they were blown to bits. Big grown up boys and middle aged men, all in their prime of life. Giving up their bodies and health so that all of us, each and every one of you, may continue living in a world of peace and dignity."

"You live, you sleep, you barely eat . . . in the cold rainy mud for months, with daily and nightly bullets and shrapnel . . . The pitiful moaning of the severely wounded and dying . . . The constant wait for death or survival adding to your discomforts and miseries . . . in a world of hell."

"No dad, no mom, no wife to speak to. All, all alone . . . in a crazy, incredible world of war."

"The American soldiers were the greatest soldiers in the world . . . with many leaders and followers. The American GI would do anything . . . go anywhere . . . as long as there was a leader . . . and a purpose."

"Now that the war is over we should no longer discriminate between the Commissioned Officers and Enlisted Men. All I can say is that some of the best men in my Army career were Privates and PFC's. So many of the Corporals and Sergeants were in many respects far above some of the Commissioned Officers. More than once I have had promotions refused by Privates because they claimed that they were there to merely fulfill an obligation. More than once I have had battlefield commissions refused by capable Sergeants."

"The Korean and Vietnam Vets are unrecognized, unappreciated and so often, so misjudged."

S/Sgt. Alex Kahn expressed the love and everlasting respect Matt Urban's GI's had for him with the following words . . . "Long after Major Matty Urban was removed from the field by three of his enlisted men—after being wounded for the seventh time—the story of his comradery, his courage and devotion to his men had spread from Africa to Germany. This seventh wound penetrated the Major's throat, entering the left side of his neck and coming out the right.

"This was a destiny of a sort, as one of the Major's favorite ways of instilling spirit into his men was by company talks. He used his voice well and enjoyed discussion, debate and defense. Here at Holloran, some of the patients who fought with the Major in one of the six campaigns he contributed to, claim that, long after his removal, the voice of Major Matty Urban—encouraging them, cheering and pleading with them, rang in their ears and was heard in their hearts."

Fred Scott, Jr., of Ocean, N.J., wrote the following which is an excerpt from an editorial recently published: "General Patton once slapped a soldier. Had he known Matt he would have hugged him, he would have kissed both cheeks, he would have proudly saluted Matt Urban. This was his kind of people, made from the same cut of cloth. They both marched to the beat of the same drummer. All soldier, from the day he put on the uniform until the day he stepped out of it."

And finally the words of Lt. Colonel Stephen W. Sprindis, Jr., who fought side by side with Matt Urban—"It is extremely difficult to put into words the heroics of this great man. His whole concept of combat leadership exhibited time and time again, from Africa to Sicily to France and Belgium, his courage, fearlessness in every confrontation with the enemy, was most *positively unparalled in all of World War II.* It was only God's will and guidance that extended and preserved this man's life on so many occasions.

"I am extremely proud to relate and corroborate a small part of Urban's front line actions. His total dedication to all GI's under his command, his disregard for personal safety, *his incredible courage above and beyond the call of duty,* with the supreme sacrifice the greater possibility but not the eventual occurrence.

"As the result of Urban's personal heroics, countless American lives were saved. I should know as I fought side by side with him, we shared the same philosophy of combat leadership. (We, as lieutenants, listened intently as General George Patton addressed us at Ft. Bragg and said "you cannot push a piece of string from the back, it will wither and stop, you must take it by the front end and pull, it will follow").

"If the Medal of Honor is not ultimately awarded to this man, who, in my opinion, *was the greatest combat soldier ever*, a serious injustice in the history of military awards will have occurred."

Concerning his personal beliefs in America, Matt Urban has the following to say—"My beliefs in America *never* needed to be reaffirmed. In America too much is too quickly forgotten. We Americans—sometimes 'cocky'—sometimes subdued—and often 'humble' need to be reminded, need to let the world know that our military, its personnel, its leaders, we, the American people are just as capable, as good, as great as any people in this world—we have been and always will be!

"As the leaders, long ago, proclaimed it then, and, we know it now—America—to me—is the great 'Land of Opportunity' in every phase of livelihood—to each, and everyone of us. A great country with the best of military, political, municipal, church and school leaders in the world! A country with the realization that our strength and our freedom lie in our belief—in the Presence of God, in unity and the love of people!"

Matt Urban's advice to the youth of America is—"Fortunately, my entire life has been involved with youngsters and young people. The beginning—your early life—your physical and mental build up as in the roots of any vegetation belong to you alone—to do as only you, yourself, control and decide. As you go along in life do not look for excuses, feel sorry for yourself because of any possible deficiencies at home, of persons, bad influences, disappointing situations. Any of these shortcomings, failures or disappointments can be, must be won over! As in boxing and other sports, you must side step or go with the punch. And, if it's as 'big' as a knockout, slowly try, try again, must be the motto!"

PART IV
THE KOREAN CONFLICT
1950-1953

For the first time in the history of warfare, soldiers of a world organization, The United Nations, fought to protect a country invaded by a belligerent aggressor. The ancient country of Korea is strategically located between China and Japan. It is a peninsula that extends toward Japan from the mainland of China. Korea had been a part of Japan from 1910 until the end of World War II. At that time, Korea was divided at the 38th parallel with the Russians occupying North Korea and the troops of the United States stationed in South Korea.

During an assembly of the United Nations in 1946, it was decided that elections be held throughout the entire country of Korea so that both North and South Korea could again become a unified whole. Russia refused to honor that mandate and the land north of the 38th parallel became a communistic country called The People's Democratic Republic of Korea. In 1948, with the blessing of the United Nations, South Korea held an election and The Republic of Korea was established below the 38th parallel.

On June 25th, 1950 the communist army of North Korea invaded South Korea. In a vote of 9 to 0, the United Nations Security Council called for a halt to the invasion and ordered North Korea to withdraw its forces. Russia was absent from the U.N. Security Council meeting and therefore could not veto the resolution. However, Russia immediately stated that the vote was illegal and refused to honor the mandate of the U.N. Security Council.

On June 27, 1950 President Truman ordered troops of the United States to help defend South Korea under the auspices of the United Nations. Ultimately, soldiers from Great Britain, Australia, Canada, France, The Phillippine Republic, Turkey, Greece, Thailand, Columbia, The Netherlands, Ethiopia, Luxembourg, Belgium, New Zealand and the Union of South Africa came to the aid of The Republic of South Korea.

By August 2, 1950 the North Korean Army drove South Korean and American troops toward the Pusan Perimeter in the far south of Korea. However, in a surprise move, after halting the North Korean advance, on September 15, the U.S. 10th Corps made an amphibious landing at Inchon on the northwest coast of South Korea. This unexpected maneuver was very successful and cut off the forces of North Korea from its units surrounding Pusan.

On the 20th of September 1950 United Nations' forces recaptured Seoul, the capital of South Korea. By October 19, Pyongyang, the capital city of North Korea fell to the U.N. army and the drive to the Yalu river which separated North Korea from Manchuria began. However, on October 20th, 1950 units of the communist army of China crossed the Yalu River from Manchuria and by October 25th U.N. troops became engaged in battle with the communist armies of both North Korea and China. Russian MIG-15 jet planes also soon entered the air war.

The Chinese and North Korean armies drove the U.N. forces south and by December 4, 1950 the Allies began evacuating Pyongyang, the capital city of North Korea. On January 10, 1951 Seoul, the capital of South Korea, again fell into communist hands. On March 15, 1951 Seoul was again liberated by the United Nation forces and a see-saw war developed.

General Douglas MacArthur, Supreme Commander of the United Nations Armed forces for most of the Korean Conflict, was relieved of his command by President Truman for *publicly* disagreeing on strategy to end the conflict. General MacArthur favored bombing Chinese staging areas in Manchuria. President Truman believed such an action would have prolonged and expanded the conflict. General MacArthur was replaced by General Ridgeway. General MacArthur returned to the United States and was given a hero's welcome. In a speech before Congress he said, "Old soldiers never die, they just fade away."

The casualties of the Korean Conflict, which was called a "police action" by President Harry S. Truman, since the United States never officially declared war, were heavy. The total casualties of the U.N. forces were 1,487,604 while Communist China and North Korea suffered approximately 2,000,000. The United States suffered 54,246 dead, 103,284 wounded, and 24 prisoners or missing in action.

The war officially ended on July 27, 1953. A demilitarized buffer zone of 2-1/2 miles was created across Korea at the location of the 38th parallel. In the establishment of the buffer zone South Korea gained about 1,500 square miles while North Korea acquired Finger Ridge at the time of cessation of hostilities. This was very expensive real estate purchased at the cost of over 1,000,000 civilian deaths in South Korea in addition to the $18,000,000,000 which America spent during the three years of fighting plus the thousands of lives lost in the armed forces of the United States. But the spread of communism was temporarilly halted in the Far East.

One hundred thirty-one gallant American servicemen earned the Medal of Honor during the Korean Conflict. Only 46 survived. The personal accounts of three of these courageous living recipients follow.

LLOYD L. "SCOOTER" BURKE

Colonel Lloyd L. "Scooter" Burke was born on September 29, 1924 in Tichnor, Arkansas, population 75. He retired from the Army in 1978 and is now a Congressional Consultant. Before enlisting in the Army in April of 1943, he was a college student at Henderson State University in Arkadelphia, Arkansas. During World War II, "Scooter" Burke served in Italy with the 401st Combat Engineer Battalion. He was honorably discharged in January of 1946 with the rank of Sergeant. In 1947 he reentered college and graduated with a B.A. in Economics in May of 1950. Having been a distinguished ROTC graduate at Henderson State, he was appointed a 2nd Lieutenant in the Regular Army upon graduation.

He has three children from his first marriage and in 1975 he acquired two step-children from his marriage to Maxine Husted. Colonel Burke's parents are of Scotch-Irish origin. He is a United Methodist by religious preference. During combat in Vietnam he lost the index finger on his left hand. He is five feet, eight inches in height and weighs 150 pounds. "Scooter" Burke is a handsome, average sized man. He acquired the nick-name "Scooter" because of his intramural football achievements while in college. For the last 11 years of his military career, Colonel Burke was the Chief Army Liaison Officer to the United States House of Representatives in Washington, D.C.

Shortly before his retirement his superior officer stated that "Colonel Burke is one of the last of the Army's three-war soldiers. His skills and professionalism, personal conduct, dilligence, initiative, and devotion to duty have been beyond reproach during his entire 34 years of distinguished service and have earned for him the respect and admiration of all those with whom he has come in contact. His outstanding performance reflects great credit upon himself and the United States Army."

Having volunteered for duty in Korea in September of 1950, the then Lieutenant "Scooter" Burke modestly states the following concerning his actions which resulted in President Harry Truman presenting him with our nation's highest military award:

"On October 5, 1951 I was Executive Officer of "G" Company, 2nd Battalion, 5th Cavalry Regiment, 1st Cavalry Division. For the next 23 days our unit participated in the bloodiest combat of the war against a determined Chinese enemy. I was eligible for rotation home and on the 28th of October I was ordered to the rear in preparation for shipment home. However, the battle wasn't over and my men were still getting killed and wounded in trying to take a strategic hill on the Imjin River northwest of Seoul. I knew my unit was short on ammo, food and water. I organized a small party to get these needed supplies out to the unit. The unit strength of a Battalion is 750 men. We were down to less than a hundred. The unit was stalled and the morale and combat effectiveness was extremely low. I stayed on the hill and the Citation pretty well spells out what happened. I'm confident the good Lord held me in the palm of His hand and let me be successful in anything I did. As a result of our actions, we routed and broke the back of a determined enemy which permitted my decimated unit to come down from the hill."

What really happened is described in "Scooter" Burke's citation for the Medal of Honor.

1st Lt. Burke, distinguished himself by conspicuous gallantry and outstanding courage above and beyond the call of duty in action against the enemy. Intense enemy fire had pinned down leading elements of his company committed to secure commanding ground when 1st Lt. Burke left the command post to rally and urge the men to follow him toward three bunkers impeding the advance. Dashing to an exposed vantage point he threw several grenades at the bunkers, then, returning for an M1 rifle and adapter, he made a lone assault, wiping out the position and killing the crew. Closing on the center bunker he lobbed grenades through the opening and, with his pistol, killed three of its occupants attempting to surround him. Ordering his men forward he charged the third emplacement, catching several grenades in midair and hurling them back at the enemy. Inspired by his display of valor his men stormed forward, overran the hostile position, but was again pinned down by increasing fire. Securing a light machine gun and three boxes of ammunition, 1st Lt. Burke dashed through the impact area to an open knoll, set up his gun and poured a crippling fire into the ranks of the enemy, killing approximately 75. Although wounded, he ordered more ammunition, reloading and destroying two mortar emplacements and a machine gun position with his accurate fire. Cradling the weapon in his arms he then led his men forward, killing some 25 more of the retreating enemy and securing the objective. 1st Lt. Burke's heroic action and daring exploits inspired his small force of 35 troops. His unflinching courage and outstanding leadership reflect the highest credit upon himself, the infantry, and the U.S. Army.

The proudest and most humble moment of his life was when President Truman hung the Medal of Honor around his neck. He had heard that when the President presented the Medal of Honor to a soldier he said, "I would rather have this Medal than be President of the United States." "Scooter" Burke confirms this as exactly what President Truman said to him.

In retrospect Colonel Burke states, "years later I often said that the Medal was as hard to wear as it was to earn. I quickly realized that the Medal was not mine, but that it was in recognition of a grateful country to an individual that was privileged enough to live and accept it. I have always felt the Medal belongs to our country and there automatically goes with it a sense of responsibility and pride to uphold all those things that it stands for. I have tried to always maintain a keen awareness of what the Medal stands for and hopefully I've worn it in solemn remembrance of those who did not make it back. I am indeed humble and grateful to a very generous country to wear its highest military award and trust that I will wear it with dignity, respect and reverence which it so richly deserves.

"At no time was it necessary to have my personal beliefs in America reaffirmed because those beliefs have never dimmed," Colonel Burke further states.

It is of interest that Colonel Burke would have been promoted to General if he had not worked for the Army in the capacity of Chief Army Liaison Officer for the House of Representatives the last 11 years of his most distinguished military career. In a speech to the House of Representatives on June 13, 1978 the Honorable Congressman John M. Murphy of New York lionized this great American hero with a most eloquent oration, the gist of which is "Scooter Burke is a representative slice of all that is fine in America. Our Founding Fathers had men like him in mind when they declared this is a nation of free men, dedicated to life, liberty, and the pursuit of happiness—men who would live it, love it, and if need be give their lives for it. I believe that those who know him best would agree with that assessment."

Being an American, in the words of "Scooter" Burke, "means freedom, responsibility, hope and opportunity. It means pride in our compassion for our brother's needs and expressing our faith and opinions without fear. Through healthy competition and free enterprise we can fulfill any dreams we choose to dream. It means owning my own home— it means joy, laughter and happiness—just everyday good living in a free country."

His advice to the youth of America: "I would advise them to use all their talents and strive to reach their full potential without comparison to others. I would remind them that we are all capable of doing far more than we think by hard work and proper motivated thinking. That true happiness comes from self-respect and high principles. To give serious thought to words like duty, honor, God and country before it is too late. To open their ears that they may hear the call of responsibility and service to keep it great."

RAYMOND GILBERT DAVIS

Raymond G. Davis was born in Fitzgerald, Georgia on January 13, 1915. After completing the second grade in Fitzgerald, his family moved to Atlanta where he graduated from Atlanta Technical High School. During his youth in Atlanta he recalls catfish seining in the Chattahoochee river, swimming in Oglethorp's Silver Lake, and refreshing drinks from the Cascade Spring which he passed daily while walking to school, and playing sandlot ball. More serious youthful ventures include home-grown produce sales, a downtown Atlanta confectionary delivery route and the making of Parkerhouse rolls at the Lee Baking Company. This job paid the major costs of his education at Georgia Tech where he graduated in 1938 with honors, earning a B.S. in Chemical Engineering. Having been a member of the ROTC program while attending college, he accepted an appointment as a 2nd Lieutenant in the Marine Corps on June 27, 1938. He retired 34 years later with the rank of Four-Star General.

Both of General Davis' parents were born in Indiana. His father was of Dutch extraction and his mother Irish. He is married to the former Willa K. Heanfner of Lincolnton, North Carolina. They have three children, Raymond G. Jr., Gordon M., and Willa Kay, all of whom are married. Raymond Davis is of the Methodist faith.

During World War II, he took part in combat in the Pacific theater on Guadalcanal Island. He was commander of the 1st Special Weapons Battalion at New Guinea and Cape Gloucester and later, while on Cape Gloucester, he became the

Commanding Officer of the 1st Battalion, 1st Marines, 1st Marine Division. Raymond Davis, then a major, was awarded the Navy Cross for his actions while commanding the 1st Battalion at Peleiu in September of 1944. He was wounded during the campaign and received the Purple Heart.

Following his return to the United States in November of 1944, he saw duty at the Marine Corps School in Quantico, Virginia and then with the 1st Provisional Marine Brigade in Guam. In May of 1949 he was appointed Inspector-Instructor of the 9th Marine Corps Reserve Infantry Battalion in Chicago, Illinois.

During the Korean conflict, Lieutenant Colonel Davis commanded the famous 1st Battalion of the 7th Marines from August to December of 1950. He earned the Medal of Honor for heroism during the 1st Marine Division's historic fight to break out of the Chosen Reservoir area during the month of December, 1950.

Initially assigned as Deputy Commanding General of the Provisional Corps of Marines in Vietnam, General Davis was reassigned as Commanding General of the 3rd Marine Division in May of 1968. For meritorious service in that capacity through April of 1969, he earned the Distinguished Service Medal.

Upon his return to the United States, he was assigned duties as Deputy Education Director at Quantico, Virginia. After his promotion to Lieutenant General on July 1, 1970 he became Commanding General of the Marine Corps Development and Education Command at Quantico. On March 12, 1971 he was promoted to his present four-star rank when he assumed duties as Assistant Commandant of the Marine Corps.

On May 24, 1971 General L.F. Chapman, Jr., Commandant of the Marine Corps, stated the following concerning Raymond G. Davis: "A superior Marine leader— in and out of combat—and one of the finest Marines of all times. Can do anything, and do it superlatively well."

A listing of the military awards of General Davis include:

Medal of Honor
Navy Cross
Distinguished Service Medal—Navy
Silver Star w/Gold Star in lieu of second award
Legion of Merit w/Combat "V" and Gold Star
Bronze Star w/Combat "V"
Purple Heart
Presidential Unit Citation w/3 Stars
Navy Unit Commendation w/1 Star
American Defense w/Fleet Clasp
American Campaign
Asiatic-Pacific Campaign w/5 campaign Stars
World War II Victory Medal
National Defense w/1 campaign Star
Korean Service w/4 campaign Stars
Vietnamese Service w/3 campaign Stars
National Order of Vietnam/4th Class
National Order of Vietnam/5th Class
Cross of Gallantry w/3 Palms for subsequent awards
Republic of Vietnam Army Distinguished Service Order
Vietnam Public Health Service Medal/1st Class
United Nations Service Medal
Korean Presidential Unit Citation
Republic of Vietnam Campaign Medal

The citation of General Davis for the Medal of Honor reads:

> For conspicuous gallantry and intrepidity at the risk of his life above and beyond the call of duty as Commanding Officer of the First Battalion, Seventh Marines, First Marine Division (Reinforced), in action against enemy aggressor forces in Korea from 1 through 4 December 1950. Although keenly aware that the operation involved

breaking through a surrounding enemy and advancing eight miles along primitive icy trails in the bitter cold with every passage disputed by a savage and determined foe, Lieutenant Colonel Davis boldly led his battalion into the attack in a daring attempt to relieve a beleaguered rifle company and to seize, hold and defend a vital mountain pass controlling the only route available for two Marine regiments in danger of being cut off by numerically superior hostile forces during their redeployment to the port of Hungnam. When the battalion immediately encountered strong opposition from entrenched enemy forces commanding high ground in the path of the advance, he promptly spearheaded his unit in a fierce attack up the steep, ice-covered slopes in the face of withering fire and, personally leading the assault in a hand-to-hand encounter, drove the hostile troops from their positions, rested his men and reconnoitered the area under enemy fire to determine the best route for continuing the mission. Always in the thick of the fighting, Lieutenant Colonel Davis led his battalion over the successive ridges in the deep snow in continuous attacks against the enemy and, constantly inspiring and encouraging his men throughout the night, brought his unit to a point within 1500 yards of the surrounded rifle company by day-break. Although knocked to the ground when a shell fragment struck his helmet and two bullets pierced his clothing, he arose and fought his way forward at the head of his men until he reached the isolated Marines. On the following morning, he bravely led his battalion in securing the vital mountain pass from a strongly entrenched and numerically superior hostile force, carrying all his wounded with him, including 22 litter cases and numerous ambulatory patients. Despite repeated savage and heavy assaults by the enemy, he stubbornly held the vital terrain until the two regiments of the division had deployed through the pass and, on the morning of 4 December, led his battalion into Hagaru-ri intact. By his superb leadership, outstanding courage and brilliant tactical ability,

Lieutenant Colonel Davis was directly instrumental in saving the beleaguered rifle company from complete annihilation and enabled the two Marine regiments to escape possible destruction. His valiant devotion to duty and unyielding fighting spirit in the face of almost insurmountable odds enhance and sustain the highest traditions of the United States Naval Service."

To General Raymond G. Davis being an American means "responsibility for freedom for self and others."

His advice to the Youth of America is vividly illustrated in a speech General Davis has made to many junior high schools, high schools and colleges which is titled, "A Challenge To Youth."

"It is a very great pleasure to be with you today and to be able to share my thoughts concerning the challenges which face each of you in the future. You are the potential strength on which our nation must draw in these troubled times. *Therefore,* I could ask no greater reward from my discussion with you than to have you raise your sights and resolve to strive for success in the future. *Your* success will insure our nation's strength. The sign posts are well marked on the competitive road ahead. Through the marvels of scientific survey and analysis you are forewarned what the competition will be. Unfortunately, the road is strewn with those who have dropped out. Studies show that more than one-third of your age group have no desire to face the challenge. They want neither physical nor mental contest. They disdain leadership, discipline and participation. These young people will not be launched into a successful future. They pose no real competition for those of you who *have* set your sights. The sign posts say 'don't join them. Don't be mislead by their claim of a miraculous new life based on the belief in Nothing.'

"Nothing has a potent popularity. Its shape flashes out in placards which proclaim 'down with everything.' It takes form in the mindless destruction of campus buildings, the ambush of legal due process, the well trod road to Canada, or the 'I don't want to get involved' apology. Nothing is the god who encourages the 'cop out' and the 'put on', the retreat from reality. 'There is nothing worth fighting for' is the password.

"I can have no truck with that sentiment. I am confounded and deeply concerned with this grasping after 'Nothing' for I see it as the epitome of all that Americans oppose. For me, nothingness is irresponsibility at its worst.

"To make nothingness a god is, in reality, to be a slave. To write off our heritage, to demand adolescently that irresponsibility be king. It is to fetter oneself with the heavy chains of discontent.

"Nothingness, as a belief, highlights the need for leadership within your generation. There is a growing minority of American youth setting a pattern of conduct and self destruction far worse than the young in any civilized country on earth. Statistics show we suffer a higher ratio of drug abuse, a greater incident of veneral disease, and a higher frequency of crimes committed by those under 25 years of age.

"You must not ignore this situation. You dare not accept the leadership of those who contribute to it. You must resist this type of leadership and accept only that which leads to self-improvement and success.

"Our nation's continued strength depends on you. That strength must not be depleted, for such a circumstance could only mean the death of freedom—freedom throughout the world. The challenge is yours! *You* must be of great spirit!

"This great spirit can manifest itself in countless ways. One of these is inherent to the words of John Stuart Mill which I saw inscribed over a mantlepiece in Vietnam:

> War is an ugly thing, but not the ugliest of things;
> the decayed and degraded state of moral and

patriotic feeling which thinks that nothing is worth war is worse.

A man who has nothing for which he is willing to fight; nothing that he cares about more than his own personal safety; is a miserable creature who has no chance of being free, unless made and kept by the exertions of better men than himself.

"You must be those 'better men' who will protect our nation. The banner responsibility in maintaining our freedom will soon be passed to you. It is worth fighting for!

"I am not totally dismayed, because I see in your faces the will to succeed—the will to become the leaders of the strongest nation on earth. I saw this same great spirit in the faces of the young men I commanded in Vietnam.

"The great reward of my service there was the opportunity to know these young Americans, many of them recent graduates of schools such as yours. I was fortunate to be able to share their aspirations, their ideals and their reactions. I witnessed the compassion which moved them and the courage which sustained them.

"Too often when we speak of the war in Vietnam, or fail to speak of it because some find it distasteful, we forget America's greatest asset—our fine young men and women who are fighting or have fought in that country. They are truly magnificent and a credit to all youth.

"A typical infantry man in Vietnam operated in the mountains and on enemy trails and in the enemy hide-a-ways. The American fighting man stayed out for as long as 60 days at a time. He cut or blasted a hole in the forest to get supplies and replacements by helicopters. After long periods on the trail, units were rotated to rear bases, but in a few days the men were ready, and often anxious, to go out again. This aggressive, can-do attitude was indicative of their strong desire to get on with the job.

"Also typical, in a different role, was Corporal Jackson and his Combined Action Platoon. The Marine Corps had great success with the CAP program which places a squad of Marines with a platoon of South Vietnamese Popular Forces in a village or hamlet to protect the people from the Viet Cong.

"Corporal Jackson had ten Marines, one Navy Corpsman, and 35 popular force troops (native troops) in his unit to provide security for three hamlets. He conducted troop training and supported the village rebuilding program. The village leaders sought his assistance and advice, entrusted their stores of rice and other goods to his care, and reported to him when the Viet Cong mined a bridge or a road. What more rewarding experience could a 20-year old American such as Corporal Jackson have than to assume such responsibility and to see and feel the faith and rising hopes of these people? Not one of the scores of villages where we established teams like that of Corporal Jackson's fell back into Communist hands.

"Isn't it ironic that we seldom hear about men like Corporal Jackson? They are the men who know how it is to crawl through the deep jungle after the enemy. They know the shock, the grief, and the growing old over-night. They have lost friends in no-name villages and heard the anguished wail of orphaned children and bewildered old people. They also know the value of trusted comrades and the fuller meaning of manhood which comes to those who serve. These young men have competed for the greatest stakes of all—life and death.

"It is very reassuring to know that these young Americans, who will assume much of the leadership in the coming generation, have had their characters forged in a crucible of gallant service to others. It is great to see them break from shells of self-interest; realize the rich reward that comes from service and sacrifice; and broaden their experience and understanding of problems which face our world. They gained the virtues of self-reliance, discipline, obedience to law, integrity and loyalty, and a contempt for cowardice, softness and surrender to private interest. These are virtues that we must all possess, for they are the firm rocks upon which successful states and great societies are built.

"I have a good feeling about what these young men and women can make of themselves. As of October 1968, more than 800,000 men and women who served in the armed forces in Vietnam went back to school that fall under the GI Bill. Percentage-wise a record number of these veterans were going for their college degree—two out of every three. Those working for degrees represented 122 percent more than veterans of World War II and 33 percent more than the veterans of the Korean Conflict. That was three years ago. Today, the number taking advantage of this opportunity has further increased. I see this as a good sign that our young veterans are ready and willing to take their proper place in society.

"The great challenge for all of us is to undergo the vital infusion of spirit demonstrated by these veterans. Essential though it is to continue technical development and social and scientific exploration, a prerequisite to our success will always be the availability of dedicated, smart, highly skilled individuals—large numbers of men and women of great spirit! Whatever else we do, the proper nurturing of young Americans will ensure that the bright torch of our great heritage as champions of freedom with justice continues to light the way in this troubled world. You are those young Americans who can possess and relay that essential spirit to all of us.

"Adversity builds character in the strong, but it can destroy the weak. Our greatest need is to kindle this burning spirit in those who possess the adequate physical and mental ability, but who lack the heart. To those of great heart who suffer from physical or mental defects, we must offer even more support.

"Your great challenge, as individuals, is to choose your intellectual endeavors wisely, and combine this choice with self-discipline and unselfish service which offer *you* the best opportunity to participate in the effort to keep a strong America. this requires more than dreamers who occupy themselves with distant concerns. It requires active participants who tackle the problems and ills immediately at hand.

"Don't drop out! Aspire to leadership roles! The late Vince Lombardi—best of all pro football coaches—ofttimes proclaimed that 'leaders are not born, they are made.' They are *made* by strong effort and desire.

"I know that as young Americans with great potential, you will make the effort as you prepare yourselves through education and self-improvement to accept the responsibility and challenge which are surely yours.

"The responsibility and challenge you accept must lead to the improvement of our society through necessary change. Unfortunately, change is often slow in coming, but you must not lose heart. You must not resort to violence, which is a waste of energy. The famous soul singer, James Brown, has said:

The energy being used for violence should be used to build the community up . . . if housing is bad and the retailers unfair, then don't terrorize—organize . . . Don't tear down the community, build it up . . .

"I pledge you full support in your efforts! I know that a bright future can be yours."

HIROSHI HERSHEY MIYAMURA

Early in 1942, after Japan attacked Pearl Harbor on December 7, 1941 the Federal government of the United States shipped the 71,484 Japanese-American citizens, commonly referred to as Nisei, together with 40,869 alien Japanese living on the west coast to relocation camps in several of our western states, classifying them as potential security risks. For the most part, these industrious, patriotic American citizens had their land, homes and life-time holdings confiscated, impossible to ever adequately make restitution for same. The underlying reason for this action probably stemmed from the heinous acts of sabotage perpetrated by Germanic American citizens residing on the east coast during World War I and racial prejudice. In an attempt to prove themselves as first class American citizens, the young Nisei men of military age petitioned our leaders to be allowed to fight in World War II. From this patriotic request was formed the famous all Japanese-American Combat team, the 442d, which fought so valiantly in Europe during World War II.

As a teen-ager, Hiroshi Miyamura joined the 100th Infantry Battalion of the 442d Combat Team after graduating from high school in Gallup, New Mexico in 1943. By the time he arrived overseas, the war in Europe was over. After his honorable discharge, he joined the Army reserves in 1946 for two years. In September of 1949, Hiroshi reinlisted in the reserves and after being called to active duty was ultimately assigned as a machine gun squad leader in H Company, 7th Infantry Regiment, 3rd Infantry Division in Korea.

It is of interest that the woman he married after World War II in Gallup, New Mexico, Tsuruko Tsuchimori, was, as a teenager, incarcerated in one of the relocation camps for Japanese-Americans. They now have three fine children— Mike, age 26, Pat, age 25, and a daughter, Kelly, age 21. Both Hiroshi's and Tsuruko's parents were born in Kumamoto, Japan, before immigrating to the United States. For many years, Hiroshi's father, named Y.Miyamura, ran a fine restaurant in Gallup, New Mexico. His mother, Torrie died in 1937. Hiroshi was raised by his father and affirms that Mr. Miyamura was responsible for building his character and developing his deep love for America and the American way of life. Hiroshi has five sisters and one brother. His brother served in the Air Force during the Korean Conflict. His father died in December of 1965.

Hiroshi Miyamura was born in Gallup, New Mexico on October 6, 1925. He is self-employed, operating an Exxon Service Station in Gallup. After being discharged at the end of World War II, he attended the Milwaukee School of Engineering in Milwaukee, Wisconsin.

During his youth he was a member of the Japanese Free Methodist Church. While attending a church conference in Pacific Palasades in 1937, he was informed that his mother had died. For many years after his mother's untimely death, he felt a resentment toward God. However, before he returned to active duty in the Army in 1949, he had many conversations with different pastors of his church. He states, "I learned how wrong I was. Although I do not attend church regularly, I still believe in God."

Standing five feet, nine and one-half inches tall, Hiroshi weighs 150 pounds. During his two year confinement as a POW of the Chinese, his weight dropped to 98 pounds. He is a handsome man with dark, expressive eyes. He is the only living Japanese-American citizen to have received the Medal of Honor.

On the night of April 24, 1951, near the Imjin River in Korea, his super-human actions began which resulted in his being awarded our nation's highest honor. His citation tells it all:

MIYAMURA, HIROSHI H.

Rank and organization: Corporal, U.S. Army, Company H, 7th Infantry Regiment, 3rd Infantry Division. Place and date: Near Taejon-ni, Korea, 24 and 25 April 1951. Entered service at: Gallup, New Mexico. Birth: Gallup, New Mexico. G.O. No: 85, 4 November 1953. Citation: Cpl. Miyamura, a member of Company H, distinguished himself by conspicuous gallantry and intrepidity above and beyond the call of duty in action against the enemy. On the night of 24 April, Company H was occupying a defensive position when the enemy fanatically attacked, threatening to overrun the position. Cpl. Miyamura, a machine gun squad leader, aware of the imminent danger to his men unhesitatingly jumped from his shelter wielding his bayonet in close hand-to-hand combat killing approximately 10 of the enemy. Returning to his position, he administered first aid to the wounded and directed their evacuation. As another savage assault hit the line, he manned his machine gun and delivered withering fire until his ammunition was expended. He ordered the squad to withdraw while he stayed behind to render the gun inoperative. He then bayoneted his way through infiltrated enemy soldiers to a second gun implacement and assisted in its operation. When the intensity of the attack necessitated the withdrawal of the company, Cpl. Miyamura ordered his men to fall back while he remained to cover their movement. He killed more than 50 of the enemy before his ammunition was depleted and he was severely wounded. He maintained his magnificent stand despite his painful wounds, continuing to repel the attack until his position was overrun. When last seen he was fighting ferociously against an overwhelming number of enemy soldiers. Cpl. Miyamura's indomitable heroism and consummate devotion to duty reflect the utmost glory on himself and uphold the illustrious traditions of the military service.

In his own words, Sgt. Miyamura (he was promoted to Sergeant while in prison camp), describes what happened to him for the next two years. "After allowing my men to go back and regroup without company, I started to make my way back to join them. Our own artillery started bombing our positions thinking that everyone of our troops were gone.

"As I made my way down one of the many trenches dug for our previous fights, I ran into an enemy soldier (Chinese). We recognized each other immediately. I fired my MI rifle at the same time falling backwards to the ground—he at the same instantly threw a concussion grenade at me. I kicked it back toward him and it went off. I did not know at the time, but a small fragment hit me in the leg. I laid there for what I thought was a few seconds. Realizing that the enemy was dead, I jumped out of the trench, ran and crawled all the way down the hill, approximately 400 yards. At the bottom of the hill I saw one of our own tanks just pulling back from its position. Trying desperately to get the driver's attention, I ran into our own barbed wire entanglement and slashed my hand very badly. I crawled under the wire but the tank was gone. I then ran a few hundred yards and fell into a ravine. I laid there for a while, exhausted and weak. I'm guessing, two or three hours.

"The attack started approximately at midnight on April 25th. About 6 o'clock I heard burp gun-fire all around me. That woke me up. I estimated the whole Chinese Army went by me. I do not know if they saw me or not. After the mass was gone, a Chinese soldier spoke in English, 'Get up. We will not harm you. We have a lenient policy.' "

"He had a .45 cal. hand gun pointed at me as he was talking. I was taken to an area where some of my company were also taken prisoner. They were fellows from Sgt. Anello's squad of machine gunners. Some were wounded, so I helped them the best I could, then realized that I was also wounded.

"After making us walk with the Chinese troops as they advanced approximately 50 miles south of our position, we were then marched back toward the north. There were about 30 of us POW's. We were weak from hunger, lack of sleep and the cold. We had only the clothes on our back and the nights were so cold we could not sleep much. Sgt. Anello was shot in the buttocks and we could no longer help him walk so the Chinese soldiers told us to leave him. That was the last time I saw him until he came through Gallup in 1956 to tell me he had made it back. Our own troops found him in time.

"As we marched on, we became weaker. The Chinese made each one of us carry our own food which they called emergency rations. It was a very fine powder made from soy beans, millet, rice and barley. You ate it dry and then drank water. The water made the powder expand, which made you feel a little better. But if you ate too much at one time, you had no rations for later. One bag was to last for about one week. We later learned to mix it with water and make patties, then toast them over a fire. This could only be done when we stopped for the day.

"It took us a little over a month (approximately 500 miles) to get to our POW compound which was called camp '5.' By the time we arrived after riding a ferry across the Yellow River and about two miles from the Manchurian border, most of us were in pretty bad shape. Most had dysentary from the water we drank from streams along the march. We were not given better food for the first year in camp. Many of the boys died from malnutrition because they couldn't or wouldn't eat what was given to us. Also, the wounded were not given medical treatment or supplies. North Korea did not recognize the Geneva Convention treaty nor did they recognize our Red Cross. However, once the Armistice talks started, we were given better food and athletic equipment to keep our spirits up. We spent much of each day going out into the forest to gather wood for heating and cooking. We talked a lot of home.

"When they tried to brainwash us, we just turned them off by not saying a word. Those that spoke up against it were beaten or put into holds without food for days at a time.

"I think that what made each one of us survive that life was the belief that we had such a wonderful country, families, and friends to go back to. We wanted to survive. For you have to have the will to live in order to survive any ordeal.

"What a wonderful sight it was to see Old Glory flying in the breeze as we crossed over to our side at Freedom Village near Kaesong!"

As Sgt. Hiroshi H. Miyamura entered Freedom Village, an American Officer approached him, asking, "Are you Cpl. Hiroshi Miyamura?"

When Sgt. Miyamura nodded his head in affirmation, the American Officer told him that he had been awarded THE MEDAL OF HONOR! Later, after he had been returned to the United States, President Eisenhower hung the Medal around his neck in a formal ceremony at the White House. In Sgt. Hiroshi Miyamura's words, "At that moment I felt this must all be a dream. To have the most respected President and General of the Army present me with my MEDAL OF HONOR!"

"I felt that no matter what race, color, or creed, the government and the people of our country are the most generous in showing their gratitude for deeds of heroism. To be recognized by my country for something that I felt was my duty was overwhelming. I am very proud and honored, but also humble for the honor bestowed upon me.

"Being an American means that I live in a country where I can be as equal as the next person, regardless of race, color or creed. That I can voice my opinions, can run for the Presidency, pursue any goal that I may want to obtain, have the freedom of religion and the pursuit of happiness.

"I think that the majority of the youth of today take their wonderful country and freedom for granted. I think the youth should be reminded that we live in a true democratic country and as responsible citizens should serve our country in whatever capacity that need be to keep it so. Our forefathers paid dearly for this Freedom."

In November 1980 Hiroshi Miyamura and other members of the famed 442nd Regimental Combat Team were honored with a parade and commemoration services at Sacramento, California. At that time Miyamura was presented the California Medal of Valor, the state's highest award.

PART V
THE VIETNAM WAR
1963-1973

Vietnam, together with the countries of Laos and Cambodia, is part of that area in Southeast Asia which is called Indochina because of its proximity to India and China. France colonized Indochina during the nineteenth century and Vietnam became one of France's most wealthy possessions. After Germany overran France in the early days of World War II, Vietnam was occupied by Germany's axis partner in the Far East, Japan. When Japan surrendered to end World War II in September of 1945, Ho Chi Minh, who had organized the Communist Party of Indochina in 1930, declared Vietnam to be an independent Republic. However, France decided to reclaim Vietnam as its own colony. That decision precipitated the First Vietnam War which lasted eight long years from 1946 until 1954 when the French forces were defeated at Dien Bien Phu.

The involvement of the United States in Vietnam began in 1950 when President Truman furnished France with a military advisement team. From 1950 until the fall of Dien Bien Phu in 1954, America supported France with equipment and President Eisenhower sent 200 U.S. Air Force technicians to Vietnam to assist France in maintaining the aircraft they used during the war. The American involvement was intended to thwart the spread of communism in Southeast Asia (the domino theory).

At the Geneva armistice in 1954, Vietnam was divided into two parts, North Vietnam and South Vietnam, at the 17th parallel, with the understanding that a National election would be held in two years to reunite the country. This decision was similar to the separation of Korea into North and South Korea at the 38th parallel at the end of World War II.

However, the South Vietnamese decided not to honor the agreement reached in Geneva to hold national elections. This determination resulted in civil war and the United States became involved, step by step. Under President Kennedy the American military advisors were increased in number and by the time Lyndon Johnson became President in 1963 there were 15,000 "advisors" assisting the south Vietnamese. Then in 1965 23,000 American military "advisors" were ordered into actual combat.

By 1969 our military forces in Vietnam had escalated to 543,000 and the monetary expenditure was in the billions of dollars. At the end of America's involvement in the Vietnam War in 1973, approximately 2,800,000 soldiers, sailors, marines and airmen had served in the war. Fifty-one thousand Americans had been killed, 1,400 were missing, and 270,000 had been wounded. Of those wounded, 21,000 were disabled.

Two years after the peace treaty of 1973 had been signed and the American forces withdrawn, the North Vietnamese invaded South Vietnam. On April 30, 1975 Saigon fell to the North Vietnamese communists.

Two hundred thirty-nine gallant Americans earned the Medal of Honor during the Vietnam War, only 86 survived. Of these great heroes, 13 personal accounts follow on the remaining pages of *The Spirit of America.*

WEBSTER ANDERSON

Sergeant First Class Webster Anderson is retired from the U.S. Army and works part time as a TV technician. He lost both legs and his right hand in combat on October 15, 1967 at Tam Ky, Vietnam, while serving as a section chief in Battery A, 2nd Battalion, 230th Artillery of the 101st Airborne Infantry Division. He is married to Ida Davis Anderson. They have three children—a daughter, Vonnie, age 19 and two sons, Webster Anderson II, 17, and Daine, who is 10. His father, Forezell Anderson Black is 75. His mother, Blanch Robb Anderson Black is deceased.

Since his retirement at age 36, Webster Anderson has completed high school and two years of technical school. He was born at Winnsboro, South Carolina on July 15, 1933. The Anderson family are Baptists and Webster attends church regularly. His faith and love for his country have been reaffirmed many times, due to interactions with people he has met, especially since he has been retired from military service. In his own words, "I try to be a better person knowing that I'm not alone in my feelings about this country."

President Richard Nixon presented Sgt. Anderson with the Medal of Honor in the East Room of the White House on November 24, 1969. His parents and family were present at the ceremony. Webster recalls that event as a high point in his life—"It was and is now a wonderful feeling and hard to believe it was happening to me."

His citation for the Medal of Honor reads:

ANDERSON, WEBSTER

Rank and organization: Sergeant First Class, U.S. Army, Battery A, 2nd Battalion, 320th Artillery, 101st Airborne Infantry Division (Airmobile). Place and date: Tam Ky, Republic of Vietnam, 15 October 1966. Entered service at Winnsboro, S.C. Born: 15 July 1933, Winnsboro, S.C. Citation: Sfc. Anderson (then S/Sgt), distinguished himself by conspicuous gallantry and intrepidity in action while serving as chief of section in Battery A, against a hostile force. During the early morning hours, Battery A's defensive position was attacked by a determined North Vietnamese Army Infantry unit supported by heavy mortar, recoiless rifle, rocket propelled grenade and automatic weapon fire. The initial enemy onslaught breached the battery defensive perimeter. Sfc. Anderson with complete disregard for his personal safety, mounted the exposed parapet of his howitzer position and became the mainstay of the defense of the battery position. Sfc. Anderson directed devastating direct howitzer fire on the assaulting soldiers attempting to overrun his gun section position. While protecting his crew and directing their fire against the enemy from his exposed position, two enemy grenades exploded at his feet knocking him down and severely wounding him in the legs. Despite the excruciating pain and though not able to stand, Sfc. Anderson valorously propped himself on the parapet and continued to direct howitzer fire upon the closing enemy and to encourage his men to fight on. Seeing an enemy grenade land within the gunpit near a wounded member of his guncrew, Sfc. Anderson heedless of his own safety, seized the grenade and attempted to throw it over the parapet to save his men. As the grenade was thrown from the position it exploded and Sfc. Anderson was again greviously wounded. Although only partially conscious and severely wounded Sfc. Anderson refused medical evacuation and continued to encourage his men in the defense of the position. Sfc. Anderson by his inspirational leadership, professionalism, devotion to duty and complete disregard for his welfare was able to maintain the defense of his section's position and to defeat a determined attack. Sfc. Anderson's gallantry and extraordinary heroism at the risk of his life above and beyond the call of duty are in the highest traditions of the military service and reflect great credit upon himself, his unit, and the U.S. Army.

"Being an American to me cannot be put into words," states Webster Anderson. "Because it is very, very great to be an American. The government of the United States is the greatest in the world."

To the Youth of America, Webster Anderson emplores— "To believe in America, to love it. And to work hard to make it better. And to defend it."

HARVEY C. BARNUM, JR.

Harvey C. Barnum, Jr. was born on July 21, 1940 in Waterbury, Connecticut. He graduated from Cheshire High School in Cheshire, Connecticut in 1958 where he was president of his senior class. During his high school years, he played football and baseball, was a member of the Boy Scouts of America, the "C" Club, and the Gym Leaders Club. In 1962 he received a B.A. Degree in Economics from St. Anselm College in Manchester, New Hampshire. He joined the Marine Corps' Platoon Leaders Class program while in college and accepted a Marine Reserve commission upon graduation. After several assignments, he was appointed to the regular Marine Corps in 1964.

Currently, Lieutenant Colonel Harvey C. Barnum, Jr. is attending the Naval War College at Newport, Rhode Island. He is five feet, eight inches in height and weighs 168 pounds. He is married to the former Dorothy Thelma Lanier of York, South Carolina. His parents are Mr. and Mrs. H. Curtis Barnum of Cheshire, Connecticut. He is of the Roman Catholic faith.

In addition to the Medal of Honor, Lt. Col. Barnum has been awarded two Bronze Stars with Combat V, the Navy Commendation Medal, the Navy Achievement Medal with Combat V, the Purple Heart, the Combat Action Ribbon, the Presidential Unit Citation, the Army Presidential Unit Citation, the Navy Unit Citation, the Meritorious Unit Citation twice, and the Vietnamese Cross of Gallantry.

From December, 1965 until February, 1966, the then

Lieutenant Barnum served on temporary duty in Vietnam. As an artillery forward observer with Company H, 2nd Battalion, 9th Marines, 3rd Marine Division. Lieutenant Barnum's action on December 18, 1965 earned him our nation's highest award, the Medal of Honor. His citation reads:

BARNUM, HARVEY C. JR.

Rank and organization: Captain (then Lt.), U.S. Marine Corps, Company H, 2nd Battalion, 9th Marines, 3rd Marine Division (Rein). Place and date: Ky Phu in Quang Tin Province, Republic of Vietnam. 18 December 1965. Entered service at: Cheshire, Conn. Born: 21 July 1940, Cheshire, Conn. Citation: For conspicuous gallantry and intrepidity at the risk of his life above and beyond the call of duty. When the company was suddenly pinned down by a hail of extremely accurate enemy fire and was quickly separated from the remainder of the battalion by over 500 meters of open and fire-swept ground, and casualties mounted rapidly, Lt. Barnum quickly made a hazardous reconnaissance of the area, seeking targets for his artillery. Finding the rifle company commander mortally wounded and the radio operator killed, he, with complete disregard for his own safety, gave aid to the dying commander, then removed the radio from the dead operator and strapped it to himself. He immediately assumed command of the rifle company, and moving at once into the midst of the heavy fire, rallying and giving encouragement to all units, reorganized them to replace the loss of key personnel and led their attack on enemy positions from which deadly fire continued to come. His sound and swift decision and his obvious calm served to stabilize the badly decimated units and his gallant example as he stood exposed repeatedly to point out targets served as an inspiration to all. Provided with two armed helicopters, he moved fearlessly through enemy fire to control the air attack against the firmly entrenched enemy while skillfully directing one platoon in a successful counterattack on the key enemy positions. Having thus cleared a small area, he requested and directed the landing of two transport helicopters for the evacuation of the dead and wounded. He then assisted in the mopping up and final seizure of the battalion's objective. His gallant initiative and heroic conduct reflected great credit upon himself and were in keeping with the highest traditions of the Marine Corps and the U.S. Naval Service.

"Being an American means that I live in and have allegiance to the country that is the leader of the free world, a country that affords an opportunity for each individual to live in an atmosphere of mental and physical security, freedom to choose the way of life each desires, and under a democratic system that protects our freedom while allowing each individual to speak out and influence the governing process of our nation. Being an American also means that I should be prepared to shoulder my portion of the load, make personal sacrifices and accept and discharge the responsibilities of a concerned citizen. America is a land of opportunity, an example for the members of the free world to look up to, a nation that does not hesitate to reach out and help a man, a nation in need. However, being an American means we must all strive to preserve for all mankind the freedoms inherent in a democratic system. Being a true American is a sobering responsibility if we stop to take inventory of the responsibilities that each of us share as well as the glory and the benefits we reap. Being an American can be a fantastic experience if we logically and sincerely support our government and all that it stands for while at the same time remain prepared to make personal sacrifices to ensure that the democratic system survives. And for me, being an American allows me to do all this while serving my country as a United States Marine."

Lt. Colonel Barnum's advice to the youth of America is—"The youth of today are growing up in a world of instant communications, the emergence of various radical groups, a worldly political scene that is ringed with a great deal of unrest and the presence of continual worldly communist aggression. Coupled with the permissiveness of society, the lack of personal discipline, the luxuries associated with life in the United States and the worldly turmoil referred to above, I feel it is paramount that the youth of today review the events of history so that they do not launch off into the future blindly. By continuing to live the good life, not looking into the future, living day by day, reaping all the benefits of being an American but not willing to undergo personal sacrifices for the good of the country so that democracy might flourish, joining dissident groups who speak out against our government, its judicial system and the military can only lead to disaster.

"The future of our country in the 21st century lies in the hands of the youth of today. In order for the American ideal, the democratic system and the freedoms inherent in it to flourish, our youth must be willing to make any and all sacrifices for our country, dedicate themselves completely to the principles and philosophies of liberty and freedom so that this nation and the principles for which it stands will flourish. Eternal vigilance cannot be bought with words and wishes. This eternal vigilance comes high—it comes in vast expenditures of money, vast human effort, vast human sacrifice. It comes in terms of interrupted lives for the youth of our land, long separations from loved ones; frequently it comes in severe personal hardships and inconveniences. Make no mistake—it always calls for sacrifices—sometimes small but generally great. As Americans, we must remain ready and willing to sacrifice our lives if necessary for liberty, for justice, for freedom, for honor. If we accepted less, we would be selling our country short. Don't join the side of the fuzzy-thinking cloud sitters, the cynics, the misguided who would sell cheaply the sacrifices in which they take no part and have never taken a part. We are indeed a privileged people, yet as President Eisenhower said in his inaugural address, "A people that values its privileges above its principles soon loses both." I ask the youth of our land to stand on their own two feet, face up to reality, tighten up their boot straps if need be, exhibit patriotism, love of country and the willingness to accept and discharge the responsibilities of citizenship. By your daily actions and deeds you can keep this American spirit alive. Each of you must realize that life alone is simple existence. But life lived with honor is the birthright you must leave future generations so that for them as for you, those beautiful, much respected, time worn words, 'Life, Liberty, and the Pursuit of Happiness' will have meaning. You are our bond with the past, our hope for the future—Good Luck and God Speed."

PATRICK HENRY BRADY

On January 6, 1968 Lt. Colonel Patrick Henry Brady saved the lives of 51 seriously wounded servicemen in Vietnam. Although he doesn't directly relate his heroic actions on that day to the saving of two lives when he was a child, there is a definite correlation of his earlier life-saving accomplishments with the incredible feat he achieved in Vietnam as an ambulance helicopter pilot. He seemed predestined to do what was called a mission impossible by his peers since two aircraft had previously been shot down while others had made unsuccessful attempts at rescue that day.

Pat Brady was born on October 1, 1936 at Philip, South Dakota. His mother LaVona and his father Michael are both of Irish ancestry. He is six feet tall and weighs 185 pounds, a typical handsome Irishman with no physical impairments. His current rank is Colonel and he holds a B.A. degree from the University of Seattle, class of 1959. In 1972 he earned an M.B.A. from Notre Dame in South Bend, Indiana. It is of interest that his father, Michael Brady, served with Darby's Rangers during World War II.

Although he credits several people and concepts in forming his character, he acknowledges that his wife, Nancy, has been the most influential person in his life. They have five children, two boys and three girls, ranging in age from 23 to 11 months. He is an orthodox Catholic. And in his words, "My faith is, or I try to make it, the most important thing in my life. In combat I used faith as a substitute for fear.

"There were many men who should have been awarded the

Medal of Honor, but the system requires witnesses and others who will take the time and effort to process it. I was just lucky to have both," Colonel Brady states.

His citation for the Medal of Honor reads:

BRADY, PATRICK HENRY
   Rank and organization: Major, U.S. Army, Medical Service Corps, 54th Medical Detachment, 67th Medical Group, 44th Medical Brigade. Place and date: Near Chu Lai, Republic of Vietnam, 6 January 1968. Entered service at Seattle, Wash. Born: 1 October 1936, Philip, S. Dak. Citation: For conspicuous gallantry and intrepidity in action at the risk of his life above and beyond the call of duty, Maj. Brady distinguished himself while serving in the Republic of Vietnam commanding a UH-1H ambulance helicopter, volunteered to rescue wounded men from a site in enemy held territory which was reported to be heavily defended and to be blanketed by fog. To reach the site he descended through heavy fog and smoke and hovered slowly along a valley trail, turning his ship sideward to blow away the fog with the backwash from his rotor blades. Despite the unchallenged, close-range enemy fire, he found the dangerously small site, where he successfully landed and evacuated two badly wounded South Vietnamese soldiers. He was then called to another area completely covered by dense fog where American casualties lay only 50 meters from the enemy. Two aircraft had proviously been shot down and others had made unsuccessful attempts to reach this site earlier in the day. With unmatched skill and extraordinary courage, Maj. Brady made four flights to this embattled landing zone and successfully rescued all the wounded. On his third mission of the day Maj. Brady once again landed at a site surrounded by the enemy. The friendly ground force, pinned down by enemy fire, had been unable to reach and secure the landing zone. Although his aircraft had been badly damaged and his controls partially shot away during his initial entry into this area, he returned minutes later and rescued the remaining

injured. Shortly thereafter, obtaining a replacement aircraft, Maj. Brady was requested to land in an enemy minefield where a platoon of American soldiers was trapped. A mine detonated near his helicopter, wounding two crew members and damaging his ship. In spite of this, he managed to fly six severely injured patients to medical aid. Throughout that day Maj. Brady utilized three helicopters to evacuate a total of 51 seriously wounded men, many of whom would have perished without prompt medical treatment. Maj. Brady's bravery was in the highest traditions of the military service and reflects great credit upon himself and the U.S. Army.

He received the Medal of Honor from President Nixon, 9 October 1969 on the White House lawn. His parents and family were present for the ceremony.

In reflecting on his actions that day in Vietnam, Colonel Brady states—"The only fear I ever experienced was that I might not get the patient. I hope that was not grounded in pride but rather a genuine concern for the pain of others—but I did not like to be told that any mission was impossible or that because someone else had tried and failed that I also would fail. I was driven to try. I found two new rescue techniques just because I tried when others would not, but they could have done the same had they but tried. My skill as a pilot was a result of my trying, not any particular gift. The day I earned the Medal was not much different than many others except that I had an audience who watched me go into the fog and come out with their wounded buddies."

In response to the question, "What does being an American mean to you in your own words?" Lt. Colonel Patrick Brady replied—"To me, it somehow relates to the Catholic Doctrine of grace. Freedom is like grace, a treasure chest we all draw from often through no merit of our own, but because of the sacrifice of others. For grace, we have Christ and that treasure is inexhaustable, but freedom is not so and must be replenished by our own sacrifices. We cannot draw on the sacrifices of those before us. Sacrifice is really love in action and America will survive if we remain a loveable people. But we seem to be becoming less loveable, less worthy of sacrifice."

His advice to the youth of America is—"Freedom is not free, but the sacrifices freedom requires can be enjoyable. Tough times are the best times—the most memorable. Comfort is the enemy. Force yourself to spend a part of each day on the three parts of your being: physical, mental, spiritual. Don't be a peer fink—decide what is worthwhile and stick to it, regardless of what your peers are saying or doing— most don't really say what they mean. No relationship will last except that with yourself and your God."

WESLEY L. FOX

In response to the question, "What did you do to be awarded the Congressional Medal of Honor?" Major Wesley L. Fox modestly answered: "I provided guidance to an outstanding group of young Marines."

In addition to the Medal of Honor, Wesley Fox has received the Bronze Star, two Navy Commendations, four Purple Hearts, two Silver Vietnamese Crosses of Gallantry, the Vietnamese Honor Medal, the Combat Action Medal, the Navy Presidential Unit Citation, the Army Presidential Unit Citation, the Navy Unit Citation, four Meritorious Unit Citations, the Korean Presidential Unit Citation, the Vietnam Unit Cross of Gallantry w/ Palm, the Civic Action ribbon, five Good Conduct medals, the Korean Service award w/three stars, the Vietnam Service award w/seven stars, the United Nations Service award, the Vietnam Campaign ribbon, two National Defense ribbons, the Navy/Marine Corps Parachute Insignia, the Scuba Diver badge, and the Canadian Parachutist wings.

His citation for the Medal of Honor reads:

FOX, WESLEY L.
Rank and organization: Captain, U.S. Marine Corps, Company A, 1st Battalion, 9th Marines, 3rd Marine Division. Place and date: Quang Tri Province, Republic of Vietnam, 22 February 1969. Entered service at: Leesburg, Va. Born: 30 September 1931, Herndon, Va. Citation: For conspicuous gallantry and intrepidity at the risk of his life above and beyond the call of duty while serving as commanding officer of Company A, in action

against the enemy in the northern A Shau Valley, Capt. (then 1st Lt.) Fox's company came under intense fire from a large well concealed enemy force. Capt. Fox maneuvered to a position from which he could assess the situation and confer with his platoon leaders. As they departed to execute the plan he had devised, the enemy attacked and Capt. Fox was wounded along with all of the other members of the command group, except the executive officer. Capt. Fox continued to direct the activity of his company. Advancing through heavy enemy fire, he personally neutralized one enemy position and calmly ordered an assault against the hostile emplacements. He then moved through the hazardous area coordinating aircraft support with the activities of his men. When his executive officer was mortally wounded, Capt. Fox reorganized the company and directed the fire of his men as they hurled grenades against the enemy and drove the hostile forces into retreat. Wounded again in the final assault, Capt. Fox refused medical attention, established a defensive posture, and supervised the preparation of casualties for medical evacuation. His indomitable courage, inspiring initiative, and unwavering devotion to duty in the face of grave personal danger inspired his marines to such aggressive action that they overcame all enemy resistance and destroyed a large bunker complex. Capt. Fox's heroic actions reflect great credit upon himself and the Marine Corps, and uphold the highest traditions of the U.S. Naval Service.

Wesley Lee Fox received the Medal of Honor at the White House in Washington from President Nixon in the presence of his immediate family. He has spent 30 years on active duty in the Marines, 16 of which have been in the enlisted ranks, and the last 14 as an officer. His highest enlisted rank was First Sergeant while his current officer rank is that of Major. Major Fox was born on September 30, 1931 in Herndon, Virginia. He attended Warren County High School in Front Royal,

Virginia before entering service. He has earned a B.S. in Business at Western State College in Gunnison, Colorado in June of 1977 while on active duty.

He is married to the former Dotti Lu Bossinger of Lewistown, Pennsylvania. They have three daughters—Dixie Lee, Amy Lu, and Nichole. His parents are Mr. and Mrs. John W. Fox of Leesburg, Virginia. It is of interest that until their oldest daughter, Dixie Lee was born, his petite wife, Dotti Lu, made parachute jumps with her husband. Major Fox is of French/English and German/Dutch ancestry. He is of the Methodist faith.

To Major Wesley Fox, being an American means: "That one can take things for granted, his freedom, rights, education, food, shelter, and even the fact that someone else will fight to insure those rights. Being an American also means that the sky is the limit. If you want it bad enough, you can get it regardless of the position you were in when you started. But most important, being an American is knowing that the majority of my people are those who will stand up and be counted."

His advice to the youth of America is—"As a people, all of the happenings, the good and the bad, to each of us as an individual are brought on by the manner in which we are perceived and received by those around us. If each of us could respect the individual rights of our neighbor, to include his right to always see us as the very best person within ourselves, we could all enjoy a warm, happy, meaningful life."

DAVID H. MCNERNEY

David McNerney was born of Irish ancestry on July 2, 1931 in Lowell, Massachusetts. In 1949 he graduated from St. Thomas High School in Houston, Texas. He retired from the Army in December of 1969 with the rank of 1st Sergeant. His present occupation is Customs Inspector with the U.S. Customs Service. He and his wife, Parmelia, live in Crosby, Texas. They have no children.

Both of his parents, deceased, are buried in Houston, Texas. During World War I his father, Edward McNerney, was the 1st Sergeant of Company K, 104 Infantry Regiment, 26th Infantry Division. He was badly wounded in France and received the Distinguished Service Cross (our second highest military award), the Silver Star, two Purple Hearts, and the Croix de Guerre from France. Edward McNerney was a career employee of the U.S. Department of Agriculture.

David has a deep pride in his family. This is evidenced not only in the achievements of his father during World War I but in the accomplishments of his brothers and sisters. Ruth Mary was an Army Nurse during World War II and now is employed as a nurse in the V.A. Hospital in Houston. Edward Jr. served on the U.S.S. submarine Dace in the Pacific during World War II. The Dace sank the Japanese heavy cruiser, Maya, during the battle of Leyte. Richard P., a Captain in the U.S. Air Force Reserves, flew combat as a Navy Lieutenant in Vietnam and was awarded the Distinguished Flying Cross and 12 Air Medals. He holds a PhD. in chemistry and is head of research at Vector Cable in Houston. His youngest sister,

Susan M., a graduate of the University of Houston, was a school teacher before her marriage.

In retrospect, David McNerney states that "all of us have tried to give as well as take from our country. We all seem to feel a deep obligation to the United States—probably from our father, who didn't say much but who certainly set an example as an American."

David is five feet, ten inches in height, and weighs 150 pounds. He has scars on the right side of his rib cage due to wounds received in Vietnam. Raised as a Catholic, he attended a Catholic grade school as well as a Catholic high school.

He was presented the Medal of Honor on September 19, 1968 by President Lyndon Johnson at the White House. His wife, Parmelia, together with his brothers and sisters, attended the ceremony. Richard P. McNerney, his youngest brother, was flown from Vietnam to witness David's award.

The citation of David H. McNerney's Medal of Honor reads:

> McNERNEY, DAVID H.
> Rank and organization: First Sergeant, U.S. Army, Company A, 1st Battalion, 8th Infantry, 4th Infantry Division. Place and date: Polei Doc, Republic of Vietnam, 22 March 1967. Entered service at: Fort Bliss, Tex. Born: July 2, 1931, Lowell, Mass. Citation: 1st Sgt. McNerney distinguished himself when his unit was attacked by a North Vietnamese battalion near Polei Doc. Running through the hail of enemy fire to the area of heaviest contact, he was assisting in the development of a defensive perimeter when he encountered several enemy at close range. He killed the enemy but was painfully injured when blown from his feet by a grenade. In spite of this injury, he assaulted and destroyed an enemy machine gun position that had pinned down five of his comrades beyond the defensive line. Upon learning his commander and artillery forward observer had been

killed, he assumed command of the company. He adjusted artillery fire to within 20 meters of the position in a daring measure to repulse enemy attacks. When the smoke grenades used to mark the position were gone, he moved into a nearby clearing to designate the location to friendly aircraft. In spite of enemy fire he remained exposed until he was certain the position was spotted and then climbed into a tree and tied the identification panel to its highest branches. Then he moved among his men readjusting their position, encouraging the defenders and checking the wounded. As the hostile assaults slackened, he began clearing a helicopter landing site to evacuate the wounded. When explosives were needed to remove large trees, he crawled outside the relative safety of the perimeter to collect demolition material from abandoned rucksacks. Moving through a fusillade of fire he returned with the explosives that were vital to the clearing of the landing zone. Disregarding the pain of his injury and refusing medical evacuation First Sgt. McNerney remained with his unit until the next day when the new commander arrived. First Sgt. McNerney's outstanding heroism and leadership were inspirational to his comrades. His actions were in keeping with the highest traditions of the U.S. Army and reflect great credit upon himself and the Armed Forces of his country.

David speaks of his feelings concerning his country—"I believe I am very chauvinistic when it comes to my country. As far back as I can remember it was present. The fact that my father was employed by the government—the pledge of allegiance—Fourth of July—talk of World War I—the things that happened in my formative years. I will never forget the invasion of Poland and the talk that we would soon be at war—the war itself: Pearl Harbor, Corregidor, sinking of the cruiser Houston, my brother as a submarine sailor, my father's record in World War I . . . I would have to be made of wood not to be full of pride for the United States and the people in it.

"I believe that every person should have some tangible goal or object that guides or influences him with utter disregard for the intangibles: God, ideals, beliefs, a sense of belonging to something good and great, an everlasting motivation that enables a person to produce to the maximum of his capabilities . . . a pride in himself and his fellow citizens that so much has been accomplished and continues to be accomplished every day. Possibly these disjoined ideals and beliefs are not coming across as I would like, but they all contribute to being an American.

"For the young people of America I have a few thoughts. Somewhere I must have read that ultimately all each individual has in this world is his or her name. What else identifies us? What else do we carry to the grave? What else is our means of immortality? It should be one of our most cherished possesions and we are the sole master of that name. What we do or fail to do with that NAME is our responsibility. Also I believe that knowledge is mandatory, especially historical knowledge. From this we learn where we were and where we are going. A knowledge of the history of the United States helps form our opinions of what we are and what has been accomplished."

MICHAEL J. NOVOSEL

A feature article, titled "Dean of the Dust-Offers," written by L. James Binder, editor of ARMY, in the August 1971 issue, vividly relates the saga of Michael J. Novosel, the oldest member of the U.S. Army to be awarded the Medal of Honor during the Vietnam war.

"Every few years, the government publishes a new volume updating the nation's roster of Medal of Honor winners. There is seldom anything lyrical or dramatic about the wording of the citations which make up the bulk of these publications, but there is no more fascinating reading anywhere.

"As the eye takes in the terse accounts of incredible acts of bravery and sacrifice in battle, the mind instinctively gropes for pictures of the kind of man who single-handedly fights off wave after wave of enemy attacks in force or who dashes repeatedly into hostile fire to rescue wounded comrades. Being human—and American—we tend to think of such a superman as being 10 feet tall, brawny and young in years, and as fierce as a jungle tiger.

"Relatively few of us are ever privileged to meet a Medal of Honor holder, and so it is apt to come as a shock of sorts when this unconsciously held image is found to have been false. There is something very special about a man who wears the Medal of Honor but it is not necessarily physical mass, youth or meanness.

"No better living proof is CWO Michael J. Novosel, a recent recipient who is old enough to be the father of most of the men who have fought in Vietnam. At 48 (he will be 49 next month), he is the Army's oldest Medal of Honor winner of the war. The soft-spoken Mr. Novosel is no giant: he is five feet, four inches tall and weighs less than 150 pounds. As for meanness, he wasn't even carrying a weapon during those 2-1/2 desperate hours on 2 October 1969, when his repeated bravery in the face of heavy Viet Cong gunfire brought him an award of the Medal in ceremonies at the White House this summer.

"The account of what he did in snatching 29 wounded South Vietnamese soldiers from under the blazing guns of an encircling enemy force is one of the most stirring stories of heroism of the war. But even if there had been no Medal of Honor, Michael Novosel would have been a remarkable man. How else could you describe a person who enlisted in the Army nearly a year before Pearl Harbor, ended World War II flying B-29's over Japan, gave up an airline pilot's job and an Air Force lieutenant colonel's commission to serve in the Vietnam war, and who the year before the action that resulted in the Medal was found to be suffering from glaucoma? These and other highlights of his life bespeak of the qualities which make considerations like mere size insignificant in comparison.

"Mr. Novosel won his Medal as a 'dustoff' pilot, that almost legendary breed of helicopter flier whose record in rescuing wounded men during battle is one of the proudest chapters of this or any other war. When the word went out for him to pick up the injured during intense fighting in the Plain of Reeds, Kien Tuong Province, near Cambodia's enemy-dominated Parrot's Beak, he was on his second tour of Vietnam as a member of the 82nd Medical Detachment, 45th Medical Company, of the 68th Medical Group.

"Three compaines of crack South Vietnamese Special Forces had attacked a large enemy bunker system hidden in six-foot elephant grass within rifle distance of Cambodia. The site of a huge training center, complete with a full-size model of a triangular South Vietnamese fire base, the bunker was occupied by a large Viet Cong force armed with mortars, rockets, heavy automatic weapons and small arms. In the heavy combat that followed, the well-entrenched VC inflicted severe casualties on the South Vietnamese attackers, pinning down two compaines for six hours and damaging several helicopter gunships and Air Force fighters which were sent in to cover their withdrawal. Many wounded men were still scattered throughout the three-kilometer area, and at 4:00 p.m. Capt. Harry L. Purdy, who was circling above in his command and control (C&C) helicopter, radioed for a dustoff ship.

"Mr. Novosel had already been in the air for seven hours on other missions that day when he and his three-men crew were dispatched to evacuate the wounded. Flying through heavy thunderstorms and rain, he reached the battle area in clear weather and began looking for injured soldiers.

"The most cogent account of what happened in the next 2-1/2 hours is in the citation accompanying Mr. Novosel's Medal. It reads in part:

> He unhesitatingly maneuvered his helicopter into a heavily fortified and defended enemy training area where a group of wounded Vietnamese soldiers were pinned down by a large enemy force. Flying without gunship or other cover and exposed to intense machine gunfire, Warrant Officer Novosel was able to locate and rescue a wounded soldier. Since all communications with the beleaguered troops had been lost, he repeatedly circled the battle area, flying at low level under continuous heavy fire to attract the attention of the scattered friendly troops. This display of courage visibly raised their morale, as they recognized this as a signal to assemble for evacuation. On six occasions, he and his crew were forced

out of the battle area by the intense enemy fire, only to
circle and return from another direction to land and
extract additional troops. Near the end of the mission, a
wounded soldier was spotted close to the enemy bunker.
Fully realizing that he would attract a hail of enemy fire,
Warrant Officer Novosel nevertheless attempted the
extraction by hovering the helicopter backward. As the
man was pulled on board, enemy automatic weapons
opened fire at close range, damaged the aircraft and
wounded Warrant Officer Novosel. He momentarily lost
control of the aircraft, but quickly recovered and
departed under withering enemy fire. In all, 15 extremely
hazardous extractions were performed in order to
remove wounded personnel. As a result of his selfless
conduct, the lives of 29 soldiers were saved.

"But citations cannot tell the whole story, any more than
can any of the men who took part in the action of 2 October
1969. All can agree on a chronological set of highlights, but
few after action reports describe how it feels to dive time and
again into the very muzzles of blazing hostile weapons, or
what is on the mind of a crew member as his helicopter sits on
the ground in a hail of bullets while a soldier with his intestines
hanging out drags himself slowly toward you through the
grass.

"Sp. 4 Joseph Horvath, crew chief on Mr. Novosel's Huey,
recalls receiving heavy automatic weapons fire 'from all sides'
as the ship first made its way along the fiery gantlet. 'I never
heard so much enemy fire before,' the veteran dustoffer
recalled. 'We made several passes . . . and I saw many gun
flashes from bunkers which are all around us. These bunkers
are all over the place.' The rest of Horvath's account tells of
repeated landings, of being driven away only to return again
by another route, and of such feats as hanging out of the
hovering craft on a litter strap to scoop up a wounded soldier
from the elephant grass below. And around the ship the
shooting, always the shooting.

"CW2 Tyron Chamberlain, the co-pilot, tells the same story of passes, landings and near landings, and adds that during the entire 2-1/2 hours 'we could hear the enemy machine guns firing at us.' When the crew returned to base that night, he notes at the end of his report, it had flown 'a total of 11 hours this day.'

"Said Sp. 4 Herbert Heinold, the craft's medical aid man: 'as soon as we touched down we started receiving fire (but) we stayed till we got the wounded aboard. Numerous times, we tried to get down to pick up survivors but the intensity of the fire was too great; it was coming from all sides, so we tried again . . . The VC knew what we were trying to do and they opened up on us everytime we came close for pickups. At one time, I saw gun flashes coming from at least a half-dozen places.'

"Capt. Purdy adds a note not covered in the citation: 'Mr. Novosel was instrumental in the successful withdrawal of the main South Vietnamese force because, between runs to pick up wounded, he guided the troops around high-water areas which dot the marshy Plain of Reeds and to waiting U.S. Navy boats.'

"One of the things that stands out in Mr. Novosel's recollection of the rescues was of his first attempt to find a wounded soldier that the C&C ship had seen from high above. 'Then we spotted him and all of a sudden we started seeing others all over. It happens that way all the time, but then you don't know if they're friendly troops or VC.'

"Another time, he recalls, he was taking especially heavy fire during one of his passes and he radioed up to Capt. Purdy that 'They're most unfriendly down here.' Capt. Purdy replied that he had strayed across the border into Cambodia, at that time forbidden to U.S. or South Vietnamese incursion despite the enemy's huge concentration of troops and weapons there.

"He even picked up two unwounded South Vietnamese

soldiers who apparently had thrown their weapons away during the action and, despite their protests, flew them back to their units.

"The part of the action he remembers most vividly was the last rescue, made just as impending darkness was forcing a return to base. The bullet-scarred ship was filled with wounded soldiers when crew chief Horvath saw a South Vietnamese soldier lying near one of the bunkers from where enemy soldiers had been firing at them. Mr. Novosel warned the crew to stay low because he expected heavy fire, brought the helicopter around and low, and began backing it toward the wounded soldier. Backing is a ticklish maneuver which is supposed to protect the crew from gunfire from the rear. Horvath seized the injured soldier by the hand and was pulling him aboard when a VC opened up from pointblank range with an AK-47, spraying the plexiglas window in front and below Mr. Novosel, and hitting the door and the rotor.

"Plexiglas and copper-bullet fragments tore into his right calf and thigh (they are still there), something struck the control stick injuring his hand, and another bullet hit the bottom of his shoe. Shock and the impact of the bullets made him lose control of the helicopter.

"I can remember saying 'Aw, hell, I'm hit.' I was disgusted, but I think the main reason was to warn the co-pilot, because you can be hit one second and be unconscious the next, he said.

"He recovered instantly, however, and climbed the ship out of the elephant grass. Meanwhile, the wounded man had slipped from the ship but was seized by the hand by Horvath as he fell and finally was pulled inside the ship about 60 feet in the air.

"Mr. Novosel, who was back flying the next day, thinks often about the VC soldier who wounded him. 'He must have been scared out of his wits, coming that close to take on something like a helicopter. I can just imagine his leader in that bunker telling him to get outside and get that bastard: he's been around long enough.'

"What was he thinking as he dove repeatedly into the gunfire? What kept him going as the odds kept falling

" 'The simple fact is that I was absolutely sure that I was not going to be hit. I felt that I was invulnerable. I know it was a false sense of security, but it kept me going.'

" 'Conversely, I knew when I headed into that bunker backwards that I was going to be hit. Don't ask me how, but I knew it.'

(The rest of the crew escaped injury from enemy action, but Horvath suffered cuts when he fell while pulling a wounded man aboard. The helicopter, which was struck repeatedly by gunfire, had its VHF radio and air-speed indicator knocked out.)

" 'People ask me questions like, was I thinking of my family when I went in there and, if I was, how could I risk my life that way,' Mr. Novosel said. 'I suppose if I was thinking hard about them I probably wouldn't have done it but if everyone who ever went to war kept worrying about his family there wouldn't be anybody left to fight—kind of like saying, suppose they had a war and nobody showed up.'

" 'You keep going because that is what you are supposed to do and because there are people down there who need you. I knew that those Vietnamese soldiers were in a bad way and I felt that I could at least try to get them out. Actually, I had a few things going for me—like the elephant grass. I just did not pose a very good target.'

" 'You always tell yourself, too, that the enemy might actually let you come right in and pick up the wounded without firing a shot. That has happened to me before. I'd know that they were there and could have blasted me if they wanted. But this time they opened up.'

"Because the enemy rarely respects the large red crosses on the sides and front of dustoff ships, at least enough to hold his fire, some of the craft carry door guns. But not Mr. Novosel's chopper, nor does he carry sidearms himself. 'Guns are a hinderance on a mission like ours,' he said. 'They take up weight and space that could be used for patients.'

"One of the techniques Mr. Novosel used that day brings whistles of wonder from his oldest son, Michael Jr., a husky 21-year-old who is also a dustoff pilot with one full tour of Vietnam already on his record. It is called a 'running landing' and consists of bringing the helicopter down and then skidding it along the ground to present a more difficult target to the enemy while crewmen reach out and scoop up the wounded. It is a tricky maneuver at best, even when the pilot does not have to contend with high elephant grass and soft, marshy ground. It is also supposed to be against regulations— but then so is flying a dustoff ship into heavy gunfire.

"The veteran flyer admits that he broke several rules that day but asserts that sometimes regulations have to be ignored when there are wounded who need prompt attention. Both Novosels, for example, say they have carried as many as 26 Vietnamese or 18 Americans at one time. Dustoff ships are supposed to hold 7 Americans or a few more of the smaller Vietnamese.

"Mr. Novosel has 'extracted' more than 5,500 wounded soldiers and Vietnamese civilians during his two tours, more often than not from areas where the enemy was still shooting. 'Sure, we take a lot of fire,' he said, 'because usually when we are called it means that people are in a bind.'

"One indication of how busy a dustoffer's life is was Mr. Novosel's log for the last year he was in Vietnam. He accumulated 1,407 hours in the air which averages out to be about four hours of flying time, seven days a week. Another gauge is the 60 Oak Leaf Clusters he has for his Air Medal;

basically, to be eligible for one medal it takes 25 combat assault hours or at least 25 missions, or 50 support missions for at least 50 hours.

(He also has three awards of the Distinguished Flying Cross, the Bronze Star, the Purple Heart, and the Vietnamese Cross of Gallantry, the latter for the action in Kein Tuong Province.)

"In conversation with him about his war record, he talks easily and modestly about his own exploits but reserves his superlatives for all those who man Vietnam's medical evacuation ships.

" 'I don't know of any dustoff pilot who wouldn't have done the same thing if he had been in my shoes,' he says.

"A dustoff (or medevac) crewman is a proud and clannish kind of soldier whose performance in the war is given a large share of the credit for the high survival rate among the wounded. Flight in and out of dangerous places under heavy fire is routine, and the system has been so highly developed that medical care facilities are seldom more than an hour away by air.

" 'The kids I worked with are the most dedicated people in the world,' said the Medal of Honor winner. 'They keep going into all kinds of tough situations, in all kinds of weather, day and night. The country owes a lot to the corps, much more than it has been given. On top of that, they have to fly into some of the most difficult and hardest places to find imaginable—and under life or death deadlines—with less navigational equipment than Lindberg had.'

"Mr. Novosel's son, a chief warrant officer second class, served in his father's unit in Vietnam after graduating from flight training and was, in fact, qualified under the elder Novosel's supervision. He is credited with evacuating more than 2,200 wounded persons during his tour. Both he and his father are stationed at Fort Bragg, N.C., where the son flies helicopters and his father a C-47 as a member of the U.S. Army' parachute team, the 'Golden Knights.' Mr. Novosel and his wife, Ethel, are the parents of three other children: Patricia, a student at Georgia Southwestern College; Jean, 17; and John, 8.

"A native of Etna, Pa., Mr. Novosel began his 16 years of active duty and 14 years of reserve service on 7 February 1941, when he enlisted in the Regular Army. In those pre-Pearl Harbor days, he recalls, the chief impetus was his desire to become an aircraft mechanic, a skill he could make into a career when he became a civilian again. 'We were just out of the Depression and the Army seemed like a good place to get an education,' he said. 'Besides, I'd wanted to fly all of my life.'

"If the Army had been scrupulous about using a measuring tape and scales, Mr. Novosel might never have got out of the repair hangers. At five feet, four inches and about 125 pounds, he was considerably under the five feet, eight inch and 160 pounds which were the minimum for acceptance to flight training. Nevertheless, 13 months after enlisting he traded his staff sergeant's stripes for a flying cadet's uniform. He simply told the Army he was considerably bigger than he was and in those days of rapid build-up it chose to believe him.

"After receiving his wings in December 1942, at the Army Air Field at Lake Charles, La., he became an instructor and later a test pilot at Laredo, Texas.

" 'I flew every kind of bomber we had and three kinds of fighter planes besides,' he says of those days.

"But the urge to see action was great and he finally was assigned to the Pacific Theater where he piloted B-29s in a 'few raids' over Japan before the war ended. He stayed in the Air Force after the war, and as a Captain commanded the 99th Bombardment Squadron on Tinian, in the Marianas. In 1949, he left active duty and bought a restaurant in Fort Walton Beach, Fla.

"He left his successful business to volunteer for service in the Korean War and, as a major, was in just long enough to complete a course at the Air Command and Staff School. Back off active duty, he spent several years managing a private club and a post exchange at Fort Walton Beach before going to work in 1959 for Southern Airways as an airliner pilot.

"When the Vietnam conflict began to broaden in the early 1960's, Mr. Novosel was a lieutenant colonel in the Air Force Reserve. Feeling that he could be of help to the effort, he 'made inquiries' about going back on active duty but soon learned that the Air Force was overstrength in its senior officer grades. So he obtained four years of military leave from Southern Airways and rejoined the Army on 29 June 1964, as a warrant officer.

"There is nothing complicated or especially highsounding about Mr. Novosel's reply today when asked why he interrupted a good civilian career, took a sharp reduction in rank and volunteered to go back to war at an age when many military men are thinking about retirement. He answers, 'Because I thought I could be of help.' If pressed for a more easily understood explanation, he adds: 'I felt that because of my military background I could do something to help the country (South Vietnam) out of its predicament.'

"His first medevac experience in an emergency situation was as a member of the Special Forces in 1965 when he carried wounded civilians to hospitals when the United States intervened in the Dominican Republic civil crisis. The next three years included a year's tour of dustoff duty in Vietnam where he evacuated his first 2000 patients. Then in 1968, his leave from Southern Airways was up and he applied for discharge.

"But his hopes of going back into a healthier branch of aviation was dashed during his discharge physical. Army physicians found that he had glaucoma, a serious eye disease which can result in progressive loss of vision. Doctors were able to check the affliction, but Southern physical requirements prevented him from resuming his job as a commercial pilot.

"The Army let him go on flying on a waiver, however, and in 1969, Mr. Novosel—who is proud of the fact that he has never been grounded—was back in Vietnam. He still is required to apply medication to his eyes four times a day, although he has 20/20 vision and apparently has suffered no ill effects from the disease.

"When the officer to whom he reported back in Vietnam saw his record, he assumed that Mr. Novosel would want a relatively safe assignment to fixed-wing duty. 'I knew, though, that they needed dustoff pilots and I asked to go back to the helicopter,' he recalls.

"As a member of the Golden Knights, he flies on jumps and plays golf as often as he can. He has made three jumps since joining the team but gave it up after the third one 'because I'm getting too old.' His plans for the future are to retire in four years, probably back to Fort Walton Beach where he still owns a house.

"He has been asked the inevitable question about his views of the war: 'I have no quarrel with our being there' is as close as he will come to commenting on our commitment. Other remarks, though, indicate that he considers the question immaterial to a soldier with a duty to perform.

"He is voluble about the quality of the American fighting man and the effect opposition to the war has had on him. . . . But he does not belong to that breed of old campaigner who feels the Army is going to hell in a handbasket because it is letting soldiers wear their hair longer and making other compromises to accommodate youthful life styles:

" 'I don't care how long a man's hair is or whether he goes strictly by the book or not. What I want to know, can he do his job. I look for little things, like a cook or clerk going to the trouble of moving an oil drum out of the way because a helicopter might have to land where it's standing. That's the kind of man I want in my outfit.'

"He is an easy going man but his eyes glint in anger when he talks about the public's attitude toward those fighting in Vietnam:

" 'Our soldiers keep going and have been doing a tremendous job in spite of all kinds of opposition at home. A soldier feels like he's hated and there isn't anything he can do about it—it isn't his fault he's in Vietnam. Afterward he goes back to an environment which at best merely tolerates him. It's a tribute to his toughness that he holds up.'

"Allegations that our troops are less than first rate fighting men also get short shrift:

" 'In all my time in Vietnam, I never saw an American soldier do anything even approaching cowardice.'

"No accolade to courage ever came from a higher authority."

Michael J. Novosel was born on September 3, 1922 at Etna, Pennsylvania, the son of Croatian immigrants. His father, Michael, died in 1945. His mother, Catherine is 92 years of age. He is a high school graduate with three years of college.

Born and reared as a Roman Catholic, Mr. Novosel believes in God very strongly and that everything he has done has been because of Him. "I have survived 38 years of military flying—in thunderstorms, severe weather, fog, ice and snow, and enemy action in three wars—and I know that God is with me. However, I have tended to lose touch with man's organized religious manifestations, and do not feel God's presence in temples dedicated to him as when I see the sun rise and set; the rain fall, the snow covering the earth, the white puffs of cumulus building up to a thunderstorm before my very eyes. In the temples, I don't see those who want for food or drink; I don't see the naked; I cannot feel the misery of the sick and lame—nor can I commiserate with them. I know that the temple builders and temple worshippers mean well and most are sincere. But all that I see there is a freshly scrubbed, freshly deodorized and perfumed Christianity, dressed in new clothes and new shoes with a new hair style belonging as often as not to some credit card company. When the one hour session of religious hypnosis is over, they get back into their mortgaged cars and return to their mortgaged homes and God is forgotten for another week. These are my thoughts on religion, on God, on people. Yet I feel no animosity toward the individuals I have described—How can I? I see some of myself in all of them."

"As a child in school I used to pity other children of other countries because they could not be, or, were not Americans. I felt extremely fortunate to be an American. I still feel that way.

"America affords its citizens ample opportunity for success, for enjoying life, for service to country, and to mankind. The individual can be productive or if he chooses—nonproductive. I have enjoyed having had the opportunity to serve my country in three wars, and having my oldest son with me in one of those wars. My wife and I have raised and educated four children. Three are married and have children of their own—our youngest son is still with us, but is preparing himself for one of the service academies. America has made all this possible for me, my wife and my children."

Michael Novosel's advice to the youth of America is—"Measure up to your responsibilities. When in school be a good student—listen to the teachers and do your part in the learning process. Obey and respect your parents—there is nothing as demoralizing to a parent as the attitude of an ungrateful child. All of this will make you a good citizen and a viable part of the American system. Then you can become involved in the social, economic and political facets of American Democracy. If you are involved, don't listen to detractors within our society. Do not believe them when they say that 'Everyone is in on the take'—'They all do it; he just got caught at it'—'He was hounded out of office by an antagonistic press.' You will hear this from time to time, but have faith in the system—it hasn't failed us yet."

CHARLES C. ROGERS

Major General Charles C. Rogers was born in Claremont, West Virginia on September 6, 1929, the son of a coal miner. His father is a veteran of World War II, and his brother also served for four years during the second World War. He is married with three daughters, ages 24, 22, and 20. General Rogers, a very modest man, was reluctant to appear in THE SPIRIT OF AMERICA. In a letter to this writer, dated 23 October 1980, he stated—"I am reluctantly answering your questionnaire, for I have always tried to keep the Medal of Honor and my activities relative to it very low key in my life with only limited success, I might add. Nevertheless, I have attempted to answer your questionnaire simply and forthrightly. Hopefully, it will be of some help to you."

After completing high school in Mount Hope, West Virginia, Charles Rogers entered West Virginia State College Institute, graduating there with a B.S. in Chemistry and Mathematics. He was commissioned a 2nd Lieutenant in the Field Artillery, having been a member of the ROTC program at West Virginia State. He also holds a Masters' degree in Counseling from Shippensburg State College in Shippensburg, Pennsylvania, and is a graduate of the Army Command and General Staff College and the U.S. Army War College.

Although he has been wounded three times, General Rogers, who is five feet, five inches tall and weighs 145 pounds, has no physical impairments. He is a Baptist, deeply religious, and intends to study for the ministry upon retirement from the Army.

President Richard Nixon presented General Rogers with the Medal of Honor in a ceremony at the White House on May 14, 1970. His mother, father, brother and sisters, together with his wife, Margarete, and their three daughters were present. Upon receiving our nation's highest military award Charles C. Rogers felt great pride and humility. However, he states that "my thoughts centered on the soldiers who were wounded and those who died under my command during that action."

His citation for the Medal of Honor reads:

> The President of the United States of America, authorized by Act of Congress, March 3, 1863, has awarded in the name of The Congress the Medal of Honor to
>
> LIEUTENANT COLONEL CHARLES C. ROGERS for conspicuous gallantry and intrepidity in action at the risk of his life above and beyond the call of duty:
>
> Lieutenant Colonel Charles C. Rogers, Field Artillery, distinguished himself by conspicuous gallantry and intrepidity in action on 1 November 1968, while serving as Commanding Officer, 1st Battalion, 5th Artillery, 1st Infantry Division during the defense of a forward fire support base in the Republic of Vietnam. In the early morning hours, the fire support base was subjected to a concentrated bombardment of heavy mortar, rocket and rocket propelled grenade fire. Simultaneously the position was struck by a human wave ground assault, led by sappers who breached the defensive barriers with bangalore torpedoes and penetrated the defensive perimeter. Colonel Rogers with complete disregard for his own safety moved through the hail of fragments from bursting enemy rounds to the embattled area. He aggressively rallied the dazed artillery crewmen to man their howitzers and he directed their fire on the assaulting enemy. Although knocked to the ground and wounded by an exploding round, Colonel Rogers sprang to his feet

and led a small counterattack force against an enemy element that had penetrated the howitzer positions. Although painfully wounded a second time during the assault, Colonel Rogers pressed the attack killing several of the enemy and driving the remainder from the positions. As a second human wave attack was launched against another sector of the perimeter, Colonel Rogers directed artillery fire on the assaulting enemy and led a second counterattack against the charging forces. His valorous example rallied the beleaguered defenders to repulse and defeat the enemy onslaught. Colonel Rogers moved from position to position through the heavy enemy fire, giving encouragement and direction to his men. At dawn the determined enemy launched a third assault against the fire base in an attempt to overrun the position. Colonel Rogers moved to the threatened area and directed lethal fire on the enemy forces. Seeing a howitzer inoperative due to casualties, Colonel Rogers joined the surviving members of the crew to return the howitzer to action. While directing the position defense, Colonel Rogers was seriously wounded by fragments from a heavy mortar round which exploded on the parapet of the gun position. Although too severely wounded to physically lead the defenders, Colonel Rogers continued to give encouragement and direction to his men in the defending and repelling of the enemy attack. Colonel Rogers' dauntless courage and heroism inspired the defenders of the fire support base to the heights of valor to defeat a determined and numerically superior enemy force. His relentless spirit of aggressiveness, conspicuous gallantry and intrepidity in action at the risk of his own life above and beyond the call of duty are in the highest traditions of the military service and reflect great credit upon himself, his unit and the United States Army.

An account of the Fight at Fire Support Base RITA on 1 November 1968 as recounted by Major General Charles C. Rogers vividly describes that terrible night.

"During the days just prior to the action of 1 November, the 1st Brigade, 1st Division, had engaged in a considerable number of actions with the enemy and had beaten him quite badly on numerous occasions. We in the Artillery had, of course, supported all these operations, and the enemy had taken heavy casualties as a result of the operation. About four nights before the big attack on Fire Support Base RITA (FSB RITA) we had observed the headlights of large numbers of trucks across the border in Cambodia driving down toward the borders. As we watched from helicopters, we observed that as the trucks approached the border they would turn off their lights and we could observe them no more. We were convinced they were transporting arms and ammunition to be used against us. Subsequently, we fired H&I (Harrasing and Interdiction) fires in the border area on the South Vietnamese side (we were not authorized to fire across the border). We were fortunate enough to strike an ammunition storage area during the course of our firing into that area. We achieved 128 secondary explosions, making it clear that we had, indeed, hit a major ammunition storage area. Perhaps more than any other single factor, this lead to the attack on the Fire Support Base RITA several nights later. Captured soldiers and documents indicated that the enemy believed he could have no success at all in the Fishhook area unless he destroyed our Artillery in the FSB RITA.

"As you are aware, just after midnight on 1 November 1968, we fired a mad minute as we had done at irregular intervals throughout each night. (Since the evening before was Halloween, the soldiers who participated in the operation have subsequently called this action in FSB RITA 'the Halloween Party').

"At the time we started firing our mad minute, I was inside my Tactical Operations Center (TOC), lying under the radio complex, asleep, for I had a premonition that this night was

258

going to be something special and, therefore, I did not sleep as normal in my bunker. As we started to fire the mad minute, I awoke and asked my Operations Officer what was going on. He informed me, and I lay back again to resume my sleep. After a minute or so, I noted that all the noise of the mad minute did not end, and I heard a tremendous amount of noise of rockets and mortars impacting in our position. I got on the telephone and called the Battery Commander of the 155mm battery on the west flank and asked him what was going on over there. He indicated that we were under heavy ground attack and that North Vietnamese Army soldiers (NVA's) were running all over the positions throwing satchel charges. I grabbed my steel pot and flack jacket and rushed out of my TOC and saw immediately that all of our Cavalry units and personnel carriers on the west flank had been hit with RPG's (Rocket Propelled Grenades) and were burning, and the ammunition in them was exploding with great ferocity. I instantly realized that with the personnel carriers knocked out, there was nothing on the west flank between my howitzer battery and the perimeter. I ran to the 155mm Howitzer Battery to direct the defense of the western flank. I saw NVA soldiers running freely throughout the position and shot at several of them while on a dead run. I came to the Howitzer Battery and found that few of my soldiers were manning the howitzers or the machine guns mounted on them. Because of the ferocity of the action and the intensity of the incoming rocket and mortar fire, most of my soldiers were in bunkers for protection. I went from howitzer to howitzer and ordered them out of the bunkers and then man the howitzers in direct and indirect fire. I moved from howitzer to howitzer giving fire commands to accomplish this. As I was beside one howitzer, I was squatting and firing my pistol at the NVA soldiers, when suddenly First Sergeant (now CSM) Ira Whitaker shouted, 'Hit the ground, Colonel, there are three

NVA soldiers over there.' As I started falling forward, I looked to the right and saw three soldiers about 75-100 meters away standing with aimed rifles, and I saw the red burst of a rifle one soldier was firing toward me. As I was falling forward, something smashed in my face and knocked me backwards. I was dazed for some little time, but I quickly regained my composure and realized I was choking on my own blood, for a rifle round had apparently ricochetted off the self propelled howitzer into my face, on the left side of my nose, and the bullet protruded down into my mouth. With my fingers, I pulled the bullet from the roof of my mouth and threw it on the ground; the wound continued to bleed profusely (I believe the bullet ricochetted into my face, for, in my view, if it had been fired directly into my face it almost surely would have gone through my head).

"There was a dead NVA soldier right by the howitzer, and the battery mascot, an old mutt, smelled him suspiciously. A little later on, to the left front of this howitzer, we noted that several NVA soldiers were behind a log pile and were firing and throwing grenades at my howitzers. We could not depress the howitzer low enough to fire at this log pile, so I called for three volunteers to accompany me out to this position to destroy the enemy at that point. We crawled out toward the area where the enemy was behind the logs, and then as we partially stood up to begin our assault, a rocket propelled grenade exploded at our feet. I remember seeing a bright red burst of fire as I was blown backwards through the air. One of the soldiers with me was killed instantly. The other two (one of whom was SP James Sutton) were not wounded, although I received many fragments on both legs. Fortunately no bones were broken and I could still move along, although, thereafter most of my movement was done by crawling or by some upright movement utilizing a rifle as a crutch. Nevertheless, we still crawled out to where the enemy was hidden behind the log pile and, with grenade and rifle fire, we eliminated the enemy at that point. We then moved toward the howitzer, dragging the dead soldier with us. Subsequently, SP Sutton and I helped other wounded personnel back to the aid station. A little later I moved back to the 155mm battery again, and noted that directly to the west of our position the enemy had again broken through the perimeter and was throwing satchel charges and shooting at my howitzers. I asked for two volunteers to join me. Two cannoners and I moved out to the endangered area and with rifle and grenade fire, cleared the enemy from that area. We held that area until friendly infantrymen came and relieved us on that western flank.

"About an hour or so later, the enemy again broke through, this time on the southwest part of the perimeter at a different howitzer. I picked up two volunteers, crawled to the embattled area and we killed all the enemy soldiers that had come through the perimeter, and who had been throwing satchel charges and shooting at my soldiers. We crawled back into the battery area, and as I was stopped near one howitzer, the .50 calibre machine gunner, who was on top of the self propelled howitzer firing the machine gun, was hit by enemy fire. He fell off the howitzer on the ground, dead at our feet. I ordered one soldier standing nearby to get back up on the machine. I'll never forget the expression in that soldier's eyes as he looked at his dead comrade at his feet, and then looked at me, hesitatingly for a moment. Then he grabbed the box of ammunition and hastily climbed up to the machine gun, and started spraying deadly machine gun fire toward the perimeter. His eyes told me he was scared to death—but not so scared that he wouldn't do what he had to do. Subsequently, another one of my machine gunners was killed by an RPG round which went through his chest. A little later I moved back to my 105mm howitzer battery and found that under the intense mortar and rocket barrage, quite a number of these soldiers had given up the manning of their howitzers and had moved into the bunkers. I ordered them to get out of the bunkers and man the howitzers. I remember one private said to me, 'Sir, we can't come out; we'll be killed out there.' At that time I was standing out in the open and I shouted at the soldier, 'Don't you see me standing here? I'm not getting killed—get your butt out of that bunker!' The soldier came out on the double, and so did all the others and quickly manned their howitzers and started firing direct and indirect fire as the situation dictated.

"One of my howitzers was firing self-illuminating ammunition to give us visibility in the gun positions; two were firing indirect fire, and the other three were engaged in direct fire, utilizing beehive ammunition which was highly effective against enemy personnel. Just about daylight, when it appeared that the fight was essentially over and the battle had been won, moving about on a rifle, I was congratulating my men for their great fight and the great courage they had displayed under intense fire. All at once we were subjected to the most intense mortar and rocket barrage I had ever experienced. The rounds were impacting all over the gun position in very large numbers; then the enemy broke through the northern part of the perimenter in especially large numbers and was pouring into the gun positions. We swung the howitzers around to the north and fired heavy volumes of beehive ammunition directly into the enemy ranks. As we cut down one group, another group would come in right behind them, wave after wave. I was astonished to see that in spite of our killing large numbers of them, they continued to come. I moved from howitzer to howitzer, giving direct fire commands in firing the beehive ammunition, set to detonate 1/10 per second after they cleared the tube of the howitzer. The rounds were, therefore, exploding a lethal volume of beehive ammunition into the enemy ranks about 100-150 meters from the howitzer. As I moved over to the howitzer in which the battery commander, Captain Rick Callahan (presently an instructor at West Point), was giving fire commands and directing the efforts of this particular howitzer crew in countering the enemy. I noted an enemy mortar round which impacted about 70 meters to the east of where I was standing. A few moments later I noted another round had impacted about 30 meters east of where I was standing. At that time I remember thinking, 'Oh boy, I bet the next round is coming right in this parapet.' The next thing I remember, I was sailing through the air. I saw other soldiers also sailing through the air and I saw the howitzer blown into the air. When I landed, (according to my S3, Major Ken Smith, who was watching the incident, I was blown about 40 feet into the air), I landed on my shoulders and back and slammed against a bunker. As I looked up at my feet above my head against the bunker, I could see my left boot was blown off and my left leg blown completely open. My right boot and trouser leg was blown completely open and blood was flowing freely from both legs. I tried to move my left toes to determine the extent of injury and I found I could not move them at all. I thought my leg was broken, but I subsequently found after operations in the hospitals of Long Binh and in Japan, that the sciatic nerve had been severed and a big chunk of the sciatic muscle had been blown out.

"I swung my feet down to the ground and looked to the left and saw the howitzer was lying on its side with its wheels spinning. Then I saw a number of my soldiers scattered around the howitzer. I crawled over to several of them and pulled them against the parapet to give them some protection. I found that the howitzer chief, a young Hawaiian corporal, had been killed by the mortar round. After that, I crawled into a bunker for I was unable to move further. A few moments later, Major Smith and a Medical Service Captain came in with a stretcher and picked me up. Considering that this was the third time I was wounded, Major Smith said, 'Colonel, you have more lives that a cat!' I had them take me to my TOC for from there I could continue to direct the defense of the position. As daylight came and as the fog lifted, we called helicopter gun ships to attack the enemy along the perimeter and in the jungles nearby. Next, we called the Air Force fighter bombers which came in and strafed all around our perimeter, dropping hard bombs and napalm just outside the perimeter and the surrounding jungles. During the course of these later actions, the enemy withdrew, dragging large numbers of his bodies with him. After the fight, we found 28 bodies inside the perimeter. Helicopter pilots and air observers indicated they counted at least 300 bodies outside the perimeter in the jungle.

"It is worthy of special mention, in my view, that Major Ken Smith, my battalion S3, had gone back to the base camp the evening before to prepare some operational reports. When the activity started in FSB RITA, he was unable to get back to assist. Enemy fire and rocket propelled grenade activity were simply too intense for helicopters to get into our positions. These factors were further magnified by the fact that the area was heavily fogged, so Major Smith could only content himself with listening to reports of the action on the radio.

"As the action intensified, I had significant numbers of soldiers seriously wounded, dictating emergency evacuation. Even with the risk of Med Evac helicopters being shot down in the effort, Major Smith forced his way into a Med Evac helicopter, and the first one that was able to get into FSB RITA under the withering fire brought Major Smith. The Med Evac helicopter succeeded in evacuating a few of our critically wounded soldiers. The courage of Major Smith and that of Med Evac personnel had no bounds that morning. In fact, I was tremendously impressed with the courage and heroism in numerous instances wherein soldiers laid their lives on the line in defending their howitzers and FSB RITA. In my life I have never been so impressed with men under emergency circumstances as I was during the fight at FSB RITA.

"Of all those persons, none was more conspicuous in action and bravery than was First Sergeant Whitaker, who, on numerous occasions, exposed himself and moved from howitzer to howitzer, inspiring his soldiers to man their howitzers and machine gun and fight off a very determined attack of their positions. When a rocket propelled grenade hit one of his outposts (manned by cooks and wiremen), First Sergeant Whitaker took off through the gun position, darting left and right through a hail of enemy fire to get to the outpost where his men had been hit. Several minutes later I saw First Sergeant Whitaker stand up and make a dash, zig-zag pattern, back to the gun position. Throughout the course of the fight, First Sergeant Whitaker inspired and motivated his soldiers to unusual levels of accomplishment in defense of the battery position. His heroic action resulted in his subsequent award of the Distinguished Service Cross, our second highest award for heroism.

"FSB RITA was manned by very human soldiers—men, who under the intense fire of the enemy, acted normally and sought cover to protect life and limb. But they were uncommonly heroic men, in that with a little motivation and leadership on the part of their senior personnel, comported themselves in the manner of men more concerned with duty than with their own lives. The Mess Steward of Battery B, SFC Fox, who always managed to get involved in the actions that the howitzers crews were involved in, was characteristically visible during the fight of FSB RITA. his many heroic actions that night resulted in his later being awarded the Silver Star. It would not be far off the mark to say that every man engaged in the intense battle of FSB RITA was a hero of a very high order, and each comported himself in such a manner as to make any commander proud to be associated with them.

"I am often asked what the Medal of Honor means to me. I always reply—I don't consider the Medal a personal honor. Rather, I consider it a living honor to those who fought, to those who were wounded, and to those who died under my command. This Medal honors them, and I wear it as a tribute to their memory."

Being an American to Major General Charles C. Rogers means "being a citizen of the greatest country in the world. Though our country isn't perfect, as free citizens in a democratic society we have the power to affect change when change is warranted. It means being free to compete in life and to rise to levels commensurate with my ability. It means feeling free, unhampered; it means feeling proud. It feels good to be a citizen of a country which millions of people all over the world admire and of which they would also love to be citizens. It means being a descendant of a proud people, a possessor of a beautiful and inspiring culture, a possessor of a proud tradition and history."

To the youth of America, General Rogers advises—"Learn, prepare yourself for leadership. Love this country, and work fervently to make it better. It deserves your best effort."

JAMES BOND STOCKDALE

Suffering as a prisoner of war in Hoa Lo Prison in Hanoi, North Vietnam for almost eight years, most of the time in solitary confinement in a box-cell ten feet long and four feet wide, only reinforced Vice Admiral James B. Stockdale's bedrock belief and love of God, country and honor.

He was born in Abingdon, Illinois on December 23, 1923. His parents were descendants of American pioneer families of Scotch-Irish origin. His father, at age 30, volunteered for and served in the U.S. Navy during World War I. His background is liberally sprinkled with war veterans throughout the years including a great, great, great, great grandfather who was a company commander in George Washington's Army at the Battle of Yorktown where the British surrendered.

James B. Stockdale has been married to Sybil Bailey Stockdale for 33 years and they have four sons, ranging in age from 30 to 18. During his youth, he was a member of the Methodist Church in Abingdon, Illinois. Throughout his Navy career he attended services of several Protestant denominations, principally Presbyterian. In the spring of 1980 he was confirmed as a member of the Episcopal Church.

Before attending the United States Naval Academy, Admiral Stockdale had one year at Monmouth College in Illinois. He graduated from the Naval Academy in 1946 and completed Naval flight school in 1950. In 1960 through 1962 he was in graduate school at Stanford University studying political science and other subjects. As president of the Naval War College, he taught a course in philosophy, entitled

"Foundations of Moral Obligation." This was the first time that discipline had been offered as a classroom subject at the Naval War College. After retiring from active duty, James B. Stockdale assumed the presidency of the Citadel in Charleston, South Carolina. While there he taught a philosophy class. He has six honorary doctorate degrees.

Although the pain and anguish of his long time confinement and torture is etched in his countenance, James Stockdale is a ruggedly handsome man of 57. He is five feet, eight inches in height and weighs 168 pounds. He is unable to bend his left leg at the knee and unable to raise his left arm above shoulder height. These impairments are the direct result of torture injuries suffered as a prisoner of war in North Vietnam.

He received the Medal of Honor for resisting the attempts of prison torture guards to extract material from him which would have brought harm to his fellow American prisoners. His superhuman effort in attempting to give his life so that others might live occurred in early September, 1969 in the main torture room (#18) of Hoa Lo Prison in Hanoi, North Vietnam. He was 45 at that time.

President Gerald Ford conferred the Congressional Medal of Honor on Vice Admiral James Stockdale on March 4, 1976 in the White House. His wife, four sons, and a daughter-in-law were present. His parents both had died while he was held prisoner.

As President Ford placed the Medal of Honor around his neck, James Stockdale's thoughts "drifted back to his youth when he was a midshipman at the Naval Academy in the year of 1945. He was frustrated there as were most of his classmates when World War II ended and they sort of died on third base without having partaken in real military action in that war. It was at that time (summer of 1945) that his cousin, Marine Captain Robert H. Dunlap, was decorated with the Congressional Medal of Honor by President Truman. He had always admired Bobby Dunlap as his number one hero. In a way, as he received his medal in 1976, he felt as though he had finally closed a loop in his life's highest aspiration."

In response to the question, "Do you feel that having received the CMH has changed your life?" James Stockdale replied:

"Yes. In the first place I have joined new friends who have a new dimension. I speak, of course, of my fellow members of the Congressional Medal of Honor Society. I've learned to feel new obligations as a citizen and particularly to repel the natural urge to let the receipt of such an award to go to one's head. And of course another way in which my life has been changed is in the acquisition of a new confidence, a new peace of mind. Knowing that one will be remembered for having received the Congressional Medal of Honor long after he is dead takes a lot of pressure out of his natural striving for recognition and success in old age."

James B. Stockdale was shot down by an enemy guided missile while on an aerial mission over North Vietnam. He was forced to parachute behind enemy lines where he was captured.

The citation for which Vice Admiral James B. Stockdale received our nation's highest award reads:

STOCKDALE, JAMES B.
Rank and organization: Rear Admiral (then Captain). U.S. Navy. Place and date: Hoa Lo Prison, Hanoi, North Vietnam, 4 September 1969. Entered service at Abingdon, Ill. Born: 23 December 1923, Abingdon, Ill. Citation: For conspicuous gallantry and intrepidity at the risk of his life above and beyond the call of duty while senior naval officer in the Prison of War camps of North Vietnam. Recognized by his captors as the leader in the Prisoners' of War resistance to interrogation and in their refusal to participate in propaganda exploitation, Rear Adm. Stockdale was singled out for interrogation and

attendant torture after he was detected in a covert communications attempt. Sensing the start of another purge, and aware that his earlier efforts at self-disfiguration to dissuade his captors from exploiting him for propaganda purposes had resulted in a cruel and agonizing punishment, Rear Adm. Stockdale resolved to make himself a symbol of resistance, regardless of personal sacrifice. He deliberately inflicted a near-mortal wound to his person in order to convince his captors of his willingness to give up his life rather than capitulate. He was subsequently discovered and revived by the North Vietnamese who, convinced of his indomitable spirit, abated in their employment of excessive harassment and torture toward all of the Prisoners of War. By his heroic action, at great peril to himself, he earned the everlasting gratitude of his fellow prisoners and of his country. Rear Adm. Stockdale's valiant leadership and extraordinary courage in a hostile environment sustain and enhance the finest traditions of the U.S. Naval Service.

In his own words Admiral Stockdale vividly describes the situation in the Hanoi Prisoner of War prison . . . "My action requires more explanation than many because first I must make clear what I mean by saying that we Americans in Hanoi were held in an extortionist prison regime. By extortionist regime I mean one in which the name of the game for the enemy was to apply fear, guilt, pain, solitude and degradation to force Americans to turn against one another, to give up military information and to provide propaganda detrimental to their government's aims. Once any of us were caught in the most commonplace act that they could relate to the breaking of their so-called camp regulations, we were physically tortured so that the North Vietnamese might realize their above ends. In their eyes, the 'highest crime' under their system was for one of us to 'incite the other criminals to oppose the camp authority.' (That's what we Americans call

military leadership.) For several years I had been earmarked as a leader of resistance and on at least two occasions I had been found out to have been the boss of elaborate clandestine resistance organizations. Enemy purges followed this discovery in every instance, and on the first occasion the result had been the death of at least one of my fellow Americans. By September, 1969 I had been caught up in a third prison bust and did not at that time know the total results of the second purge. (Leaders are always moved and isolated after busts.) In short, I was at the end of my string, having been tortured 13 times; I was getting tired of men being hurt or killed as a result of these purges for which I, in a sense, was becoming responsible. With this background I think the best description of my situation as I endured my 14th torture period was put by an editor of *NEWSWEEK Magazine* and I will just quote the way he summarized it in the August 6, 1979 edition. 'As the linchpin of a clandestine resistance movement uniting hundreds of prisoners in scattered camps, Stockdale feared, after days of torture, that he might disclose the names of co-conspirators. To convince his captors he would rather die, the senior Navy POW dragged himself (in leg irons) to the tiny window in his solitary-confinement cell, broke the glass with a stool, and slashed his wrists with the broken shards until he passed out. 'It was clear to me I had to stop the interrogation,' he recalls matter-of-factly today. 'If it cost my life, it cost it.' "
THEY NEVER GOT THE INFORMATION.

In his words, James B. Stockdale states, "Being an American means to me first, to be lucky to have freedom and second, to be obliged to defend it."

In an essay, "Freedom: Our Most Precious National Treasure" written for *Parade Magazine* in celebration of the 4th of July, 1980, James B. Stockdale summarizes his thoughts on freedom in the last two paragraphs—"This nation has come a long way since the drafting of the

Constitution and the milestones are littered with human sacrifice. We've fought wars around the globe in freedom's name and have paid a terrible price for our most fundamental national belief. Today, there are men and women who may lay down their lives for this country and the freedom for which it stands.

"We all bear the painful costs of freedom. As we formally celebrate the commitment to break from England and to protect our natural rights, let's hug to our breasts our freedom—our most precious national treasure—knowing that it, like a child, is imperfect and demanding but undeniably good. Let's keep our centuries-old habit of protecting that child of America, that freedom. She's getting more rare and precious everyday."

His advice to the youth of America is . . . "to remember that this ship of state is not powered by a perpetual motion machine. Americans have to work and try and pray and sometimes fight to keep it on course. Each young man in America must remember that it is his job to do his part. If America ever comes under the sway of free loaders and passive 'observers of the passing scene,' she will be on her way to the ash-can of history."

JAMES A. TAYLOR

When President Lyndon Johnson placed the Medal of Honor around Major Taylor's neck (he was then a Captain), James Taylor was "totally numb and bursting with pride and love of country." His only regret was that his father (deceased) was not able to share that great moment in his life with him.

"My childhood was not difficult nor was it easy. My father, Allen Issac Taylor, was a strong disciplinarian, yet an extremely tolerant individual. I learned the meaning of the word, responsibility, (individual, family, and country) at a very early age. My father taught me to be a respectful, yet stern person with a deep love and understanding for my country and my fellow man. My father was my idol, the key to my personal growth and development," James Taylor confides.

James Taylor was born on December 31, 1937 at Arcata, California. he graduated from Arcata Union High in 1955, received a B.S. in Criminology from the University of Tampa in 1972 and a Master of Arts in Education from Pepperdine University in Hawaii in 1975. Also he has attended numerous military schools including the Command and General Staff College at Ft. Levenworth, Kansas.

He retired from the service on September 1, 1979 with the rank of regular Army Major. "I was a 'Mustang,' coming up through the ranks—ten years enlisted and 14 years commissioned service." At the present, James Taylor is a salesperson for John Breahear Reality in San Jose, California and is the District Director of the Congressional Medal of Honor Society in California. He is married to Sandra Rose

Dimmick Taylor of Mt. Vernon, Washington. They have two children—a son, Mark Allen and a daughter, Theresa Rose. James is a handsome man, weighing 180 pounds and is five feet, nine inches in height. He is Southern Baptist with a great love for God and his Country. Due to service connected disabilities, James has a high frequency hearing loss and chronic back, knee and stomach pains.

His citation for the Medal of Honor reads:

TAYLOR, JAMES ALLEN
Rank and organization: Captain (then 1st Lt.), U.S. Army, Troop B, 1st Cavalry, American Division. Place and date: West of Que Son, Republic of Vietnam, 9 November 1967. Entered service at San Francisco, Calif. Born: 31 December 1937, Arcata, Calif. Citation: Capt. Taylor, Armor, was serving as executive officer of Troop B, 1st Squadron. His troop was engaged in an attack on a fortified position west of Que Son when it came under intense enemy recoilless rifle, mortar, and automatic weapons fire from an enemy strong point located immediately to its front. One armored cavalry assault vehicle was hit immediately by recoilless rifle fire and all five crew members were wounded. Aware that the stricken vehicle was in grave danger of exploding, Capt. Taylor rushed forward and personally extracted the wounded to safety despite the hail of enemy fire and exploding ammunition. Within minutes a second armored cavalry assault vehicle was hit by multiple recoilless rifle fire. Despite the continuing intense enemy fire, Capt. Taylor moved forward on foot to rescue the wounded men from the burning vehicle and personally removed all crewmen to the safety of a nearby dike. Moments later the vehicle exploded. As he was returning to his vehicle, a bursting mortar round painfully wounded Capt. Taylor, yet he valiantly returned to his vehicle to relocate the medical evacuation landing zone to an area closer to the front lines. As he was moving his vehicle, it came under machine gun fire from an enemy position not 50 yards away. Capt. Taylor engaged the

position with his machine gun, killing the three-man crew. Upon arrival at the new evacuation site, still another vehicle was struck. Once again Capt. Taylor rushed forward and pulled the wounded from the vehicle, loaded them aboard his vehicle, and returned them safely to the evacuation site. His actions of unsurpassed valor were a source of inspiration to his entire troop, contributed significantly to the success of the overall assault on the enemy position, and were directly responsible for saving the lives of a number of his fellow soldiers. His actions were in keeping with the highest traditions of the military profession and reflect great credit upon himself, his unit and the U.S. Army.

Concerning his feelings at that time, Major James A. Taylor states—"At the time my unit was engaged in the action which resulted in my being awarded the CMH; I was performing my duties in a manner in which I was trained. I feel I was reacting to an intense situation that called for me to reach down and grab something extra to insure the safety of my people and to get the job at hand done.

"Being an American to me is life itself. Freedom to choose and attain my personal goals, and free to take the risks of being myself as I desire.

"My advice to young Americans: The United States was formed by a courageous group of dedicated people. Many lives were sacrificed, many tears were shed, many hard-trying situations overcome. These sacrifices have continued throughout our history. If America is to remain a free nation, young America must continue to pick-up and carry forward the Stars and Stripes forever, or they face grave dangers. Life, love and the pursuit of happiness must be a goal, an endeavor of all Americans. Obstacles must be hurdled in a state of total unity by all. If we are ever destroyed, it will be from within, not from without by a hostile force. Love it, fight for it, or leave it."

LEO K. THORSNESS

Leo Thorsness was a prisoner of war in North Vietnamese prison camps in the Hanoi area for 6 hellish years. He has permanent injuries in his knees, back and shoulders due to ejecting from his plane during combat in North Vietnam in April of 1967 at near sonic speed. Also his maltreatment as a prisoner of war contributed to his physical disabilities for he was beaten, tortured and confined in solitary for almost a year since the North Vietnamese classified him as a troublemaker.

He was born at Walnut Grove, Minnesota on February 14, 1932. His mother is Norwegian/German and his father Norwegian. Having enlisted in the Air Force in 1951, he was commissioned in 1954. He completed his first degree and also his Masters' while on active duty. Currently, he is the director of civic affairs for Litton Industries in Beverly Hills, California after having retired from the Air Force with the rank of Colonel.

During his six years as a prisoner of war his wife, Gaylee, taught school in her home town of Sioux Falls, South Dakota where she returned from their last duty station with their daughter, Dawn. "He's more appreciative of things now that he used to take for granted," she said. "But he hasn't changed in personality. If anything, he's more red, white, and blue—more dedicated to his country—than before."

Having been raised a Lutheran, Colonel Thorsness attended Protestant Chapel with his wife and daughter during his military career. "There is no doubt in my mind that I was able to sustain my spirit and desire to make it through some sessions of torture because of the extra strength I received from Christ," he humbly states.

In October of 1973, with his wife and daughter present, Colonel Thorsness was presented the Congressional Medal of Honor by President Nixon at the White House in Washington, D.C. His personal feelings at being awarded our nation's highest military honor was one of humility and pride. He feels there are others who should have received the Medal of Honor. "As a POW I saw men, under worse conditions or under greater stress than they will ever be in combat, display courage and bravery unsurpassed under any conditions— combat or otherwise," Colonel Thorsness concludes. His belief in America was reaffirmed many times during his six long years as a POW by watching communism in action.

Colonel Thorsness was on his 93rd combat mission when his plane was hit by fire from enemy MIGS. His evacuation of his crippled F-105 was vividly described by Robert K. Ruhl in an article in *Airman,* December 1974. ' "It felt like we took a missile right up the tailpipe. The plane quivered and shuddered. There was instant knowledge we were out of business." '

"The THUD filled with smoke, and Thorsness put his head against the canopy but couldn't see out. The stick flopped in his hand. 'Go, Harry!' he shouted to his backseater, and Johnson—with an obscenity and 'I'm gone'—shot out of the aircraft as it began to tumble.

"Thorsness grabbed for the handles on either side of his seat to release his cockpit canopy, squeezed the exposed seat— ejection triggers and blasted into the windstream at 600 knots.

"He hurtled into an unflinching wall of air. His legs flew out and his knees bent grotesquely inward, causing severe damage to his knees. His flight suit ripped open. his helmet snapped off and his pockets tore away. His parachute opened, though, and his survival radio stayed with him.

"Descending in his parachute toward the mountains and foothills, Thorsness called to the strike force, but couldn't establish communications.

"Thorsness' parachute caught a dry limb as he crashed through a tree in a mountainous area, leaving him bobbing on the end of his shroud lines. It took him more than a half-hour to work himself free. Once on the ground, he crawled away to await rescue. Shock had not yet yielded to the searing pain in his knees.

"Twenty young male villagers, some with guerilla rifles, some with wooden training rifles and some with machetes, were looking for him. The last thing he saw, just before they pulled a bag over his head, was a machete at his chest.

" 'I waited and nothing happened. They took off the bag in a few minutes and cut off my clothes, even my boots. I don't think they knew how to use zippers. I resisted walking, but they insisted and won.' The villagers later allowed him to borrow a machete to cut bamboo splints which he wrapped in banana leaves and wound tightly around his badly damaged knees with vines.

"He walked ten hours, passed out and was later borne on a fishnet litter into six years of hell.

"He was beaten, tortured, confined for almost a year in solitary and broken by indescribably inhumane treatment. Today he uses a knobby, wooden cane given to him by friends, and has undergone three operations on his back and knees."

"I credit my making it, with my sanity and a certain amount of honor, with my values—God, country and family, in that order.

"They were something you could reach out and hold onto. Your clothes were gone, you were tied up with wires and made up into a suitcase. They put you in positions where you didn't think you could last another second, another minute, but you survived. But they couldn't get your values from you."

Leo Thorsness could have returned to his air base on the day he was shot down but he opted to continue on his mission even when his aircraft was critically short on fuel. This unselfish action is documented in his citation for the Medal of Honor as follows:

> For conspicuous gallantry and intrepidity in action at the risk of his life above and beyond the call of duty. As pilot of an F-105 aircraft, Lt. Col. Thorsness was on a surface-to-air missile suppression mission over North Vietnam. Lt. Col. Thorsness and his wingman attacked and silenced a surface-to-air missile site with air-to-ground missiles, and then destroyed a second surface-to-air missile site with bombs. In the attack on the second missile site, Lt. Col. Thorsness circled the descending parachutes to keep the crewmembers in sight and relay their position to the Search and Rescue Center. During this maneuver, a MIG-17 was sighted in the area. Lt. Col. Thorsness immediately initiated an attack and destroyed the MIG. Because his aircraft was low on fuel, he was forced to depart the area in search of a tanker. Upon being advised that two helicopters were orbiting over the downed crew's position and that there were hostile MIG's in the area posing a serious threat to the helicopters, Lt. Col. Thorsness, despite his low fuel condition, decided to return alone through a hostile environment of surface-to-air missile and anti-aircraft defenses to the downed crew's position. As he approached the area, he spotted four MIG-17 aircrafts and immediately initiated an attack on the MIG's, damaging one and driving the others away from the rescue scene. When it became apparent that an aircraft in the area was critically low on fuel and the crew would have to abandon the aircraft unless they could reach a tanker, Lt. Col. Thorsness, although critically short on fuel himself, helped to avert further possible loss of life and a friendly aircraft by recovering at a forward operating base, thus allowing the aircraft in emergency fuel condition to refuel safely. Lt. Col. Thorsness' extraordinary heroism, self-sacrifice, and personal

bravery involving conspicuous risk of life were in the highest traditions of the military service, and have reflected great credit upon himself and the U.S. Air Force.

To Leo K. Thorsness being an American means "The same to me as others relative to the rights and privileges we all enjoy—except I appreciate them more than most in that I lived without them for six years and had more time to realize what we take for granted—until it's taken away. That includes the 'standard' privileges such as freedom to assemble, religion, etc., but also such simple things as drinking water you don't have to boil, flush toilets, buying a car, right to change jobs— or move to another state without permission of the government, etc.

"Because of the time we all had to think, another difference in our attitudes about America from those who have never lived under another form of government, is the responsibility that goes with our freedom. That includes such major areas as the media—freedom to express themselves but responsibility not to abuse that right; for example, if they say 'news' then it should be news and not an editorial or opinion . . . if they want to editorialize they should call it what it is. Another example would be the 'right' of a 16 year old to get a license to drive a car, and the 'responsibility' not to get spaced out on drugs or booze and kill someone with that car he has the right to operate. The bottom line is simply that for every right or privilege we have there is an equal and matching responsibility. It is not because I am a recipient of the CMH I feel that—rather that I was a POW."

Colonel Thorsness' advice to the youth of America is—"If you are lucky enough to be born an American, you have an obligation to fight for your country, if and when our duly elected government says they need you. Freedom does not come easy or cheap. If the youth have never experienced the strife or trials of life—it is only because someone else has fought their battle for them so that they can have the 'good life.' When their turn comes, if they refuse, they or their kids won't have the 'good life.' It only takes one generation to completely fail in their responsibilities, and we can lose it all."

JAY R. VARGAS

Leutenant Colonel Jay R. Vargas, U.S. Marine Corps, is a handsome man of Hispanic/Italian ancestry. He has damage to his right kidney and minor loss of vision due to combat wounds in Vietnam. Standing five feet, 11 inches, he weighs 160 pounds. Based on his physical appearance, personality and high level achievements in high school, college and the Marines, one is tempted to describe him as "The All American Boy," and man.

He was born July 29, 1938 in Winslow, Arizona and is of the Catholic faith. Jay graduated from Winslow High, where he was a standout performer in all sports, achieving All-State recognition in baseball.

Attending Arizona State on a scholarship, he continued his excellence in baseball, twice achieving first team All-Conference honors. While at the university, he was elected President, "Chain Gang" Men's Honorary Club, President, Letterman's Club, and Vice-President, Kappa Phi Kappa. He graduated in 1961 with a B.S. degree in Education.

He graduated from the U.S. Marine Corps Officer's School, Quantico, Virginia, in June 1962. He also has completed the junior officer's course in Amphibious Warfare and is a graduate of the Command and Staff College, Quantico, Virginia. He has served successfully as Platoon Commander; Company Executive Officer; Assistant S-3; Company Commander; Series Commander; S-3 Operations Officer; a Formal Schools Instructor (Operations/Intelligence) Staff Planning School: Headquarters Commander: Executive

Officer, 3rd Reconnaissance Battalion, 3rd Marine Division; Aide-de-Camp to the Deputy Commanding General, Fleet Marine Force, Pacific; and as Assistant Professor, NROTC Unit, University of New Mexico. Presently, he is assigned as the Head, Operations Branch, Headquarters Marine Corps, Washington, D.C.

His medals and decorations include: the Congressional Medal of Honor, the Silver Star, the Purple Heart w/four Gold Stars, the Combat Action ribbon, the Navy Unit Commendation ribbon, the National Defense Service medal, the Vietnam Service medal w/four Bronze Stars, the Vietnamese Gallantry Cross w/Silver Star and Palm, and the Republic of Vietnam Campaign medal.

In July of 1970, Lieutenant Colonel Jay Vargas was one of the 50 recipients in the United States to receive the American Academy of Achievement's "Golden Plate Award" presented to national leaders in all professional fields.

He was awarded the National Collegiate Athletic Association's Commemorative Plaque by the United States Collegiate Athletic Directors and Coaches, in Houston, Texas, for excelling in collegiate athletics and having made a significant contribution to his country.

In January of 1974, he completed his Master of Arts degree in Education with "Honors" at the United States International University in San Diego, California.

Lieutenant Colonel Jay Vargas and his wife, the former Dorothy Jean Johnson, of San Diego, California, are the parents of three girls. His mother, Teresa Vargas, originally from Caltrano, Italy is deceased. His father, a retired newspaperman, and his three brothers reside in Arizona.

On May 14, 1970 Jay Vargas was presented with the Medal of Honor by President Nixon at the White House in Washington, D.C. His entire family was present.

The citation for which Lieutenant Colonel Jay Vargas received our nation's highest award reads:

> The President of the United States in the name of the Congress takes pleasure in presenting the MEDAL OF HONOR to
>   MAJOR JAY R. VARGAS, USMC
> for service as set forth in the following
> CITATION:
> For conspicuous gallantry and intrepidity at the risk of his life above and beyond the call of duty while serving as Commanding Officer, Company G, Second Battalion, Fourth Marines, Ninth Marine Amphibious Brigade in action against enemy forces in the Republic of Vietnam from 30 April to 2 May 1968. On 1 May 1968, though suffering from wounds he had incurred while relocating his unit under heavy enemy fire the preceeding day, Major (then Captain) Vargas combined Company G with two other companies and led his men in an attack on the fortified village of Dai Do. Exercising expert leadership, he maneuvered his marines across 700 meters of open rice paddy while under intense enemy mortar, rocket and artillery fire and obtained a foothold in two hedgerows on the enemy perimeter, only to have elements of his company become pinned down by the intense enemy fire. Leading his reserve platoon to the aid of his beleaguered men, Major Vargas inspired his men to renew their relentless advance, while destroying a number of enemy bunkers. Again wounded by grenade fragments, he refused aid as he moved about the hazardous area reorganizing his unit into a strong defense perimeter at the edge of the village. Shortly after the objective was secured, the enemy commenced a series of counterattacks and probes which lasted throughout the night but were unsuccessful as the gallant defenders of Company G stood firm in their hard-won enclave. Reinforced the following morning, the marines launched a renewed assault through Dai Do on the village of Dink To, to which the enemy retaliated with a massive counterattack

resulting in hand-to-hand combat. Major Vargas remained in the open, encouraging and rendering assistance to his marines when he was hit for the third time in the three day battle. Observing his battalion commander sustain a serious wound, he disregarded his excruciating pain, crossed the fire-swept area and carried his commander to a covered position, then resumed supervising and encouraging his men while simultaneously assisting in organizing the battalion's perimeter defense. His gallant actions uphold the highest traditions of the Marine Corps and the United States Naval Service.

The following narrative, eye-witness account of Lieutenant Colonel (then Captain) Jay B. Vargas' heroic and sustained actions on the days of April 30 to May 2, 1968 in Vietnam vividly describes what occurred:

"At 1600 on April 30, 1968, an intense enemy artillery barrage commenced on the defensive perimeter of Golf Company 2nd Battalion, 4th Marines located near the village of Lam Uan. At 1730, the company, commanded by Captain Vargas, was ordered to proceed by helicopter to the Battalion CP located at Mai Xa Chanh, in order to prepare to join in a heavy battle the following day involving BLT 2/4 and major elements of the 320th NVA (North Vietnam Army) division. The intensity of the artillery barrage increased as the helicopters arrived for the lift-out. While constantly exposing himself to the deadly incoming rounds, Captain Vargas ran from unit to unit, organizing helo-teams and supervising the loading of equipment. Only the 81mm Mortars and a portion of the 2nd Platoon were able to be placed aboard the helicopters before the barrage became so intense that the scheme had to be abandoned in favor of an overland route to the base camp. At 1925, as darkness was setting in, Captain Vargas organized and executed the withdrawal of his Company from the landing zone by foot. During the march overland to the Battalion CP, Company G was subjected to increasingly heavy artillery and mortar fire. Over 400 incoming rounds fell on the men that afternoon and evening. On several occasions, when elements or individuals became disorientated or lost in the darkness, Captain Vargas personally moved through the intense fire, issuing calm and clear orders, encouraging his men, and ensuring an orderly tactical withdrawal. He was wounded by shrapnel during this move, but ignored his wounds, refusing treatment in order to move up and down the column to ensure that his unit was intact. Captain Vargas' cool professionalism enabled Company G to arrive at the BLT CP with light casualties and the remainder of his night was spent organizing and preparing, to the most minute detail, for the planned assault the following day.

"At 1040, 1 May 1968, Company G arrived by Mike Boat at a point one kilometer southeast of its objective—the village of Dai Do. Disembarking, Captain Vargas skillfully deployed his unit and moved forward across 700 meters of rice paddy, northwest to the objective. From the moment his unit hit the beach they were continually bombarded with heavy artillery, rocket, and mortar fire. Nonetheless, his skill and inspiration enabled the Company to cross the LOD as an effective combat force. Bravo Company 1/3, had made the beach landing in conjunction with Company G and was moving in support of the attack on their left flank. In the movement toward the objective, this unit also came under intense enemy fire, resulting in the loss of the Company Commander and rendering the Platoon Commander a casualty. The individual that assumed command of Company B at this point became hysterical on the radio net, expressing the desire to pull back in the face of the intense enemy fire. Captain Vargas broke in on the net, took control of the situation, and began steadily talking the individual down to a level of rationalization. His encouragement brought the man to his senses. Captain Vargas then began issuing orders to the man, who in turn, responded to them effectively. As they approached the village, the Company came under heavy small arms and automatic weapons fire from the North Vietnamese forces in the trench-lines and well fortified positions. Through clever use of artillery, smoke screen, and overhead machine gun fire, Captain Vargas was able to gain a precious foot-hold in the first two hedgerows marking the outer edge of the heavily fortified village. The assault, however, was stalled at this point as friendly casualties began to mount and as his left flank platoon became pinned down by the overwhelming firepower of the well-entrenched enemy. Assessing the situation immediately Captain Vargas personally led his reserve platoon around to the left and to the aid of his beleaguered men. Swiftly and with calm resolve, he led an assault which eliminated one weapons bunker after another, simultaneously guiding the movement of his right flank platoon, thereby enabling the assaulting units to move relentlessly forward. In the close fighting that ensued, Captain Vargas sustained wounds from grenade fragments. Once again completely ignoring them, he moved up and down the assault lines, inspiring his men to superhuman feats and maintaining the momentum of the attack. During this particular action, eight enemy soldiers fell dead at his own hand. Shortly after the objective was secured, the North Vietnamese launched a savage counter-attack, and Captain Vargas ordered his men into a tight perimeter defense at the edge of the village. Wave upon wave of the counter-attack was beaten off and Company G subsequently held its position after inflicting heavy casualties upon the enemy. Thereafter, throughout the night, the enemy continued heavy probes of the perimeter, but Captain Vargas' well-organized defense prevented any successful penetration. The Company, at this juncture, was isolated from the remaining units which were participating in the encounter. Company B, 1/3 had been ordered to come to their assistance but was unable to penetrate the heavy enemy opposition, and was ordered to withdraw to a more secure area. Throughout the night, Captain Vargas surrounded himself with artillery fire to protect his small force of 68 men. At times he called in artillery to within 50 meters of his own position. Not a single friendly casualty was taken during the night.

"The following morning, 2 May 1968, Company E linked up with Company G, and together with Company H in support, the village of Dai Do was again swept of the enemy which had reentered during the night. By 0800, Companies E and G were vigorously engaged with well fortified North Vietnamese at the northern portion of the village. Heavy casualties were taken by the Assault Companies, yet throughout the remainder of the morning they steadily advanced through the entrenched enemy with the assistance of artillery and close air support. By 1300, the village of Dinh To, north, had been secured, but a massive enemy counter-attack forced the friendly units to pull back to the southern edge of Dai Do to reorganize and consolidate. At 1550, Company G, with an effective strength of only 53, and together with Company F in support, spearheaded an attack once again through Dai Do, and on toward the villages of Dinh To and Thoun Do. With the attack in progress, and while Company G was still moving forward, the enemy launched a battalion sized counter-attack. A fierce and brutal hand to hand battle ensued. Captain Vargas, remaining in the thick of the battle, rallied his men and directed an orderly withdrawal back through Dai Do. Painfully wounded by shrapnel and from an RPG rocket round—his third wound in as many days—he again refused treatment and continued to expose himself and coordinate the activity of those of his men still capable of fighting. Through his inspiration and example, his company fought savagely with grenades, small arms, and bayonets to contain the enemy attack long enough to make withdrawal, and to establish a hasty defense. Captain Vargas was everywhere—running 25 meters here, and under direct fire, to clear a jammed M-16 rifle, advancing another 50 meters there, to resupply a grenadier who had completely exhausted his M-79, and who was totally unarmed. When the Battalion Commander became seriously wounded during this engagement, Captain Vargas carried him to safety and returned to the scene of the fire fight to assist and direct his men. The majority of his Company now within the hastily established perimeter defense, Captain Vargas set about to assist the wounded still within the village. Each time he entered the village, now swarming with enemy troops, he was forced to fight his way in with hand grenades and small-arms fire. With complete disregard for his own personal safety, he made these trips repeatedly, shooting his way in, and carrying out the wounded. He personally accounted for seven enemy dead in this action and more significantly, saved at least as many lives. When all that was humanly possible to assist the wounded had been accomplished, and now reeling from his own wounds, he still refused evacuation and remained behind to help organize the BLT perimeter defense. At 1130, reinforcements arrived from the Mai Xa Chanh base camp and by darkness, the BLT maneuver elements had consolidated its perimeter at the southern edge of Dai Do. The night was quiet and no significant contact with the enemy was experienced the following day. The three day encounter netted 805 enemy KIA. Friendly casualties were 72 KIA and 297 medevacs. The facts contained in this account have been substantiated by eye-witnesses."

Jay Vargas "loves being an American. I am so honored but most of all just being part of America as one of her sons is my honor. America is so strong yet so forgiving."

To the youth of America—"Be honest, speak from your heart, love your fellow men regardless of color, creed or religion. Above all, remember those who have fought for your freedom. Always set the example; take care of your fellow man, and always seek some way to improve America."

GARY GEORGE WETZEL

Gary Wetzel of Milwaukee, Wisconsin is the only living Medal of Honor recipient whose parents both served in our armed forces during World War II. Capt. William F. Dismukes, an eye-witness to SP4 Wetzel's superhuman act of courage on the 8th of January, 1968 stated the following concerning the 20 year old soldier's actions on that eventful day in Vietnam—"Our mission was to insert a blocking force in a large LZ (Landing Zone) on the east bank of the Can Giuoc River five miles south of Can Giuoc. The Viet Cong was trying to break contact with the 9th Division troops to the east and were moving west to where their reserves was waiting in well prepared positions in the lines east of the river. The blocking force was inserted in the northwest corner of the large LZ along the river and were immediately caught in a crossfire from bunkers in the trees along the north and west sides. The majority of the infantrymen were wounded or pinned down in the open rice paddy as soon as they left the ships.

"We were flying in the number four position of the first element. I had control of the ship with the A/C (Aircraft Commander) following through to take the ship if necessary. Looking out the right side I could see the LZ under the aircraft ahead. It looked like about 30 or 40 acres of wet rice paddy bounded on all sides by heavy stands of palm and banana trees. An air strike had been placed across the river by mistake and our gunships had time for only one pass on the tree lines before we started our approach. The lead ship took us in close to the west tree line. At 50 feet from touchdown we were met by heavy automatic weapons fire but continued on in. Just before touchdown a rocket propelled grenade was fired from a bunker to our left front and exploded in the left chin bubble. I was knocked unconscious by the blast.

"The explosion tore out the left front of the cockpit and mortally wounded the aircraft commander. The gunner and the crew chief were thrown out of the aircraft and reached cover behind nearby dikes. The two passengers who went out the left door were killed within five feet of the aircraft and three were wounded and pinned down 15 feet from the aircraft on the right side. The sixth man never left the cabin. The aircraft settled by itself into the water less than 30 meters from the tree line beside a low dike. The rest of the flight took off after dropping their troops. Two of the aircraft went down within 500 meters of the LZ. Their crews were extracted before the Viet Cong could get to them. Any attempt to rescue my crew would have been suicidal. The automatic weapons fire from the two tree lines was so heavy the few infantrymen not wounded or killed in the LZ could not lift their heads out of the water without drawing heavy fire from the enemy gunners.

"The engine was still running when I came to, so I shut it down and reached over for the aircraft commander. The Viet Cong in the trees were tearing the aircraft apart with their fire. I saw the crew chief, Specialist 4 Jarvis, coming back across the rice paddy to help me. He was knocked down by a hand grenade but got back up and climbed into the aircraft behind my seat. Together we started to pull the aircraft commander across the radio pedestal. Wetzel got up from the dike on the other side and waded up to the aircraft. He was starting to open the left door when the second rocket propelled grenade hit the doorframe a foot away, tearing his left side to pieces and mutilating his left arm. He hung onto the aircraft for a moment and then pulled himself up into the cockpit to push the aircraft commander out of his seat. The aircraft commander was halfway over the radio when Wetzel fell back out of the aircraft. I saw him start to crawl back toward his machine gun. I looked up and saw the Viet Cong coming out of their bunkers. They were forming an assault wave in the trees to sweep the LZ. There was almost no return fire from the LZ to stop them!

"Wetzel managed to climb back into the gunner's well behind his machine gun despite his terrible wounds and turned back the assault wave. While the full attention of the enemy gunners was turned on him the other men in the LZ reached cover behind the paddy dike that ran alongside the aircraft and formed a weak defense behind it that held until dark. I crawled under the tail boom of the aircraft in an attempt to reach the dike but was immediately wounded and pinned down. I lay in the open rice paddy until dark and then joined up with an artillery observer behind the dike.

"The artillery observer had just gotten in contact with his unit and the first rounds were starting to hit around the bunkers in the trees. Our gunships had been orbiting in the LZ since we first went in and I contacted them through the artillery unit. They had withheld their fire until they were sure of our position. I directed them to the tree line and under their fire we were able to pull back across the rice paddy with our dead and wounded. We formed a perimeter on high ground 600 meters to the east and by midnight had secured enough area for Med Evac aircraft to come in. I have no idea how Wetzel survived, as badly wounded as he was, but he had been brought into the perimeter with the rest of the wounded and was sent out on the first aircraft. I saw him the next morning in the 93rd Evacuation Hospital. He had been in surgery all night and the doctors said they had almost lost him. They had taken as much shrapnel out of him as possible and had amputated his left arm below the elbow. While I was there he asked me if I thought his family would be proud of him. I told him I was sure that they would be."*

Gary Wetzel received the Medal of Honor at the White House from President Lyndon Johnson on November 19, 1968. His citation reads:

WETZEL, GARY GEORGE

Rank and organization: Specialist Fourth Class (then Pfc), U.S. Army, 173d Assault Helicopter Company. Place and date: Near Ap Dong An, Republic of Vietnam, 8 January 1968. Entered service at: Milwaukee, Wis. Born: 29 September 1947. South Milwaukee, Wis. Citation: Sp4c. Wetzel, 173d Assault Helicopter Company, distinguished himself by conspicuous gallantry and intrepidity at the risk of his life, above and beyond the call of duty. Sp4c. Wetzel was serving as door gunner aboard a helicopter which was part of an insertion force trapped in a landing zone by intense and deadly hostile fire. Sp4c. Wetzel was going to the aid of his aircraft commander when he was blown into a rice paddy and critically wounded by two enemy rockets that exploded just inches from his location. Although bleeding profusely due to the loss of his left arm and severe wounds in his right arm, chest, and left leg. Sp4c. Wetzel staggered back to his original position in his gun-well and took the enemy forces under fire. His machine gun was the only weapon placing effective fire on the enemy at that time. Through a resolve that overcame the shock and intolerable pain of his injuries, Sp4c. Wetzel remained at his position until he had eliminated the automatic weapons emplacement that had been inflicting heavy casualties on the American troops and preventing them from moving against the strong enemy force. Refusing to attend to his own extensive wounds, he attempted to return to the aid of his aircraft commander

---

*Article "EYEWITNESS TO VALOR," *U.S. ARMY DIGEST*, by Captain John L. Hopper as told by Captain William F. Dismukes, August 1969.

but passed out from loss of blood. Regaining consciousness, he persisted in his efforts to drag himself to the aid of his fellow crewmen. After an agonizing effort, he came to the side of his crew chief who was attempting to drag the wounded aircraft commander to the safety of a nearby dike. Unswerving in his devotion to his fellow man, Sp4c. Wetzel assisted his crew chief even though he lost consciousness once again during this action. Sp4c. Wetzel displayed extraordinary heroism in his efforts to aid his fellow crewman. His gallant actions were in keeping with the highest traditions of the U.S. Army and reflect great credit upon himself and the Armed Forces of his country.

Gary Wetzel is one of ten children born to George and Helen Wetzel, his World War II veteran parents of South Milwaukee, Wisconsin. He attended Oak Creek High School before enlisting in the Army. He received his high school diploma (GED) while in service. Presently he is a heavy equipment operator involved in the construction industry.

An interview after Gary Wetzel returned to civilian status relates the credo of this gallant young hero. "Gary has aged markedly since that ill-fated day in Vietnam. It is as if the energy he mustered in that rice paddy was borrowed from his future. Gary doesn't look like the stereotyped hero. No sharp, angular features of an Audie Murphy or towering stature of a John Wayne. Gary is rather short, stocky, red-bearded and speaks plainly. The pain he suffered is not etched in his face. It is seated deep in his eyes. His left hand is a metal hook. When Gary talks, you start to see that he is just another guy. Perhaps that is what makes him so special.

" 'I'd been shot down four times before,' Gary recalls, 'But that last time was by far the worst. When we were airborne we estimated that there were 800 to 1000 Viet Cong in the trees bordering that rice paddy. After we were shot down guys were dying all around me. Just like I'd heard before, your whole life starts unwinding in front of you. I thought of mistakes made in the past . . . my girl Bonnie back home . . . then when the pilot died, he was my buddy, I got angrier than hell. I had to get back to that machine gun in the chopper.'

" 'There's a lot I don't remember. Something was driving me . . . a strength I'd never felt before. I just kept shooting and watching the Cong drop. I don't know how long it went on, but I was told later that we were down in that rice paddy for about 12 hours. I think I went through 800 rounds of ammo and at least six .45 clips.'

"When the enemy finally retreated, Gary began dragging the wounded to cover by the helicopter where the medic, also wounded, gave first aid.

" 'Later I saw some of those guys at the hospital,' Gary says. 'They thanked me. That was worth more to me than a dozen medals.'

"As a result of injuries, Gary needed a total of 400 stitches as doctors worked on him that same night. He was on the critical list at Bien Hoa hospital for 11 days, and eventually was to have five operations and several skin grafts to patch up his torn body.

"If extenuating circumstances turn ordinary people into heroes, then Gary has had his share of experiences. When he was 15 years old he saw an elderly lady struck by a car. He rushed to her and quickly began administering mouth to mouth resuscitation to keep her alive until the ambulance arrived. Another time he drove up on a car which had gone off a highway and was wrapped around a tree, pinning its young passengers inside. He immediately began to tear apart the twisted metal and ably directed firemen rescue efforts. The two inside the car lived."*

Gary feels deeply about America. "Freedom, the right to

*Author, publication and date unknown.

speak and do as I feel as long as what I do doesn't interfere with the rights of others. That's important."

Concerning the youth of America, Gary feels that they should be proud and willing to give two years of their life to their country upon reaching the age of eighteen. "After all, they have had twelve years of the best schools in the best country in the world for free," he concludes.

APPENDIX I
ORDER OF PRECEDENCE OF
MILITARY DECORATIONS

The following is the order of precedence for military decorations of the United States, based on degrees of valor and meritorious achievement, and the date each medal was established:

U.S. ARMY AND U.S. AIR FORCE

1. Medal of Honor (1862)
2. Distinguished Service Cross (1918)
   Air Force Cross (1960)
3. Defense Distinguished Service Medal (1970)
4. Distinguished Service Medal (1918)
5. Silver Star (1918)
6. Defense Superior Service Medal (1976)
7. Legion of Merit (1942)
8. Distinguished Flying Cross (1926)
9. Soldier's Medal (1926)
   Airman's Medal (1960)
10. Bronze Star (1942)
11. Meritorious Service Medal (1969)
12. Air Medal (1942)
13. Joint Service Commendation Medal (1963)
14. Army Commendation Medal (1945)
    (formerly Commendation Ribbon)
    Air Force Commendation Medal (1958)
15. Purple Heart (1782)

U.S. NAVY AND MARINE CORPS

1. Medal of Honor (1862)
2. Navy Cross (1919)
3. Defense Distinguished Service Medal (1970)
4. Distinguished Service Medal (1918)
5. Silver Star (1918)
6. Defense Superior Service Medal (1976)
7. Legion of Merit (1942)
8. Navy and Marine Corps Medal (1942)
9. Bronze Star (1942)
10. Meritorious Service Medal (1969)
11. Air Medal (1942)
12. Joint Service Commendation Medal (1967)
13. Navy Commendation Medal (1944)
    (formerly Navy Commendation Ribbon)
14. Purple Heart (1782)

APPENDIX II
MEDAL OF HONOR
RECIPIENTS
1863-1978

"IN THE NAME OF THE CONGRESS
OF THE UNITED STATES"

PREPARED BY THE

COMMITTEE ON
VETERANS' AFFAIRS
UNITED STATES SENATE

FEBRUARY 14, 1979

COMMITTEE ON VETERANS' AFFAIRS

ALAN CRANSTON, California, *Chairman*

HERMAN E. TALMADGE, Georgia
JENNINGS RANDOLPH, West Virginia
RICHARD (DICK) STONE, Florida
JOHN A. DURKIN, New Hampshire
SPARK M. MATSUNAGA, Hawaii

ALAN K. SIMPSON, Wyoming
STROM THURMOND, South Carolina
ROBERT T. STAFFORD, Vermont
GORDON J. HUMPHREY, New Hampshire

PART II.—MEDAL OF HONOR RECIPIENTS BY STATE
1863-1978

[(b) indicates State of birth; *posthumous award; †second award]

ALABAMA

ARMY-AIR FORCE

BOLDEN, Paul L., S/Sgt., 30th Inf. Div. (Madison) (b. Iowa).
BOLTON, Cecil H., 1st Lt., 104th Inf. Div. (Huntsville) (b. Fla.).
(b) DAVIS, Charles W., Maj., 25th Inf. Div. (Montgomery).
(b) ERWIN, Henry E., S/Sgt., 20th Air Force (Bessemer).
  *EVANS, Rodney J., Sgt., 1st Cav. Div. (Florala) (b. Mass.).
(b) HOWARD, Robert L., 1st Lt., USA (Montgomery).
  JOHNSTON, Gordon, 1st Lt., U.S. Sig. Cp. (Birmingham) (b. N.C.).
(b) LAWLEY, William R., Jr., 1st Lt., A.C. (Birmingham).
(b) *LEONARD, Matthew, P/Sgt., 1st Inf. Div. (Birmingham).
(b) MANNING, Sidney E., Cpl., 42d Div. (Flomaton).
(b) *MICHAEL, Don Leslie, Sp.4c., 173d Airborne Brig. (Florence).
(b) MIZE, Ola L., M/Sgt., 3d Inf. Div. (Gadsden).
(b) *SEAY, William W., Sgt., 48th Trans. Gp. (Brewton).
  SPRAYBERRY, James M., Capt., 1st Cav. Div. (Montgomery) (b. Ga.).

NAVY-MARINE CORPS

(b) *GRAY, Ross Franklin, Sgt., USMCR (Marvel Valley).
(b) HOUGHTON, Edward J., Ordinary Seamen, USN (Mobile).
(b) *INGRAM, Osmond K., GMlc. USN.
(b) McLAUGHLIN, Alford L., Pfc., 1st Marine Div., Reinf., USMC (Leeds).
(b) *NEW, John Dury, Pfc., USMC.
(b) WILSON, Harold E., T/Sgt., 1st Marine Div., Reinf., USMCR (Birmingham).

ARIZONA

ARMY-AIR FORCE

(b) ALCHESAY, Sgt., Indian Scouts.
  BACON, Nicky Daniel, S/Sgt., 21st Inf., Americal Div. (Phoenix) (b. Ark.).
(b) BLANQUET, Indian Scouts, U.S. Army.
(b) CHIQUITO, Indian Scouts, U.S. Army.
(b) ELSATSOOSU Cpl., Indian Scouts, U.S. Army.
  FERGUSON, Frederick E., CWO, 1st Cav. Div. (Phoenix) (b. Tex.).
  HERRERA, Silvestre S., Pfc., 36th Inf. Div. (Phoenix) (b. Tex.).
(b) JIM, Sgt., Indian Scouts, U.S. Army.
(b) KELSAY, Indian Scouts, U.S. Army.
(b) KOSOHA, Indian Scouts, U.S. Army.
  *LAUFFER, Billy Lane, Pfc., 1st Air Cav. Div. (Phoenix) (b. Ky.).
(b) *LUKE, Frank, Jr., 2d Lt., 1st Pur. Gp., Air Service (Phoenix).
(b) MACHOL, Pvt., Indian Scouts, U.S. Army.
(b) NANNASADDIE, Indian Scouts, U.S. Army.
(b) NANTAJE (NANTAHE), Indian Scouts, U.S. Army.
(b) ROWDY, Sgt., Co. A., Indian Scouts.
  THOMPSON, Max, Sgt., 1st Inf. Div. (Prescott) (b. N.C.).

ARIZONA—Continued

NAVY-MARINE CORPS

*AUSTIN, Oscar P., Pfc., USMC (Phoenix) (b. Tex.).
*JIMINEZ, Jose Francisco, L/Cpl., USMC (Phoenix) (b. Mexico).
*†PRUITT, John Henry, Cpl., 2d Div., USMC (Phoenix) (b. Ark.). (Awarded both
    Army and Navy Medals of Honor.)
(b)   VARGAS, M. Sando, Jr., Maj. USMC (Winslow).

ARKANSAS

ARMY-AIR FORCE

(b)   BRITT, Maurice L., Capt., 3d Inf. Div. (Lonoke).
(b)   BURKE, Lloyd L., 1st Lt., 1st Cav. Div. (Stuttgart).
(b)   *COLLIER, Gilbert G., Sgt., 40th Inf. Div. (Tichnor).
      DONLON, Roger Hugh C., Capt., USA (Fort Chaffee) (b. N.Y.).
      ELLIS, William, 1st Sgt., 3d Wis. Cav. (Little Rock) (b. England).
(b)   FACTOR, Pompey, Pvt., Indian Scouts.
(b)   *GILLILAND, Charles L., Cpl., 3d Inf. Div. (Yellville).
(b)   HENDRIX, James R., S/Sgt., 4th Armd. Div. (Lepanto).
(b)   *LLOYD, Edgar H., 1st Lt., 80th Inf. Div. (Blytheville).
(b)   PAYNE, Issac, Trumpeter, 24th U.S. Infantry, Indian Scouts.
(b)   *TERRY, Seymour W., Capt., 96th Inf. Div. (Little Rock).

NAVY-MARINE CORPS

      FRANKS, William J., Seaman, USN (b. N.C.).
(b)   GORDON, Nathan Green, Lt., USN (Morrilton).
      WATSON, Wilson Douglas, Pvt., USMCR (b. Ala.).
(b)   *WILLIAMS, Jack, PM3c., USNR (Harrison).

CALIFORNIA

ARMY-AIR FORCE

      BACA, John Phillip, Sgt., 1st Cav. Div. (Fort Ord) (b. R.I.).
      *BELLRICHARD, Leslie A., Pfc., 8th Inf. Div. (Oakland) (b. Wis.).
      BROPHY, James, Pvt., 8th U.S. Cav. (Stockton) (b. Ireland).
      CAVAIANI, Jon R., S/Sgt., U.S. Army Vietnam Tr. Adv. Gp. (b. England).
(b)   CRAFT, Clarence B., Pfc., 96th Inf. Div. (Santa Ana).
      CROCKER, Henry H., Capt., 2d Mass. Cav. (b. Conn.).
      DEAN, William F., Maj. Gen., 24th Inf. Div. (b. Ill.).
      *DESIDERIO, Reginald B., Capt., 25th Inf. Div. (San Francisco) (b. Pa.).
(b)   *DEVORE, Edward A., Jr., Spec. 4, 9th Inf. Div. (Harbor City).
(b)   DOOLITTLE, James H., Brig. Gen., A.G., USA (Berkeley).
      DUNAGAN, Kern W., Maj., 46th Inf., Americal Div. (Los Angeles) (b. Ariz.).
      ELWOOD, Edwin L., Pvt., 8th U.S. Cav. (b. Mo).
(b)   *EVANS, Donald W., Sp4c., 4th Inf. Div. (Covina).
(b)   *GONZALES, David M., Pfc., 32d Inf. Div. (Pacoima).
      *HARMON, Roy W., Sgt., 91st Inf. (Pixley) (b. Okla.).
      HARVEY, Raymond, Capt., 7th Inf. Div. (Pasadena) (b. Pa.).
      HEARTERY, Richard, Pvt., 6th U.S. Cav. (San Francisco) (b. Ireland).
(b)   HERNANDEZ, Rodolfo P., Cpl., Cmbt. Team.
(b)   HIGH, Frank C., Pvt., 2d Oreg. Vol. Inf. (Picard).
      HOLDERMAN, Nelson M., Capt., 77th Div. (Santa Ana) (b. Nebr.).
      HOOPER, Joe R., S/Sgt., 101st Airborne Div. (Los Angeles) (b. S.C.).
(b)   *INGALLS, George Alan, Spec. 4, 1st Cav. Div. (Yorba Linda).
      JENNINGS, Delbert O., S/Sgt., 1st Air Cav. Div. (San Francisco) (b. N. Mex.).
      *KANDLE, Victor L., 1st Lt., 3d Inf. Div. (Redwood City) (b. Wash.).
(b)   KATZ, Phillip C., Sgt., 91st Div. (San Francisco).
      LEAHY, Cornelius J., Pvt., 36th Inf., U.S. Vol. (San Francisco) (b. Ireland).
      LITTRELL, Gary Lee, Sgt., (Los Angeles) (b. Ky.).
      McMAHON, Martin T., Capt., U.S. Vol. (b. Canada).

CALIFORNIA—Continued

ARMY-AIR FORCE

*MILLER, Oscar F., Maj., 91st Div. (Los Angeles) (b. Ark.).
*MOLNAR, Frankie Zoly, S/Sgt., 4th Inf. Div. (Fresno) (b. W. Va.).
*MOON, Harold H., Jr., Pvt., 24th Inf. Div. (Gardena) (b. N. Mex.).
(b) *MUNEMORI, Sadao S., Pfc., 442d Combat Team (Los Angeles).
(b)   PENRY, Richard Allen, Sgt., 199th Inf. Brig. (Petaluma).
*PIERCE, Larry S., Sgt., 173d Airborne Brig. (Fresno) (b. Okla.).
(b)   QUINN, Peter H., Pvt., 4th U.S. Cav. (San Francisco).
REGAN, Patrick, 2d Lt., 20th Div. (Los Angeles) (b. Mass.).
(b) *ROARK, Anund C., Sgt., 4th Inf. Div. (Los Angeles).
(b) *ROBERTS, Harold W., Cpl., 344th Bn., Tank Corps (San Francisco).
ROCCO, Louis R., WO, U.S. Mil. Assist. Com. (Los Angeles) (b. N. Mex.).
(b)   RODRIGUEZ, Joseph C., Sgt., 7th Inf. Div. (San Bernardino).
SEIBERT, Lloyd M., Sgt., 91st Div. (Salinas) (b. Mich.).
(b)   SHIELS, George F., Surg., U.S. Vol. (San Francisco).
*SHOCKLEY, William R., Pfc., 32d Inf. Div. (Selma) (b. Okla.).
(b)   TAYLOR, James Allen, Capt., 1st Cav., Ameri. Div. (San Francisco).
TURNER, George B., Pfc., 14th Armd. Div. (Los Angeles) (b. Tex.).
(b) *VIALE, Robert M., 2d Lt., 37th Inf. Div. (Ukiah).
(b) *VILLEGAS, Ysmael R., S/Sgt., 32 Inf. Div. (Casa Blanca).
*VON SCHLICK, Robert H., Pvt., 9th U.S. Inf. (San Francisco) (b. Germany).
WARE, Keith L., Lt. Col., 3d Inf. Div. (Glendale) (b. Colo.).
(b)   WAYBUR, David C., 1st Lt., 3d Inf. Div. (Piedmont).
WEAVER, Amos, Sgt., 36th Inf., U.S. Vol. (San Francisco) (b. Ind.).
WEST, Chester H., 1st Sgt., 91st Div. (Los Banos) (b. Colo.).
WILLISTON, Edward B., 1st Lt., 2d U.S. Arty. (San Francisco) (b. Vt.).
(b) *YOUNG, Robert H., Pfc., 1st Cav. Div. (Vallejo).

NAVY-MARINE CORPS

(b) *ANDERSON, James, Jr., Pfc., 3d Marine Div. (Los Angeles).
BOYDSTON, Erwin Jay, Pvt., USMC (b. Colo.).
BROCK, George F., CM2d., USN (b. Ohio).
BURNES, James, Pvt., USMC (b. Mass.).
(b) *CALLAGHAN, Daniel Judson, Rear Adm., USN.
(b)   CLAUSEY, John J., CGM, USN (San Francisco).
COLEMAN, John, Pvt., USMC (b. Ireland).
COVINGTON, Jessie Whitfield, SC3d, USN (b. Tenn.).
*CREEK, Thomas E., L/Cpl., USMC (San Diego) (b. Mo.).
DAHLGREN, John Olof, Cpl., USMC (b. Sweden).
(b)   FINN, John William, Lt., USN (Los Angeles).
FISHER, Frederick Thomas, GM1c., USN (b. England).
(b) *FOSTER, Paul Hellstrom, Sgt., USMCR (San Francisco).
(b) *GONSALVES, Harold, Pfc., USMCR (Alameda).
HALFORD, William, Cox., USN (b. England).
HANSEN, Hans A., Seaman, USN (b. Germany).
HEISCH, Henry William, Pvt., USMC (b. Germany).
HENRECHON, George Francis, MM2d, USN (b. Conn.).
HULBERT, Henry Lewis, Pvt., USMC (b. England).
ITRICH, Franz Anton, CCM, USN (b. Germany).
*JOHNSON, Ralph H., Pfc., USMC (Oakland) (b. S.C.).
(b) *JONES, Herbert Charpiot, Ens., USNR (Los Angeles).
(b) *KELSO, Jack W., Pvt., USMC, 1st Marine Div. (Caruthers).
*KOELSCH, John Kelvin, Lt. (jg.), USN (Los Angeles) (b. England).
LAVERTY, John, Flc., USN (b. Ireland).
(b) *MATTHEWS, Daniel P., Sgt., USMC, 1st Marine Div. (Van Nuys).
(b) *MAXAM, Larry Leonard, Cpl., USMC (Burbank).
McALLISTER, Samuel, Ordinary Seaman, USN (b. Ireland).
McGONAGLE, William L., Capt., USN (Thermal) (b. Kans.).
McNALLY, Michael Joseph, Sgt., USMC (b. N.Y.).
(b)   MOORE, Albert, Pvt., USMC (Merced).

CALIFORNIA—Continued

NAVY-MARINE CORPS

(b) *OBREGON, Eugene A., Pfc., USMC, 1st Marine Div. (Los Angeles).
ORNDOFF, Harry Westley, Pvt., USMC (b. Ohio).
*PERKINS, William Thomas, Jr., Cpl., USMC (Northridge) (b. N.Y.).
PHARRIS, Jackson Charles, Lt., USN (b. Ga.).
(b) PHILLIPS, Reuben Jasper, Cpl., USMC (Cambria).
(b) *PHIPPS, Jimmy W., Pfc., USMC (Reseda).
(b) PITTMAN, R. A., Sgt., USMC (Stockton).
*POYNTER, James I., Sgt., USMCR, 1st Marine Div. (Donney) (b. Ill.).
(b) SILVA, France, Pvt., USMC (Haywards).
SMITH, Eugene P., CWT, USN (b. Ill.).
STOLTENBERG, Andrew V., GM2c., USN (b. Norway).
SWETT, James Elms, 1st Lt., USMCR (b. Wash.).
WESTERMARK, Axel, Seaman, USN (b. Finland).
†WILLIAMS, Louis, Captain of Hold, USN (b. Norway).
(b) WOODS, Samuel, Seaman, USN.
*WORLEY, Kenneth L., L/Cpl., USMCC, 1st Mar. Div. (Fresno) (b. N. Mex.).
ZION, William, Pvt., USMC (b. Ind.).

COLORADO

ARMY-AIR FORCE

*CHILES, Marcellus H., Capt., 89th Div. (Denver) (b. Ark.).
DIX, Drew Dennis, S/Sgt., USA (Denver) (b. N.Y.).
(b) CRAWFORD, William J., Pvt., 36th Inf. Div. (Pueblo).
(b) *FRYAR, Elmer E., Pvt., 11th Airborne Div. (Denver).
FUNK, Jesse N., Pfc., 89th Div. (Calhan) (b. Mo.).
GROVE, William R., Lt. Col., 36th Inf., U.S. Vol. (Denver) (b. Iowa).
*LINDSTROM, Floyd K., Pfc., 3d Inf. Div. (Colorado Springs) (b. Nebr.).
*MARTINEZ, Joe P., Pvt., 7th Inf. Div. (Ault) (b. N. Mex.).
MAXWELL, Robert D., T5g., 3d Inf. Div. (Larimer Co.) (b. Idaho).
(b) *McWETHY, Edgar Lee, Jr., Spec. 5, 1st Cav. Div. (Leadville).
(b) *PUCKET, Donald D., 1st Lt., 98th Bomb. Gp. (Boulder).
*WALKER, Kenneth N., Brig. Gen., 5th Bomb Comd. (b. N. Mex.).
WALLACE, George W., 2d Lt., 9th U.S. Inf. (Denver) (b. Kans.).
*WICKERSHAM, J. Hunter, 2d Lt., 89th Div. (Denver) (b. N.Y.).
YOUNG, Gerald O., Capt., USAF (Colorado Springs) (b. Ill.).

NAVY-MARINE CORPS

*COKER, Ronald L., Pfc., USMC (Denver) (b. Nebr.).
McCANDLESS, Bruce, Comdr., USN (b. D.C.).
(b) MURPHY, Raymond G., 2d Lt., USMC, 1st Marine Div. (Pueblo).
ROSS, Donald Kirby, Machinist, USN (Denver) (b. Kans.).
SITTER, Carl L., Capt., USMC, 1st Marine Div. (Pueblo) (b. Mo.).
(b) UPTON, Frank Monroe, Quartermaster, USN (Loveland).

CONNECTICUT

ARMY-AIR FORCE

BABCOCK, John B., 1st Lt., 5th U.S. Cav. (Stonington) (b. La.).
(b) BACON, William W., Pvt., 14th Conn. Inf. (Berlin).
(b) BAIRD, George W., 1st Lt. and Adj., 5th U.S. Inf. (Milford).
(b) BECKWITH, Wallace A., Pvt., 21st Conn. Inf. (New London).
BEEBE, William S., 1st Lt., Ord. Dept., USA (Thompson) (b. N.Y.).
(b) BRIGGS, Elijah A., Cpl., 2d Conn. Hvy. Arty. (Salisbury).
(b) BUCK, F. Clarence, Cpl., 21st Conn. Inf. (Windsor).
(b) BURKE, Daniel W., 1st Sgt., 2d U.S. Inf.
(b) CANFIELD, Heth, Pvt., 2d U.S. Cav. (New Medford).
CORLISS, George W., Capt., 5th Conn. Inf. (New Haven) (b. N.Y.).
(b) CURTIS, John C., Sgt. Maj., 9th Conn. Inf. (Bridgeport).
DALY, Michael J., Capt., 3d Inf. Div. (Southport) (b. N.Y.).
FLYNN, Christopher, Cpl., 14th Conn. Inf. (b. Ireland).
(b) FORSYTH, Thomas H., 1st Sgt., 4th U.S. Cav. (Hartford).

CONNECTICUT—Continued

ARMY-AIR FORCE

FOX, Nicholas, Pvt., 28th Conn. Inf. (Greenwich).
GRAY, Robert A., Sgt., 21st Conn. Inf. (Groton) (b. Pa.).
(b) GIBBS, Wesley, Sgt., 2d Conn. Hvy. Arty. (Salisbury).
*HARTELL, Lee R., 1st Lt., 2d Inf. Div. (Danbury) (b. Pa.).
(b) HICKOK, Nathan E., Cpl., 8th Conn. Inf. (Danbury).
HINCKS, William B., Sgt. Maj., 14th Conn. Inf. (Bridgeport) (b. Maine).
(b) HOOPER, William B., Cpl., 1st N.J. Cav. (Willimantic).
HORNE, Samuel B., Capt., 11th Conn. Inf. (Winsted) (b. Ireland).
(b) HUBBELL, William S., Capt., 21st Conn. Inf. (North Stonington).
(b) JACKSON, Frederick R., 1st Sgt., 7th Conn. Inf. (New Haven).
JOHNSTON, William J., Pfc., 45th Inf. Div. (Colchester) (b. N.Y.).
(b) LANFARE, Aaron S., 1st Lt., 1st Conn. Cav. (Branford).
(b) LEVITOW, John L., Sgt., USAF (New Haven).
*LIBBY, George D., Sgt., 24th Inf. Div. (Waterbury) (b. Maine).
(b) *MAGRATH, John D., Pfc., 10th Mtn. Div. (East Norwalk).
(b) MARSH, Charles H., Pvt., 1st Conn. Cav. (New Milford).
MURPHY, James T., Pvt., 1st Conn. Arty. (b. Canada).
NEVILLE, Edwin M., Capt., 1st Conn. Cav. (Waterbury).
(b) O'NEILL, William, Cpl., 4th U.S. Cav. (Tariffville).
(b) PALMER, John G., Cpl., 21st Conn. Inf. (Montville).
(b) *SHEA, Daniel John, Pfc., 196th Light Inf. Brig., Ameri. Div. (Norwalk).
SIMONDS, William Edgar, Sgt. Maj., 25th Conn. Inf. (Canton).
(b) SODERMAN, William A., Pfc., 2d Inf. Div. (West Haven).
(b) TINKHAM, Eugene M., Cpl., 148th N.Y. Inf. (Sprague).
(b) TUCKER, Allen, Sgt., 10th Conn. Inf. (Sprague).
(b) WHITAKER, Edward W., Capt., 1st Conn. Cav. (Ashford).
WILSON, Christopher W., Pvt., 73d N.Y. Inf. (West Meriden) (b. Ireland).
WRIGHT, Robert, Pvt., 14th U.S. Inf. (Woodstock) (b. Ireland).

NAVY-MARINE CORPS

(b) BARNUM, Harvey C., Jr., Capt., USMC (Cheshire).
CRANDALL, Orson L., CBM, USN (b. Mo.).
(b) HARDING, Thomas, Captain of Forecastle, USN (Middletown).
(b) HILL, Frank, Pvt., USMC (Hartford).
(b) KELLOG, Allan Jay, Jr., Gy/Sgt., 1st Mar. Div. (Bethel).
(b) MANNING, Henry J., Quartermaster, USN (New Haven).
(b) PECK, Oscar E., Second Class Boy, USN (Bridgeport).
(b) *REEVES, Thomas J., CRM, USN (Thomaston).
(b) ROSE, George, Seaman, USN (Stamford).
(b) RYAN, Richard, Ordinary Seaman, USN.
*TALBOT, Ralph, 2d Lt., USMC (b. Mass.).

DELAWARE

ARMY-AIR FORCE

(b) BUCKINGHAM, David E., 1st Lt., 4th Del. Inf. (Pleasant Hill).
(b) CONNOR, James P., Sgt., 3d Inf. Div. (Wilmington).
(b) DU PONT, Henry A., Capt., 5th U.S. Arty. (Wilmington).
(b) MAYBERRY, John B., Pvt., 1st Del. Inf. (Smyrna).
McCARREN, Bernard, Pvt., 1st Del. Inf. (Wilmington) (b. Ireland).
(b) *NELSON, William L., Sgt., 9th Inf. Div. (Wilmington).
PIERCE, Charles H., Pvt., 22d U.S. Inf. (Delaware City) (b. Md.).
(b) POSTLES, James Parke, Capt., 1st Del. Inf. (Wilmington).
(b) SEWARD, Griffin, Wagoner, 8th U.S. Cav. (Dover).
SHILLING, John, 1st Sgt., 3d Del. Inf. (Felton) (b. England).
(b) SMITH, S. Rodmond, Capt., 4th Del. Inf. (Wilmington).
TANNER, Charles B., 2d Lt., 1st Del. Inf. (Wilmington) (b. Pa.).

NAVY-MARINE CORPS

(b) CHADWICK, Leonard, Apprentice First Class, USN (Middletown).

DELAWARE—Continued

Navy-Marine Corps

(b) HAND, Allexander, Quartermaster, USN.

DISTRICT OF COLUMBIA

Army-Air Force

BARNES, Will C., Pfc., Sig. Cp. (b. Calif.).
(b) BELL, Dennis, Pvt., 10th U.S. Cav.
BUTTERFIELD, Daniel, Brig. Gen., U.S. Vol. (b. N.Y.).
BYRNE, Bernard A., Capt., 6th U.S. Inf. (b. Va.).
CAPEHART, Charles E., Maj., 1st W. Va. Cav. (b. Pa.).
(b) CHEEVER, Benjamin H., Jr., 1st Lt., 6th U.S. Cav.
CHURCH, James Robb, Asst. Surg., 1st U.S. Vol. Cav. (b. Ill.).
(b) McALWEE, Benjamin F., Sgt., 3d Md. Inf.
(b) *McGOVERN, Robert M., 1st Lt., 1st Cav. Div.
MYERS, Fred, Sgt., 6th U.S. Cav. (b. Germany).
SHAW, George C., 1st Lt., 27th U.S. Inf. (b. Mich.).
(b) TAYLOR, William, Sgt. and 2d Lt., 1st Md. Inf.
(b) WARRINGTON, Lewis, 1st Lt., 4th U.S. Cav.
WOODRUFF, Carle A., 1st Lt., 2d U.S. Arty. (b. N.Y.).

Navy-Marine Corps

(b) BADGER, Oscar Charles, Ens., USN.
*BAUSELL, Lewis Kenneth, Cpl., USMC (b. Va.).
BEHNKE, Heinrich, S1c., USN (b. Germany).
BERKELEY, Randolph Carter, Maj., USMC (b. Va.)
CHAMBERS, Justice M., Col., USMC (b. W. Va.).
(b) COURTS, George McCall, Lt. (jg), USN.
(b) HARRINGTON, David, F1c., USN.
(b) HAYDEN, John, Apprentice, USN.
*JOHNSON, James E., Sgt., USMC, 1st Marine Div. (b. Idaho).
(b) KEEFER, Philip B., Coppersmith, USN.
(b) LIPSCOMB, Harry, WT, USN.
McDONALD, James Harper, CM, USN (b. Scotland).
MILLER, Andrew, Sgt., USMC (b. Germany).
MURPHY, John Alphonsus, Drummer, USMC (b. N.Y.).
(b) PORTER, David Dixon, Col., USMC.
(b) RUSH, John, F1c., USN.
STEWART, Peter, Gun Sgt., USMC (b. Scotland).
SUTTON, Clarence Edwin, Sgt., USMC (b. Va.).
(b) WAINWRIGHT, Richard, Jr., Lt., USN.

FLORIDA

Army-Air Force

(b) *BENNETT, Emory L., Pfc., 3d Inf. Div. (Cocoa).
*BOWEN, Hammett L., Jr., S/Sgt., 25th Inf. Div. (Jacksonville) (b. Georgia).
(b) *CUTINHA, Nicholas J., Spec. 4, 25th Inf. Div. (Fernandina Beach).
*FEMOYER, Robert E., 2d Lt., 711th Heavy Bombing Sq. (Jackson) (b. W. Va.).
McGUIRE, Thomas B., Jr., Maj., AC, 13th Air Force (MacDill Field) (b. N.J.).
(b) MILLS, James H., Pvt., 3d Inf. Div. (Fort Meade).
*NININGER, Alexander R., Jr., 2d Lt., 57th Inf., Phil. Scouts (Fort Lauderdale) (b. Ga.).
(b) *SIMS, Clifford Chester, S/Sgt., 101st Airborne Div. (Port St. Joe).
VARNUM, Charles A., Capt. 7th U.S. Cav. (Pensacola) (b. N.Y.).

Navy-Marine Corps

*CARTER, Bruce W., Pfc., 3d Mar. Div. (Jacksonville) (b. N.Y.)
(b) *CORRY, William Merrill, Jr., Lt. Comdr., USN (Quincy).
(b) *JENKINS, Robert H., Pfc., USMC (Interlachen).

NAVY-MARINE CORPS

(b)   LASSEN, Clyde Everett, Lt., USN (Fort Myers).
(b)   *LOPEZ, Baldomero, 1st Lt., USMC, 1st Marine Div. (Tampa).
      McCAMPBELL, David, Comdr., USN (b. Ala.).
(b)   *McTUREOUS, Robert Miller, Jr., Pvt., USMC (Altoona).
      *ORMSBEE, Francis Edward, Jr., CMM, USN (b. R.I.).
      *SMEDLEY, Larry Eugene, Cpl., USMC, 1st Mar. Div. (Orlando) (b. Va.).

GEORGIA

ARMY-AIR FORCE

(b)   BROWN, Bobbie E., Capt., 1st Inf. Div. (Atlanta).
(b)   CARTER, Mason, 1st Lt., 5th U.S. Inf. (Augusta).
      *DURHAM, Harold Bascom, Jr., 2d Lt., 1st Inf. Div. (Atlanta) (b. N.C.).
      GARLINGTON, Ernest A., 1st Lt., 7th U.S. Cav. (Athens) (b. S.C.).
(b)   JACKSON, Joe M., Lt. Col., USAF (Newnan).
(b)   *JOHNSTON, Donald R., Spec. 4, 1st Cav. Div. (Columbus).
(b)   LEE, Daniel L., 1st Lt., 117th Cav. Rec. Sq. (Alma).
      McCLEERY, Finnis D., Plat. Sgt., 198th Inf. Brig. Ameri. Div. (Fort Benning) (b.
      Tex.).
(b)   *McKIBBEN, Ray, Sgt., 17th Cav. (Felton).
(b)   McKINNEY, John R., Sgt., 33d Inf. Div. (Woodcliff).
(b)   RAY, Ronald Eric, Capt., 25th Inf. Div. (Cordelle).
(b)   *STORY, Luther H., Pfc., 2d Inf. Div. (Buena Vista).
(b)   *WILBANKS, Hilliard A., Capt., 21st Tact. Air Support Squadron (Cornelia).

NAVY-MARINE CORPS

(b)   DAVIS, Raymond G., Lt. Col., USMC, 1st Marine Div. (Atlanta).
(b)   *DAVIS, Rodney Maxwell, Sgt., USMC, 1st Mar. Div. (Macon).
(b)   *DYESS, Aquilla James, Lt. Col., USMCR (Augusta).
(b)   *ELROD, Henry Talmage, Capt., USMC (Ashburn).
(b)   LELAND, George W., GM, USN (Savannah).
(b)   LIVINGSTON, James E., Capt., USMC (McRae).
(b)   *PHILLIPS, Lee H., Cpl., USMC, 1st Marine Div. (Ben Hill).
(b)   PLESS, Stephen W., Maj., USMC, 1st Mar. Aircraft Wing (Newman).
(b)   *THOMASON, Clyde, Sgt., USMCR (Atlanta).

HAWAII

ARMY-AIR FORCE

(b)   *KAWAMURA, Terry Teruo, Cpl., 173d Airborne Brig. (Wahiawa).
(b)   *MENDONCA, LeRoy A., Sgt., 3d Inf. Div. (Honolulu).
(b)   *PILILAAU, Herbert K., Pfc., 2d Inf. Div. (Oahu).
(b)   *SMITH, Elmelindo R., P/Sgt., 8th Inf. Div. (Honolulu).
(b)   *YANO, Rodney J. T., Sgt., 11th Armd. Cav. Reg. (Kaelakekua, Kona).

IDAHO

ARMY-AIR FORCE

(b)   BLEAK, David B., Sgt., 40th Inf. Div. (Shelley).
(b)   BROSTROM, Leonard C., Pfc., 7th Inf. Div. (Preston).
      FISHER, Bernard Frances, Maj., 1st Air. Com. (Kuna) (b. Calif.).
(b)   NEIBAUR, Thomas C., Pvt., 42d Inf. Div. (Sugar City).
(b)   *SCHOONOVER, Dan D., Cpl., 7th Inf. Div. (Boise).
(b)   *VAN NOY, Junior, Pvt., Engr. Boat and Shore Regt. (Preston).

NAVY-MARINE CORPS

(b)   MYERS, Reginald R., Maj. USMC, 1st Marine Div. (Boise).
      *REASONER, Frank S., 1st Lt., USMC, 3d Marine Div. (Kellogg) (b. Wash.).

317

ILLINOIS

ARMY-AIR FORCE

(b)   ALLEN, Abner, P., Cpl., 39th Ill. Inf. (Bloomington).
ALLEX, Jake, Cpl., 33d Div. (Chicago) (b. Serbia, now Yugoslavia).
ANDERSON, Johannes S., 1st Sgt., 33d Div. (Chicago) (b. Finland).
AYERS, John G. K., Pvt., 8th Mo. Inf. (Pekin) (b. Mich.).
BAKER, JOHN F., Jr., Sgt., 25th Inf. Div. (Moline) (b. Iowa).
BANCROFT, Neil, Pvt., 7th U.S. Cav. (Chicago) (b. N.Y.).
(b)   BATSON, Matthew A., 1st Lt., 4th U.S. Cav. (Carbondale).
BENDER, Stanley, S/Sgt., 3d Inf. Div. (Chicago) (b. W. Va.).
(b)   BERG, George, Pvt., 17th U.S. Inf. (Mt. Erie).
(b)   BERTOLDO, Vito R., Sgt., 42d Inf. Div. (Decatur).
(b)   BICKFORD, Matthew, Cpl., 8th Mo. Inf. (Trivolia).
BLACK, John C., Lt. Col., 37th Ill. Inf. (Danville) (b. Miss.).
BLACK, William P., Capt., 37th Ill. Inf. (Danville) (b. Ky.).
*BLANCHFIELD, Michael R., Spec. 4, 173d Airb. Brig. (Wheeling) (b. Minn.).
(b)   BLODGETT, Welis H., 1st Lt., 37th Ill. Inf. (Chicago).
BOURKE, John G., Pvt., 15th Pa. Cav. (Chicago) (b. Pa.).
BOWEN, Emmer, Pvt., 127th Ill. Inf. (Hampshire) (b. N.Y.).
BURRITT, William W., Pvt., 113th Ill. Inf. (Chicago) (b. N.Y.).
CALLAHAN, John H., Pvt., 122d Ill. Inf. (Macoupin County) (b. Ky.).
CAPRON, Horace, Jr., Sgt., 8th Ill. Cav. (b. Md.).
(b)   CHOATE, Clyde L., S/Sgt., 601st T. D. Bn. (Anna).
CHURCHILL, Samuel J., Cpl., 2d Ill. Light Arty. (De Kalb County) (b. Vt.).
COLBY, Carlos W., Sgt., 97th Ill. Inf. (Madison County). (b. N.H.).
COOK, John H., Sgt., 119 Ill. Inf. (Quincy) (b. England).
COX, Robert M., Cpl., 55th Ill. Inf. (Prairie City) (b. Ohio).
CREED, John, Pvt., 23rd Ill. Inf. (Chicago) (b. Ireland).
CUNNINGHAM, James S., Pvt., 8th Mo. Inf. (Bloomington) (b. Pa.).
CUTTS, James M., Capt., 11th U.S. Inf. (b. D.C.).
(b)   DANIELS, James T., Sgt., 4th U.S. Cav. (Richland County).
DARROUGH, John S., Sgt., 113th Ill. Inf. (Concord) (b. Ky.).
(b)   DAVIS, Martin K., Sgt., 116th Ill. Inf. (Stonington).
DICKIE, David, Sgt., 97th Ill. Inf. (Gillespie) (b. Scotland).
(b)   DUNHAM, Russell E., T/Sgt., 3d Inf. Div. (Brighton).
DUNNE, James, Cpl., Chicago Mercantile Btry., Ill. Light Arty. (Chicago) (b. Mich.).
ELLIS, Michael B., Sgt., 1st Div. (East St. Louis) (b. Mo.).
FARQUHAR, John M., Sgt. Maj., 89th Ill. Inf. (Chicago) (b. Scotland).
FISHER, John H., 1st Lt., 55th Ill. Inf. (Chicago) (b. Pa.).
FOX, Henry, Sgt. 106th Ill. Inf. (Lincoln) (b. Germany).
FRASER (FRAZIER), William W., Pvt., 97th Ill. Inf. (Alton) (b. Scotland).
FREEMEYER, Christopher, Pvt., 5th U.S. Inf. (Chicago) (b. Germany).
GAGE, Richard J., Pvt., 104th Ill. Inf. (Ottawa) (b. N.H.).
(b)   GARMAN, Harold A., Pvt., 5th Inf. Div. (Albion).
(b)   GERSTUNG, Robert E., T/Sgt., 79th Inf. Div. (Chicago).
GESCHWIND, Nicholas, Capt., 116th Ill. Inf. (Pleasant Hill) (b. France).
*GIBSON, Eric G., T5, 3d Inf. Div. (Chicago) (b. Sweden).
(b)   *GOETTLER, Harold Ernest, 1st. Lt., 50th Aero Sq., Air Serv. (Chicago).
GOLDIN, Theodore, Pvt., 7th U.S. Cav. (Chicago) (b. Wis.).
(b)   GOLDSBERY, Andrew E., Pvt., 127th Ill. Inf. (St. Charles).
(b)   GOULD, Newton T., Pvt., 113th Ill. Inf. (Elk Grove Village).
GUMPERTZ, Sydney G., 1st Sgt., 33d Div. (Chicago) (b. Calif.).
(b)   HALL, John, Pvt., 8th U.S. Cav. (Logan County).
*HAMMOND, Lester, Jr., Cpl., Cmbt. Team (Quincy) (b. Mo.).
HANEY, Milton L., Chaplain, 55th Ill. Inf. (Bushnell) (b. Ohio).
HAPEMAN, Douglas, Lt. Col., 104th Ill. Inf. (Ottawa) (b. N.Y.).
*HARDENBERGH, Henry M., Pvt., 39th Ill. Inf. (Bremen) (b. Ind.).
*HARVEY, Carmel Bernon, Jr., Spec. 4, 5th Cav. Div. (Chicago) (b. W. Va.).
HENRY, James, Sgt., 113th Ill. Inf. (Kankakee) (b. Ohio).
HIGGINS, Thomas J., Sgt., 99th Ill. Inf. (Barry) (b. Canada).
HIGHLAND, Patrick, Cpl., 23d Ill. Inf. (Chicago) (b. Ireland).
(b)   HILL, Ralyn M., Cpl., 129th Inf., 33d Div. (Oregon).
(b)   HOBDAY, George, Pvt., 7th U.S. Cav. (Pulaski County).

ILLINOIS—Continued

HOLLAND, Lemuel F., Cpl., 104th Ill. Inf. (La Salle County) (b. Ohio).
HOUGHTON, George L., Pvt., 104th Ill. Inf. (Brookfield) (b. Canada).
HOWE, Orion P., Mus., 55th Ill. Inf. (Waukegan) (b. Ohio).
HYATT, Theodore, 1st Sgt., 127th Ill. Inf. (Gardner) (b. Pa.).
HYDE, Henry J., Sgt., 1st U.S. Cav. (Princeton) (b. Maine).
HYMER, Samuel, Capt., 115th Ill. Inf. (Rushville) (b. Ind.).
JOHNS (JONES), Elisha, Cpl., 113th Ill. Inf. (Martintonk) (b. Ohio).
JOHNSON, Andrew, Pvt., 116th Ill. Inf. (Assumption) (b. Ohio).
JOHNSON, Harold I., Pfc., 356th Inf., 89th Div. (Chicago) (b. Kans.).
JOHNSTON, David, Pvt., 8th Mo. Inf. (Warshaw County) (b. Pa.).
JOSSELYN, Simeon T., 1st Lt., 13th Ill. Inf. (Amboy) (b. N.Y.).
(b) KAYS, Kenneth M., Pfc., 101st Airborne Div. (Fairfield).
(b) KELLER, Leonard B., Sgt., 9th Inf. Div. (Rockford).
KELLEY, Leverett M., Sgt., 36th Ill. Inf. (Rutland) (b. N.Y.).
†KELLY, John Joseph, Pvt., 2d Div., USMC (Chicago). (Also awarded Navy Medal of Honor.)
(b) KELLY, John J. H., Cpl., 5th U.S. Inf. (Schuyler County).
KLOTH, Charles H., Pvt., Ill. Light Arty. (Chicago) (b. Europe).
(b) KNIGHT, Joseph F., Sgt., 6th U.S. Cav. (Danville).
KRETSINGER, George, Pvt., Chicago Mercantile Btry., Ill. Light Arty. (Chicago) (b. N.Y.).
(b) *KROTIAK, Anthony L., Pfc., 37th Inf. Div. (Chicago).
(b) *KRYZOWSKI, Edward C., Capt., 2d Inf. Div. (Cicero).
LABILL, Joseph S., Pvt., 6th Mo. Inf. (Vandalia) (b. France).
LARRABEE, James W., Cpl., 55th Ill. Inf. (Mendota) (b. N.Y.).
LOMAN, Berger, Pvt., 33d Div. (Chicago) (b. Norway).
(b) LOWER, Robert A., Pvt., 55th Ill. Inf. (Elmwood).
(b) LUCAS, George W., Pvt., 3d Mo. Cav. (Mt. Sterling).
(b) LYNCH, Allen James, Sgt., 1st Cav. Div. (Airmobile) (Chicago).
(b) MARSH, George, Sgt., 104th Ill. Inf. (Brookfield).
(b) McCLERNAND, Edward J., 2d Lt., 2d U.S. Cav. (Springfield).
McCONNELL, Samuel, Capt., 119th Ill. Inf. (Bushnell) (b. Ohio).
(b) McCORNACK, Andrew, Pvt., 127th Ill. Inf. (Rutland).
McDONALD, John Wade, Pvt., 20th Ill. Inf. (Wayneville) (b. Ohio)
McGRAW, Thomas, Sgt., 23d Ill. Inf. (Chicago) (b. Ireland).
McGUIRE, Patrick, Pvt., Ill. Light Arty. (Chicago) (b. Ireland).
(b) McKEEN, Nineveh S., 1st Lt., 21st Ill. Inf. (Marshall).
MERRIFIELD, James K., Cpl., 88th Ill. Inf. (Manlius) (b. Pa.).
(b) MICHAEL, Edward S., 1st Lt., AC (Chicago).
MILLER, Henry A., Capt., 8th Ill. Inf. (Decatur) (b. Germany).
MILLER, Jacob C., Pvt., 113th Ill. Inf. (Geneva) (b. Ohio).
(b) *MONROE, James H., Pfc., 1st Cav. Div. (Wheaton).
(b) MOORE, Wilburen F., Pvt., 117th Ill. Inf. (Lebanon).
MORELOCK, Sterling, Pvt., 1st Div. (Oquawka) (b. Md.).
MORFORD, Jerome, Pvt., 55th Ill. Inf. (Bridgers Corner) (b. Pa.).
(b) *MOSKALA, Edward J., Pfc., 96th Inf. Div. (Chicago).
(b) MURPHY, Robinson B., Mus., 127th Ill. Inf. (Oswego).
MURPHY, Thomas C., Cpl., 31st Ill. Inf. (Pekin) (b. Ireland).
(b) NEWMAN, Marcellus J., Pvt., 111th Ill. Inf. (Richview).
O'DEA, John, Pvt., 8th Mo. Inf. (Clinton) (b. Ireland).
O'DONNELL, Menomen, 1st Lt., 11th Mo. Inf. (b. Ireland).
(b) OGDEN, Carlos C., 1st Lt., 79th Inf. Div. (Fairmount).
(b) *OLIVE, Milton L., III, Pfc., 173d Airborne Brig. (Chicago).
PALMER, George H., Mus., 1st Ill. Cav. (b. N.Y.).
PARKS. James W., Cpl., 11th Mo. Inf. (Xenia) (b. Ohio).
PAYNE, Thomas H. L., 1st Lt., 37th Ill. Inf. (Mendota) (b. Mass.).
PENTZER, Patrick H., Capt., 97th Ill. Inf. (Gillespie) (b. Mo.).
PEREZ, Manuel, Jr., 11th Airborne Div. (Chicago) (b. Okla.).
PIKE, Edward M., 1st Sgt., 33d Ill. Inf. (Bloomington) (b. Maine).
(b) POPE, Thomas A., Cpl., 33d Div. (Chicago).
POST, Philip Sidney, Col., 59th Ill. Inf. (Galesburg) (b. N.Y.).
POWERS, Wesley J., Cpl., 147th Ill. Inf. (Virgil) (b. Canada).

319

ARMY-AIR FORCE

PUTNAM, Winthrop D., Cpl., 77th Ill. Inf. (Peoria) (b. Mass.).
(b) REBMANN, George F., Sgt., 119th Ill. Inf. (Browning).
REED, William, Pvt., 8th Mo. Inf. (Pekin) (b. Pa.).
(b) *ROBINSON, James W., Sgt., 1st Inf. Div. (Hinsdale).
RUNDLE, Charles W., Pvt., 116th Ill. Inf. (Oakley) (b. Ohio).
(b) SANFORD, Jacob, Pvt., 55th Ill. Inf. (Prairie City).
SCHENCK, Benjamin W., Pvt., 116th Ill. Inf. (Maroa) (b. Ohio).
SCHOFIELD, John M., Maj., 1st Mo. Inf. (Freeport) (b. N.Y.).
(b) SCHROEDER, Henry F., Sgt., 16th U.S. Inf. (Chicago).
*SEBILLE, Louis J., USAF (Chicago) (b. Mich.).
SHAPLAND, John, Pvt., 104th Ill. Inf. (Ottawa) (b. England).
(b) SIMMONS, William T., Lt., 11th Mo. Inf. (Green County).
SLAGLE, Oscar, Pvt., 104th Ill. Inf. (Manlius) (b. Ohio).
SMALLEY, Reuben S., Pvt., 104th Ill. Inf. (Brookfield) (b. Pa.).
(b) SPALDING, Edward B., Sgt., 52d Ill. Inf. (Rockford).
SPRAGUE, Benona, Cpl., 116th Ill. Inf. (Chencys Grove) (b. N.Y.).
STEPHENS, William G., Pvt., Ill. Light Arty. (Chicago) (b. N.Y.).
STOCKMAN, George H., 1st Lt., 6th Mo. Inf. (Chicago) (b. Germany).
STOKES, George, Pvt., 122d Ill. Inf. (Jerseyville) (b. England).
SUMNER, James, Pvt., 1st U.S. Cav. (Chicago) (b. England).
(b) TAYLOR, Henry H., Sgt., 45th Ill. Inf. (Galena).
TOOMER, William, Sgt., 127th Ill. Inf. (Chicago) (b. Ireland).
(b) *TRUEMPER, Walter E., 2d Lt., 8th AF (Caurora).
(b) VERNAY, James D., 2d Lt., 11th Ill. Inf. (Lacon).
(b) VOKES, Leroy H., 1st Sgt., 3d U.S. Cav. (Lake County).
WARD, Thomas J., Pvt., 116th Ill. Inf. (Macon County) (b. W. Va.).
(b) WARDEN, John, Cpl., 55th Ill. Inf. (Lemont).
WEBBER, Alason P., Mus., 86th Ill. Inf. (b. N.Y.).
WHEATON, Loyd, Lt. Col., 8th Ill. Inf. (b. Mich.).
WHITE, Patrick H., Capt., Chicago Mercantile Btry., Ill. Light Arty. (Chicago) (b. Ireland).
(b) WHITMORE, John, Pvt., 119th Ill. Inf. (Camden).
(b) *WICKAM, Jerry Wayne, Cpl., 11th Arm. Cav. Reg. (Leaf River).
(b) WIDICK, Andrew J., Pvt., 116th Ill. Inf. (Decatur).
WILLIAMS, Ellwood N., Pvt., 28th Ill. Inf. (Havanna) (b. Pa.).
(b) WILSON, Arthur H., 2d Lt., 6th U.S. Cav. (Springfield).
(b) WILSON, Charles, Cpl., 5th U.S. Inf. (Beardstown).
WOOD, Richard H., Capt., 97th Ill. Inf. (Woodburn) (b. N.J.).

NAVY-MARINE CORPS

ASTEN, Charles, Quarter Gunner, USN (b. Nova Scotia).
*BAILEY, Kenneth D., Maj., USMC (Danville) (b. Okla.).
(b) *BIGELOW, Elmer Charles, WT1c., USNR (Hebron).
*BRUCE, Daniel D., Pfc., USMC, 1st Marine Div. (Chicago) (b. Ind.).
(b) *BURKE, Robert C., Pfc., USMC (Monticello).
(b) CATHERWOOD, John, Ordinary Seaman, USN (Springfield).
(b) COURTNEY, Henry C., Seaman, USN (Springfield).
(b) *CROMWELL, John Philip, Capt., USN (Henry).
(b) CRONAN, Willie, BM, USN (Chicago).
*DE LA GARZA, Emilio A., Jr., Cpl., USMC, 1st Marine Div. (Chicago) (b. Ind.).
DOW, Henry, BM, USN (b. Scotland).
(b) DUNLAP, Robert Hugo, Capt., USMCR (Abingdon).
(b) *FARDY, John Peter, Cpl., USMC (Chicago).
FERRELL, John H., Pilot, USN (b. Tenn.).
FLUCKEY, Eugene Bennett, Comdr., USN (b. D.C.).
GRBITCH, Rade, Seaman, USN (b. Austria).
(b) HELMS, John Henry, Sgt., USMC (Chicago).
HOLYOKE, William E., BM1c., USN (b. N.H.).
(b) HULL, James L., F1c., USN (Patoka).
HYLAND, John, Seaman, USN (b. Ireland).
IZAC, Edouard Victor Michel, Lt., USN. (b. Iowa).

ILLINOIS—Continued

NAVY-MARINE CORPS

(b) JOHNSTON, William P., Landsman, USN (Chicago).
(b) †KELLY, John Joseph, Pvt., USMC (Chicago). (Also awarded Army Medal of Honor.)
(b) LEIMS, John Harold, 2d Lt., USMCR (Chicago).
(b) *LESTER, Fred Faulkner, HA1c., USN (Downers Grove).
(b) McCARTHY, Joseph Jeremiah, Capt., USMCR·(Chicago).
      McCORMICK, Michael, BM, USN (b. Ireland).
      MEYER, William, CM, USN (b. Germany).
(b) MOLLOY, Hugh, Ordinary Seaman, USN (b. Ireland).
(b) MULLIN, Hugh P., Seaman, USN (Richmond).
(b) *OSBORNE, Weedon E., Lt. (jg.), Dental Corps, USN (Chicago).
(b) *OZBOURN, Joseph William, Pvt., USMC (Herrin).
      ROBERTS, Charles Church, MM1c., USN (b. Mass.).
      ROBINSON, Robert Guy, Gun. Sgt., USMC (b. N.Y.).
(b) SCHILT, Christian Frank, 1st Lt., USMC (Richland County).
(b) STOCKDALE, James B., Rear Adm., USN (Abingdon).
      UPHAM, Oscar J., Pvt., USMC (b. Ohio).
(b) *WEBER, Lester W., L/Cpl., USMC (Hinsdale).
(b) WILLIAMS, Ernest Calvin, 1st Lt., USMC (Broadwell).
(b) *WILSON, Robert Lee, Pfc., USMC (Centralia).
(b) *WITEK, Frank Peter, Pfc., USMCR (b. Conn.).

INDIANA

ARMY-AIR FORCE

(b) ANDERSON, Marion T., Capt., 51st Ind. Inf. (Kokomo).
      ARCHER, James W., 1st Lt. and Adj., 59th Ind. Inf. (Spencer) (b. Ill.).
(b) ARMSTRONG, Clinton L., Pvt., 83d Ind. Inf. (Franklin).
      BANKS, George L., Sgt., 15th Ind. Inf. (Allen County).
(b) BIDDLE, Melvin E., Pfc., 517th Para. Inf. Rgt. (Anderson).
(b) BIEGLER, George W., Capt., 28th Inf., U.S. Vol. (Terre Haute).
(b) BLASDEL, Thomas A., Pvt., 83d Ind. Inf. (Guilford).
      BOX, Thomas J., Capt., 27th Ind. Inf. (Bedford).
      BROUSE, Charles W., Capt., 100th Ind. Inf. (Indianapolis).
      BROWN, Lorenzo D., Pvt., 7th U.S. Inf. (Indianapolis) (b. N.C.).
(b) BRUNER, Louis J., Pvt., 5th Ind. Cav. (Clifty Brumer).
(b) BUCKLES, Abram J., Sgt., 18th Ind. Inf. (Muncie).
(b) CHAMBERLAIN, Orville T., 2d Lt., 74th Ind. Inf. (Elkhart).
(b) CHISMAN, William W., Pvt., 83d Ind. Inf. (Wilmington).
(b) CONAWAY, John W., Pvt., 83d Ind. Inf. (Hartford).
(b) CUMMINS, Andrew J., Sgt., 10th U.S. Inf. (Alexandria).
      DAVIS, John, Pvt., 17th Ind. Mtd. Inf. (Indianapolis) (b. Ky.).
      DAVIS, Sammy L., Sgt., 9th Inf. Div. (Martinsville) (b. Ohio).
      DOUGALL, Allan H., 1st Lt. and Adj., 88th Ind. Inf. (New Haven) (b. Scotland).
(b) EVANS, Coron D., Pvt., 3d Ind. Cav. (Jefferson County).
(b) FERRIER, Daniel T., Sgt., 2d Ind. Cav. (Delphi).
      FOUT, Frederick W., 2d Lt., 15th Btry., Ind. Light Arty. (Indianapolis) (b. Germany).
      FRANTZ, Joseph, Pvt., 83d Ind. Inf. (Osgood) (b. France).
      GRAHAM, Thomas N., 2d Lt., 15th Ind. Inf. (Westville).
(b) GRAVES, Thomas J., Pvt., 17th U.S. Inf. (Millville).
(b) GREEN, Francis C., Sgt., 8th U.S. Cav. (Mt. Vernon).
(b) HELMS, David H., Pvt., 83d Ind. Inf. (Farmers Retreat).
      HOLMES, William T., Pvt., 3d Ind. Cav. (Indianapolis) (b. Ill.).
(b) HORNADAY, Simpson, Pvt., 6th U.S. Cav. (Hendricks County).
(b) HOUGH, Ira, Pvt., 8th Ind. Inf. (Henry County).
      HUDSON, Aaron R., Pvt., 17th Ind. Mtd. Inf. (La Porte County) (b. Ky.).
      JOHNSON, Ruel M., Maj., 100th Ind. Inf. (Goshen).
      JORDAN, Absalom, Cpl., 3d Ind. Cav. (North Madison) (b. Ohio).
(b) KENDALL, William W., 1st Sgt., 49th Ind. Inf. (Dubois County).
      KISTERS, Gerry H., 2d Lt., 2d Armd. Div. (Bloomington) (b. Utah).

321

ARMY-AIR FORCE

KUDER, Jeremiah, Lt., 74th Ind. Inf. (Warsaw) (b. Ohio).
LAWTON, Henry W., Capt., 30th Ind. Inf. (Ft. Wayne) (b. Ohio).
(b)　LYTTON, Jeptha L., Cpl., 23d U.S. Inf. (Lawrence County).
McCALL, Thomas E., S/Sgt., 36th Inf. Div. (Veedersburg) (b. Kans.).
(b)　*McGEE, William D., Pvt., 76th Inf. Div. (Indianapolis).
(b)　*MICHAEL, Harry J., 2d Lt., 80th Inf. Div. (Milford).
(b)　NOLAN, Joseph A., Artificer, 45th Inf., U.S. Vol. (South Bend).
(b)　OPEL, John N., Pvt., 7th Ind. Inf. (Decatur County).
(b)　OVERTURF, Jacob H., Pvt., 83d Ind. Inf. (Holton).
ROOD, Oliver P., Pvt., 20th Ind. Inf. (Terre Haute) (b. Ky.).
(b)　RUSSELL, Milton, Capt., 51st Ind. Inf. (North Salem).
RYAN, Peter J., Pvt., 11th Ind. Inf. (Terre Haute) (b. Ireland).
(b)　*SESTON, Charles H., Sgt., 11th Ind. Inf. (New Albany).
(b)　SHEPHERD, William, Pvt., 3d Ind. Cav. (Dillsboro).
SMALLEY, Reuben, Pvt., 83d Ind. Inf. (Poston) (b. N.Y.).
STEINMETZ, William, Pvt., 83d Ind. Inf. (Sunmans) (b. Ky.).
STERLING, John T., Pvt., 11th Ind. Inf. (Marion County) (b. Ill.).
(b)　STOLTZ, Frank, Pvt., 83d Ind. Inf. (Sunmans).
(b)　SUTHERLAND, John A., Cpl., 8th U.S. Cav. (Montgomery County).
TAYLOR, Richard, Pvt., 18th Ind. Inf. (Martin County) (b. Ala.).
THOMPSON, William P., Sgt., 20th Ind. Inf. (Tippecanoe County) (b. N.Y.).
(b)　WALKER, Allen, Pvt., 3d U.S. Cav. (Patriot).
(b)　WEISS, Enoch R., Pvt., 1st U.S. Cav. (Kosciusko County).
(b)　*WETHERBY, John C., Pvt., 4th U.S. Inf. (Martinsville).
(b)　WHITEHEAD, John M., Chaplain, 15th Ind. Inf. (Westville).
(b)　WOODFILL, Samuel, 1st Lt., 5th Div. (Bryantsburg).
(b)　YOUNT, John P., Pvt., 3d U.S. Cav. (Putnam County).

NAVY-MARINE CORPS

(b)　*ABRELL, Charles G., Cpl., USMC, First Marine Div. (Terre Haute).
(b)　ANTRIM, Richard Nott, Comdr., USN (Peru).
BADDERS, William, C.M.M., USN (Indianapolis) (b. Ill.).
(b)　BEARSS, Hiram Iddings, Col., USMC (Peru).
(b)　BUCHANAN, Allen, Lt. Comdr., USN (Evansville).
(b)　CAMPBELL, William, BM, USN.
DITZENBACK, John, Quartermaster, USN (b. N.Y.).
(b)　HILL, Frank E., SC1c., USN (La Grange).
(b)　INGRAM, Jonas Howard, Lt. (jg.), USN (Jeffersonville).
(b)　*SCOTT, Norman, Rear Adm., USN (Indianapolis).
(b)　SHOUP, David Monroe, Col., USMC (Tippacanoe).
(b)　WILKES, Perry, Pilot, USN.
*WINDRICH, William G., S/Sgt., USMC, 1st Marine Div. (Hammond) (b. Ill.).

IOWA

ARMY-AIR FORCE

BEBB, Edward J., Pvt., 4th Iowa Cav. (Henry County) (b. Ohio).
(b)　BEYER, Arthur O., Cpl., 603d T.D. Bn. (St. Ansgar).
BIRDSALL, Horatio L., Sgt., 3d Iowa Cav. (Keokuk) (b. N.Y.).
BIRKHIMER, William E., Capt., 3d U.S. Arty. (b. Ohio).
BOQUET, Nicholas, Pvt., 1st Iowa Inf. (Burlington) (b. Germany).
(b)　BRAS, Edgar A., Sgt., 8th Iowa Inf. (Louisa County).
(b)　BRILES, Herschel F., S/Sgt., 899th Tank Destroyer Battalion (Fort Des Moines).
(b)　*CHRISTENSEN, Dale Eldon, 2d Lt., 112th Cav. Regt. (Gray).
COSGRIFF, Richard H., Pvt., 4th Iowa Cav. (Wapello) (b. N.Y.).
(b)　DAY, George E., Col., USAF. (Sioux City).
(b)　DETHLEFSEN, Merlyn Hans, Maj., U.S. Air Force (Greenville).
DUNLAVY, James, Pvt., 3d Iowa Cav. (Davis County) (b. Ind.).
(b)　*EDWARDS, Junior D., Sfc., 2d Inf. Div. (Indianaola).
ELSON, James M., Sgt., 9th Iowa Inf. (Shellsburg) (b. Ohio).
FANNING, Nicholas, Pvt., 4th Iowa Cav. (Independence) (b. Ind.).

IOWA—Continued

GODLEY, Leonidas M., 1st Sgt., 22d Iowa Inf. (Ashland) (b. W. Va.).
HAYS, John H., Pvt., 4th Iowa Cav. (Oskaloosa) (b. Ohio).
(b) HEALEY, George W., Pvt., 5th Iowa Cav. (Dubuque).
HERINGTON, Pitt B., Pvt., 11th Iowa Inf. (Tipton) (b. Mich.).
*HIBBS, Robert John, 2d Lt., 1st Inf. Div. (Des Moines) (b. Nebr.).
HILL, James, 1st Lt., 21st Iowa Inf. (Cascade) (b. England).
KALTENBACH, Luther, Cpl., 12th Iowa Inf. (Honey Creek). (b. Germany).
(b) KNOX, John W., Sgt., 5th U.S. Inf. (Burlington).
(b) *LINDSEY, Darrell R., Capt., Air Corps (Storm Lake).
MAY, William, Pvt., 32d Iowa Inf. (Maysville) (b. Pa.).
MAYES, William B., Pvt., 11th Iowa Inf. (De Witt) (b. Ohio).
MILLER, James P., Pvt., 4th Iowa Cav. (Henry County) (b. Ohio).
MORGAN, Richard H., Cpl., 4th Iowa Cav. (Taylor) (b. Ind.).
(b) NEPPEL, Ralph G., Sgt., 83d Inf. Div. (Glidden).
(b) *PIKE, Emory J., Lt. Col., 82d Div. (Des Moines).
POWER, Albert, Pvt., 3d Iowa Cav. (Davis County) (b. Ohio).
SLOAN, Andrew J., Pvt., 12th Iowa Inf. (Colesburg) (b. Pa.).
SMITH, Henry I., 1st Lt., 7th Iowa Inf. (Shell Rock Hall) (b. England).
(b) STANLEY, Eben, Pvt., 5th U.S. Cav. (Decatur County).
STRAUB, Paul F., Surg., 36th Inf., U.S. Vol. (b. Germany).
SWAN, Charles A., Pvt., 4th Iowa Cav. (Mt. Pleasant) (b. Pa.).
(b) *THORSON, John F., Pfc., 7th Inf. Div. (Armstrong).
TIBBETS, Andrew W., Pvt., 3d Iowa Cav. (Appanoose County) (b. Ind.).
(b) TITUS, Calvin Pearl, Mus., 14th U.S. Inf. (Vinton).
(b) TWOMBLY, Voltaire P., Cpl., 2d Iowa Inf. (Keosauqua).
(b) WELCH, George W., Pvt., 11th Mo. Inf. (Keokuk).
WILLIAMSON, James A., Col., 4th Iowa Inf. (Des Moines) (b. Ky.).
YOUNG, Calvary M., Sgt., 3d Iowa Cav. (Hopeville) (b. Iowa).

(b) DEIGNAN, Osborn, Cox., USN (Sheart).
FITZ, Joseph, Ordinary Seaman, USN (b. Austria).
(b) FLETCHER, Frank Friday, Rear Adm., USN (Oskaloosa).
(b) FLETCHER, Frank Jack, Lt., USN (Marshalltown).
(b) HOWARD, Jimmie E., Gunnery Sgt., 1st Marine Div. (Burlington).
(b) PIERCE, Francis J., PhM1c., USN (Earlville).

KANSAS

(b) ADAMS, Stanley T., M/Sgt., 24th Inf. Div. (Olathe).
(b) *BLECKLEY, Erwin R., 2d Lt., 130th Field Arty., Obs., 50th Aero Sq., A. S.
(Wichita).
*COWAN, Richard Eller, Pfc., 2d Inf. Div. (Wichita) (b. Nebr.).
(b) EHLERS, Walter D., S/Sgt., 1st Inf. Div. (Manhattan).
(b) FERGUSON, Arthur M., 1st Lt., 36th Inf., U.S. Vol. (Burlington).
FUNSTON, Frederick, Col., 20th Kans. Vol. Inf. (Iola) (b. Ohio).
(h) HENDERSON, Joseph, Sgt., 6th U.S. Cav. (Leavenworth).
HUNTSMAN, John A., Sgt., 36th Inf., U.S. Vol. (Lawrence) (b. Iowa).
JOHNSON, Leon W., Col., 9th Air Force (Moline) (b. Mo.).
*PEDEN, Forrest E., T5g., 3d Inf. Div. (Walthena) (b. Mo.).
*PITTS, Riley L., Capt., 25th Inf. Div. (Wichita) (b. Okla.).
(b) ROBB, George S., 1st Lt., 93d Div. (Salina).
(b) TREMBLEY, William B., Pvt., 20th Kans. Vol. Inf. (Kansas City).
(b) WHITE, Edward, Pvt., 20th Kans. Vol. Inf. (Kansas City).

(b) *DAVENPORT, Jack A., Cpl., USMC, 1st Marine Div. (Mission).
(b) FOSTER, Paul Frederick, Ens., USN (Wichita).
(b) *TIMMERMAN, Grant Frederick, Sgt., USMC (Americus).

KENTUCKY

ARMY-AIR FORCE

(b) BELL, J. Franklin, Col., 36th Inf., U.S. Vol. (Shelbyville).
(b) *COLLIER, John W., Cpl., 25th Inf. Div. (Worthington).
(b) *CRAIN, Morris E., T/Sgt., 36th Inf. Div. (Paducah).
(b) CRUSE, Thomas, 2d Lt., 6th U.S. Cav. (Owensboro).
(b) DAY, William L., 1st Sgt., 5th U.S. Cav. (Barron County).
(b) DODD, Carl H., 1st Lt., 24th Inf. Div. (Kenvir).
(b) HARDAWAY, Benjamin F., 1st Lt., 17th U.S. Inf. (Benleyville).
(b) HARRIS, William M., Pvt., 7th U.S. Cav. (Madison County).
     HAWTHORNE, Harry L., 2d Lt., 2d U.S. Arty. (b. Minn.).
(b) HORSFALL, William H., Drummer, 1st Ky. Inf. (Campbell County).
     HUGHES, Oliver, Cpl., 12th Ky. Inf. (Albany) (b. Tenn.).
     JONES, William H., Farrier, 2d U.S. Cav. (Louisville) (b. N.C.).
(b) KERR, John B., Capt., 6th U.S. Cav. (Hutchison Station).
     *LONG, Donald Russell, Sgt., 1st Inf. Div. (Ashland) (b. Ohio).
(b) MATTINGLY, Henry B., Pvt., 10th Ky. Inf. (Marion County).
(b) McDONALD, Franklin M., Pvt., 11th U.S. Inf. (Bowling Green).
     McGINTY, John J., III, 2d Lt., 3d Mar. Div. (Louisville) (b. Mass.).
(b) *NASH, David P., Pfc., 9th Inf. Div. (Whitesville).
(b) NASH, James J., Pvt., 10th U.S. Inf. (Louisville).
     PHOENIX, Edwin, Cpl., 4th U.S. Cav. (b. Mo.).
(b) ROSS, Wilburn, K., Pvt., 3d Inf. Div. (Strunk).
(b) SANDLIN, Willie, Sgt., 33d Div. (Hyden).
(b) SCOTT, George D., Pvt., 7th U.S. Cav. (Mt. Vernon).
(b) SHAW, Thomas, Sgt., 9th U.S. Cav. (Covington).
(b) *SMITH, David M., Pfc., 2d Inf. Div. (Livingston).
(b) SPURRIER, Junior J., S/Sgt., 35th Inf. Div. (Riggs).
(b) *SQUIRES, John C., Sgt., 3d Inf. Div. (Louisville).
     *STEWART, Jimmy G., S/Sgt., 1st Cav. Div. (Ashland) (b. W. Va.).
(b) STIVERS, Thomas W., Pvt., 7th U.S. Cav. (Madison County).
(b) SULLIVAN, Thomas, Pvt., 1st U.S. Cav. (Covington).
     WALKER, Dr. Mary E., Contract Acting Assistant Surgeon, U.S. Army
        (Louisville) (b. N.Y.).
(b) WEST, Ernest E., Pfc., 25th Inf. Div. (Wurtland).
(b) WESTON, John F., Maj., 4th Ky. Cav.
(b) WOODS, Brent, Sgt., 9th U.S. Cav. (Louisville).

NAVY-MARINE CORPS

(b) BARBER, William E., Capt., USMC, 1st Marine Div. (West Liberty).
     BOERS, Edward William, Seaman USN (b. Ohio).
(b) BUSH, Richard Earl, Cpl., USMCR (Glasgow).
(b) CLARY, Edward Alvin, WT, USN (Foxport).
(b) HOLT, George, Quarter Gunner, USN.
(b) NOBLE, Daniel, Landsman, USN.
(b) *PHELPS, Wesley, Pfc., USMCR (Neafus).
(b) SKAGGS, Luther, Jr., Pfc., USMC (Henderson).

LOUISIANA

ARMY-AIR FORCE

(b) ANDERSON, Charles W., Pvt., 1st N.Y. (Lincoln) Cav.
     BEAUFORT, Jean J., Cpl., 2d La. Inf. (New Orleans) (b. France).
     *BENNETT, Steven L., Capt., 20th Tac. Air Sup. Sqr. (Lafayette) (b. Tex.).
(b) *FOURNET, Douglas B., 1st Lt., 1st Cav. Div. (Airmobile) (Lake Charles).
     GREELY, Adolphus W., Maj. Gen., U.S. Army, retired (b. Mass.).
(b) HUNT, Fred O., Pvt., 5th U.S. Inf. (New Orleans).
(b) *JOHNSON, Leroy, Sgt., 32d Inf. Div. (Oakdale).
     KANE, John R., Col., A.C. (Shreveport) (b. Tex.).
     NOVOSEL, Michael J., Chief War. Off., 68th Medical Group, (Kenner) (b. Pa.).
(b) ROACH, Hampton M., Cpl., 5th U.S. Cav. (Concord).
(b) SCHOWALTER, Edward R., Jr., 1st Lt., 7th Inf. Div. (Metairie).
(b) STANCE, Emanuel, Sgt., 9th U.S. Cav. (Carroll Parish).

ARMY-AIR FORCE

(b)   WHITTINGTON, Hulon B., Sgt., 2d Armd. Div. (Bastrop).
(b)   WILLIAMS, Moses, 1st Sgt., 9th U.S. Cav. (Carrollton, La.).
(b)   WISE, Homer L., S/Sgt., 36th Inf. Div. (Baton Rouge).

NAVY-MARINE CORPS

(b)   *CLAUSEN, Raymond M., Pfc., 1st Mar. Aircraft Wing (New Orleans).
(b)   DE BLANC, Jefferson Joseph, 1st Lt., USMCR (Lockport).
      FREEMAN, Martin, Pilot, USN (b. Germany).
      *GILMORE, Howard Walter, Comd., USN (b. Ala.).
(b)   OSBORNE, John, Seaman, USN (New Orleans).
(b)   RYAN, Thomas John, Ensign, USN (New Orleans).
(b)   †WEISBOGEL, Albert, Captain of the Mizzen Top, USN (New Orleans).
      WILKINSON, Theodore Stark, Ens., USN (b. Md.).
(b)   WILLIAMS, John, Captain of Maintop, USN (New Orleans).

MAINE
ARMY-AIR FORCE

(b)   AMES, Adelbert, 1st Lt., 5th U.S. Arty. (Rockland).
(b)   BAILEY, James E., Sgt., 5th U.S. Cav. (Dexter).
(b)   BELCHER, Thomas, Pvt., 9th Maine Inf. (Bangor).
(b)   BLISS, Zenas R., Col., 7th R.I. Inf. (Johnston).
(b)   BOWMAN, Alonzo, Sgt., 6th U.S. Cav. (Washington Township).
(b)   *BUKER, Brian Leroy, Sgt., 1st Spec. Forces (Benton).
(b)   CHAMBERLAIN, Joshua L., Col., 20th Maine Inf. (Brunswick).
(b)   CHASE, John F., Pvt., Maine Light Arty. (Augusta).
(b)   CLARK, Charles A., Lt. and Adj., 6th Maine Inf. (Sangorville).
(b)   CONDON, Clarence M., Sgt., 3d U.S. Arty. (Southbrooksville).
(b)   DAHLGREN, Edward C., 2d Lt., 36th Inf. Div. (Portland).
      DOHERTY, Thomas M., Cpl., 21st U.S. Inf. (Newcastle) (b. Ireland).
(b)   ESTES, Lewellyn G., Capt., and Ass't. Adj. Gen., Vol. (Penobscot).
(b)   FERNALD, Albert E., 1st Lt., 20th Maine Inf. (Winterport).
      *FOURNIER, William G., Sgt., 25th Inf. Div. (Winterport) (b. Conn.).
(b)   *GOODBLOOD, Clair, Cpl., 3d Inf. Div. (Burnham).
(b)   HANSCOM, Moses C., Cpl., 19th Maine Inf. (Bowdoinham).
(b)   HASKELL, Frank W., Sgt. Maj., 3d Maine Inf. (Waterville).
(b)   HAYNES, Asbury F., Cpl., 17th Maine Inf. (Edingburgh).
(b)   HESSELTINE, Francis S., Col., 13th Maine Inf. (Bangor).
(b)   HOWARD, Oliver O., Brig. Gen., U.S. Vol. (Leeds).
      HYDE, Thomas W., Maj., 7th Maine Inf. (Bath) (b. Italy).
(b)   KNOWLES, Abiather J., Pvt., 2d Maine Inf. (La Grange).
(b)   LITTLEFIELD, George H., Cpl., 1st Maine Inf. (Skowhegan).
(b)   *LORING, Charles J., Jr., Maj., USAF (Portland).
      MATTOCKS, Charles P., Maj., 17th Maine Inf. (Portland) (b. Vt.).
      *McMAHON, Thomas J., Spec. 4, 196th Inf. Brig. Amer. Div. (Lewiston) (b. D.C.).
(b)   *McMASTERS, Henry A., Cpl., 4th U.S. Cav. (Augusta).
(b)   MERRIAM, Henry C., Lt. Col., 73d U.S. Colored Troops (Houlton).
(b)   MERRILL, Augustus, Capt., 1st Maine Vet. Inf. (Lyndon).
(b)   MILLETT, Lewis L., Capt., 25th Inf. Div. (Mechanic Falls).
(b)   MORRILL, Walter G., Capt., 20th Maine Inf. (Brownville).
(b)   ROBERTS, Otis O., Sgt., 6th Maine Inf. (Dexter).
(b)   *SKIDGEL, Donald Sidney, Sgt., 1st Cav. Div. (Caribou).
(b)   SMITH, Charles H., Col., 1st Maine Cav. (Hollis).
(b)   SMITH, Joseph S., Lt. Col. and Commissary, 2d Army Corps (Wiscasset).
(b)   SMITH, William, Pvt., 8th U.S. Cav. (Bath).
(b)   SPURLING, Andrew B., Lt. Col., 2d Maine Cav. (Cranberry Isles).
(b)   TAYLOR, Wilbur N., Cpl., 8th U.S. Cav. (Hamden).
(b)   THAXTER, Sidney W., Maj., 1st Maine Cav. (Bangor).
(b)   TOBIE, Edward P., Sgt. Maj., 1st Maine Cav. (Lewiston).
(b)   TOZIER, Andrew J., Sgt., 20th Maine Inf. (Plymouth).
      *WAUGH, Robert T., 1st Lt., 85th Inf., Div. (Augusta) (b. R.I.).

325

MAINE—Continued

ARMY-AIR FORCE

WHEELER, Henry W., Pvt. 2d Maine Inf. (Bangor) (b. Ark.).
(b) WHITTIER, Edward N., 1st Lt., Maine Light Arty. (Gorham).
(b) WOOD, H. Clay., 1st Lt., 11th U.S. Inf. (Winthrop).
ZEAMER, Jay, Jr., Maj., U.S. Army Air Corps (Machias) (b. Pa.)

NAVY-MARINE CORPS

(b) ANGLING, John, Cabin Boy, USN (Portland).
(b) BIBBER, Charles J., GM, USN (Portland).
(b) BICKFORD, John F., Captain of Top, USN (Tremont).
(b) BOWMAN, Edward R., Quartermaster, USN (Eastport).
(b) DAVIS, Samuel W., Ordinary Seaman, USN.
(b) DUNCAN, Adam, BM, USN.
(b) DUNN, William, Quartermaster, USN.
(b) FARLEY, William, BM, USN (Whitehead).
(b) FOSS, Herbert Louis, Seaman, USN (Belfast).
(b) FRISBEE, John B., GM, USN.
(b) GIDDINGS, Charles, Seaman, USN (Bangor).
(b) HAYDEN, Cyrus, Carpenter, USN (York).
(b) KENDRICK, Thomas, Cox., USN (Bath).
(b) MACK, John, Seaman, USN.
(b) McCULLOCK, Adam, Seaman, USN.
McLEOD, James, Captain of Foretop, USN (b. Scotland).
(b) POOLE, William B., Quartermaster, USN.
RICE, Charles, Coal Heaver, USN (b. Russia).
ROBINSON, John, Captain of the Hold, USN (b. Cuba).
(b) SCHONLAND, Herbert Emery, Comdr., USN (Portland).
(b) SEWARD, Richard, Paymaster's Steward, USN (Kittery).
(b) *SMITH, Charles H., Cox., USN.
(b) STERLING, James E., Coal Heaver, USN.
(b) TAYLOR, Thomas, Cox., USN (Bangor).
(b) TRIPP, Othniel, CBM, USN.
(b) VERNEY, James W., CQM, USN.
(b) WILLIAMS, Anthony, Sailmaker's Mate, USN (b. Mass.).
(b) YOUNG, Horatio N., Seaman, USN (Calaise).

MARYLAND

ARMY-AIR FORCE

(b) BARNES, William H., Pvt., 38th U.S. Colored Troops (St. Marys County).
(b) BEAUFORD, Clay, 1st Sgt., 5th U.S. Cav. (Washington County).
(b) BOYNE, Thomas, Sgt., 9th U.S. Cav. (Prince Georges County).
(b) BUFFINGTON, John E., Sgt., 6th Md. Inf. (Carroll County).
(b) CADWALLADER, Abel G., Cpl., 1st Md. Inf. (Baltimore).
(b) CARTER, Joseph F., Capt., 3d Md. Inf. (Baltimore).
CLARKE, Powhatan H., 2d Lt., 10th U.S. Cav. (Baltimore) (b. La.).
(b) *COSTIN, Henry G., Pvt. 29th Div. (Baltimore).
(b) CRIST, John, Sgt., 8th U.S. Cav. (Baltimore).
DEETLINE, Frederick, Pvt., 7th U.S. Cav. (Baltimore) (b. Germany).
(b) DONAHUE, John L., Pvt., 8th U.S. Cav. (Baltimore County).
(b) DORSEY, Decatur, Sgt., 39th U.S. Colored Troops (Baltimore County).
(b) FLEETWOOD, Christian A., Sgt. Maj., 4th U.S. Colored Troops (Baltimore).
(b) GALT, Sterling A., Artificer, 36th Inf., U.S. Vol. (Pawneytown).
*GRAHAM, James A., Capt., 1st Mar. Div. (Prince Georges) (b. Pa.).
GREAVES, Clinton, Cpl., 9th U.S. Cav. (Prince Georges County) (b. Va.).
(b) HARRIS, James H., Sgt., 38th U.S. Colored Troops (St. Marys County).
HART, John W., Sgt., 6th Pa. Res. (Cumberland) (b. Germany).
(b) HILTON, Alfred B., Sgt., 4th U.S. Colored Troops (Harford County).
(b) *HOOKER, George, Pvt., 5th U.S. Cav. (Frederick).
*JACHMAN, Isadore S., S/Sgt., U.S. Army (Baltimore) (b. Germany).
(b) *JECELIN, William R., S/Sgt., 25th Inf. Div. (Baltimore).
(b) KOOGLE, Jacob, 1st Lt., 7th Md. Inf. (Frederick).

326

ARMY-AIR FORCE

MATHEWS, William H., 1st Sgt., 2d Md. Vet. Inf. (b. England).
(b) MAUS, Marion P., 1st Lt., 1st U.S. Inf. (Tennallytown).
*McDONALD, Phill G., Pfc., 4th Inf. Div. (Hyattsville) (b. W. Va.).
McGONNIGLE, Andrew J., Capt. and Asst. Quartermaster, U.S. Vol. (Cumberland) (b. N.Y.).
(b) McMILLAN, Albert W., Sgt., 7th U.S. Cav. (Baltimore).
MYERS, William H., Pvt., 1st Md. Cav. (Baltimore) (b. Pa.).
(b) OLIVER, Francis, 1st Sgt., 1st U.S. Cav. (Baltimore).
(b) PENNSYL, Josiah, Sgt., 6th U.S. Cav. (Frederick County).
PHELPS, Charles E., Col., 7th Md. Inf. (Baltimore) (b. Vt.).
*PORTER, Donn F., Sgt., 25th Inf. Div. (Baltimore) (b. Pa.).
(b) PORTER, Samuel, Farrier, 6th U.S. Cav. (Montgomery County).
(b) SCHNEIDER, George, Sgt., 3d Md. Vet. Inf. (Baltimore).
(b) SHEA, Joseph H., Pvt., 92d N.Y. Inf. (Baltimore).
(b) *SHERIDAN, Carl V., Pfc., 9th Inf. Div. (Baltimore).
(b) SKINNER, John O., Contract Surg., U.S. Army.
(b) SMITH, Andrew J., Sgt., 8th U.S. Cav. (Baltimore).
(b) SMITH, Francis M., 1st Lt. and Adj., 1st Md. Inf. (Frederick).
(b) SMITH, Otto, Pvt., 8th U.S. Cav. (Baltimore).
(b) TAYLOR, Charles, 1st Sgt., 3d U.S. Cav. (Baltimore).
THOMPSON, John, Cpl., 1st Md. Inf. (Baltimore) (b. Denmark).
TUCKER, Jacob R., Cpl., 4th Md. Inf. (Baltimore) (b. Pa.).
(b) WALLEY, Augustus, Pvt., 9th U.S. Cav. (Reisterstown).
(b) *WALMSLEY, John S., Jr., USAF (Baltimore).
WEINERT, Paul H., Cpl., 1st U.S. Arty. (Baltimore) (b. Germany).
(b) WIEDORFER, Paul J., Pvt., 80th Inf. Div. (Baltimore).

NAVY-MARINE CORPS

ANDREWS, John, Ordinary Seaman, USN (b. Pa.).
BROWN, John, Captain of Afterguard, USN (b. Denmark).
(b) BROWN, William H., Landsman, USN (Baltimore).
(b) BUCK, James, Quartermaster, USN (Baltimore).
(b) CARR, William M., Master at Arms, USN (Baltimore).
(b) CHATHAM, John Purnell, GM2d, USN (Worcester).
CONNOR, Thomas, Ordinary Seaman, USN (b. Ireland).
(b) DIGGINS, Bartholomew, Ordinary Seaman, USN (Baltimore).
(b) HAMMANN, Charles Hazeltine, Ens., USNRF (Baltimore).
(b) HAYDEN, Joseph B., Quartermaster, USN.
(b) JARRETT, Berrie H., Seaman, USN (Baltimore).
JOHANSON, John P., Seaman, USN (b. Sweden).
(b) JONES, Thomas, Cox., USN (Baltimore).
(b) LAKIN, Daniel, Seaman, USN (Baltimore).
(b) MAGEE, John W., F2d, USN.
(b) McDONNELL, Edward Orrick, Ens., USN (Baltimore).
(b) McNAIR, Frederick Vallette, Lt., USN.
MORTON, Charles W., BM, USN (b. Ireland).
(b) †MULLEN, Patrick, BM, USN (Baltimore).
NORRIS, Thomas R., Lt., USN (Silver Spring) (b. Fla.).
PRESTON, Arthur Murray, Lt., USNR (Silver Spring) (b. D.C.).
(b) *RICKETTS, Milton Ernest, Lt., USN (Baltimore).
(b) RINGOLD, Edward, Cox., USN (Baltimore).
(b) *SHUCK, William E., Jr., S/Sgt., USMC, 1st Marine Div. (Cumberland).
(b) SHUTES, Henry, Captain of Forecastle, USN (Baltimore).
(b) SWEARER, Benjamin, Seaman, USN (Baltimore).
*TALLENTINE, James, Quarter Gunner, USN (b. England).
(b) *TAYLOR, Karl G., Sr., S/Sgt., 3d Mar. Div. (Laurel).
(b) TRUETT, Alexander H., Cox., USN (Baltimore).
WRIGHT, William, Yeoman, USN (b. England).

MASSACHUSETTS

ARMY-AIR FORCE

(b)   ADAMS, John G. B., 2d Lt., 19th Mass. Inf. (Groveland).
(b)   ALLEN, Nathaniel M., Cpl., 1st Mass. Inf. (Boston).
(b)   ANDERSON, Frederick C., Pvt., 18th Mass. Inf.
(b)   *BARNES, John A., III, Pfc., 173d Airborne Brig. (Needham).
       BAYBUTT, Philip, Pvt., 2d Mass. Cav. (Fall River) (b. England).
(b)   *BEAUDOIN, Raymond O., 1st Lt., 30th Inf. Div. (Holyoke).
(b)   BESSEY, Charles A., Cpl., 3d U.S. Cav. (Reading).
       BOODY, Robert, Sgt., 40th N.Y. Inf. (Amesbury) (b. Maine).
(b)   BOSS, Orlando, Cpl., 25th Mass. Inf. (Fitchburg).
(b)   BOWDEN, Samuel, Cpl., 6th U.S. Cav. (Salem).
       BRETT, Lloyd M., 2d Lt., 2d U.S. Cav. (Malden) (b. Maine).
       BROWN, John H., Capt., 12th Ky. Inf. (Charlestown) (b. Canada).
(b)   BRYANT, Andrew S., Sgt., 46th Mass. Inf. (Springfield).
(b)   BUFFUM, Robert, Pvt., 21st Ohio Inf. (Salem).
(b)   BURT, James M., Capt., 2d Armd. Div. (Lee).
       CALLEN, Thomas J., Pvt., 7th U.S. Cav. (Boston) (b. Ireland).
       CARNEY, William H., Sgt., 54th Mass. Colored Inf. (New Bedford) (b. Va.).
(b)   CARSON, Anthony J., Cpl., 43d Inf., U.S. Vol. (Malden).
       CARTER, Robert G., 2d Lt., 4th U.S. Cav. (Bradford) (b. Maine).
       CASEY, David, Pvt., 25th Mass. Inf. (Northbridge) (b. Ireland).
(b)   CHANDLER, Henry F., Sgt., 59th Mass. Inf. (Andover).
       COSGROVE, Thomas, Pvt., 40th Mass. Inf. (E. Stoughton) (b. Ireland).
(b)   *CRAIG, Gordon M., Cpl., 1st Cav. Div. (East Bridgewater).
(b)   CRANDALL, Charles, Pvt., 8th U.S. Cav. (Worcester).
(b)   DAWSON, Michael, Trumpeter, 6th U.S. Cav. (Boston).
(b)   DEANE, John M., Maj., 29th Mass. Inf. (Freetown).
(b)   DeCASTRO, Joseph H., Cpl., 19th Mass. Inf. (Boston).
(b)   *DeFRANZO, Arthur F., S/Sgt., 1st Inf. Div. (Saugus).
(b)   DELAND, Frederick N., Pvt., 40th Mass. Inf. (Sheffield).
(b)   DODGE, Francis S., Capt., 9th U.S. Cav. (Danvers).
       DOWNEY, William, Pvt., 4th Mass. Cav. (Fall River) (b. Ireland).
(b)   DUFFEY, John, Pvt., 4th Mass. Cav. (New Bedford).
       EDDY, Samuel E., Pvt., 37th Mass. Inf. (Chesterfield) (b. Vt.).
       ELLIOTT, Russell C., Sgt., 3d Mass. Cav. (Boston) (b. N.H.).
(b)   ELLSWORTH, Thomas F., Capt., 55th Mass. Inf. (Boston).
       *FALLS, Benjamin F., Color Sgt., 19th Mass. Inf. (Lynn) (b. N.H.).
       FERRIS, Eugene W., 1st Lt. and Adj., 30th Mass. Inf. (Lowell) (b. Vt.).
(b)   FOLEY, Robert F., Capt., 25th Inf. Div. (Newton).
(b)   GARDNER, Charles N., Pvt., 32d Mass. Inf. (Norwell).
       GARDNER, Robert J., Sgt., 34th Mass. Inf. (Berkshire County) (b. N.Y.).
(b)   GARLAND, Harry, Cpl., 2d U.S. Cav. (Boston).
(b)   GAYLORD, Levi B., Sgt., 29th Mass. Inf. (Boston).
(b)   GIBSON, Edward H., Sgt., 27th Inf., U.S. Vol. (Boston).
(b)   GIFFORD, David L., Pvt., 4th Mass. Cav. (Dartmouth).
(b)   GOODMAN, David, Pvt., 8th U.S. Cav. (Paxton).
(b)   GRACE, Peter, Sgt., 83d Pa. Inf. (Berkshire).
(b)   *GRANT, Joseph Xavier, Capt., 25th Inf. Div. (Cambridge).
(b)   HADDOO, John, Cpl., 5th U.S. Inf. (Boston).
(b)   HALL, George J., S/Sgt., 34th Inf. Div. (Stoneham).
(b)   HANLEY, Richard P., Sgt., 7th U.S. Cav. (Boston).
       HANNA, Marcus A., Sgt., 50th Mass. Inf. (Rockport) (b. Maine).
       HARBOURNE, John H., Pvt., 29th Mass. Inf. (Boston) (b. England).
(b)   HASKELL, Marcus M., Sgt., 35th Mass. Inf. (Chelsea).
       HOLEHOUSE, James (John), Pvt., 7th Mass. Inf. (Fall River) (b. England).
(b)   HOMAN, Conrad, Color Sgt., 29th Mass. Inf. (Roxbury).
       HOOKER, George W., 1st Lt., 4th Vt. Inf. (Boston) (b. N.Y.).
(b)   HOWE, William H., Sgt., 29th Mass. Inf. (Haverhill).
(b)   HUNTER, Charles A., Sgt., 34th Mass. Inf. (Spencer).
(b)   JELLISON, Benjamin H., Sgt., 19th Mass. Inf. (Newburyport).
       JOHNS, Henry T., Pvt., 49th Mass. Inf. (Hinsdale).
       *JOHNSON, Elden H., Pvt., 3d Inf. Div. (E. Weymouth) (b. N.J.).
       KARPELES, Leopold, Sgt., 57th Mass. Inf. (Springfield) (b. Hungary).

ARMY-AIR FORCE

(b) LEONARD, Edwin, Sgt., 37th Mass. Inf. (Agawan).
(b) LEWIS, William B., Sgt., 3d U.S. Cav. (Boston).
LORD, William, Musician, 40th Mass. Inf. (Lawrence) (b. England).
LOVERING, George M., 1st Sgt., 4th Mass. Inf. (E. Randolph) (b. N.H.).
(b) LOWTHERS, James, Pvt., 6th U.S. Cav. (Boston).
LUNT, Alphonso M., Sgt., 38th Mass. Inf. (Cambridge) (b. Maine).
(b) LUTHER, James H., Pvt., 7th Mass. Inf. (Dighton).
MacGILLIVARY, Charles A., Sgt., 44th Inf. Div. (Boston) (b. Canada).
MAHONEY, Jeremiah, Sgt., 29th Mass. Inf. (Fall River).
(b) MANNING, Joseph S., Pvt., 29th Mass. Inf.
(b) MARLAND, William, 1st Lt., Mass. Light Arty. (Andover).
(b) MATHEWS, George W., Asst. Surg., 36th Inf., U.S. Vol. (Worcester).
(b) MATTHEWS, David A., Cpl., 8th U.S. Cav. (Boston).
(b) MAXHAM, Lowell M., Cpl., 7th Mass. Inf. (Taunton).
(b) MAYNARD, George H., Pvt., 13th Mass. Inf. (Waltham).
(b) McKINLEY, Daniel, Pvt., 8th U.S. Cav. (Boston).
(b) MILES, Nelson A., Col., 61st N.Y. Inf. (Roxbury).
(b) MOSHER, Louis C., 2d Lt., Philippine Scouts (Brockton).
MOYLAN, Myles, Capt., 7th U.S. Cav. (Essex) (b. Ireland).
MURPHY, Daniel J., Sgt., 19th Mass. Inf. (Lowell) (b. Pa.).
(b) *MURPHY, Frederick C., Pfc., 65th Inf. Div. (Weymouth).
(b) NEE, George H., Pvt., 21st U.S. Inf. (Boston).
(b) NEILON, Frederick S., Sgt., 6th U.S. Cav.
(b) O'REGAN, Michael, Pvt., 8th U.S. Cav. (Fall River).
(b) OSBORNE, William, Sgt., 1st U.S. Cav. (Boston).
(b) OSBORNE, William H., Pvt., 29th Mass Inf. (Scituate).
(b) *OUELLETTE, Joseph R., Pfc., 2d Inf. Div. (Lowell).
(b) *PERKINS, Michael J., Pfc., 101st Inf., 26th Div. (Boston).
(b) PINKHAM, Charles H., Sgt., Maj., 57th Mass. Inf. (Grafton).
PLUNKETT, Thomas, Sgt., 21st Mass. Inf. (West Boylston) (b. Ireland).
*PRUSSMAN, Ernest W., Pfc., 8th Inf. Div. (Brighton) (b. Md.)
PYM, James, Pvt., 7th U.S. Cav. (Boston) (b. England)
(b) REED, Charles W., Bug., 9th Independent Btry., Mass. Light Arty. (Charlestown).
(b) RICE, Edmund, Maj., 19th Mass. Inf. (Boston).
RICH, Carlos H., 1st Sgt., 4th Vt. Inf. (Northfield) (b. Canada).
ROBINSON, John H., Pvt., 19th Mass. Inf. (Roxbury) (b. Ireland).
(b) SAXTON, Rufus, Brig. Gen., U.S. Vol. (Greenfield).
SCANLAN, Patrick, Pvt., 4th Mass. Cav. (Spencer) (b. Ireland).
(b) SINGLETON, Frank, Sgt., 6th U.S. Cav. (See Nielon, Frederick, true name, above).
SLADEN, Joseph A., Pvt., 33d Mass. Inf. (Lowell) (b. England)
(b) SMITH, Thomas, Pvt., 1st U.S. Cav. (Boston).
(b) SNOW, Elmer T., Trumpeter, 3d U.S. Cav. (Hardwick).
STRONG, James N., Sgt., 49th Mass. Inf. (Pittsfield).
SWEATT, Joseph S. G., Pvt., 6th Mass. Inf. (Lowell) (b. N.H.).
(b) TAGGART, Charles A., Pvt., 37th Mass. Inf. (North Blanford).
TERRY, John D., Sgt., 23d Mass. Inf. (Boston) (b. Maine).
TOBIN, John M,. 1st Lt. and Adj., 9th Mass. Inf. (Boston) (b. Ireland).
TOLAN, Frank, Pvt., 7th U.S. Cav. (Boston) (b. N.Y.).
TRACY, Charles H., Sgt., 37th Mass. Inf. (Springfield) (b. Conn.).
(b) *TURNER, Charles W., Sfc., 2d Inf. Div, (Boston).
(b) TURPIN, James H., 1st Sgt., 5th U.S. Cav. (Boston).
(b) WALKER, Frank O., Pvt., 46th Inf., U.S. Vol. (Burlington).
(b) WARD, James, Sgt., 7th U.S. Cav. (Boston).
(b) WARREN, Francis E., Cpl., 49th Mass. Inf. (Hinsdale).
WELCH, Richard, Cpl., 37th Mass. Inf. (Williamstown) (b. Ireland).
WHITMAN, Frank M., Pvt., 35th Mass. Inf. (Ayersville) (b. Maine).
WHITTLESEY, Charles W., Maj., 308th Inf., 77th Div. (Pittsfield) (b. Wisconsin).
(b) WILBUR, William H., Col., West. Task Force, N.A. (Palmer).
*WILKIN, Edward G., Cpl., 45th Inf. Div. (Longmeadow) (b. Vt.).
WOOD, Leonard, Asst. Surg., U.S. Army (b. N.H.).
(b) WRIGHT, Samuel C., Pvt., 29th Mass. Inf. (Plympton).

NAVY-MARINE CORPS

(b)   ADAMS, John Mapes, Sgt., USMC (Haverhill).
ADRIANCE, Harry Chapman, Cpl., USMC (b. N.Y.).
ARTHER, Matthew, Signal Q.M., USN (Boston) (b. Scotland).
(b)   ATKINSON, Thomas E., Yeoman, USN (Salem).
(b)   BAKER, Benjamin F., Cox., USN (Dennisport).
(b)   BARNUM, James, BM, USN.
BAZAAR, Philip, Ordinary Seaman, USN (b. Chile, South America).
BEYER, Albert, Coxs., USN (Boston) (b. Germany).
BOIS, Frank, Q.M., USN (Northampton) (b. Canada).
(b)   BOND, William, BM, USN (Boston).
(b)   BRADLEY, Alexander, Landsman, USN (Boston).
BRENNAN, Christopher, Seaman, USN (b. Ireland).
(b)   *CADDY, William Robert, Pfc., USMCR (Quincy).
CAMPBELL, Daniel, Pvt., USMC (b. Canada).
(b)   *CARON, Wayne Maurice, H.C.M. 3rd c., USN (Middleboro).
(b)   CARR, William Louis, Pvt., USMC (Peabody).
(b)   CHANDLER, James B., Cox., USN.
(b)   CHARETTE, George, G.M. 1c., USN (Lowell).
(b)   CONNOLLY, Michael, Ordinary Seaman, USN (Boston).
COONEY, James, Pvt., USMC (b. Ireland).
CRAMEN, Thomas, BM., USN (b. Ireland).
DEMPSEY, John, Seaman, USN (b. Ireland).
(b)   DENEEF, Michael, Captain of Top, USN.
(b)   DENNIS, Richard, BM., USN.
(b)   *DEWERT, Richard David, Hospital Corpsman, USN (Taunton).
(b)   DORAN, John J., BM2d., USN.
(b)   ENRIGHT, John, Landsman, USN (Lynn).
FORSTERER, Bruno Albert, Sgt., USMC (b. Germany).
(b)   GILE, Frank S., Landsman, USN.
(b)   GILL, Freeman, GM1c., USN (Boston).
GISBURNE, Edward A., E3c., USN (b. R.I.)
GRADY, John, Lt., USN (b. Canada).
GRIFFITHS, John, Captain of Forecastle, USN (b. Wales).
(b)   GRISWOLD, Luke M., Ordinary Seaman, USN.
HAMILTON, Thomas W., Quartermaster, USN (b. Scotland).
(b)   HANDRAN, John, Seaman, USN.
*HANSON, Robert Murray, 1st Lt., USMCR (b. India).
(b)   HARCOURT, Thomas, Ordinary Seaman, USN (Boston).
HARRINGTON, Daniel, Landsman, USN (b. Ireland).
(b)   HARRISON, George H., Seaman, USN.
(b)   HART, William, M1c., USN.
(b)   HATHAWAY, Edward W., Seaman, USN (Plymouth).
(b)   HILL, Walter Newell, Capt., USMC (Haverhill).
(b)   HORTON, James, GM, USN.
(b)   HORTON, James, Capt. of Top, USN (Boston).
(b)   HORTON, Lewis A., Seaman, USN (Bristol).
HOWARD, Peter, BM, USN (b. France).
(b)   HUDNER, Thomas Jerome, Jr., Lt. (jg.), USN (Fall River).
HUNT, Martin, Pvt., USMC (b. Ireland).
(b)   JAMES, John H., Captain of Top, USN (Boston).
(b)   *JULIAN, Joseph Rodolph, Plat. Sgt., USMCR (Sturbridge).
KEARNEY, Michael, Pvt., USMC (b. Ireland).
(b)   KELLY, Francis, WT., USN (Boston).
(b)   KELLY, Thomas G., Lt., Comdr., USN, River Assault Div. 152 (Boston).
KENNA, Barnett, Quartermaster, USN (b. England).
KERSEY, Thomas, Ordinary Seaman, USN (b. Canada).
KYLE, Patrick J., Landsman, USN (b. Ireland).
LAFFEY, Bartlett, Seaman, USN (b. Ireland).
*LOGAN, Hugh, Captain of Afterguard, USN (b. Ireland).
(b)   LYLE, Alexander Gordon, Lt. Comdr., Dental Corps, USN (Gloucester).

NAVY-MARINE CORPS

(b)   LYONS, Thomas, Seaman, USN (Salem).
      MACKENZIE, John, CBM, USN (b. Conn).
      MADDIN, Edward, Ordinary Seaman, USN (b. Canada).
      McDONALD, John, BM, USN (b. Scotland).
(b)   McFARLAND, John, Captain of Forecastle, USN (Boston).
(b)   MIHALOWSKI, John, TM1c., USN (Worcester).
      MILLER, Harry Herbert, Seaman, USN (b. Canada).
      MILLER, James, Quartermaster, USN (b. Denmark).
      MILLER, Willard, Seaman, USN (b. Canada).
(b)   MOORE, William, BM, USN (Boston).
      MULLER, Frederick, Mate, USN (b. Denmark).
(b)   NEWLAND, William, Ordinary Seaman, USN (Medway).
      NUGENT, Christopher, Orderly Sgt., USMC (b. Ireland).
(b)   O'BRIEN, Oliver, Cox., USN (Boston).
(b)   O'CALLAHAN, Joseph Timothy, Comdr., USNR (Boston).
      OLSEN, Anton, Ordinary Seaman, USN (b. Norway).
(b)   *OUELLET, David G., Seaman, USN (Newton).
(b)   PARKER, William, Captain of Afterguard, USN (Boston).
      PILE, Richard, Ordinary Seaman, USN (b. West Indies).
(b)   POPE, Everett Parker, Capt., USMC (Milton).
(b)   *POWER, John Vincent, 1st Lt., USMC (Worcester).
      PRANCE, George, Captain of Maintop, USN (b. France).
      PRENDERGAST, Thomas Francis, Cpl., USMC (b. Ireland).
      PRESTON, John, Landsman, USN (b. Ireland).
      PROVINCE, George, Ordinary Seaman, USN (b. N.Y.).
(b)   REGAN, Jeremiah, Quartermaster, USN (Boston).
      RILLEY, John Phillip, Landsman, USN (b. Pa.).
(b)   ROUNTRY, John, F1c., USN.
(b)   RYAN, Francis T., Cox., USN.
(b)   SADLER, William, Captain of Top, USN (Boston).
(b)   SAUNDERS, James, Quartermaster, USN.
      SAVAGE, Auzella, Ordinary Seaman, USN (b. Maine).
(b)   SCANNELL, David John, Pvt., USMC (Boston).
(b)   SCOTT, Joseph Francis, Pvt., USMC (Boston).
      SEACH, William, Ordinary Seaman, USN (b. England).
(b)   SMITH, John, Captain of Forecastle, USN (Boston).
(b)   STACY, William B., Seaman, USN.
(b)   STANLEY, William A., Shell Man, USN.
      STEVENS, Daniel D., Quartermaster, USN (b. Tenn.).
(b)   STICKNEY, Herman Osman, Comdr., USN (Pepperell).
      SULLIVAN, Edward, Pvt., USMC (b. Ireland).
(b)   SULLIVAN, James F., BM, USN (Lowell).
      SWANSON, John, Seaman, USN (b. Sweden).
(b)   SWEENEY, William, Landsman Engineers' Force, USN (Boston).
      TALBOTT, William, Captain of Forecastle, USN (b. Maine).
      THIELBERG, Henry, Seaman, USN (b. Germany).
      THOMPSON, William, Sig. Quartermaster, USN (Boston) (b. N.J.).
(b)   TROY, William, Ordinary Seaman, USN (Boston).
(b)   *VITTORI, Joseph, Cpl., USMCR, 1st Marine Div. (Beverly).
(b)   *WALSH, William Gary, Gun. Sgt., USMCR (Roxbury).
(b)   WILLEY, Charles H., Machinist, USN (Boston).
      WILLIAMS, Augustus, Seaman, USN (b. Norway).
(b)   WILLIS, George, Cox., USN (Boston).

MICHIGAN

ARMY-AIR FORCE

      ALBER, Frederick, Pvt., 17th Mich. Inf. (Manchester) (b. Germany).
(b)   †BALDWIN, Frank D., Capt., 19th Mich. Inf.; 1st Lt., 5th U.S. Inf. (Constantine).
      BALLEN, Frederick, Pvt., 47th Ohio Inf. (Adrian) (b. Germany).
      BARRELL, Charles L., 1st Lt., 102d U.S. Colored Troops (Leighton).

(b)   BENNETT, Orson W., 1st Lt., 102d U.S. Colored Troops (Union City).
(b)   BONDSTEEL, James Leroy, S/Sgt., 1st Inf. Div. (Jackson).
      BRANDLE, Joseph E., Pvt., 17th Mich. Inf. (Colon) (b. Ohio).
      *BRYANT, William Maud, Sfc., 1st Special Forces (Detroit) (b. Ga.).
(b)   CAWETZKA, Charles, Pvt., 30th Inf., U.S. Vol. (Wayne).
(b)   CHRISTIANCY, James I., 1st Lt., 9th Mich. Cav. (Monroe County).
(b)   CLUTE, George W., Cpl., 14th Mich. Inf. (Marathon).
      COLE, Gabriel, Cpl., 5th Mich. Cav. (New Salem) (b. N.Y.).
(b)   CRAW, Demas T., Col., A.C. (Traverse City).
      †CUSTER, Thomas W., 2d Lt., 6th Mich. Cav. (Monroe) (b. Ohio).
      CUTCHEON, Byron M., Maj., 20th Mich. Inf. (Ypsilanti) (b. N.H.).
      DODD, Robert F., Pvt., 27th Mich. Inf. (Hamtramck) (b. Canada).
(b)   DOUGHERTY, William, Blacksmith, 8th U.S. Cav. (Detroit).
(b)   *ESSEBAGGER, John, Jr., Cpl., 3d Inf. Div. (Holland).
(b)   FALCONER, John A., Cpl., 17th Mich. Inf. (Manchester).
      FALL, Charles S., Sgt., 26th Mich. Inf. (Hamburg) (b. Ind.).
(b)   FORMAN, Alexander A., Cpl., 7th Mich. Inf. (Jonesville).
      FOX, Henry M., Sgt., 5th Mich. Cav. (Coldwater) (b. Ohio).
      FRENCH, Samuel S., Pvt., 7th Mich. Inf. (Gifford) (b. N.Y.).
(b)   FURLONG, Harold A., 1st Lt., 353d Inf., 89th Div. (Detroit).
      HACK, John, Pvt., 47th Ohio Inf. (Adrian) (b. Germany).
      HADLEY, Cornelius M., Sgt., 9th Mich. Cav. (Adrian) (b. N.Y.).
(b)   HAIGHT, Sidney, Cpl., 1st Mich. Sharpshooters (Goodland).
(b)   HARRINGTON, John, Pvt., 6th U.S. Cav. (Detroit).
(b)   HASTINGS, Smith H., Capt., 5th Mich. Cav. (Quincy).
      HILL, EDWARD, Capt., 16th Mich. Inf. (Detroit) (b. N.Y.).
(b)   HODGES, Addison J., Pvt., 47th Ohio Inf. (Adrian).
(b)   HOLLAND, David, Cpl., 5th U.S. Inf. (Dearborn).
      HOLTON, Charles M., 1st Sgt., 7th Mich. Cav. (Battle Creek) (b. N.Y.).
      IRWIN, Patrick, 1st Sgt., 14th Mich. Cav. (Ann Arbor) (b. Ireland).
(b)   JOHNSON, Dwight H., Spec. 5, 4th Inf. Div. (Detroit).
(b)   JOHNSON, Oscar G., Sgt., 91st Inf. Div. (Foster City).
      KEEN, Joseph S., Sgt., 13th Mich. Inf. (Detroit) (b. England).
      KELLEY, Andrew J., Pvt., 17th Mich. Inf. (Ypsilanti) (b. Ind.).
      KEMP, Joseph, 1st Sgt., 5th Mich. Inf. (Sault Ste. Marie) (b. Ohio).
(b)   LAMBERS, Paul Ronald, Sgt., 25th Inf. Div. (Holland).
      LANE, Morgan D., Pvt., Sig. C., U.S. Army (Alleghany) (b. N.Y.).
      LEMON, Peter C., Sgt., 1st Cav. Div. (East Tawas).
(b)   LEONARD, William, Pvt., 2d U.S. Cav. (Ypsilanti).
(b)   LEWIS, Henry, Cpl., 47th Ohio Inf. (Adrian).
      LUCE, Moses A., Sgt., 4th Mich. Inf. (Hillsdale) (b. Ill.).
      McCONNELL, James, Pvt., 33d Inf., U.S. Vol. (Detroit) (b. N.Y.).
      McFALL, Daniel, Sgt., 17th Mich. Inf. (Ypsilanti) (b. N.Y.).
      McHALE. Alexander U., Cpl., 26th Mich. Inf. (Muskegon) (b. Ireland).
      MENTER, John W., Sgt., 5th Mich. Inf. (Detroit) (b. N.Y.).
      MORSE, Benjamin, Pvt., 3d Mich. Inf. (Grand Rapids) (b. N.Y.).
(b)   *MOYER, Donald R., Sfc., 25th Inf. Div. (Oakland).
(b)   MUNDELL, Walter L., Cpl., 5th Mich. Inf. (Dallas) (b. Va.).
(b)   NASH, Henry H., Cpl., 47th Ohio Inf. (Adrian).
      NOLL, Conrad, Sgt., 20th Mich. Inf. (Ann Arbor) (b. Germany).
      NORTON, Elliott M., 2d Lt., 6th Mich. Cav. (Cooper) (b. Conn.).
(b)   PETERS, Henry C., Pvt., 47th Ohio Inf. (Adrian).
      PLANT, Henry E., Cpl., 14th Mich. Inf. (Cockery) (b. N.Y.).
(b)   POLOND, Alfred, Pvt., 10th U.S. Inf. (Lapeer).
(b)   *POXON, Robert Leslie, 1st Lt., 1st Cav. Div. (Detroit).
      RANNEY, George E., Asst. Surg., 2d Mich. Cav. (Detroit) (b. N.Y.).
(b)   ROBINSON, James H., Pvt., 3d Mich. Cav. (Victor).
      ROMEYN, Henry, 1st Lt., 5th U.S. Inf. (b. N.Y.).
(b)   SANCRAINTE, Charles F., Pvt., 15th Mich. Inf. (Monroe).
(b)   *SAVACOOL, Edwin F., Capt., 1st N.Y. Cav. (Marshall).
(b)   SHAFTER, William R., 1st Lt., 7th Mich. Inf. (Galesburg).
      SHEPHARD, Irwin, Cpl., 17th Mich. Inf. (Chelsea) (b. N.Y.).

ARMY-AIR FORCE

SIDMAN, George D., Pvt., 16th Mich. Inf. (Owosso) (b. N.Y.).
(b) SJOGREN, John C., S/Sgt., 40th Inf. Div. (Rockford).
*SKIDGEL, Donald Sidney, Sgt., 1st Cav. Div. (Detroit) (b. Maine).
SMITH, Alonzo, Sgt., 7th Mich. Inf. (Jonesville) (b. N.Y.).
(b) SMITH, Maynard H., Sgt., 423d Bomb. Sq. (Detroit).
(b) SMITH, William H., Pvt., 1st U.S. Cav. (Lapeer).
SWIFT, Frederic W., Lt. Col., 17th Mich. Inf. (b. Conn.).
(b) SYPE, Peter, Pvt., 47th Ohio Inf. (Adrian).
(b) THATCHER, Charles M., Pvt., 1st Mich. Sharpshooters (Eastmanville).
*THOMAS, William H., Pfc., 38th Inf. Div. (Ypsilanti) (b. Ark.).
THOMPSON, Charles A., Sgt., 17th Mich. Inf. (Kalamazoo) (b. Ohio).
(b) TOBAN, James W., Sgt., 9th Mich. Cav. (Northfield).
VLUG, Dirk J., Pfc., 32d Inf. Div. (Grand Rapids) (b. Minn.).
(b) WARD, William H., Capt., 47th Ohio Inf. (Adrian).
(b) WATSON, Joseph, Pvt., 8th U.S. Cav. (St. Joseph).
*WETZEL, Walter C., Pfc., 8th Inf. Div. (Roseville) (b. W. Va.).
(b) WHITNEY, William G., Sgt., 11th Mich. Inf. (Quincy).
*WIGLE, Thomas W., 2d Lt., 34th Inf. Div. (Detroit) (b. Ind.).
(b) WILDER, Wilber E., 1st Lt., 4th U.S. Cav. (Detroit).
(b) WILLCOX, Orlando B., Col., 1st Mich. Inf. (Detroit).
WITHINGTON, William H., Capt., 1st Mich. Inf. (Jackson) (b. Mass.).
(b) WOODRUFF, Alonzo, Sgt., 1st U.S. Sharpshooters (Ionia).
*YNTEMA, Gordon Douglas, Sgt., 5th Special Forces Group (Holland) (b. Md.).
(b) *ZUSSMAN, Raymond, 2d Lt., 756th Tank Bn. (Detroit).

NAVY-MARINE CORPS

*CANNON, George Ham, 1st Lt., USMC (b. Mo.).
(b) CHARETTE, William R., HC3c., USN (Ludington).
(b) CRONIN, Cornelius, CQM, USN (Detroit).
(b) DEWEY, Duane E., Cpl., USMCR, 1st Marine Div. (Muskegon).
(b) *FLAHERTY, Francis C., Ens., USNR (Charlotte).
(b) GLOWIN, Joseph Anthony, Cpl., USMC (Detroit).
(b) *HAMMERBERG, Owen Francis Patrick, BM2c., USN (Daggett).
(b) SIMANEK, Robert E., Pfc., USMC, 1st Marine Div. (Detroit).
*SKINNER, Sherrod E., Jr., 2d Lt., USMCR, 1st Marine Div. (East Lansing) (b. Conn.).
(b) SMITH, Albert Joseph, Pvt., USMC (Calumet).
(b) *WILLIAMS, Dewayne T., Pfc., USMC, 1st Mar. Div. (St. Clair).
(b) ZUIDERVELD, William, HA1c., USN.

MINNESOTA

ARMY-AIR FORCE

ALBEE, George E., 1st Lt., 41st U.S. Inf. (Owatonna) (b. N.H.).
BARRICK, Jesse, Cpl., 3d Minn. Inf. (Rice County) (b. Ohio).
BELL, Harry, Capt., 36 Inf., U.S. Vol. (Minneapolis) (b. Wis.).
(b) *BIANCHI, Willibald C., 1st Lt., 45th Inf., Philippine Scouts (New Ulm).
BURGER, Joseph, Pvt., 2d Minn. Inf. (Crystal Lake) (b. Austria).
BURKARD, Oscar, Pvt., Hosp. Corps, U.S. Army (Hay Creek) (b. Germany).
CILLEY, Clinton A., Capt., 2d Minn. Inf. (Sasioja) (b. N.H.).
CLARK, William A., Cpl., 2d Minn. Inf. (Shelbyville) (b. Pa.).
(b) COLALILLO, Mike, Pfc., 100th Inf. Div. (Duluth).
†CUKELA, Louis, Sgt., 5th Reg., USMC (Minneapolis) (b. Austria). (Also awarded Navy Medal of Honor.)
FLANNIGAN, James, Pvt., 2d Minn. Inf. (Louisville) (b. N.Y.).
HANNA, Milton, Cpl., 2d Minn. Inf. (Henderson) (b. Ohio).
(b) HAWKS, Lloyd C., Pfc., 3d Inf. Div. (Park Rapids).
HOLMES, Lovilo N., 1st Sgt., 2d Minn. Inf. (Mankato) (b. N.Y.).
HUGGINS, Eli L., Capt., 2d U.S. Cav. (b. Ill.).
JOHNSON, John, Pvt., 2d Wis. Inf. (Rochester) (b. Norway).
LINDBERGH, Charles A., Capt., A.C. Res., U.S. Army (Little Falls) (b. Mich.).

333

ARMY-AIR FORCE

MALLON, George H., Capt., 33d Div. (Minneapolis) (b. Kans.).

MORGAN, George H., 2d Lt., 3d U.S. Cav. (Minneapolis) (b. Canada).

O'BRIEN, Henry D., Cpl., 1st Minn. Inf. (St. Anthony Falls) (b. Maine).

(b) *OLSON, Kenneth L., Spec. 4, 199th Inf. Brig. (Paynesville).

*PAGE, John U. D., Lt. Col., X Corps Arty. (St. Paul) (b. Malahi Island, Philippine Islands).

PAY, Byron E., Pvt., 2d Minn. Inf. (Mankato) (b. N.Y.).

PICKLE, Alonzo H., Sgt., 1st Minn. Inf. (Dover) (b. Canada).

(b) *PRUDEN, Robert J., S/Sgt., 75th Inf. Ameri. Div. (St. Paul).

*RABEL, Laszlo, S/Sgt., 173d Airborne Brig. (Minneapolis) (b. Hungary).

REED, Axel H., Sgt., 2d Minn. Inf. (Glencoe) (b. Maine).

(b) RUDOLPH, Donald E., 2d Lt., 6th Inf. Div. (Minneapolis).

SHERMAN, Marshall, Pvt., 1st Minn. Inf. (St. Paul) (b. Vt.).

(b) THORSNESS, Leo K., Lt. Col., 357th Tactical Fighter Sq. (Walnut Grove).

TRACY, John, Pvt., 8th U.S. Cav. (St. Paul) (b. Ireland).

VALE, John, Pvt., 2d Minn. Inf. (Rochester) (b. England).

(b) *WAYRYNEN, Dale Eugene, Spec. 4, 101st Airborne Div. (McGregor).

WELCH, Charles H., Sgt., 7th U.S. Cav. (Ft. Snelling) (b. N.Y).

WILSON, William O., Cpl., 9th U.S. Cav. (St. Paul) (b. Md.).

WRIGHT, Samuel, Cpl., 2d Minn. Inf. (Swan Lake) (b. Ind.).

NAVY-MARINE CORPS

CATLIN, Albertus Wright, Maj., USMC (b. N.Y.).

(b) *COURTNEY, Henry Alexius, Jr., Maj., USMCR (Duluth).

†CUKELA, Louis, Sgt., USMC (Also awarded Army Medal of Honor) (Minneapolis) (b. Austria).

(b) DYER, Jesse Farley, Capt., USMC (St. Paul).

(b) *FLEMING, Richard E., Capt., USMCR (St. Paul).

(b) *HAUGE, Louis James, Jr., Cpl., USMCR (Ada).

*KRAUS, Richard Edward, Pfc., USMCR (b. Ill.).

(b) *LA BELLE, James Dennis, Pfc., USMCR (Columbia Heights).

(b) NELSON, Oscar Frederick, MM1c., USN (Minneapolis).

(b) *RUD, George William, CMM, USN (Minneapolis).

(b) SORENSON, Richard Keith, Pvt., USMCR (Anoka).

MISSISSIPPI

ARMY-AIR FORCE

(b) BARFOOT, Van T., 2d Lt., 45th Inf. Div. (Carthage).

*DIAMOND, James H., Pfc., 24th Inf. Div. (Gulfport) (b. La.).

(b) HEARD, John W., 1st Lt., 3d U.S. Cav. (Woodstock Plantation).

(b) *HENRY, Robert T., Pvt., 1st Inf. Div. (Greenville).

*JORDAN, Mack A., Pfc., 24th Inf. Div. (Collins).

LEE, Hubert L., M/Sgt., 2d Inf. Div. (Leland) (b. Mo.).

LINDSEY, Jake W., T/Sgt., 1st Inf. Div. (Lucedale) (b. Ala.).

(b) PITTMAN, John A., Sgt., 2d Inf. Div. (Tallula).

(b) SLATON, James D., Cpl., 45th Inf. Div. (Gulfport).

(b) WELBORN, Ira C., 2d Lt., 9th U.S. Inf. (Mico).

NAVY-MARINE CORPS

(b) BROWN, Wilson, Landsman, USN (Natchez).

(b) COMMISKEY, Henry A., 1st Lt., USMC, 1st Marine Div. (Hattiesburg).

MADISON, James Jonas, Lt. Comdr., USNRF (b. N.J.).

(b) *WHEAT, Roy M., L/Cpl., 1st Marine Div. (Moselle).

(b) WILSON, Louis Hugh, Jr., Capt., USMC (Brandon).

MISSOURI

ARMY-AIR FORCE

*ADAMS, William E., Maj., 1st Aviation Brig. (b. Wyo.).
(b) BARGER, Charles D., Pfc., 89th Div. (Stotts City).
(b) BARKLEY, John L., Pfc., 3d Div. (Blairstown).
BIEGER, Charles, Pvt., 4th Mo. Cav. (St. Louis) (b. Germany).
BRANT, Abram B., Pvt., 7th U.S. Cav. (St. Louis) (b. N.Y.).
BRYAN, William C., Hospital Steward, USA (St. Louis) (b. Ohio).
(b) BURR, Herbert H., S/Sgt., 11th Armd. Div. (Kansas City).
DE PUY, Charles H., 1st Sgt., 1st Mich. Sharpshooters (St. Louis) (b. Mich.).
(b) EPPS, Joseph L., Pvt., 33d Inf., U.S. Vol. (Oklahoma, Indian Territory).
EVANS, William, Pvt., 7th U.S. Inf. (St. Louis) (b. Ireland).
FLYNN, James E., Sgt., 6th Mo. Inf. (St. Louis) (b. Ill.).
FOLLETT, Joseph L., Sgt., 1st Mo. Light Arty. (St. Louis) (b. N.J.).
(b) FORREST, Arthur J., Sgt., 354th Inf., 89th Div. (Hannibal).
(b) FRIZZELL (FRAZELL), Henry F., Pvt., 6th Mo. Inf. (Pilot Knob).
GREBE, M. R. William, Capt., 4th Mo. Cav. (St. Louis) (b. Germany).
GUERIN, Fitz W., Pvt., 1st Mo. Light Arty. (St. Louis) (b. N.Y.).
GWYNNE, Nathaniel, Pvt., 13th Ohio Cav. (Fairmont) (b. Ohio).
(b) HALL, William P., 1st Lt., 5th U.S. Cav. (Huntsville).
HAMMEL, Henry A., Sgt., 1st Mo. Light Arty. (St. Louis) (b. Germany).
(b) HATLER, M. Waldo, Sgt., 356th Inf., 89th Div. (Neosho).
HOWARD, James H., Lt. Col., A.C. (St. Louis) (b. China).
HUNT, Louis T., Pvt., 6th Mo. Inf. (Jefferson County) (b. Ind.).
(b) *KANELL, Billie G., Pvt., 25th Inf. Div. (Poplar Bluff).
(b) *KELLEY, Ova A., Pvt., 96th Inf. Div. (Norwood).
KIRBY, Dennis T., Maj., 8th Mo. Inf. (St. Louis) (b. N.Y.).
(b) *LONG, Charles R., Sgt., 2d Inf. Div. (Kansas City).
McCAMMON, William W., 1st Lt., 24th Mo. Inf. (Montgomery County) (b. Ohio).
MILLER, Archie, 1st Lt., 6th U.S. Cav. (St. Louis) (b. Ill.).
MONTROSE, Charles H., Pvt., 5th U.S. Inf. (St. Louis) (b. Minn.).
PESCH, Joseph, Pvt., 1st Mo. Light Arty. (St. Louis) (b. Germany).
*PETERSEN, Danny J., Sp4c., 25th Inf. Div. (Kansas City) (b. Kans.).
PORTER, Ambrose, Commissary Sgt., 12th Mo. Cav. (Rockport) (b. Md.).
RAY, Charles W., Sgt., 22d U.S. Inf. (St. Louis) (b. N.C.).
*RIORDAN, Paul F., 2d Lt., 34th Inf. Div. (Kansas City) (b. Iowa).
SCHOFIELD, John M., Maj., 1st Mo. Inf. (St. Louis) (b. N.Y.).
SHAW, Thomas, Sgt., 9th U.S. Cav. (Pike County) (b. Ky.)
SHEPPARD, Charles, Pvt., 5th U.S. Inf. (St. Louis) (b. Conn.).
(b) *SISLER, George K., 1st Lt., 1st Special Forces (Dexter).
(b) *SKINKER, Alexander R., Capt., 35th Div. (St. Louis).
(b) *SPECKER, Joe C., Sgt., 48th Engr. Bn. (Odessa).
(b) TAYLOR, Bernard, Sgt., 5th U.S. Cav. (St. Louis).
TROGDEN, Howell G., Pvt., 8th Mo. Inf. (St. Louis) (b. N.C.).
WAGNER, John W., Cpl., 8th Mo. Inf. (St. Louis) (b. Md.).
(b) WHERRY, William M., 1st Lt., 3d U.S. Res. Mo. Inf. (St. Louis).
*WILSON, Richard G., Pfc., 11th Abn. Div. (Cape Girardeau) (b. Ill.).
WORTICK, Joseph, Pvt., 8th Mo. Inf. (Hannibal) (b. Pa.).

NAVY-MARINE CORPS

BALCH, John Henry, PhM1c., USN (b. Kans.).
(b) BALLARD, Donald Everett, H.C.M., 2d c., USN, 3rd Mar. Div. (Kansas City).
(b) BUTTON, William Robert, Cpl., USMC (St. Louis).
(b) CARY, Robert Webster, Lt. Comdr., USN (Kansas City).
(b) *COLE, Darrell Samuel, Sgt., USMCR (Flat River).
(b) *DAVID, Albert LeRoy, Lt. (jg.), USN (Maryville).
DURNEY, Austin J., Blacksmith, USN (b. Pa.).
(b) FUQUA, Samuel Glenn, Capt., USN (Laddonia).
(b) GAIENNIE, Louis Rene, Pvt., USMC (St. Louis).
(b) HANNEKEN, Herman Henry, 2d Lt., USMC (St. Louis).
(b) HOLTZ, August, CWT, USN (St. Louis).
MARTIN, William, BM, USN (b. Prussia).

335

MISSOURI—Continued

Navy-Marine Corps

(b)   McGUIRE, Fred Henry, HA, USN (Gordonville).
(b)   O'HARE, Edward Henry, Lt., USN (St. Louis).
(b)   *PHILLIPS, George, Pvt., USMCR (Rich Hill).
(b)   *SISLER, George K., 1st Lt., 1st Special Forces (Dexter).
(b)   TOWNSEND, Julius Curtis, Lt., USN (Athens).

MONTANA

Army-Air Force

(b)   *GALT, William Wylie, Capt., 34th Inf. Div. (Stanford).
    MORAN, John E.; Capt., 37th Inf., U.S. Vol. (Cascade County) (b. Vt.).
    *PARRISH, Laverne, T4g., 25th Inf. Div. (Ronan) (b. Mo.).
    POWERS, Leo J., Pfc., 34th Inf. Div. (Alder Gulch) (b. Neb.).
    SCHAUER, Henry, Pfc., 3d Inf. Div. (Scobey) (b. Okla.).
    SMITH, Cornelius C., Cpl., 6th U.S. Cav. (Helena) (b. Ariz.).

Navy-Marine Corps

(b)   RUHL, Donald Jack, Pfc., USMCR (Columbus).

NEBRASKA

Army-Air Force

(b)   *BOOKER, Robert D., Pvt., 34th Inf. Div. (Callaway).
(b)   CO-RUX-TE-CHOD-ISH (Mad Bear), Sgt., Pawnee Scouts, USA.
(b)   *FOUS, James W., Pfc., 9th Inf. Div. (Omaha).
(b)   HAGEMEISTER, Charles Cris, Spec. 5, 1st Cav. Div. (Lincoln).
(b)   KOUMA, Ernest R., M/Sgt., 2d Inf. Div. (Dwight).
    VIFQUAIN, Victor, Lt. Col., 97th Ill. Inf. (Saline County) (b. Belgium).

Navy-Marine Corps

    *BAUER, Harold William, Lt. Col., USMC (b. Kans.).
(b)   EHLE, John Walter, F1c., USN (Kearney).
(b)   *GOMEZ, Edward, Pfc., USMCR, 1st Marine Div. (Omaha).
    GRAVES, Ora, Seaman, USN (b. Colo.).
(b)   *HANSEN, Dale Merlin, Pvt., USMC (Wisner).
    *KEITH, Miguel, L/Cpl., 3rd Mar. Amph. Force (Omaha) (b. Tex.).
(b)   KERREY, Joseph Robert, Lt. (jg.), USN, SEAL Force (Lincoln).
(b)   *PARLE, John Joseph, Ens., USNR (Omaha).
(b)   SCHMIDT, Otto Diller, Seaman, USN (Blair).
(b)   VOLZ, Jacob, Carpenter's Mate, USN (Sutton).

NEVADA

Navy-Marine Corps

    *VAN VOORHIS, Bruce Alvery, Lt. Comdr., USN (b. Wash).

NEW HAMPSHIRE

Army-Air Force

(b)   APPLETON, William H., 1st Lt., 4th U.S. Colored Troops (Portsmouth).
(b)   BARKER, Nathaniel C., Sgt., 11th N.H. Inf. (Manchester).
(b)   BATCHELDER, Richard N., Lt. Col. and Chief Qm., 2d Corps (Manchester).
(b)   BOUTWELL, John W., Pvt., 18th N.H. Inf. (Hanover).
    BRADY, James, Pvt., 10th N.H. Inf. (Kingston) (b. Mass.).
(b)   CAMP, Carlton N., Pvt., 18th N.H. Inf. (Hanover).
(b)   CARR, Chris (name changed from Karaberis, Christos H.), Sgt., 337th Inf., 85th Inf. Div. (Manchester).
    COHN, Abraham, Sgt. Maj., 6th N.H. Inf. (Campton) (b. Prussia).

ARMY-AIR FORCE

(b) COPP, Charles D., 2d Lt., 9th N.H. Inf. (Nashua).
COUGHLIN, John, Lt. Col., 10th N.H. Inf. (Manchester) (b. Vt.).
(b) CRAIG, Samuel H., Sgt., 4th U.S. Cav. (New Market).
*DILBOY, George, Pfc., 103d Inf., 26th Div. (Keene) (b. Greece).
DILLON, Michael A., Pvt., 2d N.H. Inf. (Wilton) (b. Mass.).
(b) DOW, George P., Sgt., 7th N.H. Inf. (Atkinson).
(b) GOODALL, Francis H., 1st Sgt., 11th N.H. Inf. (Bath).
(b) GRIMES, Edward P., Sgt., 5th U.S. Cav. (Dover).
(b) HADLEY, Osgood T., Cpl., 6th N.H. Vet. Inf. (Nashua).
(b) HARRIS, Moses, 1st Lt., 1st U.S. Cav. (Andover).
KARABERIS, Christos H., Sgt., 85th Inf Div. (Manchester) (Name changed to Chris Carr). (See above.)
(b) KNIGHT, Charles H., Cpl., 9th N.H. Inf. (Keene).
(b) LITTLE, Henry F. W., Sgt., 7th N.H. Inf. (Manchester).
(b) NEAL, Solon D., Pvt., 6th U.S. Cav. (Hanover).
NOLAN, John J., Sgt., 8th N.H. Inf. (Nashua) (b. Ireland).
(b) *PEASE, Harl, Jr., Capt., Bomb. Sq. (H) (Plymouth).
(b) ROBIE, George F., Sgt., 7th N.H. Inf. (Candia).
(b) ROWE, Henry W., Pvt., 11th N.H. Inf. (Candia).
SIMONS, Charles J., Sgt., 9th N.H. Inf. (Exeter) (b. India).
TABOR, William L. S., Pvt., 15th N.H. Inf. (Concord) (b. Mass.).
TILTON, William, Sgt., 7th N.H. Inf. (Hanover) (b. Vt.).
(b) WILCOX, William H., Sgt., 9th N.H. Inf. (Lempster).
(b) WILKINS, Leander A., Sgt., 9th N.H. Inf. (Lancaster).

NAVY-MARINE CORPS

ANDERSON, Robert, Quartermaster, USN (b. Ireland).
(b) FOY, Charles H., Signal Quartermaster, USN (Portsmouth).
(b) FRANKLIN, Frederick, Quartermaster, USN (Portsmouth).
(b) GEORGE, Daniel G., Ordinary Seaman, USN (Plaistow).
(b) HAM, Mark G., CM, USN (Portsmouth).
HAWKINS, Charles, Seaman, USN (b. Scotland).
JONES, John, Landsman, USN (b. Conn.).
(b) MELVILLE, Charles, Ordinary Seaman, USN (Dover).
(b) O'KANE, Richard Hetherington, Cmdr., USN (Dover).
SMITH, William, Quartermaster, USN (b. Ireland).
(b) TODD, Samuel, Quartermaster, USN (Portsmouth).
(b) WEST, Walter Scott, Pvt., USMC (Bradford).

NEW JERSEY

ARMY-AIR FORCE

BART, Frank J., Pvt., 2d Div. (Newark) (b. N.Y.).
BEECH, John P., Sgt., 4th N.J. Inf. (Trenton) (b. England).
*BENJAMIN, George, Jr., Pfc., 77th Inf. Div. (Carney's Point) (b. Pa.).
(b) BRADBURY, Sanford, 1st Sgt., 8th U.S. Cav. (Sussex County).
(b) BRANT, William, Lt., 1st N.J. Vet. Bn. (Elizabeth).
(b) *BRITTIN, Nelson V., Sfc, 24th Inf. Div. (Audubon).
BURKE, Frank (Francis X), 1st Lt., 3d Inf. Div. (Jersey City) (b. N.Y.).
(b) CARMIN, Isaac H., Cpl., 48th Ohio Inf. (Monmouth County).
CASTLE, Frederick W., Brig. Gen., USAAC (Mountain Lake) (b. Philippine Islands).
(b) *COURSEN, Samuel S., 1st Lt., 1st Cav. Div. (Madison).
CUMMINGS, Amos J., Sgt. Maj., 26th N.J. Inf. (Irvington) (b. N.Y.).
(b) DRAKE, James M., 2d Lt., 9th N.J. Inf. (Elizabeth).
*DUTKO, John W., Pfc., 3d Inf. Div. (Riverside) (b. Pa.).
EGGERS, Alan L., Sgt., 27th Div. (Summit). (b. N.Y.).
ENGLISH, Edmund, 1st Sgt., 2d N.J. Inf. (Newark) (b. Ireland).
FALLON, Thomas T., Pvt., 37th N.Y. Inf. (Freehold) (b. Ireland).
FESQ, Frank, Pvt., 40th N.J. Inf. (Newark) (b. Germany).
(b) FOLLY, William H., Pvt., 8th U.S. Cav. (Bergen County).

NEW JERSEY—Continued

ARMY-AIR FORCE

GREGG, Stephen R., 2d Lt., 36th Inf. Div. (Bayonne) (b. N.Y.).
HEYL, Charles H., 2d Lt., 23d U.S. Inf. (Camden) (b. Pa.).
(b) HOPKINS, Charles F., Cpl., 1st N.J. Inf. (Warren County).
(b) *HOSKING, Charles Ernest, Jr., M/Sgt., 1st Special Forces (Ramsey).
(b) HOWARD, James, Sgt., 158th N.Y. Inf. (Newton).
(b) JACKSON, James, Capt., 1st U.S. Cav.
JACOBS, Jack H., Capt., U.S. Military Asst. Com. (Trenton) (b. N.Y.).
LATHAM, John C., Sgt., 27th Div. (Rutherford) (b. England).
LOCKE, Lewis, Pvt., 1st N.J. Cav. (Jersey City) (b. N.Y.).
(b) MAGEE, William, Drummer, 33d N.J. Inf. (Newark).
(b) *MAY, Martin O., Pfc., 77th Inf. Div. (Phillipsburg).
*McGRAW, Francis X., Pfc., 1st Inf. Div. (Camden) (b. Pa.).
(b) MEAGHER, John, T/Sgt., 77th Inf. Div. (Jersey City).
MILES, L. Wardlaw, Capt., 77th Div. (Princeton) (b. Md.).
*MINUE, Nicholas, Pvt., 1st Armd. Div. (Carteret) (b. Poland).
(b) ORESKO, Nicholas, M/Sgt., 94th Inf. Div. (Bayonne).
*O'SHEA, Thomas E., Cpl., 27th Div. (Summit) (b. N.Y.).
OSS, Albert, Pvt., 11th N.J. Inf. (Newark) (b. Belgium).
(b) PARKER, James, Lt. Col., 45th Inf., U.S. Vol. (Newark).
(b) *SADOWSKI, Joseph J., Sgt., 4th Armd. Div. (Perth Amboy).
(b) *SAWELSON, William, Sgt., 78th Div. (Harrison).
SEWELL, William J., Col., 5th N.J. Inf. (Camden) (b. Ireland).
(b) SHEERIN, John, Blacksmith, 8th U.S. Cav. (Camden County).
(b) SMITH, Theodore F., Pvt., 1st U.S. Cav. (Rahway).
(b) SOUTHARD, David, Sgt., 1st N.J. Cav. (Ocean County).
(b) STEWART, George W., 1st Sgt., 1st N.J. Cav. (Salem).
STREILE, Christian, Pvt., 1st N.J. Cav. (Jersey City) (b. Germany).
SULLIVAN, Thomas, Pvt., 7th U.S. Cav. (Newark) (b. Ireland).
TAYLOR, Forrester L., Capt., 23d N.J. Inf. (Burlington) (b. Pa.).
(b) THOMPKINS, William H., Pvt., 10th U.S. Cav. (Paterson).
(b) *THORNE, Horace M., Cpl., 9th Armd. Div. (Keyport).
(b) TILTON, Henry R., Maj. and Surg., USA (Jersey City).
(b) TITUS, Charles, Sgt., 1st N.J. Cav. (New Brunswick).
TOFFEY, John J., 1st Lt., 33d New Jersey Inf. (Hudson) (b. N.Y.).
(b) TOMPKINS, Aaron B., Sgt., 1st N.J. Cav. (Orange).
VAN IERSEL, Ludovicus M. M., Sgt., 2d Div. (Glen Rock) (b. Holland).
(b) WANTON, George H., Pvt., 10th U.S. Cav. (Paterson).
(b) *WATTERS, Charles Joseph, Chaplain (Maj.) 173rd Airborne Brig. (Jersey City).
WILSON, John, Sgt., 1st N.J. Cav. (Jersey City) (b. England).
(b) ZABITOSKY, Fred William, Sfc., 5th Spec. Forces Group (Trenton).

NAVY-MARINE CORPS

*BARKER, Jedh C., L/Cpl., 3d Mar. Div., USMC (Park Ridge) (b. N.H.).
BASILONE, John, Sgt., USMC (Rariton) (b. N.Y.).
(b) BEHNE, Frederick, F1c., USN (Lodi).
*BENFOLD, Edward C., HC3c., USN (Camden) (b. N.Y.).
BLUME, Robert, Seaman, USN (b. Pa.).
(b) BREEMAN, George, Seaman, USN (Passaic).
CAFFERATA, Hector A., Jr., Pvt., 1st Marine Div., USMC (Montville) (b. N.Y.).
(b) *CHOLISTER, George Robert, BM1c., USN (Camden).
(b) *CONNOR, Peter S., S/Sgt., 1st Marine Div. (Rein) (Orange).
COONEY, Thomas C., Chief Machinist, USN (b. Canada).
(b) DAVIS, John, Quarter Gunner, USN (Cedarville).
(b) EILERS, Henry A., GM, USN (Newark).
(b) FRYER, Eli Thompson, Capt., USMC (Hightstown).
(b) HAMBERGER, William F., CCM, USN (Newark).
HARVEY, Harry, Sgt., USMC (b. N.Y.).
(b) KANE, Thomas, Captain of the Hold, USN (Jersey City).
(b) MAGER, George Frederick, Apprentice First Class, USN (Phillipsburg).
(b) PARKER, Alexander, BM, USN (Kensington).
PETERSEN, Carl Emil, Chief Machinist, USN (b. Germany).

338

Navy-Marine Corps

PFEIFER, Louis Fred, Pvt., USMC (b. Pa.).
(b) PRESTON, Herbert Irving, Pvt., USMC (Berkeley).
(b) ROUH, Carlton Robert, 1st Lt., USMCR (Lindenwold).
     SHIVERS, John, Pvt., USMC (b. Canada).
     SIEGEL, John Otto, BM2d., USN (b. Wisconsin).
(b) SIGLER, Franklin Earl, Pvt., USMCR (Glenridge).
(b) STRAHAN, Robert, Captain of the Top, USN.
     †SWEENEY, Robert, Ordinary Seaman, USN (b. Canada).
     TEYTAND, August P., QM3d., USN (b. West Indies).
     *TOMICH, Peter, CWT, USN (b. Austria).
(b) TOMLIN, Andrew J., Cpl., USMC (Goshin).
(b) VAN ETTEN, Hudson, Seaman, USN (Port Jervis).
(b) WEEKS, Charles H., Captain of Foretop, USN.
(b) WHITFIELD, Daniel, Quartermaster, USN (Newark).
(b) YOUNG, Edward B., Cox., USN (Bergen).

NEW MEXICO

Army-Air Force

(b) *FERNANDEZ, Daniel, Spec. 4, 25th Inf. Div. (Albuquerque).
     McDONALD, Robert, 1st Lt., 5th U.S. Inf. (Fort Sumner) (b. N.Y.).
     *MILLER, Franklin D., S/Sgt., 1st Spec. Forces (Albuquerque) (b. N.C.).
(b) MIYAMURA, Hiroshi H., Cpl., 3d Inf. Div. (Gallup).
(b) RUIZ, Alejandro Renteria, Pfc., 27th Inf. Div. (Carlsbad).
     SCOTT, Robert S., Capt., 43d Inf. Div. (Santa Fe) (b. D.C.).

Navy-Marine Corps

*BONNYMAN, Alexander, Jr., 1st Lt., USMCR (b. Ga.).

NEW YORK

Army-Air Force

ALLEN, James, Pvt., 16th N.Y. Inf. (Potsdam) (b. Ireland).
(b) ALLEN, William, 1st Sgt., 23d U.S. Inf. (Lansingburg).
(b) ANDERSON, Bruce, Pvt., 142d N.Y. Inf. (Ephratah).
(b) ARCHER, Lester, Sgt., 96th N.Y. Inf. (Fort Ann).
     *ASHLEY, Eugene, Jr., Sfc., 1st Spec. Forces (New York) (b. N.C.).
     AUSTIN, William G., Sgt., 7th U.S. Cav. (New York) (b. Tex.).
     BAKER, John, Musician, 5th U.S. Inf. (Brooklyn) (b. Germany).
(b) *BAKER, Thomas A., Sgt., 27th Inf. Div. (Troy).
(b) BARNUM, Henry A., Col., 149th N.Y. Inf. (Syracuse).
(b) BARRETT, Carlton W., Pvt., 1st Inf. Div. (Luzerne).
(b) BATES, Delavan, Col., 30th U.S. Colored Troops (Oswego County).
(b) BEIKIRCH, Gary B., Sgt., 1st Spec. Forces (Buffalo).
     BELL, Bernard P., T/Sgt., 36th Inf. Div. (New York) (b. W.Va.).
(b) BENJAMIN, John F., Cpl., 2d N.Y. Cav. (Orange County).
(b) BENJAMIN, Samuel N., 1st Lt., 2d U.S. Arty. (New York).
     BICKFORD, Henry H., Cpl., 8th N.Y. Cav. (Hartland) (b. Mich.).
(b) BLUNT, John W., 1st Lt., 6th N.Y. Cav. (Chatham, Four Corners).
(b) BOEHM, Peter M., 2d Lt., 15th N.Y. Cav. (Brooklyn).
(b) BOWEN, Chester B., Cpl., 19th N.Y. Cav. (1st N.Y. Dragoons) (Nunda).
(b) *BOYCE, George W. G., Jr., 2d Lt., 112th Cav. Regimental Cmbt. Team (New York).
     BRADLEY, Thomas W., Sgt., 124th N.Y. Inf. (Walden) (b. England).
(b) BREWER, William J., Pvt., 2d N.Y. Cav. (New York).
(b) BRINGLE, Andrew, Cpl., 10th N.Y. Cav. (Buffalo).
     BROSNAN, John, Sgt., 164th N.Y. Inf. (NewYork) (b. Ireland).
     BROWN, Edward, Jr., Cpl., 62d N.Y. Inf. (New York) (b. Ireland).
(b) BROWN, Henri Le Fevre, Sgt., 72d N.Y. Inf. (Ellicott).
(b) *BROWN, Morris, Jr., Capt., 126th N.Y. Inf. (Penn Yan).

NEW YORK—Continued

ARMY-AIR FORCE

(b) BROWNELL, Francis E., Pvt., 11th N.Y. Inf. (Troy).
(b) BRUSH, George W., Lt., 34th U.S. Colored Troops (New York).
BRUTON, Christopher C., Capt., 22d N.Y. Cav. (Riga).
BUCHA, Paul William, Capt., 101st Airborne Div. (West Point) (b. D.C.).
(b) *BUCHANAN, George A., Pvt., 148th N.Y. Inf. (Ontario County).
BUCKLEY, Denis, Pvt., 136th N.Y. Inf. (Avon) (b. Canada).
BURK, E. Michael, Pvt., 125th N.Y. Inf. (Troy) (b. Ireland).
(b) BURK, Thomas, Sgt., 97th N.Y. Inf. (Harrisburg).
BUTLER, Edmond, Capt., 5th U.S. Inf. (Brooklyn) (b. Ireland).
(b) *BUTTS, John E., 2d Lt., 9th Inf. Div. (Buffalo).
(b) CADWELL, Luman L., Sgt., 2d N.Y. Vet. Cav. (Broome).
(b) CALKIN, Ivers S., 1st Sgt., 2d N.Y. Cav. (Willsborough).
(b) CALL, Donald M., Cpl., 344th Bn., Tank Corps., U.S. Army (Larchmont Manor).
(b) CAMPBELL, James A., Pvt., 2d N.Y. Cav. (New York).
(b) CAREY, James L., Sgt., 10th N.Y. Cav. (Onondaga County).
(b) CARMAN, Warren, Pvt., 1st N.Y. Cav. (Seneca County).
(b) CARR, Eugene A., Col., 3d Ill. Cav. (Hamburg).
(b) CARTER, John J., 2d Lt., 33d N.Y. Inf. (Nunda).
CARTER, William H., 1st Lt., 6th U.S. Cav. (New York) (b. Tenn.).
CASEY, James S., Capt., 5th U.S. Inf. (New York) (b. Pa.).
*CASTLE, Frederick W., Brig. Gen., 8th AF (West Point) (b. P.I.).
(b) CATLIN, Isaac S., Col., 109th N.Y. Inf. (Oswego).
CHANDLER, Stephen E., Q.M. Sgt., 24th N.Y. Cav. (Granby) (b. Mich.).
(b) CHAPIN, Alaric B., Pvt., 142d N.Y. Inf. (Pamelia).
*CHARLTON, Cornelius H., Sgt., 25th Inf. Div. (Bronx) (b. W. Va.).
*CHELI, Ralph, Maj., Air Corps (Brooklyn) (b. Calif.).
(b) CLANCY, James T., Sgt., 1st N.J. Cav. (Albany).
(b) CLANCY, John E., Mus., 1st U.S. Arty. (New York).
(b) CLAPP, Albert A., 1st Sgt., 2d Ohio Cav. (Pompey).
(b) CLARK, Francis J., T/Sgt., 28th Inf. Div. (Salem).
(b) CLARK, Harrison, Cpl., 125th N.Y. Inf. (Chatham).
(b) CLARKE, Dayton P., Capt., 2d Vt. Inf. (Hermon).
(b) CLEVELAND, Charles F., Pvt., 26th N.Y. Inf. (Hartford).
(b) COEY, James, Maj., 147th N.Y. Inf. (New York).
(b) COLLINS, Thomas D., Sgt., 143 N.Y. Inf. (Liberty).
(b) *COLYER, Wilbur E., Sgt., 1st Div. (South Ozone, L.I.).
(b) COMPSON, Hartwell B., Maj., 8th N.Y. Cav. (Seneca Falls).
CONBOY, Martin, Sgt., 37th N.Y. Inf. (New York).
(b) CONGDON, James. Sgt., 8th N.Y. Cav. (Fairport) (Served as James Madison, see below.)
(b) CORLISS, Stephen P., 1st Lt., 4th N.Y. Hvy. Arty. (Albany).
(b) COYNE, John N., Sgt., 70th N.Y. Inf. (New York).
(b) CROSIER, William H., Sgt., 149th N.Y. Inf. (Skaneateles).
(b) CROSS, James E., Cpl., 12th N.Y. Inf. (Darien).
(b) CROWLEY, Michael, Pvt., 22d N.Y. Cav. (Rochester).
(b) CUNNINGHAM, Charles, Cpl., 7th U.S. Cav. (Hudson).
CURRAN, Richard, Asst. Surg., 33d N.Y. Inf. (Seneca Falls) (b. Ireland).
(b) CURREY, Francis S., Sgt., 30th Inf. Div. (Hurleyville).
(b) CURTIS, Newton Martin, Brig. Gen., U.S. Vol. (De Peyster).
(b) *DALESSONDRO, Peter J., T/Sgt., 9th Inf. Div. (Watervliet).
DAVIDSON, Andrew, 1st Lt., 30th U.S. Colored Troops (Oswego County) (b. Scotland).
DAVIS, John, G.M. 3c, USN (New York) (b. Germany).
DAVIS, Thomas, Pvt., 2d N.Y. Hvy. Arty. (b. Wales).
(b) *DeGLOPPER, Charles N., Pfc., 82d Airborne Div. (Grand Island).
(b) DENNY, John, Sgt., Company C, 9th U.S. Cav. (Elmira).
DI CESNOLA, Louis P., Col., 4th N.Y. Cav. (New York) (b. Italy).
(b) DICKEY, William D., Capt., 15th N.Y. Hvy. Arty. (Newburgh).
(b) *DIETZ, Robert H., S/Sgt., 38th Armd. Inf. Bn., 7th Armd. Div. (Kingston).
DILGER, Hubert, Capt., 1st Ohio Light Arty. (New York) (b. Germany).
*DOANE, Stephen Holden, 1st Lt., 25th Inf. Div. (Walton) (b. Mass.).
(b) DOCKUM, Warren C., Pvt., 121st N.Y. Inf. (Clintonville).

340

ARMY-AIR FORCE

DODDS, Edward E., Sgt., 21st N.Y. Cav. (Rochester) (b. Canada).
(b) DONALDSON, Michael A., Sgt., 165th Inf., 42d Div. (Haverstraw).
DONELLY, John S., Pvt., 5th U.S. Inf. (Buffalo) (b. Ireland).
(b) DONAVAN, William Joseph, Lt. Col., 42d Div. (Buffalo).
(b) DONLON, Roger Hugh C., Capt., U.S. Army (Saugerties).
DOODY, Patrick, Cpl., 164th N.Y. Inf. (New York) (b. Ireland).
(b) *DUNN, Parker F., Pfc., 78th Div. (Albany).
EDWARDS, David, Pvt., 146th N.Y. Inf. (Sangersfield) (b. England).
(b) EDWARDS, William D., 1st Sgt., 7th U.S. Inf. (Brooklyn).
(b) ELDRIDGE, George H., Sgt., 6th U.S. Cav. (Sacketts Harbor).
(b) EMBLER, Andrew H., Capt., 59th N.Y. Inf. (New York).
(b) EMMET, Robert Temple, 2d Lt., 9th U.S. Cav. (New York).
(b) EVANS, James R., Pvt., 62d N.Y. Inf. (New York).
(b) EVERSON, Adelbert, Pvt., 185th N.Y. Inf. (Salina).
(b) FARNSWORTH, Herbert E., Sgt. Maj., 10th N.Y. Cav. (Cattaraugus County).
(b) FISHER, Almond E., 2d Lt., 45th Inf. Div. (Brooklyn).
(b) FOURNIA, Frank O., Pvt., 21st U.S. Inf. (Plattsburg).
*FRATELLENICO, Frank R., Cpl., 101st Airborne Div. (Chatham) (b. Conn.).
(b) FREEMAN, Archibald, Pvt., 124th N.Y. Inf. (Newburgh).
(b) FREEMAN, William H., Pvt., 169th N.Y. Inf. (Troy).
(b) GAFFNEY, Frank, Pfc., 108th Inf., 27th Div. (Niagara Falls).
(b) *GARBIARZ, William J., Pfc., 1st Cav. Div. (Buffalo).
(b) GARDINER, Peter W., Pvt., 6th U.S. Cav. (Carlisle).
(b) GERE, Thomas P., 1st Lt. and Adj., 5th Minn. Inf. (Chemung County).
*GERTSCH, John G., S/Sgt., 101st Airborne Div. (Buffalo) (b. N.J.).
(b) GIFFORD, Benjamin, Pvt., 121st N.Y. Inf. (German Flats).
GILMORE, John C., Maj., 16th N.Y. Inf. (Potsdam) (b. Canada).
GINLEY, Patrick, Pvt., 1st N.Y. Light Arty. (New York) (b. Ireland).
(b) GLOVER, T. B., Sgt., 2d U.S. Cav. (New York).
(b) GOETTEL, Philip, Pvt., 149th N.Y. Inf. (Syracuse).
(b) GOHEEN, Charles A., 1st Sgt., 8th N.Y. Cav. (Groveland).
(b) GOODRICH, Edwin, 1st Lt., 9th N.Y. Cav. (Westfield).
(b) GOURAUD, George E., Capt. and Aide-de-Camp, U.S. Vol. (New York).
GRANT, Gabriel, Surg., U.S. Vol. (New York) (b. N.J.).
(b) GREENE, Oliver D., Maj. and Asst. Adj. Gen., USA (Scott).
(b) GREIG, Theodore W., 2d Lt., 61st N.Y. Inf. (Staten Island).
GRINDLAY, James G., Col., 146th N.Y. Inf. (Utica).
GRUEB, George, Pvt., 158th N.Y. Inf. (New York) (b. Germany).
(b) *GUENETTE, Peter M., Sp4c., 101st Airborne Div. (Albany).
(b) HAIGHT, John H., Sgt., 72d N.Y. Inf. (Westfield).
HALL, Francis B., Chaplain, 16th N.Y. Inf. (Plattsburg).
(b) HALL, H. Seymour, 2d Lt., 27th N.Y. Inf., and Capt., 121st N.Y. Inf. (New York).
(b) HALLOCK, Nathan M., Pvt., 124th N.Y. Inf. (Middletown).
HAMILTON, Mathew H., Pvt., 7th U.S. Cav. (New York) (b. Australia).
(b) HAMILTON, Pierpont M., Maj., A.C. (New York).
(b) HANFORD, Edward R., Pvt., 2d U.S. Cav. (Alleghany County).
(b) HARING, Abram P., 1st Lt., 132d N.Y. Inf. (New York).
(b) HARRIS, Charles D., Sgt., 8th U.S. Cav. (Albion).
(b) HART, William E., Pvt., 8th N.Y. Cav. (Pittsford).
HARVEY, Harry, Cpl., 22d N.Y. Cav. (Rochester) (b. England).
(b) HATCH, John P., Brig. Gen., U.S. Vol. (Oswego).
(b) HAWTHORNE, Harris S., Cpl., 121st N.Y. Inf. (Otego).
(b) HEERMANCE, William L., Capt., 6th N.Y. Cav. (Kinderhook).
HIBSON, Joseph C., Pvt., 48th N.Y. Inf. (New York) (b. England).
(b) HICKEY, Dennis W., Sgt., 2d N.Y. Cav. (Troy).
(b) HILL, James, Sgt., 14th N.Y. Hvy. Arty. (Lyons).
(b) HILLS, William G., Pvt., 9th N.Y. Cav. (Conewango).
[1] HOFFMAN, Charles F., Gun. Sgt., 2d Div., USMC (Brooklyn) (Real name: Ernest A. Janson).

[1] Note: Later changed name to Janson, Ernest A. Also received Navy Medal of Honor for same act and appears under Janson under Navy and Marine list.

NEW YORK—Continued

(b) HOGARTY, William P., Pvt., 23d N.Y. Inf. (New York).
HORAN, Thomas, Sgt., 72d N.Y. Inf. (Dunkirk).
(b) HOUGHTON, Charles H., Capt., 14th N.Y. Arty. (Ogdensburg).
(b) HOULTON, William, Com. Sgt., 1st W. Va. Cav. (Clymer).
(b) HUMPHREY, Charles F., 1st Lt., 4th U.S. Arty. (New York).
IRSCH, Francis, Capt., 45th N.Y. Inf. (New York).
IRWIN, Bernard J. D., Asst. Surg., U.S. Army (New York) (b. Ireland).
JACOBSON, Eugene P., Sgt. Maj., 74th N.Y. Inf. (New York).
JAMIESON, Walter, 1st Sgt., 139th N.Y. Inf. (New York) (b. France).
(b) JARVIS, Frederick, Sgt., 1st U.S. Cav. (Essex County).
JOEL, Lawrence, Spec. 6, 173d Airborne Brig. (New York) (b. N.C.).
(b) JOHNSON, Follett, Cpl., 60th N.Y. Inf. (St. Lawrence).
(b) JOHNSON, Wallace W., Sgt., 6th Pa. Res. (Waverly).
(b) JOHNSTON, Edward, Cpl., 5th U.S. Inf. (Buffalo).
JONES, William, 1st Sgt., 73d N.Y. Inf. (New York) (b. Ireland).
KAPPESSER, Peter, Pvt., 149th N.Y. Inf. (Syracuse) (b. Germany).
(b) *KAROPCZYC, Stephen Edward, 1st Lt., 25th Inf. Div. (Bethpage).
(b) KAUFMAN, Benjamin, 1st Sgt., 308th Inf., 77th Div. (Brooklyn).
KAUSS (KAUTZ), August, Cpl., 15th N.Y. Hvy. Arty. (New York) (b. Germany).
(b) *KEDENBURG, John J., Spec. 5, 1st Spec. For. (Massapequa).
KEELE, Joseph, Sgt. Maj., 182d N.Y. Inf. (Staten Island) (b. Ireland).
(b) KEENAN, Bartholomew T., Trumpeter, 1st U.S. Cav. (Brooklyn).
(b) KELLER, William, Pvt., 10th U.S. Inf. (Buffalo).
(b) KELLY, Daniel, Sgt., 8th N.Y. Cav. (Groveland).
KELLY, Thomas, Pvt., 6th N.Y. Inf. (b. Ireland).
KELLY, Thomas, Pvt., 21st U.S. Inf. (New York) (b. Ireland).
(b) KELLY, Thomas J., Cpl., 7th Armd. Div. (Brooklyn).
(b) KENYON, John S., Sgt., 3d N.Y. Cav. (Schenevus).
(b) KENYON, Samuel P., Pvt., 24th N.Y. Cav. (Oriskany Falls).
KEOUGH, John, Cpl., 67th Pa. Inf. (Albany) (b. Ireland).
(b) KIGGINS, John, Sgt., 149th N.Y. Inf. (Syracuse).
KING, Horatio C., Maj. and Qm., U.S. Vol. (Brooklyn) (b. Maine).
(b) KING, Rufus, Jr., 1st Lt., 4th U.S. Arty. (New York).
KLINE, Harry, Pvt., 40th N.Y. Inf. (Syracuse) (b. Germany).
(b) KNOX, Edward M., 2d Lt., 15th N.Y. Btry. (New York).
†*KOCAK, |Matej, Sgt., USMC (New York)| (b. Austria) (Also received Navy Medal of Honor).
KOELPIN, William, Sgt., 5th U.S. Inf. (New York) (b. Prussia).
(b) KUDER, Andrew, 2d Lt., 8th N.Y. Cav. (Groveland).
(b) LADD, George, Pvt., 22d N.Y. Cav. (Camillus).
(b) LAING, William, Sgt., 158th N.Y. Inf. (New York).
(b) LANG, George C., Spec. 4, 9th Inf. Div. (Flushing).
LANGBEIN, J. C. Julius, Musician, 9th N.Y. Inf. (New York) (b. Germany).
*LANGHORN, Garfield M., Pfc., 1st Aviation Brig. (Riverhead) (b. Va.).
LAWTON, Louis B., 1st Lt., 9th U.S. Inf. (Auburn) (b. Iowa).
(b) LEVY, Benjamin, Pvt., 1st N.Y. Inf. (New York).
LIBAIRE, Adolphe, Capt., 9th N.Y. Inf. (New York).
LITEKY, Angelo J., Chaplain (Capt.) 199th Inf. Brigade (Fort Hamilton) (b. D.C.).
(b) LOHNES, Francis W., Pvt., 1st Nebr. Vet. Cav. (Oneida County).
(b) LONG, Oscar F., 2d Lt., 5th U.S. Inf. (Utica).
(b) LONSWAY, Joseph, Pvt., 20th N.Y. Cav. (Clayton).
(b) LORISH, Andrew J., Com. Sgt., 19th N.Y. Cav. (1st N.Y. Dragoons) (Dansville).
(b) LOUE, George M., Col., 116th N.Y. Inf. (New York).
*LOZADA, Carlos James, Pfc., 173d Airborne Brig. (Bronx) (b. Puerto Rico).
*LUCAS, Andre C., Lt. Col., 101st Airborne Div. (b. D.C.).
LUDGATE, William, Capt., 59th N.Y. Vet. Inf. (New York) (b. England).
(b) LUTES, Franklin W., Cpl., 111th N.Y. Inf. (Clyde).
(b) LYMAN, Joel H., Q.M. Sgt., 9th N.Y. Cav. (E. Randolph).
MADDEN, Michael, Pvt., 42d N.Y. Inf. (New York) (b. Ireland).
(b) MADISON, James, Sgt., 8th N.Y. Cav. (Fairport) (Real name James Congdon (see above)).

MANDY, Harry J., 1st Sgt., 4th N.Y. Cav. (New York) (b. England).
(b) MARSH, Albert, Sgt., 64th N.Y. Inf. (Randolph).
(b) McBRIDE, Bernard, Pvt., 8th U.S. Cav. (Brooklyn).
McBRYAR, William, Sgt., 10th U.S. Cav. (New York) (b. N.C.).
McENROE, Patrick H., Sgt., 6th N.Y. Cav. (New York) (b. Ireland).
(b) McGINN, Edward, Pvt., 54th Ohio Inf. (New York).
(b) McHUGH, John, Pvt., 5th U.S. Inf. (Syracuse).
(b) McKAY, Charles W., Sgt., 154th N.Y. Inf. (Allegheny).
McMURTRY, George G., Capt., 77th Div. (New York) (b. Pennsylvania).
(b) McVEAGH, Charles H., Pvt., 8th U.S. Cav. (New York).
McVEANE, John P., Cpl., 49th N.Y. Inf. (Buffalo) (b. Canada).
(b) MEACH, George E., Farrier, 6th N.Y. Cav. (New York).
MEAGHER, Thomas, 1st Sgt., 158th N.Y. Inf. (Brooklyn) (b. Scotland).
(b) *MERRELL, Joseph F., Pvt., 3d Inf. Div. (Staten Island).
(b) MERRILL, George, Pvt., 142d N.Y. Inf. (Queensbury).
(b) MERRILL, John, Sgt., 5th U.S. Cav. (New York).
(b) MERRITT, John G., Sgt., 1st Minn. Inf. (New York).
(b) MEYER, Henry C., Capt., 24th N.Y. Cav. (Dobbs Ferry).
(b) MILLER, Frank, Pvt., 2d N.Y. Cav. (Jamaica).
(b) MILLER, George, Cpl., 5th U.S. Inf. (Brooklyn).
MILLER, John, Pvt., 8th N.Y. Cav. (Rochester) (b. Germany).
(b) MILLS, Albert L., Capt., U.S. Vol. (New York).
(b) MILLS, Frank W., Sgt., 1st N.Y. Mtd. Rifles (Middletown).
(b) MOFFITT, John H., Cpl., 16th N.Y. Inf. (Plattsburg).
(b) MOQUIN, George, Cpl., 5th U.S. Cav. (New York).
MORSE, Charles E., Sgt., 62d N.Y. Inf. (New York) (b. France).
*MULLER, Joseph E., Sgt., 77th Inf. Div. (New York) (b. Mass.).
MURPHY, Michael C., Lt. Col., 170th N.Y. Inf. (New York) (b. Ireland).
(b) MURPHY, Thomas, Cpl., 158th N.Y. Inf. (New York).
MURPHY, Thomas J., 1st Sgt., 146th N.Y. Inf. (New York) (b. Ireland).
(b) *MURRAY, Robert C., S/Sgt., 23d Inf. Div. (Bronx).
(b) NEAHR, Zachariah C., Pvt., 142d N.Y. Inf. (Canajoharie).
(b) NEWMAN, William H., Lt., 86th N.Y. Inf. (Orange County).
NIHILL, John, Pvt., 5th U.S. Cav. (Brooklyn) (b. Ireland).
(b) NIVEN, Robert, 2d Lt., 8th N.Y. Cav. (Rochester).
(b) NORTON, John R., Lt., 1st N.Y. Cav. (Ontario County).
(b) NORTON, Llewellyn P., Sgt., 10th N.Y. Cav. (Cortland County).
(b) NUTTING, Lee, Capt., 61st N.Y. Inf. (Orange County).
O'BEIRNE, James R., Capt., 37th N.Y. Inf. (New York) (b. Ireland).
(b) *O'BRIEN, William J., Lt. Col., 27th Inf. Div. (Troy).
(b) O'CALLAGHAN, John, Sgt., 8th U.S. Cav. (New York).
OLIVER, Paul A., Capt., 12th N.Y. Inf. (New York) (b. at Sea).
(b) O'NEIL, Richard W., Sgt., 165th Inf., 42d Div. (New York).
(b) ORR, Charles A., Pvt., 187th N.Y. Inf. (Bennington).
O'SULLIVAN, John, Pvt., 4th U.S. Cav. (New York) (b. Ireland).
(b) PACKARD, Loron F., Pvt., 5th N.Y. Cav. (Cuba).
(b) PARKS, Henry Jeremiah, Pvt., 9th N.Y. Cav. (Orangeville).
PARNELL, William R., 1st Lt., 1st U.S. Cav. (New York) (b. Ireland).
(b) PATTERSON, John H., 1st Lt., 11th U.S. Inf. (New York).
(b) PECK, Archie A., Pvt., 307th Inf., 77th Div. (Hornell).
(b) *PETERSON, George, S/Sgt., 1st Inf. Div. (Brooklyn).
(b) PFISTERER, Herman, Mus., 21st U.S. Inf. (New York).
(b) PLIMLEY, William, 1st Lt., 120th N.Y. Inf. (Catskill).
(b) PORTER, William, Sgt., 1st N.J. Cav. (New York).
(b) POTTER, Norman, F., 1st Sgt., 149th N.Y. Inf. (Pompey).
(b) POWERS, Thomas, Cpl., 1st U.S. Cav. (New York).
PRESTON, Noble D., 1st Lt. and Commissary, 10th N.Y. Cav. (Fulton).
(b) PUTNAM, Edgar P., Sgt., 9th N.Y. Cav. (Stockton).
QUINLAN, James, Maj., 88th N.Y. Inf. (New York) (b. Ireland).
RAFFERTY, Peter, Pvt., 69th N.Y. Inf. (New York) (b. Ireland).
(b) RAND, Charles F., Pvt., 12th N.Y. Inf. (Batavia).
(b) RANNEY, Myron H., Pvt., 13th N.Y. Inf. (Franklinville).

(b) *RAY, Bernard J., 1st Lt., 4th Inf. Div. (Baldwin).
(b) RAYMOND, William H., Cpl., 108th N.Y. Inf. (Penfield).
(b) READ, Morton A., Lt., 8th N.Y. Cav. (Brockport).
    REYNOLDS, George, Pvt., 9th N.Y. Cav. (New York) (b. Ireland).
    RHODES, Julius D., Pvt., 5th N.Y. Cav. (Springville) (b. Mich.).
(b) RIDDELL, Rudolph, Lt., 61st N.Y. Inf. (Hamilton).
(b) ROBERTSON, Robert S., 1st Lt., 93d N.Y. Inf. (Argyle).
(b) ROBINSON, John C., Brig. Gen., U.S. Vol. (Binghamton).
(b) ROCKEFELLER, Charles M., Lt., 178th N.Y. Inf. (New York).
(b) ROONEY, Edward, Pvt., 5th U.S. Inf. (Poughkeepsie).
(b) *ROOSEVELT, Theodore, Jr., Brig. Gen. (Oyster Bay).
(b) RUSSELL, Charles L., Cpl. 93d N.Y. Inf. (Malone).
(b) RUSSELL, James, Pvt., 1st U.S. Cav. (New York).
    RUTHERFORD, John T., 1st Lt., 9th N.Y. Cav. (Canton).
(b) SAGE, William H., Capt., 23d U.S. Inf. (Binghamton).
(b) SAGELHURST, John C., Sgt., 1st N.J. Cav. (Buffalo).
(b) SALE, Albert, Pvt., 8th U.S. Cav.
    *SANTIAGO-COLON, Hector, Spec. 4, 1st Cav. Div. (New York) (b. Puerto Rico).
(b) SARTWELL, Henry, Sgt., 123d N.Y. Inf. (Fort Ann).
(b) SCHAEFER, Joseph E., S/Sgt., 1st Inf. Div. (Long Island).
    SCHILLER, John, Pvt., 158th N.Y. Inf. (New York) (b. Germany).
    SCHMAL, George W., Blacksmith, 24th N.Y. Cav. (Buffalo) (b. Germany).
    SCHWAN, Theodore, 1st Lt., 10th U.S. Inf. (New York) (b. Germany).
(b) SCOFIELD, David H., Q.M. Sgt., 5th N.Y. Cav. (Mamaroneck).
(b) SCOTT, Robert B., Pvt., 8th U.S. Cav. (Washington County).
    SHALER, Alexander, Col., 65th N.Y. Inf. (New York) (b. Conn.).
(b) SHEA, Charles W., 2d Lt., 88th Inf. Div. (New York).
(b) SHIPLEY, Robert F., Sgt., 140th N.Y. Inf. (Wayne).
(b) *SHOUP, Curtis F., S/Sgt., 87th Inf. Div. (Buffalo).
(b) SICKLES, Daniel E., Maj. Gen., U.S. Vol. (New York).
(b) SIMMONS, John, Pvt., 2d N.Y. Hvy. Arty. (Liberty).
(b) SKELLIE, Ebenezer, Cpl., 112th N.Y. Inf. (Mina).
(b) SMITH, Charles E., Cpl., 6th U.S. Cav. (Auburn).
    SMITH, David L., Sgt., Btry. E., 1st N.Y. Light Arty. (Bath).
(b) *SMITH, George W., Pvt., 6th U.S. Cav. (Greenfield).
(b) SMITH, Richard, Pvt., 95th N.Y. Inf. (Haverstraw).
(b) SMITH, Wilson, Cpl., 3d N.Y. Light Arty. (Madison).
(b) SOVA, Joseph E., Saddler, 8th N.Y. Cav. (Chili).
    STAHEL, Julius, Maj. Gen. U.S. Vol. (New York) (b. Hungary).
(b) STANLEY, Edward, Cpl., 8th U.S. Cav. (New York).
(b) STARKINS, John H., Sgt., 34th N.Y. Btry. (Great Neck).
    STEWART, George E., 2d Lt., 19th U.S. Inf. (New York) (b. Australia).
(b) *STONE, Lester R., Jr., Sgt., 23d Inf. Div. (Americal) (Harpursville).
(b) *STRYKER, Robert F., Spec. 4, 26th Inf. Div. (Throop).
(b) SWIFT, Harlan J., 2d Lt., 2d N.Y. Militia Regt. (New York).
    THACKRAH, Benjamin, Pvt., 115th N.Y. Inf. (Johnsonville) (b. Scotland).
(b) THOMPKINS, George W., Cpl., 124th N.Y. Inf. (Port Jervis).
(b) THOMPSON, Allen, Pvt., 4th N.Y. Hvy. Arty. (Sandy Creek).
(b) THOMPSON, George W., Pvt., 2d U.S. Cav. (Victory).
(b) THOMPSON, James, Pvt., 4th N.Y. Hvy. Arty. (Sandy Creek).
    THOMPSON, J. (James) Harry, Surgeon, U.S. Vol. (New York) (b. England).
    THOMPSON, John, Sgt., 1st U.S. Cav. (New York) (b. Scotland).
(b) *THOMPSON, William, Pfc., 25th Inf. Div. (Bronx).
    THOMSON, Clifford, 1st Lt., 1st N.Y. Cav. (New York).
(b) THORN, Walter, 2d Lt., 116th U.S. Colored Troops.
    TOMPKINS, Charles H., 1st Lt., 2d U.S. Cav. (Brooklyn) (b. Va.).
(b) TOOHEY, Thomas, Sgt., 24th Wis. Inf. (New York).
(b) TOY, Frederick E., 1st Sgt., 7th U.S. Cav. (Buffalo).
(b) TRACY, Benjamin F., Col., 109th N.Y. Inf. (Oswego, N.Y.).
(b) TRACY, William G., 2d Lt., 122d N.Y. Inf. (Onondaga County).
    TRAYNOR, Andrew, Cpl., 1st Mich. Cav. (Rome) (b. N.J.).

NEW YORK—Continued

Army-Air Force

(b) TREMAIN, Henry E., Maj. and Aide-de-Camp, U.S. Vol. (New York).
(b) TRIBE, John, Pvt., 5th N.Y. Cav. (Oswego).
     *TURNER, William B., 1st Lt., 27th Div. (Garden City) (b. Mass.).
     VALENTE, Michael, Pvt., 107th Inf. 27th Div. (Ogdensburg) (b. Italy).
     *VANCE, Leon R., Jr., Lt. Col., 8th A.F. (Garden City) (b. Okla.).
(b) VANSCHAICK, Louis J., 1st Lt., 4th U.S. Inf. (Cobleskill).
(b) VAN WINKLE, Edward, Cpl., 148th N.Y. Inf. (Phelps).
     VON VEGESACK, Ernest, Maj., U.S. Vol. (New York) (b. Belgium).
(b) VOSLER, Forrest L., T/Sgt., A.C. (Rochester).
     WAALER, Reidar, Sgt., 105th M.G. Bn., 27th Div. (New York) (b. Norway).
     WAINWRIGHT, Jonathan M., Gen., Commanded USA in Philippines (Skaneateles) (b. Wash.).
(b) WALL, Jerry, Pvt., 126th N.Y. Inf. (Milo).
(b) WALLING, William H., Capt., 142d N.Y. Inf. (Hartford).
     WAMBSGAN, Martin, Pvt., 90th N.Y. Inf. (Cayuga County) (b. Germany).
(b) *WARREN, John E., Jr., 1st Lt., 25th Inf. Div. (Brooklyn).
(b) WATSON, James C., Cpl., 6th U.S. Cav. (Cochecton).
(b) WEBB, Alexander S., Brig. Gen., U.S. Vol. (New York).
(b) WEBB, James, Pvt., 5th N.Y. Inf. (Brooklyn).
     WEEKS, John H., Pvt., 152d N.Y. Inf. (Hartwick Seminary) (b. Conn.).
(b) WEIR, Henry C., Capt., and Asst. Adj. Gen., U.S. Vol. (West Point).
(b) WELCH, Michael, Sgt., 6th U.S. Cav. (Poughkeepsie).
(b) WELCH, Stephen, Sgt., 154th N.Y. Inf. (Cattaraugus County).
     *WELLS, Henry S., Pvt., 148th N.Y. Inf. (Phelps).
     WELLS, Thomas M., Chief Bugler, 6th N.Y. Cav. (DeKalb) (b. Ireland).
(b) WEST, Frank, 1st Lt., 6th U.S. Cav. (Mohawk).
     *WILL, Walter J., 1st Lt., 1st Inf. Div. (W. Winfield) (b. Pa.).
(b) *WILLETT, Louis E., Pfc., 4th Inf. Div. (Brooklyn).
(b) WILLIAMS, Le Roy, Sgt., 8th N.Y. Hvy. Arty. (Oswego).
     WINDOLPH, Charles, Pvt., 7th U.S. Cav. (Brooklyn) (b. Germany).
(b) WINEGAR, William W., Lt., 19th N.Y. Cav. (1st N.Y. Dragoons) (Springport).
(b) WISNER, Lewis S., 1st Lt., 124th N.Y. Inf. (Wallkill).
(b) WRIGHT, Raymond R., Sp 4c., 9th Inf. Div. (Mineville).
(b) YOUNG, James M., Pvt., 72d N.Y. Inf. (Chautauqua County).

Navy-Marine Corps

     AHERN, William, WT, USN (b. Ireland).
     ALLEN, Edward, BM 1c., USN (b. Holland).
     ANDERSON, William, Cox., USN (b. Sweden).
(b) APPLETON, Edwin Nelson, Cpl., USMC (Brooklyn).
(b) AUER, John F., Ordinary Seaman Apprentice, USN (New York).
     AVERY, James, Seaman, USN (b. Scotland).
     BAKER, Charles, Quarter Gunner, USN (New York) (b. D.C.).
(b) BARTER, Gurdon H., Landsman, USN (Williamsburgh).
     BASS, David L., Seaman, USN (b. Ireland).
     BATES, Richard, Seaman, USN (b. Wales).
     BELL, George, Captain of the Afterguard, USN (Brooklyn) (b. England).
(b) BENNETT, Floyd, Machinist, USN (Warrensburg).
(b) BENNETT, James H., CBM, USN (New York).
(b) BETHAM, Asa, Cox., USN (New York).
     BJORKMAN, Ernest H., Ordinary Seaman, USN (b. Sweden).
     BLAGHEEN, William, SC, USN (b. England).
(b) *BOBO, John P., 2d Lt., 3d Marine Div. (Niagara Falls).
     BOURNE, Thomas, Seaman, USN (New York) (b. England).
(b) BRADLEY, Amos, Landsman, USN (Dansville).
     BRADLEY, Charles, BM, USN (b. Ireland).
     BRADY, George F., CGM, USN (b. Ireland).
(b) BREEN, John, BM, USN (New York).
     BRINN, Andrew, Seaman, USN (b. Scotland).
(b) BROWN, Charles, Cpl., USMC (New York) (Enlisted at Hong Kong, China).
(b) BROWN, James, Quartermaster, USN (Rochester).

345

NAVY-MARINE CORPS

BROWN, John, Captain of Forecastle, USN (b. Scotland).
BROWN, Robert, Captain of Top, USN (b. Norway).
(b) BROWNELL, William P., Cox., USN (New York).
(b) BUCKLEY, Howard Major, Pvt., USMC (Croton Falls).
BURKE, Thomas, Seaman, USN (b. Ireland).
(b) BURNS, John M., Seaman, USN (Hudson).
BURTON, Albert, Seaman, USN (b. England).
BYRNES, James, BM., USN (b. Ireland).
CAHEY, Thomas, Seaman, USN (b. Ireland).
CANN, Tedford H., Seaman, USN (New York) (b. Conn.).
(b) *CAPODANNO, Vincent R., Lt. (Chaplain Corps) USNR, 1st Mar. Div. (Staten Island).
CAREY, James, Seaman, USN (Brooklyn) (b. Ireland).
CASSIDY, Michael, Landsman, USN (b. Ireland).
CAVANAUGH, Thomas, F1c., USN (b. Ireland).
CHANDRON, August, SA2d., USN (b. France).
CHAPUT, Louis G., Landsman, USN (b. Canada).
(b) CLANCY, Joseph, Chief, BM, USN (New York).
CLAUSEN, Claus Kristian, Cox., USN (New York) (b. Denmark).
COLBERT, Patrick, Cox., USN (b. Ireland).
(b) CONLAN, Dennis, Seaman, USN (New York).
†COOPER, John, Cox., USN (b. Ireland).
CORAHORGI, Demetri, F1c., USN. (b. Austria).
(b) CORCORAN, Thomas E., Landsman, USN.
(b) COREY, William, Landsman, USN (New York).
(b) COSTELLO, John, Ordinary Seaman, USN (Rouses Point).
(b) COTTON, Peter, Ordinary Seaman, USN (New York).
(b) CREELMAN, William J., Landsman, USN (Brooklyn).
(b) CREGAN, George, Cox., USN (New York).
(b) †DALY, Daniel, Gun. Sgt., USMC (Glen Cove).
DAVIS, John, GM3c., USN (New York) (b. Germany).
(b) DECKER, Percy A., BM2d., USN (New York).
DENHAM, Austin, Seaman, USN (b. England).
DENNING, Lorenzo, Landsman, USN (New York) (b. Conn.).
(b) DENSMORE, William, CBM, USN (New York).
DONNELLY, John, Ordinary Seaman, USN (b. England).
DOUGHERTY, Patrick, Landsman, USN (b. Ireland).
DUNPHY, Richard D., Coal Heaver, USN (b. Ireland).
EGLIT, John, Seaman, USN (b. Finland).
(b) ENGLISH, Thomas, SQM, USN (New York).
ERICKSON, John P., Captain of Forecastle, USN (b. England).
ERICKSON, Nick, Cox., USN (b. Finland).
EVERETTS, John, GM1c., USN (b. Canada).
(b) FARRELL, Edward, Quartermaster, USN (Saratoga).
FIELD, Oscar Wadsworth, Pvt., USMC (b. N.J.).
FITZGERALD, John, Pvt., USMC (b. Ireland).
FLANNAGAN, John, BM, USN (b. Ireland).
FLOOD, Thomas, Boy, USN (b. Ireland).
(b) FORBECK, Andrew P., Seaman, USN (New York).
(b) FOWLER, Christopher, Quartermaster, USN.
(b) FRANKLIN, Joseph John, Pvt., USMC (Buffalo).
(b) GALBRAITH, Robert, Apprentice First Class, USN (Brooklyn).
GARDNER, William, Seaman, USN (b. Ireland).
(b) GARRISON, James R., Coal Heaver, USN (Poughkeepsie).
GIBBONS, Michael, Oiler, USN (b. Ireland).
(b) GOWAN, William Henry, BM, USN (Rye).
GRAHAM, Robert, Landsman, USN (b. England).
*GRAVES, Terrence, 2d Lt., USMC (b. Tex.).
GREENE, John, Captain of Forecastle, USN (New York).
HALLING, Luovi, BM1c., USN (b. Sweden).
(b) HALSTEAD, William, Cox., USN.
(b) HAMILTON, Hugh, Cox., USN (New York).

346

(b) HARLEY, Bernard, Ordinary Seaman, USN (Brooklyn).
HARRIS, John, Captain of Forecastle, USN (b. Scotland).
(b) HARTIGAN, Charles Conway, Lt., USN (Middletown).
HILL, George, Chief Quarter Gunner, USN (b. England).
(b) HILL, William L., Captain of Top, USN (Brooklyn).
HINNEGAN, William, F2c., USN (b. Ireland).
(b) HOBAN, Thomas, Cox., USN (New York).
HOBSON, Richmond Pearson, Lieutenant, USN (b. Ala.).
HOLLAT, George, 3c Boy, USN (New York).
HOWARD, Martin, Landsman, USN (b. Ireland).
HUDSON, Michael, Sgt., USMC (b. Ireland).
(b) HUGHES, John Arthur, Capt., USMC (New York).
(b) HUSE, Henry McClaren Pinckney, Capt., USN (West Point).
(b) HUSKEY, Michael, Fireman, USN (New York).
(b) *HUTCHINS, Carlton Barmore, Lt., USN (Albany).
IRLAM, Joseph, Seaman, USN (b. England).
(b) IRVING, John, Cox., USN (Brooklyn).
IRVING, Thomas, Cox., USN (b. England).
IRWIN, Nicholas, Seaman, USN (b. Denmark).
(b) JACOBSON, Douglas Thomas, Pfc., USMCR (Rochester).
(b) †JANSON, Ernest August, Gun. Sgt., USMC (Also awarded Army Medal of Honor
under name of Hoffman, Charles F.) (Brooklyn).
JOHANSSON, Johan J., Ordinary Seaman, USN (b. Sweden).
JOHNSON, Henry, Seaman, USN (b. Norway).
JOHNSON, William, Cooper, USN (b. West Indies).
JONES, Andrew, CBM, USN (b. Ireland).
(b) JONES, John E., Quartermaster, USN (New York).
(b) JORDAN, Robert, Cox., USN (New York).
(b) KATES, Thomas Wilbur, Pvt., USMC (Shelby Center).
(b) KENYON, Charles, Fireman, USN.
KING, Hugh, Ordinary Seaman, USN (b. Ireland).
†KING, John, CWT, USN (b. Ireland).
(b) KING, Robert H., Landsman, USN.
(b) KINNAIRD, Samuel W., Landsman, USN (New York).
*†KOCAK, Matej, Sgt., 2d Div. USMC (New York) (b. Austria) (Also awarded
Army Medal of Honor).
KRAUSE, Ernest, Cox., USN (b. Germany).
KUCHNEISTER, Hermann William, Pvt., USMC (b. Germany).
(b) LAKIN, Thomas, Seaman, USN.
(b) LANN, John S., Landsman, USN (Rochester).
(b) LEE, James H., Seaman, USN.
LEJEUNE, Emile, Seaman, USN (b. France).
(b) LEONARD, Joseph, Pvt., USMC (Cohoes).
(b) LLOYD, John W., Cox, USN (New York).
LOW, George, Seaman, USN (b. Canada).
(b) LUCY, John, Second Class Boy, USN (New York).
MACHON, James, Boy, USN (b. England).
MACK, Alexander, Captain of Top, USN (b. Holland).
(b) MACKIE, John F., Cpl., USMC (New York).
MADDEN, William, Coal Heaver, USN (b. England).
MARTIN, William, Seaman, USN (b. Ireland).
(b) *McCARD, Robert Howard, Gun. Sgt., USMC (Syracuse).
(b) McCARTON, John, SP, USN (Brooklyn).
(b) McCLELLAND, Matthew, F1c., USN (Brooklyn).
(b) †McCLOY, John, CB, USN (Brewsters).
McGOWAN, John, Quartermaster, USN (b. Ireland).
McINTOSH, James, Captain of Top, USN (b. Canada).
McKENZIE, Alexander, BM, USN (b. Scotland).
(b) McKNIGHT, William, Cox., USN (Ulster County).
McNAMARA, Michael, Pvt., USMC (b. Ireland).
MILLIKEN, Daniel S., Quarter Gunner, USN (b. Maine).
(b) MILLMORE, John, Ordinary Seaman, USN (New York).

(b) MILLS, Charles, Seaman, USN (Upster).
(b) MITCHELL, Thomas, Landsman, USN (New York).
  MOORE, Charles, Landsman, USN (b. Ireland).
(b) MOORE, Francis, BM, USN (New York).
(b) MORGAN, James H., Captain of Top, USN (New York).
(b) MORRIS, John, Cpl., USMC (New York).
  MORRISON, John G., Cox., USN (Lansingburg) (b. Ireland).
  MORSE, William, Seaman, USN (b. Germany).
  MURPHY, John Edward, Cox., USN (b. Ireland).
  MURPHY, Patrick, BM, USN (b. Ireland).
(b) MURRAY, William H., Pvt., USMC (Brooklyn).
(b) NAYLOR, David, Landsman, USN (Thompsonville).
  NIBBE, John H., Quartermaster, USN (b. Germany).
(b) NICHOLS, William, Quartermaster, USN (New York).
  NOIL, Joseph B., Seaman, USN (b. Canada).
(b) *NOONAN, Thomas P., L/Cpl., 3rd Mar. Div. USMC (Brooklyn).
(b) NORDSIEK, Charles Luers, Ordinary Seaman, USN (New York).
  NORDSTROM, Isidor, CBM, USN (b. Sweden).
  NORRIS, J. W., Landsman, USN (b. England).
  OAKLEY, William, GM2d, USN (b. England).
  O'CONNELL, Thomas, Coal Heaver, USN (b. Ireland).
(b) O'DONOGHUE, Timothy, Seaman, USN (Rochester).
  OHMSEN, August, Master-at-Arms, USN (b. Germany).
(b) OMALLEY, Robert E., Sgt., 3d Mar. Div. (New York).
  OSEPINS, Christian, Seaman, USN (b. Holland).
(b) OVIATT, Miles M., Cpl., USMC (Cattarangus County).
(b) OWENS, Michael, Pvt., USMC (New York).
(b) PARKS, George, Captain of Forecastle, USN (Schenectady).
(b) PEASE, Joachim, Seaman, USN (Long Island).
(b) PERRY, Thomas, BM, USN.
(b) *PETERS, Lawrence David, Sgt., 1st Mar. Div., USMC (Binghamton).
  PETERSON, Alfred, Seaman, USN (b. Sweden).
  PHILLIPS, George F., M1c., USN (b. Mass.).
  PHINNEY, William, BM, USN (b. Norway).
(b) *POWERS, John James, Lt., USN (New York).
(b) PRICE, Edward, Cox., USN.
(b) PROVINCE, George, Ordinary Seaman, USN.
  PYNE, George, Seaman, USN (b. England).
(b) QUICK, Joseph, Cox., USN.
(b) READ, Charles, Ordinary Seaman, USN (Cambridge).
  REGAN, Patrick, Ordinary Seaman, USN (b. Ireland).
  REID, Patrick, CWT, USN (b. Ireland).
(b) RICHARDS, Louis, Quartermaster, USN (New York).
  ROANTREE, James S., Sgt., USMC (b. Ireland).
  ROBINSON, Alexander, BM, USN (b. England).
  ROBINSON, Charles, BM, USN (b. Scotland).
  ROBINSON, Thomas, Captain of Afterguard, USN (b. Norway).
(b) ROGERS, Samuel F., Quartermaster, USN (Buffalo).
  RUSSELL, Henry P., Landsman, USN (b. Canada).
(b) RUSSELL, John, Seaman, USN (New York).
(b) SCHEPKE, Charles S., GM1c., USN (New York).
(b) SCHNEPEL, Fred Jurgen, Ordinary Seaman, USN (New York).
  SCHUTT, George, Cox., USN (b. Ireland).
  SEANOR, James, Master-at-Arms, USN (b. Mass.).
  SHANAHAN, Patrick, CBM, USN (b. Ireland).
  SHARP, Hendrick, Seaman, USN (b. Spain).
  SHERIDAN, James, Quartermaster, USN (b. N.J.).
(b) SHIPMAN, William, Cox., USN (New York).
(b) SIMKINS, Lebbeus, Cox., USN (Utica).
  SIMPSON, Henry, F1c., USN (b. England).
(b) SMITH, Edwin, Ordinary Seaman, USN (New York).
(b) SMITH, James, Captain of Forecastle, USN (Albany).

(b) SMITH, James, Landsman, USN.
SMITH, James, Seaman, USN (b. Hawaii).
SMITH, John, Seaman, USN (b. Bermuda).
(b) SMITH, John, Second Captain of Top, USN (Albany).
SMITH, Oloff, Cox., USN (b. Sweden).
SMITH, Thomas, Seaman, USN (b. England).
(b) SMITH, Walter B., Ordinary Seaman, USN.
SMITH, Wilhelm, GM1c., USN (b. Germany).
(b) SMITH, Willard M., Cpl., USMC (Alleghany).
SPICER, William, GM1c., USN (b. England).
(b) SPROWLE, David, Orderly Sgt., USMC (Lisbon).
(b) STANLEY, Robert Henry, Hospital Apprentice, USN (Brooklyn).
STANTON, Thomas, USN (b. Ireland).
*STOCKHAM, Fred W., Gunnery Sgt., 6th Regt., USMC (New York) (b. Mich.).
(b) STOKES, John, Chief Master-at-Arms, USN (New York).
(b) STOUT, Richard, Landsman, USN.
(b) SULLIVAN, James, Ordinary Seaman, USN (New York).
(b) SULLIVAN, John, Seaman, USN (New York).
SULLIVAN, Timothy, Cox., USN (b. Ireland).
SUMMERS, Robert, Chief Quartermaster, USN (b. Prussia).
SUNDQUIST, Gustav A., Ordinary Seaman, USN (b. Sweden).
(b) SWATTON, Edward, Seaman, USN (New York).
(b) TAYLOR, George, Armorer, USN (Watertown).
THOMASS, Karl, Cox., USN (b. Germany).
THORDSEN, William George, Cox., USN (b. Germany).
TRIPLETT, Samuel, Ordinary Seaman, USN (b. Kans.).
(b) TROY, Jeremiah, CBM, USN (New York).
VADAS, Albert, Seaman, USN (b. Austria-Hungary).
WAGG, Maurice, Cox., USN (b. England).
WALKER, Edward Alexander, Sgt., USMC (b. Scotland).
(b) WALSH, James A., Seaman, USN (New York).
(b) WALSH, Kenneth Ambrose, 1st Lt., USMC (Brooklyn).
(b) WARD, James, Quarter Gunner, USN (New York).
WARREN, David, Cox., USN (b. Scotland).
(b) WEBSTER, Henry S., Landsman, USN (Stockholm).
WEISSEL, Adam, SC, USN (b. Germany).
WELLS, William, Quartermaster, USN (b. Germany).
WESTA, Karl, CMM, USN (b. Norway).
(b) WILCOX, Franklin L., Ordinary Seaman, USN (Paris).
WILKE, Julius A. R., BM1c., USN (b. Germany).
(b) WILKES, Henry, Landsman, USN (New York).
WILLIAMS, Frank, Seaman, USN (Buffalo) (b. Germany).
WILLIAMS, John, BM, USN (New York) (b. N.J.).
(b) WILLIAMS, Robert, Signal Quartermaster, USN (New York).
WILSON, August, Boilermaker, USN (b. Germany).
WOON, John, BM, USN (b. England).
(b) WORAM, Charles B., Seaman, USN (New York).
(b) WRIGHT, Edward, Quartermaster, USN (New York).
(b) YOUNG, William, BM, USN.

NORTH CAROLINA

ARMY-AIR FORCE

*BLACKWELL, Robert L., Pvt. 30th Div. (Hurdle Mills) (b. N. Dak.).
(b) CRUMP, Jerry K., Cpl., 3d Inf. Div. (Forest City).
(b) *EUBANKS, Ray E., Sgt., 503d Para. Inf. (LaGrange).
(b) *GEORGE, Charles, Pfc., 45th Inf. Div. (Whittier).
MURRAY, Charles P., Jr., 1st Lt., 3d Inf. Div. (Wilmington) (b. Md.).
(b) PARKER, Samuel I., 2d Lt., 1st Div. (Monroe).
(b) PATTERSON, Robert Martin, Spec. 4, 17th Cav. (Springlake).
*SIMS, Clifford Chester, S/Sgt., 101st Airborne Div. (Fayetteville) (b. Fla.).

Army-Air Force

*STOUT, Mitchell W., Sgt., 44th Arty. (b. Tenn.).
(b)   THOMPSON, Max, Sgt., 1st Inf. Div. (Canton).
(b)   *WARNER, Henry F., Cpl., 1st Inf. Div. (Troy).
(b)   *WOMACK, Bryant H., Pfc., 25th Inf. Div. (Mills Springs).

Navy-Marine Corps

(b)   ANDERSON, Edwin A., Capt., USN (Wilmington).
(b)   *HALYBURTON, William David, Jr., PhM2d., USNR (Canton).
(b)   HERRING, Rufus G., Lt., USNR (Roseboro).
(b)   JOHNSTON, Rufus Zenas, Lt., USN (Lincolnton).
(b)   PARKER, Pomeroy, Pvt., USMC (Gates County).
(b)   STATON, Adolphus, Lt., USN (Tarboro).
(b)   STODDARD, James, Seaman, USN.

NORTH DAKOTA

Army-Air Force

(b)   ANDERS, Frank L., Cpl., 1st N. Dak. Vol. Inf. (Fargo).
      BLOCH, Orville Emil, 1st Lt., 85th Inf Div. (Streeter) (b. Wis.).
      BOEHLER, Otto, Pvt., 1st N. Dak. Vol. Inf. (Wahpeton) (b. Germany).
      DAVIS, Charles P., Pvt., 1st N. Dak. Vol. Inf. (Valley City) (b. Minn.).
      DOWNS, Willis H., Pvt., 1st N. Dak. Vol. Inf. (Jamestown) (b. Conn.).
(b)   *HAGEN, Loren D., 1st Lt., U.S. Army Tr. Adv. Gp. (Fargo).
      JENSEN, Gotfred, Pvt., 1st N. Dak. Vol. Inf. (Devils Lake) (b. Denmark).
      KINNE, John B., Pvt., 1st N. Dak. Inf. (Fargo) (b. Wis.).
      LONGFELLOW, Richard M., Pvt., 1st N. Dak. Vol. Inf. (Mandan) (b. Ill.).
      ROSS, Frank F., Pvt., 1st N. Dak., Vol. Inf. (Langdon) (b. Ill.).
      SLETTELAND, Thomas, Pvt., 1st N. Dak. Inf. (Grafton) (b. Norway).
      *SMITH, Fred E., Lt. Col., 77th Div. (Bartlett) (b. Ill.).
      *WOLD, Nels, Pvt., 138th Inf., 35th Div. (Minnewaukan) (b. Minn.).

Navy-Marine Corps

      BRADLEY, Willis Winter, Jr., Comdr., USN (b. N.Y.).
      CARTER, Joseph E., Blacksmith, USN (b. England).
(b)   *GURKE, Henry, Pfc., USMC (Neche).

OHIO

Army-Air Force

(b)   ALBERT, Christian, Pvt., 47th Ohio Inf. (Cincinnati).
(b)   *ANTOLAK, Sylvester, Sgt., 3d Inf. Div. (St. Clairsville).
(b)   ASTON, Edgar R., Pvt., 8th U.S. Cav. (Clermont County).
(b)   AYERS, David, Sgt., 57th Ohio Inf. (Upper Sandusky).
(b)   *BAESEL, Albert E., 2d Lt., 37th Div. (Berea).
      *BAKER, Addison E., Lt. Col., 93d Bomb. Gp. (Akron) (b. Ill.).
      BEATY, Powhatan, 1st Sgt., 5th U.S. Colored Troops (Delaware County) (b. Va.).
      BELL, James B., Sgt., 11th Ohio Inf. (Troy).
(b)   BENNETT, Edward A., Pfc., 358th Inf., 90th Inf. Div. (Middleport).
(b)   BENSINGER, William, Pvt., 21st Ohio Inf. (Hancock County).
(b)   BICKHAM, Charles G., 1st Lt., 27th U.S. Inf. (Dayton).
(b)   BISHOP, Daniel, Sgt., 5th U.S. Cav. (Monroe County).
      BOYNTON, Henry V., Lt. Col., 35th Ohio Inf. (b. Mass.).
      BRONSON, James H., 1st Sgt., 5th U.S. Colored Troops (Delaware County) (b. Pa.).
      BROOKIN, Oscar, Pvt., 17th U.S. Inf. (Green County) (b. Wis.).
      BROWN, John H., 1st Sgt., 47th Ohio Inf. (Cincinnati) (b. Mass.).
(b)   BROWN, Robert B., Pvt., 15th Ohio Inf. (Zanesville).
(b)   BROWN, Uriah, Pvt., 30th Ohio Inf. (Miami County).
(b)   BROWN, Wilson W., Pvt., 21st Ohio Inf. (Wood County).

OHIO—Continued

(b) BUHRMAN, Henry G., Pvt., 54th Ohio Inf. (Cincinnati).
(b) BURNS, James M., Sgt., 1st W. Va. Inf. (Jefferson County).
(b) CALVERT, James S., Pvt., 5th U.S. Inf. (Athens County).
     CAPEHART, Henry, Col., 1st W. Va. Cav. (Bridgeport) (b. Pa.).
(b) CARR, Franklin, Cpl., 124th Ohio Inf. (Stark County).
(b) CARR, John, Pvt., 8th U.S. Cav. (Columbus).
     CARSON, William J., Mus., 1st Bn., 15th U.S. Inf. (North Greenfield) (b. Pa.).
(b) *CHRISTIAN, Herbert F., Pfc., 3d Inf. Div. (Steubenville).
(b) *CICCHETTI, Joseph J., Pvt., 37th Inf. Div. (Waynesburg).
(b) COCKLEY, David L., 1st Lt., 10th Ohio Cav. (Lexington).
(b) COLWELL, Oliver, 1st Lt., 95th Ohio Inf. (Champaign County).
(b) COOK, John, Bugler, 4th U.S. Arty. (Cincinnati).
(b) COONROD, Aquilla, Sgt., 5th U.S. Inf. (Bryan).
     *CRAIG, Robert, 2d Lt., 3d Inf. Div. (Toledo) (b. Scotland).
(b) CRANSTON, William W., Pvt., 66th Ohio Inf. (Woodstock).
(b) CROCKER, Ulric L., Pvt., 6th Mich. Cav.
(b) CUBBERLY, William G., Pvt., 8th U.S. Cav. (Butler County).
(b) CUMPSTON, James M., Pvt., 91st Ohio Inf. (Gallis County).
     DAVIDSON, Andrew, Asst. Surg., 47th Ohio Inf. (Cincinnati) (b. Vt.).
(b) DAVIS, Freeman, Sgt., 80th Ohio Inf. (Newcomerstown).
(b) DAVIS, Harry, Pvt., 46th Ohio Inf. (Franklin County).
(b) DAY, David F., Pvt., 57th Ohio Inf. (Dallasburg).
(b) DAY, Matthias, W., 2d Lt., 9th U.S. Cav. (Oberlin).
(b) *DE ARMOND, William, Sgt., 5th U.S. Inf. (Butler County).
(b) *DELEAU, Emile, Jr., Sgt., 36th Inf. Div. (Blaine).
(b) DE WITT, Richard W., Cpl., 47th Ohio Inf. (Oxford).
     DORSEY, Daniel, Cpl., 33d Ohio Inf. (Fairfield County) (b. Va.).
     DOWLING, James, Cpl., 8th U.S. Cav. (Cleveland) (b. Ireland).
     ENDERLIN, Richard, Mus., 73d Ohio Inf. (Chillicothe) (b. Germany).
     FERRARI, George, Cpl., 8th U.S. Cav. (Montgomery County) (b. N.Y.).
(b) FINKENBINER, Henry S., Pvt., 107th Ohio Inf. (North Industry).
     *FLEEK, Charles Clinton, Sgt., 25th Inf. Div. (Cincinnati) (b. Ky.).
     FORCE, Manning F., Brig. Gen., U.S. Vol. (Cincinnati) (b. D.C.).
(b) FREEMAN, Henry B., 1st Lt., 18th U.S. Inf. (Mount Vernon).
     FREY, Franz, Cpl., 37th Ohio Inf. (Cleveland) (b. Switzerland).
(b) GATES, George, Bugler, 8th U.S. Cav. (Delaware County).
(b) GAUNT, John C., Pvt., 104th Ohio Inf. (Damascoville).
(b) GAUSE, Isaac, Cpl., 2d Ohio Cav. (Trumbull County).
(b) GEIGER, George, Sgt., 7th U.S. Cav. (Cincinnati).
     *GIVEN, John J., Cpl., 6th U.S. Cav. (Cincinnati) (b. Ky.).
(b) GODFREY, Edward S., Capt., 7th U.S. Cav. (Ottawa).
     GRAY, John, Pvt., 5th Ohio Inf. (Hamilton County) (b. Scotland).
     GREEN, John, Maj., 1st U.S. Cav. (b. Germany).
     GREENAWALT, Abraham, Pvt., 104th Ohio Inf. (Salem) (b. Pa.).
(b) GREGG, Joseph O., Pvt., 133d Ohio Inf. (Circleville).
(b) GRIMSHAW, Samuel, Pvt., 52d Ohio Inf. (Jefferson County).
(b) GUINN, Thomas, Pvt., 47th Ohio Inf. (Clinton County).
(b) *HALL, Lewis, T5g, 25th Inf. Div. (Columbus).
(b) HALL, Newton H., Cpl. 104th Inf. (Portage County).
(b) HANKS, Joseph, Pvt., 37th Ohio Inf. (Chillicothe).
     HARRIS, David W., Pvt., 7th U.S. Cav. (Cincinnati) (b. Ind.).
(b) HARRIS, Sampson, Pvt., 30th Ohio Inf. (Olive).
(b) HARTZOG, Joshua B., Pvt., 1st U.S. Arty. (Paulding County).
(b) *HASTINGS, Joe R., Pfc., 97th Ohio Inf. (Magnolia).
     HAWKINS, Martin J., Cpl., 33d Ohio Inf. (Portsmouth) (b. Pa.).
(b) HAYES, Webb·C., Lt. Col., 31st Inf., U.S. Vol. (Freemont).
(b) HEDGES, Joseph, 1st Lt., 4th U.S. Cav.
     HELLER, Henry, Sgt., 66th Ohio Inf. (Urbana) (b. Pa.).
(b) HERDA, Frank A., Sp4c., 101st Airborne Div. (Cleveland).
(b) HOLCOMB, Daniel I., Pvt., 41st Ohio Inf. (Hartford).
     HOLLAND, Milton M., Sgt. Maj., 5th U.S. Colored Troops (Athens) (b. Austin, Tex.).

ARMY-AIR FORCE

(b)   HOWARD, Hiram R., Pvt., 11th Ohio Inf. (Urbana).
(b)   HUGHEY, John, Cpl., 2d Ohio Cav. (Highland).
(b)   HUTCHINSON, Rufus D., Sgt., 7th U.S. Cav. (Butlerville).
(b)   IMMELL, Lorenzo D., Cpl., 2d U.S. Arty. (Ross).
(b)   JAMES, Isaac, Pvt., 110th Ohio Inf. (Montgomery County).
       JARDINE, James, Sgt., 54th Ohio Inf. (Hamilton County) (b. Scotland).
       JOHN, William, Pvt., 37th Ohio Inf. (Chillicothe) (b. Germany).
(b)   JONES, David, Pvt., 54th Ohio Inf. (Fayette County).
       *KEFURT, Gus, S/Sgt., 3d Inf. Div. (Youngstown) (b. Pa.).
(b)   KELLEY, George V., Capt., 104th Ohio Inf. (Massillon).
(b)   *KESSLER, Patrick L., Pfc., 3d Inf. Div. (Middletown).
       KIMBALL, Joseph, Pvt., 2d W. Va. Cav. (Ironton) (b. N.H.).
(b)   KIRK, Jonathan C., Capt., 20th Ind. Inf. (Wilmington).
(b)   KNIGHT, William J., Pvt., 21st Ohio Inf. (Farmers Center) (Defiance County).
(b)   KOUNTZ, John S., Mus., 37th Ohio Inf. (Maumee).
(b)   KYLE, John, Cpl., 5th U.S. Cav. (Cincinnati).
(b)   *LaPOINTE, Joseph Guy, Jr., Spec. 4, 101st Airb. Div. (Englewood) (Dayton).
(b)   LARIMER, Smith, Cpl., 2d Ohio Cav. (Columbus).
       *LOGAN, John A., Maj., 33d Inf., U.S. Vol. (Youngstown) (b. Ill.).
(b)   LONGSHORE, William H., Pvt., 30th Ohio Inf. (Muskingum County).
(b)   LOYD, George, Pvt., 122d Ohio Inf. (Muskingum County).
       MASON, Elihu H., Sgt., 21st Ohio Inf. (Pemberville) (b. Ind.).
       MAYFIELD, Melvin, Cpl., 6th Inf. Div. (Nashport) (b. W. Va.).
       MAYS, Isaiah, Cpl., 24th U.S. Infantry (Columbus Barracks) (b. Va.).
(b)   McCLEARY, Charles H., 1st Lt., 72d Ohio Inf. (Sandusky County).
(b)   McCLELLAND, James M., Pvt., 30th Ohio Inf. (Harrison County).
(b)   McGONAGLE, Wilson, Pvt., 30th Ohio Inf. (Jefferson County).
       McMILLEN, Francis M., Sgt., 110th Ohio Inf. (Piqua) (b. Ky.).
(b)   MEAHER, Nicholas, Cpl., 1st U.S. Cav. (Perry County).
(b)   *METZGER, William E., Jr., 2d Lt., 8th A.F. (Lima).
(b)   MILLER, Daniel H., Pvt., 3d U.S. Cav. (Fairfield County).
       MILLER, John, Cpl., 8th Ohio Inf. (Freemont) (b. Germany).
(b)   MOREY, Delano, Pvt., 82d Ohio Inf. (Hardin County).
(b)   MORGAN, Lewis, Pvt., 4th Ohio Inf. (Delaware County).
       MURPHY, John P., Pvt., 5th Ohio Inf. (Cincinnati) (b. Ireland).
(b)   MYERS, George S., Pvt., 101st Ohio Inf. (Fairfield).
       NORTH, Jasper N., Pvt., 4th W. Va. Inf. (Ames).
       ORBANSKY, David, Pvt., 58th Ohio Inf. (Columbus) (b. Prussia).
(b)   PARROTT, Jacob, Pvt., 33d Ohio Inf. (Hardin County).
(b)   PATTERSON, John T., Principal Mus., 122d Ohio Inf. (Morgan County).
(b)   PEARSALL, Platt, Cpl., 30th Ohio Inf. (Meigs County).
(b)   *PETRARCA, Frank J., Pfc., 37th Inf. Div. (Cleveland).
(b)   PHILLIPS, Samuel D., Pvt., 2d U.S. Cav. (Butler County).
       PHISTERER, Frederick, 1st Lt., 18th U.S. Inf. (Medina County) (b. Germany).
(b)   PINN, Robert, 1st Sgt., 5th U.S. Colored Troops (Massillon).
(b)   PITTINGER, William, Sgt., 2d Ohio Inf. (Jefferson County).
(b)   POPPE, John A., Sgt., 5th U.S. Cav. (Cincinnati).
(b)   PORTER, John R., Pvt., 21st Ohio Inf. (Findley).
       POWELL, William H., Maj., 2d W. Va. Cav. (Ironton) (b. England).
(b)   PRATT, James, Blacksmith, 4th U.S. Cav. (Bellefontaine).
(b)   PRENTICE, Joseph R., Pvt., 19th U.S. Inf. (Lancaster).
(b)   RAMSBOTTOM, Alfred, 1st Sgt., 97th Ohio Inf. (Delaware County).
       REDDICK, William H., Cpl., 33d Ohio Inf. (b. Ala.).
(b)   RENNINGER, Louis, Cpl., 37th Ohio Inf. (Liverpool).
(b)   RICHARDSON, William R., Pvt., 2d Ohio Cav. (Washington).
(b)   RICHEY, William E., Cpl., 15th Ohio Inf. (Athens County).
(b)   RICHMAN, Samuel, Pvt., 8th U.S. Cav. (Cleveland).
       RICHMOND, James, Pvt., 8th Ohio Inf. (Toledo) (b. Maine).
(b)   RICKENBACKER, Edward V., 1st Lt., 94th Aero Sq., Air Serv. (Columbus).
(b)   RICKSECKER, John H., Pvt., 104th Ohio Inf. (Springfield).
(b)   ROBERTS, Gordon R., Sgt. 101st Airborne Div. (Cincinnati).
(b)   *ROBERTSON, Samuel, Pvt., 33d Ohio Inf. (Barnesville).

Army-Air Force

(b)   ROBINSON, Elbridge, Pvt., 122d Ohio Inf. (Morgan County).
      ROCK, Frederick, Pvt., 37th Ohio Inf. (Cleveland) (b. Germany).
(b)   *ROSS, Marion A., Sgt. Maj., 2d Ohio Inf. (Champagne County).
(b)   ROSSER, Ronald E., Cpl., 2d Inf. Div. (Crooksville).
      ROUNDS, Lewis A., Pvt., 8th Ohio Inf. (Huron County) (b. N.Y.).
(b)   ROWALT, John F., Pvt., 8th U.S. Cav. (Belleville).
(b)   SCHMIDT, William, Pvt., 37th Ohio Inf. (Maumee).
      SCHNELL, Christian, Cpl., 37th Ohio Inf. (Wapakoneta) (b. Va.).
(b)   *SCOTT, John M., Sgt., 21st Ohio Inf. (Finley).
(b)   SEAMAN, Elisha B., Pvt., 66th Ohio Inf. (Logan County).
      SEARS, Cyrus, 1st Lt., Ohio Light Arty. (Bucyrus) (b. N.Y.).
(b)   SHARPLESS, Edward C., Cpl., 6th U.S. Cav. (Marion County).
      SHIELDS, Bernard, Pvt., 2d W. Va. Cav. (Ironton) (b. Ireland).
(b)   *SLAVENS, Samuel, Pvt., 33d Ohio Inf. (Wakefield).
(b)   SMITH, Otis W., Pvt., 95th Ohio Inf. (Logan County).
      SPRAGUE, John W., Col., 63d Ohio Inf. (Sandusky) (b. N.Y.).
(b)   STANLEY, David S., Maj. Gen., U.S. Vol. (Congress).
      STEELE, John W., Maj. and Aide-de-Camp, U.S. Vol. (b. Vermont).
(b)   STICKELS, Joseph, Sgt., 83d Ohio Inf. (Bethany).
(b)   STOKES, Alonzo, 1st Sgt., 6th U.S. Cav. (Logan County).
(b)   STURGEON, James K., Pvt., 46th Ohio Inf. (Perry County).
(b)   SURLES, William H., Pvt., 2d Ohio Inf. (Steubenville).
(b)   SWAYNE, Wager, Lt. Col., 43d Ohio Inf. (Columbus).
(b)   THOMPSON, Freeman C., Cpl., 116th Ohio Inf. (Monroe County).
(b)   THOMPSON, Thomas, Sgt., 66th Ohio Inf. (Champagne County).
(b)   *TOWLE, John R., Pvt., 82d Airborne Div. (Cleveland).
(b)   TREAT, Howell B., Sgt., 52d Ohio Inf. (Painsville).
      TYRRELL, George William, Cpl., 5th Ohio Inf. (Hamilton County) (b. Ireland).
(b)   VANCE, Wilson, Pvt., 21st Ohio Inf. (Hancock County).
(b)   WAGEMAN, John H., Pvt., 60th Ohio Inf. (Amelia).
(b)   WALKER, James C., Pvt., 31st Ohio Inf. (Springfield).
(b)   WARD, Nelson W., Pvt., 11th Pa. Cav. (Columbiana County).
      WELSH, Edward, Pvt., 54th Ohio Inf. (Cincinnati) (b. Ireland).
      WENDE, Bruno, Pvt., 17th U.S. Inf. (Canton) (b. Germany).
(b)   WILEY, James, Sgt., 59th N.Y. Inf.
(b)   WILHELM, George, Capt., 56th Ohio Inf. (Lancaster).
(b)   WILLIAMS, William H., Pvt., 82d Ohio Inf. (Miami County).
(b)   WILSON, John A., Pvt., 21st Ohio Inf. (Wood County).
(b)   WILSON, Milden H., Sgt., 7th U.S. Inf. (Newark).
      *WINDER, David F., Pfc., 11th Inf. Brigade (Mansfield) (b. Pa.).
(b)   WOLLAM, John, Pvt., 33d Ohio Inf. (Jackson).
      WOOD, Mark, Pvt., 21st Ohio Inf. (Portage) (b. England).
(b)   *WOODFORD, Howard E., S/Sgt., 33d Inf. Div. (Barberton).
      YEAGER, Jacob F., Pvt., 101st Ohio Inf. (Tiffin) (b. Pa.).
(b)   *YOUNG, Rodger W., Pvt., 37th Inf. Div. (Clyde).

Navy-Marine Corps

(b)   BARTON, Thomas C., Seaman, USN (Cleveland).
      *BAUGH, William B., Pfc., 1st Marine Div. USMC, (Harrison) (b. Ky.).
(b)   BEASLEY, Harry C., Seaman, USN.
(b)   *BERRY, Charles Joseph, Cpl., USMC (Lorain).
      BUTTS, George, GM., USN (b. N.Y.).
(b)   *DICKEY, Douglas E., Pfc., 3d Marine Div. (Greenville).
(b)   DORMAN, John, Seaman, USN (Cincinnati).
(b)   *EPPERSON, Harold Glenn, Pfc., USMCR (Avon).
      *ESTOCIN, Michael J., Captain, USN (Akron) (b. Pa.).
(b)   *FOSTER, William Adelbert, Pfc., USMCR (Cleveland).
(b)   GARY, Donald Arthur, Lt. (jg.), USN (Findlay).
      HALEY, James, Captain of Forecastle, USN (b. Ireland).
(b)   HANFORD, Burke, M1c., USN (Toledo).
(b)   HARNER, Joseph Gabriel, BM2c., USN (Louisville).

NAVY-MARINE CORPS

JARDINE, Alexander, F1c., USN (b. Scotland).
(b) *KIDD, Isaac Campbell, Rear Adm., USN (Cleveland).
(b) *MARTIN, Harry Linn, 1st Lt., USMCR (Bucyrus).
    *MASON, Leonard Foster, Pfc., USMC (b. Ky.).
(b) McGUNIGAL, Patrick, SF1c., USN (Hubbard).
(b) McHUGH, Martin, Seaman, USN (Cincinnati).
(b) *NEWLIN, Melvin Earl, Pfc., 1st Mar. Div. (Wellsville).
(b) OSTERMANN, Edward Albert, 1st Lt., USMC (Columbus).
    *PAUL, Joe C., L/Cpl., 3d Marine Div. (Dayton) (b. Ky.).
    READ, Charles A., Cox., USN (b. Sweden).
(b) REID, George Croghan, Maj., USMC (Lorain).
(b) *SCOTT, Robert R., MM1c. USN (Massillon).
(b) SHEPARD, Louis C., Ordinary Seaman, USN.
(b) *STEIN, Tony, Cpl., USMCR (Dayton).
(b) STUPKA, Laddie, F1c., USN (Cleveland).
(b) *WARD, James R., Seaman 1c, USN (Springfield).
    WILLIAMS, Jay, Cox., USN (b. Ind.).
(b) WOOD, Robert B., Cox., USN (New Garden).

OKLAHOMA

ARMY-AIR FORCE

(b) *BURRIS, Tony K., Sfc., 2d Inf. Div. (Blanchard).
(b) CHILDERS, Ernest, 2d Lt., 45th Inf. Div. (Tulsa).
(b) CREWS, John R., S/Sgt., 63d Inf. Div. (Golden).
    EPPS, Joseph L., Pvt., 33d Inf. Div. (Oloagah) (b. Mo.).
(b) *GOTT, Donald J., 1st Lt., 8th A.F. (Arnett) (Okarche).
    HAYS, George Price, 1st Lt., 3d Div. (b. China).
(b) *HENRY, Frederick F., 1st Lt., 2d Inf. Div. (Clinton).
(b) *KINER, Harold G., Pvt., 30th Inf. Div. (Enid).
    *McGILL, Troy A., Sgt., 1st Cav. Div. (Ada) (b. Tenn.).
(b) MONTGOMERY, Jack C., 1st Lt., 45th Inf. Div. (Sallisaw).
(b) *REESE, John N., Jr., Pfc., 37th Inf. Div. (Pryor).
    SAMPLER, Samuel M., Cpl., 36th Div. (Altus) (b. Tex.).
    TREADWELL, Jack L., Capt., 45th Inf. Div. (Snyder) (b. Ala.).
    TURNER, Harold L., Cpl., 36th Div. (Seminole) (b. Mo.).

NAVY-MARINE CORPS

(b) *EVANS, Ernest Edwin, Comdr., USN (Pawnee).
(b) McCOOL, Richard Miles, Jr., Lt., USN'.
    *SCHWAB, Albert Earnest, Pfc., USMCR (Tulsa) (b. D.C.).
(b) SMITH, John Lucian, Maj., USMC (Lexington).

OREGON

ARMY-AIR FORCE

    ALLWORTH, Edward C., Capt., 5th Div. (Corvallis) (b. Wash.).
(b) *DAHL, Larry G., Sp4c., 27th Trans. Bat. (Oregon City).
(b) *HOLCOMB, John N., Sgt., 1st Cav. Div. (Corvallis).
(b) *KAUFMAN, Loren R., Sfc., 2d Inf. Div. (The Dalles).
    KILBOURNE, Charles E., 1st Lt., S.C., U.S. Vol. (Portland) (b. Va.).
(b) *KINGSLEY, David R., 2d Lt., A.C. (Portland).
    PHIFE, Lewis, Sgt., 8th U.S. Cav. (Marion) (b. Iowa).
    ROBERTSON, Marcus W., Pvt., 2d Oregon Vol. Inf. (Hood River) (b. Wis.).
(b) *STRYKER, Stuart S., Pfc., 17th Airborne Div. (Portland).
    *YABES, Maximo, 1st Sgt., 25th Inf. Div. (Eugene) (b. Calif).

NAVY-MARINE CORPS

JACKSON, Arthur J., Pfc., USMC (b. Ohio).

NAVY-MARINE CORPS

*MARTINI, Gary W., Pfc., 1st Mar. Div. (Portland) (b. Va.).

PENNSYLVANIA

ARMY-AIR FORCE

(b)   AMMERMAN, Robert W., Pvt., 148th Pa. Inf. (Center County).
      ANDERSON, Everett W., Sgt., 15th Pa. Cav. (Philadelphia) (b. La.).
(b)   ANDERSON, Thomas, Cpl., 1st W. Va. Cav. (Washington County).
(b)   APPLE, Andrew O., Cpl., 12th W. Va. Inf.
(b)   ARNOLD, Abraham K., Capt., 5th U.S. Cav. (Bedford).
(b)   BAIRD, Absalom, Brig. Gen., U.S. Vol. (Washington).
(b)   †BEAUMONT, Eugene B., Maj. and Asst. Adj. Gen., Cav. Corps, Army of the Miss.
          (Luzerne County).
(b)   BENNETT, Orren, Pvt., 141st Pa. Inf. (Towanda).
(b)   BENYAURD, William H. H., 1st Lt., Engr. (Philadelphia).
(b)   BETTS, Charles M., Lt. Col., 15th Pa. Cav. (Philadelphia).
      BEYER, Hillary, 2d Lt., 90th Pa. Inf. (Philadelphia).
(b)   BINGHAM, Henry H., Capt., 140th Pa. Inf. (Cannonsburg).
(b)   BISHOP, Francis A., Pvt., 57th Pa. Inf. (Bradford County).
(b)   BLACKMAR, Wilmon W., Lt., 1st W. Va. Cav. (Bristol).
      BLACKWOOD, William R. D., Surgeon, 48th Pa. Inf. (Philadelphia) (b. Ireland).
(b)   BLAIR, James, 1st Sgt., 1st U.S. Cav. (Schuylkill County).
(b)   BLICKENSDERFER, Milton, Cpl., 126th Ohio Inf. (Lancaster).
      BLUCHER, Charles, Cpl., 188th Pa. Inf. (b. Germany).
(b)   BONEBRAKE, Henry G., Lt., 17th Pa. Cav. (Waynesboro).
      BONNAFFON, Sylvester, Jr., 1st Lt., 99th Pa. Inf. (Philadelphia).
(b)   BOON, Hugh P., Capt., 1st W. Va. Cav. (Washington).
      BRANNIGAN, Felix, Pvt., 74th N.Y. Inf. (Allegheny County) (b. Ireland).
(b)   BREST, Lewis F., Pvt., 57th Pa. Inf. (Mercer).
      BREWSTER, Andre W., Capt., 9th U.S. Inf. (Philadelphia) (b. N.J.).
      BREYER, Charles, Sgt., 90th Pa. Inf. (Philadelphia).
(b)   BROWN, Charles, Sgt., 50th Pa. Inf. (Schuylkill County).
(b)   BROWN, Jeremiah Z., Capt., 148th Pa. Inf. (Rimmersburg).
(b)   *BROWN, Melvin L., Pfc., 1st Cav. Div. (Mahaffey).
(b)   BURNETT, George R., 2d Lt., 9th U.S. Cav. (Spring Mills).
(b)   BUZZARD, Ulysses G., Pvt., 17th U.S. Inf. (Armstrong).
(b)   CALDWELL, Daniel, Sgt., 13th Pa. Cav. (Marble Hill).
(b)   *CAREY, Alvin, S/Sgt., 2d Inf. Div. (Laughlinstown).
(b)   CARLISLE, Casper R., Pvt., Ind. Pa. Light Arty. (Allegheny County).
      CARPENTER, Louis H., Capt., 10th U.S. Cav. (Philadelphia) (b. N.J.).
(b)   CART, Jacob, Pvt., 7th Pa. Res. Corps (Carlisle).
(b)   CASEY, Henry, Pvt., 20th Ohio Inf. (Fayette County).
(b)   CHAMBERS, Joseph B., Pvt., 100th Pa. Inf. (East Brook).
(b)   CLARK, James G., Pvt., 88th Pa. Inf. (Germantown).
(b)   CLARK, Wilfred, Pvt., 2d U.S. Cav. (Philadelphia).
(b)   CLAUSEN, Charles H., 1st Lt., 61st Pa. Inf. (Philadelphia)
(b)   CLAY, Cecil, Capt., 58th Pa. Inf. (Philadelphia).
(b)   CLOPP, John E., Pvt., 71st Pa. Inf. (Philadelphia).
      COLLIS, Charles H. T., Col., 114th Pa. Inf (Philadelphia) (b. Ireland).
(b)   COMFORT, John W., Cpl., 4th U.S. Cav. (Philadelphia).
(b)   CONNELL, Trustrim, Cpl., 138th Pa. Inf. (Ft. Kennedy).
(b)   CONNER, Richard, Pvt., 6th N.J. Inf. (Philadelphia).
(b)   COOKE, Walter H., Capt., 4th Pa. Inf. Militia (Norristown).
(b)   CORCORAN, Michael, Cpl., 8th U.S. Cav. (Philadelphia).
(b)   CORSON, Joseph K., Asst. Surg., 6th Pa. Res. (35th Penn. Vol.) (Philadelphia).
(b)   *CRESCENZ, Michael J., Cpl., 196th Inf. Brig., Amer. Div. (Philadelphia).
(b)   CUNNINGHAM, Francis M., 1st Sgt., 1st W. Va. Cav. (Springfield).
(b)   DAVIDSIZER, John A., Sgt., 1st Pa. Cav. (Lewiston).
(b)   DAVIS, Charles C., Maj., 7th Pa. Cav. (Harrisburg).
      DAY, Charles, Pvt., 210th Pa. Inf. (Lycoming County) (b. N.Y.).
(b)   DEARY, George, Sgt., 5th U.S. Cav. (Philadelphia).

ARMY-AIR FORCE

(b) DE LACEY, Patrick, 1st Sgt., 143d Pa. Inf. (Scranton).
DELANEY, John C., Sgt., 107th Pa. Inf. (Honesdale) (b. Ireland).
DE LAVIE, Hiram H., Sgt., 11th Pa. Inf. (Allegheny) (b. Ohio).
(b) DE SWAN, John F., Pvt., 21st U.S. Inf. (Philadelphia).
(b) DOLBY, David Charles, Sgt., 1st Cav. Div. (Norristown).
(b) DONALDSON, John, Sgt., 4th Pa. Cav. (Butler County).
DOUGHERTY, Michael, Pvt., 13th Pa. Cav. (Philadelphia) (b. Ireland).
EDGERTON, Nathan H., Lt. and Adj., 6th U.S. Colored Troops (Philadelphia).
(b) ELLIOTT, Alexander, Sgt., 1st Pa. Cav. (North Sewickley).
(b) ENGLE, James E., Sgt., 97th Pa. Inf. (Chester).
(b) *ENGLISH, Glenn H., Jr., S/Sgt., 173d Airborne Brigade (Altoona).
EVANS, Thomas, Pvt., 54th Pa. Inf. (Cambria County) (b. Wales).
(b) EWING, John C., Pvt., 211th Pa. Inf. (Latrobe).
(b) FASNACHT, Charles H., Sgt., 99th Pa. Inf. (Lancaster County).
(b) FASSETT, John B., Capt., 23d Pa. Inf. (Philadelphia).
(b) FEASTER, Mosheim, Pvt., 7th U.S. Cav. (Schellburg).
(b) FISHER, Joseph, Cpl., 61st Pa. Inf. (Philadelphia).
(b) FLANAGHAN, Augustine, Sgt., 55th Pa. Inf. (Chest Springs).
(b) FOX, William R., Pvt., 95th Pa. Inf. (Philadelphia).
(b) FRICK, Jacob G., Col., 129th Pa. Inf. (Pottsville).
(b) FUNK, Leonard A., Jr., 1st Sgt., 82d Airborne Div. (Wilkinsburg).
FUNK, West, Maj. 121st Pa. Inf. (Philadelphia) (b. Mass.).
(b) FURMAN, Chester S., Cpl., 6th Pa. Res. (Columbia).
FURNESS, Frank, Capt., 6th Pa. Cav. (Philadelphia).
(b) GALLOWAY, George N., Pvt., 95th Pa. Inf. (Philadelphia).
(b) GALLOWAY, John, Com. Sgt., 8th Pa. Cav. (Philadelphia).
(b) GEDEON, Louis, Pvt., 19th U.S. Inf. (Pittsburgh).
(b) GILLIGAN, Edward L., 1st Sgt., 88th Pa. Inf. (Philadelphia).
GION, Joseph, Pvt., 74th N.Y. Inf. (Allegheny County).
(b) GOODMAN, William E., 1st Lt., 147th Penn. Inf. (Philadelphia).
(b) GRAUL, William, Cpl., 188th Pa. Inf. (Reading).
GRESSER, Ignatz, Cpl., 128th Pa. Inf. (Lehigh County) (b. Germany).
(b) GUNTHER, Jacob, Cpl., 8th U.S. Cav. (Schuylkill County).
(b) *HALLMAN, Sherwood H., S/Sgt., 29th Inf. Div. (Spring City).
(b) HARMON, Amzi D., Cpl., 211th Pa. Inf. (Westmoreland County).
(b) *HARR, Harry R., Cpl., 31st Inf. Div. (East Freedom).
(b) HARRIS, George W., Pvt., 148th Pa. Inf. (Bellefonte).
(b) HARTRANFT, John F., Col., 4th Pa. Militia (Norristown).
HAWKINS, Thomas, Sgt. Maj., 6th U.S. Colored Troops (Philadelphia) (b. Ohio).
HENRY, Guy V., Col., 40th Mass. Inf. (Reading) (b. Fort Smith, Indian Ter.).
(b) HENRY, John., 1st Sgt., 3d U.S. Inf. (Philadelphia) (True name John H. Shingle, see below).
(b) HERRON, Francis J., Lt. Col., 9th Iowa Inf. (Pittsburgh).
(b) HERRON, Leander, Cpl., 3d U.S. Inf. (Bucks County).
(b) HIGBY, Charles, Pvt., 1st Pa. Cav. (New Brighton).
(b) HILL, Henry, Cpl., 50th Pa. Inf. (Schuylkill County).
(b) HILL, James M., 1st Sgt., 5th U.S. Cav. (Washington County).
(b) HIMMELSBACK, Michael, Pvt., 2d U.S. Cav. (Allegheny County).
(b) HOFFMAN, Thomas W., Capt., 208th Pa. Inf. (Perrysburg).
(b) HOGAN, Franklin, Cpl., 45th Pa. Inf. (Howard).
(b) HOOVER, Samuel, Bugler, 1st U.S. Cav. (Dauphin County).
(b) HORNER, Freeman V., S/Sgt., 30th Inf. Div. (Shamokin).
(b) HOTTENSTINE, Solomon J., Pvt., 107th Pa. Inf. (Philadelphia).
HOWARD, Henderson C., Cpl., 11th Pa. Res. (Ind.).
(b) HUBBARD, Thomas, Pvt., 2d U.S. Cav. (Philadelphia).
(b) HUFF, James W., Pvt., 1st U.S. Cav. (Washington).
(b) HUIDEKOPER, Henry S., Lt. Col., 150th Pa. Inf. (Meadville).
(b) HUNTERSON, John C., Pvt., 3d Pa. Cav. (Philadelphia).
(b) ILGENFRITZ, Charles H., Sgt., 207th Pa. Inf. (York County).
JENNINGS, James T., Pvt., 56th Pa. Inf. (Bucks County) (b. England).
(b) JOHNSON, Joseph E., 1st Lt., 58th Pa. Inf. (Lower Merion).
(b) JOHNSON, Samuel, Pvt., 9th Pa. Res. (Connellsville).

356

ARMY-AIR FORCE

- (b)   KELLY, Alexander, 1st Sgt., 6th U.S. Colored Troops (Indiana County).
- (b)   KELLY, Charles E., Cpl., 36th Inf. Div. (Pittsburgh).
- (b)   *KELLY, John D., T/Sgt., 79th Inf. Div. (Cambridge Springs).
- (b)   KEPHART, James, Pvt., 13th U.S. Inf. (Venango County).
-       KERR, Thomas R., Capt., 14th Pa. Cav. (Pittsburgh) (b. Ireland).
- (b)   KINDIG, John M., Cpl., 63rd Pa. Inf. (East Liberty).
- (b)   KINSEY, John, Cpl., 45th Pa. Inf. (Lancaster County).
- (b)   KIRK, John, 1st Sgt., 6th U.S. Cav. (York).
- (b)   KIRKWOOD, John A., Sgt., 3d U.S. Cav. (Allegheny County).
- (b)   KITCHEN, George K., Sgt., 6th U.S. Cav. (Lebanon County).
- (b)   KNAPPENBERGER, Alton W., Pfc., 3d Inf. Div. (Spring Mount).
- (b)   KRAMER, Theodore L., Pvt., 188th Pa. Inf. (Danville).
- (b)   LANDIS, James P., Chief Bugler, 1st Pa. Cav.
- (b)   LAWS, Robert E., S/Sgt., 43d Inf. Div. (Altoona).
- (b)   LEONARD, William E., Pvt., 85th Pa. Inf. (Jacksonville).
- (b)   LEWIS, DeWitt Clinton, Capt., 97th Pa. Inf. (West Chester).
- (b)   LILLEY, John, Pvt., 205th Pa. Inf. (Mifflin County).
- (b)   *LOBAUGH, Donald R., Pvt., 32d Inf. Div. (Freeport).
- (b)   LOWER, Cyrus B., Pvt., 13th Pa. Res. (Laurence County).
- (b)   LUTY, Gatlieb, Cpl., 74th N.Y. Inf. (West Manchester).
- (b)   LYTLE, Leonidas S., Sgt., 8th U.S. Cav. (Warren County).
- (b)   MacLAY, William P., Pvt., 43d Inf., U.S. Vol. (Altoona).
- (b)   MARM, Walter Joseph, Jr., 1st Lt., 1st Cav. Div. (Washington).
- (b)   MARQUETTE, Charles, Sgt., 93d Pa. Inf. (Lebanon County).
- (b)   MARTIN, Sylvester H., Lt., 88th Pa. Inf. (Chester County).
-       *MATHIES, Archibald, Sgt., 8th A.F. (Pittsburgh) (b. Scotland).
- (b)   MATTHEWS, John C., Cpl., 61st Pa. Inf. (Westmoreland County).
- (b)   MATTHEWS, Milton, Pvt., 61st Pa. Inf. (Pittsburgh).
-       McADAMS, Peter, Cpl., 98th Pa. Inf. (Philadelphia) (b. Ireland).
-       McANALLY, Charles, Lt., 69th Pa. Inf. (Philadelphia) (b. Ireland).
-       McKEEVER, Michael, Pvt., 5th Pa. Cav. (Philadelphia) (b. Ireland).
- (b)   McKOWN, Nathaniel A., Sgt., 58th Pa. Inf. (Philadelphia).
- (b)   *McVEIGH, John J., Sgt., 2d Inf. Div. (Philadelphia)
- (b)   MEARS, George W., Sgt., 6th Pa. Res. (Bloomsburgh).
- (b)   MECHLIN, Henry W. B., Blacksmith, 7th U.S. Cav. (Mt. Pleasant).
- (b)   MERLI, Gino J., Pfc., 1st Inf. Div. (Peckville).
- (b)   *MESSERSCHMIDT, Harold O., Sgt., 30th Inf. Div. (Chester).
-       *MESTROVITCH, James I., Sgt., 111th Inf., 28th Div. (Pittsburgh) (b. Montenegro).
- (b)   MILLER, George W., Pvt., 8th U.S. Cav. (Philadelphia).
- (b)   MILLER, William E., Capt., 3d Pa. Cav. (West Hill).
-       MINDIL, George W., Capt., 61st Pa. Inf. (Philadelphia) (b. Germany).
- (b)   *MINICK, John W., S/Sgt., 8th Inf. Div. (Carlisle).
- (b)   MITCHELL, Alexander H., 1st Lt., 105th Pa. Inf. (Hamilton).
- (b)   MITCHELL, Theodore, Pvt., 61st Pa. Inf. (Pittsburgh).
-       MONAGHAN, Patrick, Cpl., 48th Pa. Inf. (Minersville) (b. Ireland).
- (b)   MORRIS, William, Sgt., 1st N.Y. Cav. (Philadelphia).
- (b)   MORRISON, Francis, Pvt., 85th Pa. Inf. (Drakestown).
- (b)   MOSTOLLER, John W., Pvt., 54th Pa. Inf. (Somerset County).
-       MULHOLLAND, St. Clair A., Maj., 116th Pa. Inf. (Philadelphia) (b. Ireland).
-       MUNSELL, Harvey M., Sgt., 99th Pa. Inf. (Venango County) (b. N.Y.)
- (b)   MURPHY, Edward F., Cpl., 5th U.S. Cav. (Wayne County).
- (b)   OLIVER, Charles, Sgt., 100th Pa. Inf. (Allegheny County).
- (b)   ORR, Robert L., Maj., 61st Pa. Inf. (Philadelphia).
- (b)   ORTH, Jacob G., Cpl., 28th Pa. Inf. (Philadelphia).
-       PALMER, William J., Col., 15th Pa. Cav. (Philadelphia) (b. Del.).
- (b)   PAUL, William H., Pvt., 90th Pa. Inf. (Philadelphia).
- (b)   PAYNE, Irvin C., Cpl., 2d N.Y. Cav. (Wayne County).
- (b)   PEARSON, Alfred L., Col., 155th Pa. Inf. (Pittsburgh).
- (b)   PEIRSOL, James K., Sgt., 13th Ohio Cav.
- (b)   PENNYPACKER, Galusha, Col., 97th Pa. Inf. (Valley Forge).
-       PETTY, Philip, Sgt., 136th Pa. Inf. (Tioga County) (b. England).

357

ARMY-AIR FORCE

PHILLIPS, Josiah, Pvt., 148th Pa. Inf. (Ulysses) (b. N.Y.)
(b) *PINDER, John J., T5g., 1st Inf. Div. (Burgettstown).
(b) PIPES, James M., Capt. 140th Pa. Inf. (Green County).
PITMAN, George J., Sgt., 1st N.Y. Cav. (Philadelphia) (b. N.J.)
(b) *PORT, William D., Pfc., 1st Air Cav. Div. (Petersburg).
(b) PORTER, Horace, Capt., Ord. Dept., U.S. Army (Harrisburg).
(b) PURCELL, Hiram W., Sgt. 104th Pa. Inf. (Bucks County).
PURMAN, James J., Lt., 140th Pa. Inf. (Green County).
(b) QUAY, Matthew S., Col., 134th Pa. Inf. (Beaver County).
QUINN, Alexander M., Sgt., 13th U.S. Inf. (Philadelphia) (b. N.J.)
(b) RANKIN, William, Pvt., 4th U.S. Cav. (Lewiston).
(b) RAUB, Jacob F., Asst. Surg., 210th Pa. Inf. (Weaversville).
(b) REED, George W., Pvt., 11th Pa. Inf. (Johnstown).
(b) *REESE, James W., Pvt., 48th Pa. Inf. (Chester).
REID, Robert, Pvt., 48th Pa. Inf. (Pottsville) (b. Scotland).
(b) REIGLE, Daniel P., Cpl., 87th Pa. Inf. (Adams County).
(b) REISINGER, J. Monroe, Cpl., 150th Pa. Inf. (Meadville).
(b) RESSLER, Norman W., Cpl., 7th U.S. Inf. (Dalmatia).
(b) RHODES, Sylvester D., Sgt., 61st Pa. Inf. (Wilkes-Barre).
ROBINSON, Thomas, Pvt., 81st Pa. Inf. (Tamaqua) (b. Ireland).
(b) RODENBOUGH, Theophilus, Capt., 2d U.S. Cav.
(b) *ROEDER, Robert E., Capt., 88th Inf. Div. (Summit Station).
(b) ROHM, Ferdinand F., Chief Bugler, 16th Pa. Cav. (Juniata County).
(b) ROOSEVELT, George W., 1st Sgt., 26th Pa. Inf. (Chester).
(b) ROUGHT, Stephen, Sgt., 141st Pa. Inf. (Crampton).
(b) ROUSH, J. Levi, Cpl., 6th Pa. Res. (Bedford County).
(b) ROWAND, Archibald, H., Jr., Pvt., 1st W. Va. Cav. (Pittsburgh).
(b) RUTTER, James M., Sgt., 143d Pa. Inf. (Wilkes-Barre).
SACRISTE, Louis J., 1st Lt., 116th Pa. Inf. (Philadelphia) (b. Del.).
(b) SANDS, William, 1st Sgt., 88th Pa. Inf. (Reading).
(b) *SARNOSKI, Joseph R., 2d Lt., A. C. (Simpson).
(b) *SAYERS, Foster J., Pfc., 90th Inf. Div. (Howard).
(b) SCHAFFNER, Dwite H., 1st Lt., 77th Div. (Falls Creek).
SCHEIBNER, Martin E., Pvt., 90th Pa. Inf. (Berks County) (b. Russia).
(b) SCHOONMAKER, James M., Col., 14th Pa. Cav. (Pittsburgh).
(b) SCOTT, John Wallace, Capt., 157th Pa. Inf. (Chester County).
SEITZINGER, James M., Pvt., 116th Pa. Inf. (Worcester) (b. Germany).
(b) SELLERS, Alfred J., Maj., 90th Pa. Inf. (Plumstedville).
SHAMBAUGH, Charles, Cpl., 11th Pa. Res. (Indiana County). (b. Prussia).
SHELLENBERGER, John S., Cpl., 85th Pa. Inf. (Perryopolis).
(b) SHEPHERD, Warren J., Cpl., 17th U.S. Inf. (Westover).
SHIEL, (SHIELDS), John, Cpl., 90th Pa. Inf. (Cressonville).
(b) SHINGLE, John H., 1st Sgt., 3d U.S. Cav. (Philadelphia) (Served as John Henry, see above).
(b) SHOMO, William A., Maj., A.C. (Westmoreland County).
(b) SHOPP, George J., Pvt., 191st Pa. Inf. (Reading).
(b) SILK, Edward A., 1st Lt., 100th Inf. Div. (Johnstown).
(b) *SITMAN, William S., Sfc., 2d Inf. Div. (Bellwood).
(b) SLUSHER, Henry C., Pvt., 22d Pa. Cav. (Washington County).
(b) SMITH, Robert, Pvt., 3d U.S. Inf. (Philadelphia).
(b) SMITH, Thaddeus S., Cpl., 6th Pa. Res. Inf. (Franklin County).
SNEDDEN, James, Musician, 54th Pa. Inf. (Johnstown) (b. Scotland).
(b) SOWERS, Michael, Pvt., 4th Pa. Cav. (Allegheny County).
(b) *SPEICHER, Clifton T., Cpl., 40th Inf. Div. (Gray).
(b) SPENCE, Orizoba, Pvt., 8th U.S. Cav. (Tionesta).
SPILLANE, Timothy, Pvt., 16th Pa. Cav. (Erie) (b. Ireland).
(b) SPRINGER, George, Pvt., 1st U.S. Cav. (York County).
(b) STOREY, John H. R., Sgt., 109th Pa. Inf. (Philadelphia).
(b) STRAUSBAUGH, Bernard A., 1st Sgt., 3d Md. Inf. (Warfordsburg).
(b) STRAYER, William H., Pvt., 3d U.S. Cav. (Maytown).
SWAP, Jacob E., Pvt., 83d Pa. Inf. (Springs) (b. N.Y.)
TAYLOR, Anthony, 1st Lt., 15th Pa. Cav. (Philadelphia (b. N.J.).

PENNSYLVANIA—Continued

ARMY-AIR FORCE

(b) TAYLOR, Forrester L., Capt., 23d N.J. Inf.
(b) TEA, Richard L., Sgt., 6th U.S. Cav. (Philadelphia).
(b) THOMAS, Charles L., Sgt., 11th Ohio Cav. (Philadelphia).
(b) THOMAS, Hampton S., Maj., 1st Pa. Vet. Cav. (Quakertown).
(b) THOMPSON, James B., Sgt., 1st Pa. Rifles (Perrysville).
    THOMPSON, Joseph H., Maj., 28th Div. (Beaver Falls) (b. Ireland).
    THOMPSON, Peter, Pvt., 7th U.S. Cav. **(b. Scotland).**
(b) TOMINAC, John J., 1st Lt., 3d Inf. Div. (Conemaugh).
(b) *TURNER, Day G., Sgt., 80th Inf. Div. (Nescopeck).
(b) TWEEDALE, John, Pvt., 15th Pa. Cav. (Philadelphia).
(b) VANDERSLICE, John M., Pvt., 8th Pa. Cav. (Philadelphia).
    VEALE, Moses, Capt., 109th Pa. Inf. (Philadelphia). (b. N.J.)
    WAINWRIGHT, John, 1st Lt., 97th Pa. Inf. (Westchester) (b. N.Y.)
(b) WALTON, George W., Pvt., 97th Pa. Inf. (Upper Oxford).
    WARD, Charles H., Pvt., 1st U.S. Cav. (Philadelphia) (b. England)
(b) WARFEL, Henry C., Pvt., 1st Pa. Cav. (Huntington).
(b) WEAHER, Andrew J., Pvt., 8th U.S. Cav. (Philadelphia).
(b) *WEICHT, Ellis R., Sgt., 36th Inf. Div. (Bedford).
(b) WHITE, J. Henry, Pvt., 90th Pa. Inf. (Philadelphia).
(b) WILLS, Henry, Pvt., 8th U.S. Cav. (Gracon).
(b) *WILSON, Alfred L., T5g., 26th Inf. Div. (Fairchance).
(b) WILSON, Benjamin, Pvt., 6th U.S. Cav. (Pittsburgh).
(b) WILSON, Charles E., Sgt., 1st N.J. Cav. (Bucks County).
(b) WILSON, Francis A., Cpl., 9th Pa. Inf. (Philadelphia).
(b) †WILSON, William, Sgt., 4th U.S. Cav. (Philadelphia)
(b) WITCOME, Joseph, Pvt., 8th U.S. Cav. (Mechanicsburg).
(b) WOODWARD, Evan M., 1st Lt., 2d Pa. Res. Inf. (Philadelphia).
(b) WRAY, William J., Sgt., 1st Vet. Res. Corps. (Philadelphia).
(b) WRIGHT, Albert D., Capt., 43d U.S. Colored Troops.
(b) YOUNG, Andrew J., Sgt., 1st Pa. Cav. (Carmichaelstown).

NAVY-MARINE CORPS

    ANDERSON, Aaron, Landsman, USN (Philadelphia) (b. N.C.)
    BALDWIN, Charles, Coal Heaver, USN (b. Del.).
(b) BARRETT, Edward, F2c., USN.
    *BENFORD, Edward C., HC3c., USN (b. N.Y.).
(b) BINDER, Richard, Sgt., USMC (Philadelphia).
(b) BISHOP, Charles Francis, QM2c., USN (Pittsburgh).
(b) BOONE, Joel Thompson, Lt. (Medical Corps), USN (St. Clair).
(b) BRAZELL, John, Quartermaster, USN (Philadelphia).
(b) BRUTSCHE, Henry, Landsman, USN (Philadelphia).
(b) BUCHANAN, David M., Apprentice, USN (Philadelphia).
(b) †BUTLER, Smedley, Darlington, Maj., USMC West Chester).
(b) CAMPBELL, Albert Ralph, Pvt., USMC (Williamsport).
(b) CLIFFORD, Robert T., Master-at-Arms, USN.
(b) CONNOR, William C., BM, USN.
(b) CRAWFORD, Alexander, Fireman, USN.
    CRILLEY, Frank William, CGM, USN (b. N.J.).
(b) CRIPPS, Thomas, Quartermaster, USN (Philadelphia).
(b) CROUSE, William Adolphus, WT, USN (Tannetsburg).
(b) CUTTER, George W., Landsman, USN (Philadelphia).
(b) *DAMATO, Anthony Peter, Cpl., USMC (Shenandoah).
(b) DAVIS, Joseph H., Landsman, USN (Philadelphia).
    DEAKIN, Charles, BM, USN (b. N.Y.).
    DEMPSTER, John, Cox., USN (b. Scotland).
(b) DENIG, J. Henry, Sgt., USMC (York).
(b) *DIAS, Ralph E., Pfc., USMC (Shelocta).
    DOOLEN, William, Coal Heaver, USN (b. Ireland).
    DOUGHERTY, James, Pvt., USMC (b. Ireland).

359

NAVY-MARINE CORPS

(b) *DREXLER, Henry Clay, Ens., USN (Braddock).
       DRUSTRUP, Neils, Lt., USN (b. Denmark).
(b) DU MOULIN, Frank, Apprentice, USN (Philadelphia).
(b) DUNCAN, James K. L., Ordinary Seaman, USN (Frankfort).
(b) EDWARDS, Walter Atlee, Lt. Comdr., USN (Philadelphia).
(b) *FISHER, Harry, Pvt., USMC (McKeesport).
(b) FOLEY, Alexander Joseph, Sgt., USMC (Heckersville).
(b) FRANCIS, Charles Robert, Pvt., USMC (Doylestown).
       FRY, Isaac N., Orderly Sgt., USMC.
       GAUGHIN, Philip, Sgt., USMC (b. Ireland).
       GIRANDY, Alphonse, Seaman, USN (b. West Indies).
       GRACE, H. Patrick, CQM, USN (b. Ireland).
(b) GROSS, Samuel, Pvt., USMC (Philadelphia).
(b) HAFFEE, Edmund, Quarter Gunner, USN (Philadelphia).
(b) HAMILTON, Richard, Coal Heaver, USN (Philadelphia).
(b) HAYES, John, Cox., USN (Philadelphia).
(b) *HILL, Edwin Joseph, CB, USN (Philadelphia).
       HORTON, William Charlie, Pvt., USMC (b. Ill.).
(b) HUBER, William Russel, MM, USN (Harrisburg).
(b) IAMS, Ross Lindsey, Sgt., USMC (Graysville).
       JOHNSEN, Hans, Chief Machinist, USN (b. Norway).
(b) JOHNSON, John, Seaman, USN (Philadelphia).
       JOHNSON, Peter, F1c., USN (b. England).
(b) JONES, William, Captain of Top, USN (Philadelphia).
       *KELLY, John D., Pfc., USMC, 1st Marine Div. (Homestead) (b. Ohio).
       KILLACKEY, Joseph, Landsman, USN (b. Ireland).
       LAVERTY, John, Fireman, USN (b. N.Y.).
(b) LAWSON, John, Landsman, USN.
       LEAR, Nicholas, Quartermaster, USN (b. R.I.).
       LEON, Pierre, Captain of Forecastle, USN (b. La.).
(b) LEVERY, William, Apprentice First Class, USN.
       LLOYD, Benjamin, Coal Heaver, USN (b. England).
(b) LOWRY, George Maus, Ens., USN (Eve).
(b) MacNEAL, Harry Lewis, Pvt., USMC (Philadelphia).
       MAHONEY, George, F1c., USN (b. Mass.).
(b) MARM, Walter Joseph, Jr., 1st Lt., 1st Cav. Div. (Washington).
       MARTIN, Edward S., Quartermaster, USN (b. Ireland).
       MARTIN, James, Sgt., USMC (b. Iceland).
(b) MATHIAS, Clarence Edward, Pvt., USMC (Royalton).
       MATTHEWS, Joseph, Captain of Top, USN (b. Malta).
       *MAUSERT, Frederick W., III, Sgt., 1st Marine Div. USMC, (Dresher) (b. N.Y.).
(b) McWILLIAMS, George W., Landsman, USN.
(b) MILLER, Hugh, BM, USN (Philadelphia).
(b) MITCHELL, Joseph, GM1c., USN (Philadelphia).
(b) MOORE, George, Seaman, USN (Philadelphia).
(b) *MORGAN, William D., Cpl., USMC, 3rd Mar. Div. (Pittsburgh).
       O'NEAL, John, BM, USN (b. Ireland).
       ORTEGA, John, Seaman, USN (b. Spain).
(b) PAIGE, Mitchell, Platoon Sgt., USMC (Charleroi).
       PETERS, Alexander, BM1c., USN (b. Russia).
       PETTY, Orlando Henderson, Lt., Medical Corps, USNRF (b. Ohio).
(b) *PROM, William R., L/Cpl., USMC, 3rd Mar. Div. (Pittsburgh).
(b) PURVIS, Hugh, Pvt., USMC (Philadelphia).
       QUICK, John Henry, Sgt., USMC (b. W. Va.).
(b) *RAMER, George H., 2d Lt., 1st Marine Div. USMCR (Lewisburg).
       RANNAHAN, John, Cpl., USMC (b. Ireland).
(b) *REEM, Robert D., 2d Lt., 1st Marine Div. USMC (Elizabethtown).
(b) RUSH, William Rees, Capt., USN (Philadelphia).
(b) SAPP, Isaac, Seaman, Engineers' Force, USN (Philadelphia).
(b) SCHMIDT, Oscar, Jr., OGM, USN (Philadelphia).
(b) SEMPLE, Robert, Chief Gunner, USN (Pittsburgh).
       SINNETT, Lawrence C., Seaman, USN (b. W. Va.).

Navy-Marine Corps

(b)   SNYDER, William E., Chief Electrician, USN (South Bethlehem).
(b)   STEWART, James A., Cpl., USMC (Philadelphia).
      SUNDQUIST, Axel, CCM, USN (b. Russia).
      *TAYLOR, Karl Gorman, Sr., S/Sgt., 3rd Mar. Div. USMC (Avella) (b. Md.).
(b)   TAYLOR, William G., Captain of Forecastle, USN (Philadelphia).
      THAYER, James, Ship's Corporal, USN (b. Ireland).
      THOMPSON, Henry A., Pvt., USMC (b. England).
      THORNTON, Michael, Seaman, USN (b. Ireland).
(b)   TROUT, James M., F2d., USN (Philadelphia).
(b)   VANTINE, Joseph E., F1c., USN (Philadelphia).
(b)   VAUGHN, Pinkerton R., Sgt., USMC (Downingtown).
      WHITE, Joseph, Cox., USN (b. D.C.).
      WILLIAMS, Henry, CM, USN (b. Canada).
(b)   WILLIAMS, John, Seaman, USN.
      WILLIAMS, Peter, Seaman, USN (b. Norway).
      WILLIAMS, William, Landsman, USN (b. Ireland).
      WILLIS, Richard, Cox., USN (b. England).

RHODE ISLAND

Army-Air Force

(b)   AVERY, William B., Lt., 1st N.Y. Marine Arty., U.S. Army (Providence).
      BABCOCK, William J., Sgt., 2d R.I. Inf. (South Kingston) (b. Conn.).
(b)   BARBER, James A., Cpl., 1st R.I. Light Arty. (Westerly).
(b)   BLISS, George N., Capt., 1st R.I. Cav. (Tiverton).
(b)   BUCKLYN, John K., 1st Lt., 1st R.I. Light Arty. (Foster Creek).
      BURBANK, James H., Sgt., 4th R.I. Inf. (Providence) (b. Holland).
(b)   CHILD, Benjamin H., Cpl., 1st R.I. Light Arty. (Providence).
(b)   CORCORAN, John, Pvt., 1st R.I. Light Arty. (Pawtucket).
      ENNIS, Charles, D., Pvt., 1st R.I. Light Arty. (Charleston) (b. Conn.).
      HAVRON, John H., Sgt., 1st R.I. Light Arty. (Providence) (b. Ireland).
(b)   LAWTON, John S., Sgt., 5th U.S. Cav. (Bristol).
(b)   LEWIS, Samuel E., Cpl., 1st R.I. Light Arty. (Coventry).
(b)   McDONALD, George E., Pvt., 1st Conn. Hvy. Arty. (Warwick).
      McGAR, Owen, Pvt., 5th U.S. Inf. (Pawtucket) (b. Mass.).
(b)   MOLBONE, Archibald, Sgt., 1st R.I. Light Arty. (West Greenwich).
      PARKER, Thomas, Cpl., 2d R.I. Inf. (Providence) (b. England).
(b)   *PETERS, George J., Pvt., 17th Airborne Div. (Cranston).
(b)   POTTER, George W., Pvt., 1st R.I. Arty. (Coventry).
      TAYLOR, Joseph, Pvt., 7th R.I. Inf. (Burrilville) (b. England).
      WELSH, James, Pvt., 4th R.I. Inf. (Slatersville) (b. Ireland).

Navy-Marine Corps

      BRADLEY, George, Chief Gunner, USN (b. N.Y.).
      *CHAMPAGNE, David B., Cpl., USMC, 1st Marine Div. (Wakefield) (b. Md.).
      EADIE, Thomas, CGM, USN (b. Scotland).
(b)   EDWARDS, John, Captain of Top, USN (Providence).
(b)   GILLICK, Matthew, BM, USN (Providence).
(b)   HAYES, Thomas, Cox., USN.
      MOORE, Philip, Seaman, USN (b. Canada).
(b)   READ, George E., Seaman, USN.
(b)   WALSH, Michael, Chief Machinist, USN (Newport).

SOUTH CAROLINA

Army-Air Force

(b)   ANDERSON, Webster, Sfc., 101st Airborne Div. (Winnsboro).
(b)   ATKINS, Thomas E., Pfc., 32d Inf. Div. (Campobello).
(b)   *BARKER, Charles H., Pfc., 7th Inf. Div. (Pickens).
(b)   DOZIER, James C., 1st Lt., 30th Div. (Rock Hill).

SOUTH CAROLINA—Continued

ARMY-AIR FORCE

(b) FOSTER, Gary Evans, Sgt., 30th Div. (Inman).
(b) *HALL, Thomas Lee, Sgt., 30th Div. (Fort Mill).
(b) *HERIOT, James D., Cpl., 30th Div. (Providence).
(b) HILTON, Richmond H., Sgt., 30th Div. (Westville).
(b) KENNEDY, John T., 2d Lt., 6th U.S. Cav. (Orangeburg).
(b) *KNIGHT, Noah O., Pfc., 3d Inf. Div. (Jefferson).
(b) MABRY, George L., Jr., Lt. Col., 4th Inf. Div. (Sumter).
(b) *McWHORTER, William A., Pfc., 32d Inf. Div. (Liberty).
(b) *SMITH, Furman L., Pvt., 34th Inf. Div. (Central).
(b) VILLEPIGUE, John C., Cpl., 30th Div. (Camden).
(b) WILLIAMS, Charles Q., 1st Lt., 5th Special Forces Group (Charleston).

NAVY-MARINE CORPS

(b) ELLIOTT, Middleton Stuart, Surg., USN (Beaufort).
      FLOYD, Edward, Boilermaker, USN (b. Ireland).
(b) *HOWE, James D., L/Cpl., 1st Mar. Div. USMC (Fort Jackson, S.C.).
(b) KENNEMORE, Robert S., S/Sgt., 1st Mar. Div. USMC (Greenville).
      *McGINTY, John J. III, 2d Lt., 3d Mar. Div. (Laurel Bay) (b. Mass.).
(b) MOFFETT, William A., Comdr., USN.
(b) *OWENS, Robert Allen, Sgt., USMC (Greenville).
(b) SULLIVAN, Daniel Augustus Joseph, Ens., USNRF (Charleston).
(b) THORNTON, Michael Edwin, Petty Officer, Naval Advisory Group (Greenville).
(b) TRUESDELL, Donald LeRoy, Cpl., USMC (Lugoff).
(b) *WATKINS, Lewis G., S/Sgt., 1st Mar. Div. USMC (Seneca).
(b) WHEELER, George Huber, SF1c. USN.
(b) WILLIAMS, James E., BMFC, USN (Rock Hill).

SOUTH DAKOTA

ARMY-AIR FORCE

      HILLOCK, Marvin C., Pvt., 7th U.S. Cav. (Lead City) (b. Mich.).
      *OLSON, Arlo L., Capt., 3d Inf. Div. (Toronto) (b. Iowa).
      WILSON, William O., Cpl., 9th U.S. Cav. (b. Md.).

NAVY-MARINE CORPS

(b) FOSS, Joseph Jacob, Capt., USMCR (Sioux Falls).
      *LITTLETON, HERBERT A., Pfc., 1st Mar. Div. USMCR (Black Hawk) (b. Ark.).

TENNESSEE

ARMY-AIR FORCE

(b) ADKINSON, Joseph B., Sgt., 30th Div. (Atoka).
(b) CANTRELL, Charles P., Pvt., 10th U.S. Inf. (Nashville).
(b) CECIL, Josephus S., 1st Lt., 19th U.S. Inf. (New River).
(b) COLLINS, Harrison, Cpl., 1st Tenn. Cav. (Hawkins County).
(b) COOLEY, Raymond H., S/Sgt., 25th Inf. Div. (Richard City).
(b) COOLIDGE, Charles H., T/Sgt., 36th Inf. Div. (Signal Mountain).
(b) *DUKE, Ray E., Sfc., 24th Inf. Div. (Whitwell).
(b) *GARDNER, James A., 1st Lt., 101st Airborne Div. (Memphis).
(b) GILLESPIE, George L., 1st. Lt., Corps of Engrs., U.S. Army (Chattanooga).
(b) GRANT, George, Sgt., Co. E, 18th U.S. Inf. (Raleigh).
(b) GREER, Allen J., 2d Lt., 4th U.S. Inf. (Memphis).
(b) HUFF, Paul B., Cpl., 82d Airborne Div. (Cleveland).
      JENKINS, Don J., S/Sgt., 9th Inf. Div. (Nashville) (b. Ky.).
(b) JORDAN, George, Sgt., 9th U.S. Cav. (Williamson County).
(b) KARNES, James E., Sgt., 30th Div. (Knoxville).
(b) LAWSON, Gaines, 1st Sgt., 4th East Tenn. Inf. (Hawkins County).
      *LEMERT, Milo, 1st Sgt., 30th Div. (Crossville) (b. Iowa).
(b) *LYELL, William F., Cpl., 7th Inf. Div. (Old Hickory).

TENNESSEE—Continued

ARMY-AIR FORCE

(b) McGAHA, Charles L., M/Sgt., 25th Inf. Div. (Cosby).
(b) McGARITY, Vernon, T/Sgt., 99th Inf. Div. (Model).
(b) MORRIS, William W., Cpl., 6th U.S. Cav. (Stewart County).
(b) STRIVSON, Benoni, Pvt., 8th U.S. Cav. (Overton).
(b) TALLEY, Edward R., Sgt., 30th Div. (Russellville).
(b) WARD, Calvin John, Pvt., 30th Div. (Morristown).
     WELD, Seth L., Cpl., 8th U.S. Inf. (Altamont) (b. Md.).
(b) YORK, Alvin C., Cpl., 82d Div. (Pall Mall).

NAVY-MARINE CORPS

(b) BONNEY, Robert Earl, CWT, USN (Nashville).
(b) HARRISON, Bolden Reush, Seaman, USN (Savannah).
(b) *KINSER, Elbert Luther, Sgt., USMCR (Greeneville).
(b) *RAY, David Robert, HC2dc., 1st Mar. Div. USN, (McMinnville).
(b) *SINGLETON, Walter K., Sgt., 3rd Marine Div. (Memphis).
(b) *WILLIS, John Harland, PhM1c., USN (Columbia).

TEXAS

ARMY-AIR FORCE

(b) ADAMS, Lucian, S/Sgt., 3d Inf. Div. (Port Arthur).
(b) *BARKELEY, David B., Pvt., 89th Div. (San Antonio).
(b) *CARSWELL, Horace S., Jr., Maj., AC, 308th Bomb. Gp. (San Angelo).
(b) *COLE, Robert G., Lt. Col., 101st Airborne Div. (San Antonio).
(b) *DAVIS, George Andrew, Jr., Maj., USAF (Lubbock).
(b) EDWARDS, Daniel R., Pfc., Co. C, 1st Div. (Bruceville).
     EVERHART, Forrest E., T/Sgt., 90th Inf. Div. (Texas City) (b. Ohio).
(b) FIELDS, James H., 1st Lt., 4th Armd. Div. (Houston).
(b) *FOWLER, Thomas W., 2d Lt., 1st Armd. Div. (Wichita Falls).
     GARCIA, Marcario, S/Sgt., 4th Inf. Div. (Sugarland) (b. Mexico).
     *HANSON, Jack G., Pfc., 7th Inf. Div. (Galveston) (b. Miss.).
(b) *HARRIS, James L., 2d Lt., 756th Tank Bn. (Hillsboro).
(b) HOWZE, Robert L., 2d Lt., 6th U.S. Cav. (Overton).
     *HUGHES, Lloyd H., 2d Lt., A.C. (San Antonio) (b. La.).
(b) KEARBY, Neel E., Col., A.C. (Dallas).
(b) *KEATHLEY, George D., S/Sgt., 85th Inf. Div. (Lamesa).
(b) *KIMBRO, Truman, T4g., 2d Inf. Div. (Houston).
(b) *KNIGHT, Jack L., 1st Lt., 124th Cav. Reg. (Weatherford).
(b) *KNIGHT, Raymond L., 1st Lt., A.C. (Houston).
(b) *LAW, Robert D., Spec. 4, 1st Inf. Div. (Fort Worth).
     *LEE, Milton A., Pfc., 101st Airborne Div. (San Antonio) (b. La.).
(b) *LEONARD, T. W., 1st Lt., 893d T.D. Bn. (Dallas).
(b) LOGAN, James M., Sgt., 36th Inf. Div. (Luling).
(b) LOPEZ, Jose M., Sgt., 2d Inf. Div. (Brownsville).
(b) *MARTINEZ, Benito, Cpl., 25th Inf. Div. (Fort Hancock).
(b) *MATHIS, Jack W., 1st Lt., A.C. (San Angelo).
(b) McCLEERY, Finnis D., P/Sgt., 6th U.S. Inf. (San Angelo).
(b) McLENNON, John, Musician, 7th U.S. Inf.
     McNERNEY, David H., 1st Sgt., 4th Inf. Div. (Fort Bliss) (b. Mass.).
(b) MORGAN, John C., 2d Lt., A.C. (Entered service: London, England).
(b) MURPHY, Audie L., 1st Lt., 3d Inf. Div. (Hunt County, near Kingston).
     PAINE, Adam, Indian Scouts, U.S. Army (Fort Duncan) (b. Fla.).
     *PENDLETON, Charles F., Cpl., 3d Inf. Div. (Forth Worth) (b. Tenn.).
     *ROBINSON, James E., Jr., 1st Lt., 63d Inf. Div. (Waco) (b. Ohio).
(b) RODRIGUEZ, Cleto, T/Sgt., 37th Inf. Div. (San Antonio).
(b) SASSER, Clarence Eugene, Spec. 5, 9th Inf. Div. (Rosharon).
(b) SHELTON, George M., Pvt., 23d U.S. Inf. (Bellington).
(b) *STEINDAM, Russell A., 1st Lt., 25th Inf. Div. (Austin).
     STONE, James L., 1st Lt., 1st Cav. Div. (Houston) (b. Ark.).
     *WALLACE, Herman C., Pfc., 76th Inf. Div. (Lubbock) (b. Okla.).
     WARD, John, Sgt., 24th U.S. Inf., Indian Scouts (Fort Duncan) (b. Ark.).

TEXAS—Continued

ARMY-AIR FORCE

*WATKINS, Travis E., M/Sgt., 2d Inf. Div. (Overton) (b. Ark.).
(b) **WHITELEY, Eli, 1st Lt., 3d Inf. Div. (Georgetown).**
(b) *YOUNG, Marvin R., S/Sgt., 25th Inf. Div. (Odessa).

NAVY-MARINE CORPS

*ANDERSON, Richard Allen, L/Cpl., 1st Mar. Div. (Edinburg) (b. D.C.).
(b) *BORDELON, William James, S/Sgt., USMC (San Antonio).
BULKELEY, John Duncan, Lt. Comdr., USN (b. N.Y.).
*CREEK, Thomas E., L/Cpl., 3rd Mar. Div. USMC, (Amarillo) (b. Mo.).
(b) *DEALEY, Samuel David, Comdr. USN (Dallas).
(b) *GONZALEZ, Alfredo, Sgt., 1st Mar. Div. USMC, (Edinburg).
*GUILLEN, Ambrosio, S/Sgt., 1st Mar. Div. USMC, (b. Colo.).
(b) HARRELL, William George, Sgt., USMC (Rio Grande City).
(b) HARRISON, William Kelly, Comdr., USN (Waco).
*HAWKINS, William Dean, 1st Lt., USMC (El Paso) (b. Kans.).
(b) HAYDEN, David E., HA1c., USN (Florence).
(b) *HUTCHINS, Johnnie David, Sfc., USNR (Weimer).
*KILMER, John E., Hospital Corpsman, USN (b. Ill.).
(b) *LUMMUS, Jack, 1st Lt., USMCR (Ennie).
(b) *MITCHELL, Frank N., 1st Lt., 1st Marine Div. USMC, (Roaring Springs).
(b) *MORELAND, Whitt L., Pfc., 1st Marine Div. USMCR, (Austin).
(b) O'BRIEN, George H., Jr., 2d Lt., 1st Marine Div. USMCR, (Big Spring).
(b) *ROAN, Charles Howard, Pfc., USMCR (Claude).
(b) WHEELER, George H., SF1c., USN (San Antonio).
*WILSON, Alfred M., Pfc., 3rd Mar. Div. USMC, (Abilene) (b. Ill.).

UTAH

ARMY-AIR FORCE

THACKER, Brian Miles, 1st Lt., 92d Arty. (Salt Lake City) (b. Ohio).
*VALDEZ, Jose F., Pfc., 3d Inf. Div. (Pleasant Grove) (b. N. Mex.).

NAVY-MARINE CORPS

(b) *BENNION, Mervyn Sharp, Capt., USN (Vernon).
(b) HALL, William E., Lt. (jg.), USNR (Storrs).
(b) WAHLEN, George Edward, PhM2c., USN (Ogden).

VERMONT

ARMY-AIR FORCE

(b) BATES, Norman F., Sgt., 4th Iowa Cav.
(b) BEATTY, Alexander M., Capt., 3d Vt. Inf. (Ryegate).
(b) BENEDICT, George G., 2d Lt., 12th Vt. Inf. (Burlington).
(b) BUTTERFIELD, Frank G., 1st Lt., 6th Vt. Inf. (Rockingham).
(b) CLARK, John W., 1st Lt. and Regimental Qm., 6th Vt. Inf. (Montpelier).
COFFEY, Robert J., Sgt., 4th Vt. Inf. (Montpelier) (b. Canada).
DAVIS, George E., 1st Lt., 10th Vt. Inf. (Burlington) (b. Mass.).
DOLLOFF, Charles W., Cpl., 1st Vt. Inf. (St. Johnsbury) (b. N.Y.).
(b) DOWNS, Henry W., Sgt., 8th Vt. Inf. (Newfane).
DRURY, James, Sgt., 4th Vt. Inf. (Chester) (b. Ireland).
EVANS, Ira H., Capt., 116th U.S. Colored Troops (Barre) (b. N.H.).
(b) GOULD, Charles G., Capt., 5th Vt. Inf. (Windham).
(b) GRANT, Lewis A., Col., 5th Vt. Inf. (Winhall).
HACK, Lester G., Sgt., 5th Vt. Inf. (Salisbury) (b. N.Y.).
HARRINGTON, Ephraim W., Sgt., 2d Vt. Inf. (Kirby) (b. Maine).
(b) HAWKINS, Gardner C., 1st Lt., 3d Vt. Inf. (Woodstock).
(b) HENRY, William W., Col., 10th Vt. Inf. (Waterbury).
(b) HOLTON, Edward A., 1st Sgt., 6th Vt. Inf. (Williston).
(b) HOWARD, Squire E., 1st Sgt., Vt. Inf. (Townshend).

364

VERMONT—Continued

INGALLS, Lewis J., Pvt., 8th Vt. Inf. (Belvidere) (b. Mass.).
(b) JEWETT, Erastus W., 1st Lt., 9th Vt. Inf. (St. Albans).
(b) JOHNDRO, Franklin, Pvt., 118th N.Y. Inf. (Highgate Falls).
JOHNSTON, Willie, Mus., 3d Vermont Inf. (St. Johnsbury) (b. N.Y.).
(b) LIVINGSTON, Josiah O., 1st Lt. and Adj., 9th Vt. Inf. (Marshfield).
LONERGAN, John, Capt., 13th Vt. Inf. (Burlington) (b. Ireland).
LYON, Frederick A., Cpl., 1st Vt. Cav. (Burlington) (b. Mass.).
(b) McCORMICK, Michael, Pvt., 5th U.S. Inf. (Rutland).
(b) NICHOLS, Henry C., Capt., 73d U.S. Colored Troops (Brandon).
(b) NOYES, William W., Pvt., 2d Vt. Inf. (Montpelier).
(b) PECK, Cassius, Pvt., 1st U.S. Sharpshooters (Brookfield).
(b) PECK, Theodore S., 1st Lt., 9th Vt. Inf. (Burlington).
PINGREE, Samuel E., Capt., 3d Vt. Inf. (Hartford) (b. N.H.).
RIPLEY, William Y. W., Lt. Col., 1st U.S. Sharpshooters (Rutland).
(b) ROBBINS, Augustus J., 2d Lt., 2d Vt. Inf. (Grafton).
(b) SARGENT, Jackson, Sgt., 5th Vt. Inf. (Stowe).
SCOTT, Alexander, Cpl., 10th Vt. Inf. (Winooski) (b. Canada).
(b) SCOTT, Julian A., Drummer, 3d Vt. Inf. (Johnson).
(b) SEAVER, Thomas O., Col., 3d Vt. Inf. (Pomfret).
(b) SPERRY, William J., Maj., 6th Vt. Inf.
SWEENEY, James, Pvt., 1st Vt. Cav. (Essex) (b. England).
(b) THOMAS, Stephen, Col., 8th Vt. Inf. (Montpelier).
TRACY, Amasa A., Lt. Col., 2d Vt. Inf. (Middlebury) (b. Maine).
VEAZEY, Wheelock G., Col., 16th Vt. Inf. (Springfield) (b. N.H.).
(b) WELLS, William, Maj., 1st Vt. Cav. (Waterbury).
(b) WHEELER, Daniel D., 1st Lt., 4th Vt. Inf. (Cavendish).
WOODBURY, Eri D., Sgt., 1st Vt. Cav. (St. Johnsbury) (b. N.H.).

(b) BLAIR, Robert M., BM, USN (Peacham).
BREAULT, Henry, Torpedoman Second Class, USN (b. Conn.).
BRESNAHAN, Patrick Francis, WT., USN (b. Mass.).
(b) EDSON, Merritt Austin, Col., USMC (Rutland).
RAMAGE, Lawson Paterson, Comd., USN (b. Mass.).

VIRGINIA

(b) ADAMS, James F., Pvt., 1st W. Va. Cav. (Cabell County).
(b) AYERS, James F., Pvt., 6th U.S. Cav. (Collinstown).
(b) BROWN, Benjamin, Sgt., 24th U.S. Inf. (Spotsylvania County).
(b) DERVISHIAN, Ernest H., 2d Lt., 34th Inf. Div. (Richmond).
(b) DOSS, Desmond T., Pfc., 77th Inf. Div. (Lynchburg).
*FAITH, Don C., 7th Inf. Div. (Arlington) (b. Ind.).
(b) *FOLLAND, Michael Fleming, Cpl., 199th Inf. Brig. (Richmond).
(b) *GAMMON, Archer T., S/Sgt., 6th Armd. Div. (Roanoke).
(b) GARDINER, James, Pvt., 36th U.S. Colored Troops (Gloucester).
(b) GILLENWATER, James R., Cpl., 36th Inf., U.S. Vol. (Rye Cove).
(b) GREGORY, Earl D., Sgt., 29th Div. (Chase City).
(b) GRESHAM, John C., 1st Lt., 7th U.S. Cav. (Lancaster Courthouse).
(b) JAMES, Miles, Cpl., 36th U.S. Colored Troops (Norfolk).
(b) JOHNSON, Henry, Sgt., 9th U.S. Cav. (Boynton).
(b) *JONES, William A., III, Col., USAF, 602d Spec. Oper. Sq. (Norfolk).
(b) LEE, Fitz, Pvt., 10th U.S. Cav. (Dinwiddie Co.).
(b) *MILLER, Gary L., 1st Lt., 1st Inf. Div. (Covington).
(b) *MONTEITH, Jimmie W., Jr., 1st Lt., 1st Inf. Div. (Richmond).
(b) MORRIS, Charles B., S/Sgt., 173d Airborne Brig. (Roanoke).
NETT, Robert P., Capt., 77th Inf. Div. (Lynchburg) (b. Conn.).
(b) *PEREGORY, Frank D., T/Sgt., 29th Inf. Div. (Charlottesville).
(b) RATCLIFF, Edward, 1st Sgt., 38th U.S. Colored Troops (James County).
(b) *SARGENT, Ruppert L., 1st Lt., 25th Inf. Div. (Hampton).

VIRGINIA—Continued

ARMY-AIR FORCE

(b) *SHEA, Richard T., Jr., 1st Lt., 7th Inf. Div. (Portsmouth).
(b) SMITH, James (Ovid), Pvt., 2d Ohio Inf. (Fredericksburg).
(b) STEWART, Benjamin F., Pvt., 7th U.S. Inf. (Norfolk).
(b) VEAL, Charles, Pvt., 4th U.S. Colored Troops (Portsmouth).
(b) WHITEHEAD, Patton G., Pvt., 5th U.S. Inf. (Russell County).
(b) *WILKINS, Raymond H., Maj., A.C. (Portsmouth).
(b) WOODALL, Zachariah, Sgt., 6th U.S. Cav. (Alexandria).

NAVY-MARINE CORPS

(b) ATKINS, Daniel SC1c., USN (Brunswick).
   BARROW, David D., Seaman, USN (Norfolk) (b. N.C.).
   BLAKE, Robert, Contraband, USN.
(b) BRIGHT, George Washington, Coal Passer, USN (Norfolk).
   BUCK, James, QM, USN (Norfolk) (b. Md.).
(b) BYRD, Richard Evelyn, Comdr., USN (Winchester).
(b) FOX, Wesley L., Capt., USMC, 3d Mar. Div. (Herndon).
(b) GARVIN, William, Captain of Forecastle, USN.
(b) HICKMAN, John, F2c., USN (Richmond).
(b) *HAMMOND, Francis C., Hospital Corpsman, USN (Alexandria).
(b) JORDAN, Thomas, Quartermaster, USN (Portsmouth).
(b) LANGHORNE, Cary DeVall, Surg., USN (Lynchburg).
(b) LANNON, James Patrick, Lt., USN (Alexandria).
   LEE, Howard V., Maj., 3d Mar. Div. (Dumfries) (b. N.Y.).
   LUCAS, Jacklyn Harold, Pfc. USMCR (Norfolk) (b. N.C).
   MEREDITH, James, Pvt., USMC (b. Nebr.).
(b) MIFFLIN, James, Engineer's Cook, USN (Richmond).
   MONTGOMERY, Robert William, Captain of Afterguard, USN (b. Ireland).
   NEIL, John, Quarter Gunner, USN (b. Newfoundland).
(b) NEVILLE, Wendell Cushing, Lt. Col., USMC (Portsmouth).
(b) O'CONNER, James F., Landsman Engineers' Force, USN (Portsmouth).
(b) PENN, Robert, F1c., USN (City Point).
   ROBERTS, James, Seaman, USN (b. England).
(b) SHACKLETTE, William Sidney, Hospital Steward, USN (Delaplane).
   SMITH, Frank Elmer, Oiler, USN (b. Mass.).
   SMITH, Thomas, Seaman, USN (b. Ireland).
(b) STREET, George Levick, III, Comdr., USN (Richmond).
(b) TAYLOR, Richard H., Quartermaster, USN.
   TORGERSON, Martin T., GM3c., USN (b. Norway).
(b) UPSHUR, William Peterkin, Capt., USMC (Richmond).
(b) VANDEGRIFT, Alexander Archer, Maj. Gen., USMC (Charlottesville).
   VOLZ, Robert, Seaman, USN (b. Calif.).

WASHINGTON

ARMY-AIR FORCE

   *ALBANESE, Lewis, Pfc., 1st Cav. Div. (Seattle) (b. Italy).
(b) BJORKLUND, Arnold L., 1st Lt., 36th Inf. Div. (Seattle).
   BRADY, Patrick Henry, Maj., 44th Med. Brig. (Seattle) (b. S. Dak.).
   BRONSON, Deming, 1st Lt., 91st Div. (Seattle) (b. Wis.).
   DROWLEY, Jesse R., S/Sgt., Americal Inf. Div. (Spokane)(b. Mich.).
   FLEMING, James P., Capt., 20th Spec. Oper. Sq. (Pullman) (b. Mo.).
(b) *GRANDSTAFF, Bruce Alan, Plat. Sgt., 4th Inf. Div. (Spokane).
   HAWK, John D., Sgt., 90th Inf. Div. (Bremerton) (b. Calif.).
(b) KERSTETTER, Dexter J., Pfc., 33d Inf. Div. (Centralia).
(b) KINSMAN, Thomas James, Spec. 4, 9th Inf. Div. (Renton).
   *LEISY, Robert Ronald, 2nd Lt., 1st Cav. Div. (Seattle) (b. Calif.).
   LYON, Edward E., Pvt., 2d Oreg. Vol. Inf. (Amboy) (b. Wis.).
(b) *MANN, Joe E., Pfc., 101st Airborne Div. (Seattle).
   McCARTER, Lloyd G., Pvt., 503d Parachute Inf. Regt. (Tacoma) (b. Idaho).
   *PENDLETON, Jack J., S/Sgt., 30th Inf. Div. (Yakima) (b. N. Dak.).
   SCHAUER, Henry, Pfc., 3d Inf. Div. (Palouse) (b. Okla.).

WASHINGTON—Continued

ARMY-AIR FORCE

STEVENS, Hazard, Capt. and Asst. Adj. Gen., U.S. Vol. (Olympia) (b. R.I.).
(b) WILSON, Benjamin F., 1st Lt., 7th Inf. Div. (Vashon).
(b) WILSON, John M., 1st Lt., U.S. Engrs. (Olympia).

NAVY-MARINE CORPS-COAST GUARD

(b) *ANDERSON, Richard Beatty, Pfc., USMC (Tacoma).
     BOYINGTON, Gregory, Maj., USMCR (b. Idaho).
(b) BUSH, Robert Eugene, HA1c., USNR (Tacoma).
     DAVIS, Raymond E., QM3c., USN (Seattle) (b. Minn.).
     FADDEN, Harry D., Cox., USN (b. Oreg.).
(b) GALER, Robert Edward, Maj., USMC (Seattle).
(b) *KEPPLER, Reinhardt John, BM1c., USN (Ralston).
     *MONEGAN, Walter G., Jr., Pfc., 1st Marine Div. USMC (Seattle) (b. Mass.).
     *MUNRO, Douglas Albert, SM1c., USCG (S. Cle Elum) (b. Canada).
(b) *ROOKS, Albert Harold, Capt., USN (Colton).
(b) *SHIELDS, Marvin G., CMTC, Seabee Team 1104 (Port Townsend).
     VAN WINKLE, Archie, S/Sgt., 1st Marine Div. USMCR (Arlington) (b. Alaska).
     WINANS, Roswell, 1st Sgt., USMC (b. Indiana).

WEST VIRGINIA

ARMY-AIR FORCE

     APPLE, Andrew O., 12th W. Va. Inf. (New Cumberland) (b. Pa.).
     BARRINGER, William H., Pvt., 4th W. Va. Inf. (Jackson County).
(b) *BELCHER, Ted, Sgt., 25th Inf. Div. (Accoville).
(b) *BENNETT, Thomas W., Cpl., 14th Inf. Div. (Morgantown).
     BOURY, Richard, Sgt., 1st W. Va. Cav. (Wirt Courthouse) (b. Ohio).
(b) BUCKLEY, John C., Sgt., 4th W. Va. Inf. (Fayette County).
     BUMGARNER, William, Sgt., 4th W. Va. Inf. (Mason City).
(b) CRISWELL, Benjamin C., Sgt., 7th U.S. Cav. (Marshall County).
(b) CURTIS, Josiah M., 2d Lt., 12th W. Va. Inf. (Ohio County).
(b) DURHAM, James R., 2d Lt., 12th W. Va. Inf. (Clarksburg).
(b) ECKES, John N., Pvt., 47th Ohio Inf. (Weston).
     GAUJOT, Antoine A., Cpl., 27th Inf., U.S. Vol. (Williamson) (b. Mich.).
     GAUJOT, Julien E., Capt. 1st U.S. Cav. (Williamson) (b. Mich.).
     *HARTSOCK, Robert W., S/Sgt., 25th Inf. Div. (Fairmont) (b. Md.).
(b) *HEDRICK, Clinton M., T/Sgt., 17th Airborne Div. (Riverton).
     INSCHO, Leonidas H., Cpl., 12th Ohio Inf. (Charleston) (b. Ohio).
(b) *KELLEY, Jonah E., S/Sgt., 78th Inf. (Keyser).
     *KYLE, Darwin K., 2d Lt., 3d Inf. Div. (Racine) (b. Ky.).
(b) McCAULSLIN, Joseph, Pvt., 12th W. Va. Inf. (Ohio County).
(b) *McDONALD, Phill G., Pfc., 4th Inf. Div. (Beckley).
     McELHINNY, Samuel O., Pvt., 2d W. Va. Cav. (Point Pleasant) (b. Ohio).
(b) McWHORTER, Walter F., Commissary Sgt., 3d W. Va. Cav. (Harrison County).
(b) MOORE, George G., Pvt., 11th W. Va. Inf. (Tyler County).
     PARSONS, Joel, Pvt., 4th W. Va. Inf. (Mason City).
(b) *POMEROY, Ralph E., Pfc., 7th Inf. Div. (Quinwood).
(b) REEDER, Charles A., Pvt., 12th W. Va. Inf. (Harrison County).
(b) ROGERS, Charles Calvin, Lt. Col., 1st Inf. Div. (Institute).
     SCHORN, Charles, Chief Bugler, 1st W. Va. Cav. (Mason City) (b. Germany).
(b) SHAHAN, Emisire, Cpl., 1st W. Va. Cav. (Preston County).
(b) SHANES, John, Pvt., 14th W. Va. Inf. (Monongalia County).
(b) SHOEMAKER, Levi, Sgt., 1st W. Va. Cav. (Monongalia County).
(b) SUMMERS, James C., Pvt., 4th W. Va. Inf. (Kanawha).
(b) VAN MATRE, Joseph, Pvt., 116th Ohio Inf. (Mason County).
     WHITE, Adam, Cpl., 11th W. Va. Inf. (Parkersburg) (b. Switzerland).
(b) WOODS, Daniel A., Pvt., 1st Va. Cav. (Ohio County).

NAVY-MARINE CORPS

(b) COX, Robert Edward, CGM, USN (St. Albans).

NAVY-MARINE CORPS

(b)   FRAZER, Hugh Carroll, Ens., USN (Martinsburg).
(b)   JONES, Claud Ashton, Comdr., USN (Fire Creek).
      *MARTINI, Gary W., Pfc., 1st Marine Div. (Charleston) (b. Va.).
(b)   NICKERSON, Henry Nehemiah, BM, USN (Edgewood).
      *THOMAS, Herbert Joseph, Sgt., USMCR (b. Ohio).
(b)   WILLIAMS, Hershel Woodrow, Cpl., USMCR (Quiet Dell).

WISCONSIN

ARMY-AIR FORCE

(b)   ANDERSON, Beauford T., S/Sgt., 96th Inf. Div. (Soldiers Grove).
(b)   ANDERSON, Peter, Pvt., 31st Wis. Inf. (Lafayette County).
(b)   BONG, Richard I., Maj., A.C. (Poplar).
(b)   *BURR, Elmer J., 1st Sgt., 32 Inf. Div. (Menasha).
      CABLE, Joseph A., Pvt., 5th U.S. Inf. (b. Mo.).
(b)   COATES, Jefferson, Sgt., 7th Wis. Inf. (Boscobel).
      CROFT, James E., Pvt., Wis. Light Arty. (Janesville) (b. England).
      DURHAM, John S., Sgt., 1st Wis. Inf. (Malone) (b. N.Y.).
      ELLIS, Horace, Pvt., 7th Wis. Inf. (Chippewa Falls) (b. Pa.).
(b)   *ENDL, Gerald L., S/Sgt., 32d Inf. Div. (Janesville).
      FRITZ, Harold A., Capt., 11th Air Cav. Reg. (Milwaukee) (b. Ill.).
(b)   *GRUENNERT, Kenneth E., Sgt., 32d Inf. Div. (Helenville).
(b)   *HANDRICH, Melvin O., M/Sgt., 25th Inf. Div. (Manawa).
(b)   HILL, Frank E., Sgt., 5th U.S. Cav. (Mayfield).
      HILLIKER, Benjamin F., Mus., 8th Wis. Inf. (Waupaca) (b. N.Y.).
(b)   INGMAN, Einar H., Sgt., 7th Inf. Div. (Tomahawk).
(b)   *JERSTAD, John L., Maj., A.C. (Racine).
      JOHNSON, John, Pvt., 2d Wis. Inf. (Janesville) (b. Norway).
      MacARTHUR, Arthur, Jr., 1st Lt. and Adj., 24th Wis. Inf. (Milwaukee) (b.
        Mass.).
      MacARTHUR, Douglas, Gen., USA (Ashland) (b. Ark.).
(b)   McGRATH, Hugh J., Capt., 4th U.S. Cav. (Eau Claire).
(b)   *MILLER, Andrew, S/Sgt., 95th Inf. Div. (Two Rivers).
      *MITCHELL, William C., Maj. Gen., A.C. (Milwaukee) (b. Nice, France).
(b)   MOORE, Daniel B., Cpl., 11th Wis. Inf. (Mifflin).
(b)   *MOWER, Charles E., Sgt., 24th Inf. Div. (Chippewa Falls).
(b)   NEWMAN, Beryl R., 1st Lt., 34th Inf. Div. (Baraboo).
(b)   *OLSON, Truman O., Sgt., 3d Inf. Div. (Cambridge).
      O'CONNOR, Albert, Sgt., 7th Wis. Inf. (Columbia County) (b. Canada).
      POND, George F., Pvt., 3d Wis. Cav. (Fairwater) (b. Ill.).
      POND, James B., 1st Lt., 3d Wis. Cav. (Janesville) (b. N.Y.).
(b)   *RED CLOUD, Mitchell, Jr., Cpl., 24th Inf. Div. (Merrillan).
(b)   ROBBINS, Marcus M., Pvt., 6th U.S. Cav. (Elba).
      SICKLES, William H., Sgt., 7th Wis. Inf. (Columbia County) (b. N.Y.).
(b)   *SIJAN, Lance P., Capt., USAF (Milwaukee).
(b)   SLACK, Clayton K., Pvt., 124th M. G. Bn., 33d Div. (Madison).
(b)   STUMPF, Kenneth E., S/Sgt., 25th Inf. Div. (Menasha).
(b)   *SUDUT, Jerome A., 2d Lt., 25th Inf. Div. (Wausau).
      TRUELL, Edwin M., Pvt., 12th Wis. Inf. (Manston) (b. Mass.).
      WALLER, Francis A., Cpl., 6th Wis. Inf. (Desoto) (b. Ohio).
(b)   WETZEL, Gary George, Spec. 4, 173rd Assault Helicopter Comp. (Milwaukee).
(b)   WINDUS, Claron A., Bugler, 6th U.S. Cav. (Janesville).

NAVY-MARINE CORPS

(b)   *AGERHOLM, Harold Christ, Pfc., USMCR (Racine).
      CASTLE, Guy Wilkinson Stuart, Lt., USN.
(b)   *CHRISTIANSON, Stanley R., Pfc., 1st Marine Div. USMC (Mindoro).
(b)   DE SOMER, Abraham, Chief Turret Capt., USN (Milwaukee).
(b)   MODRZEWSKI, Robert J., Maj., 3d Marine Div. (Milwaukee).
(b)   *PETERSON, Oscar Verner, CWT, USN (Prentice).
      *VAN VALKENBURGH, Franklin, Capt., USN (b. Minn.).

WISCONSIN—Continued

NAVY-MARINE CORPS

YOUNG, Cassin, Comdr., USN (b. D.C.).
(b)   YOUNG, Frank Albert, Pvt., USMC (Milwaukee).

WYOMING

ARMY-AIR FORCE

(b)   BAKER, Edward L., Jr., Sgt. Maj., 10th U.S. Cav. (Laramie County).
    *CAREY, Charles F., Jr., T/Sgt., 100th Inf. Div. (Cheyenne) (b. Okla.).
(b)   ROBERTS, Charles D., 2d Lt., 17th U.S. Inf. (Fort Russell).

PUERTO RICO

ARMY-AIR FORCE

(b)   *RUBIO, Euripides, Capt., 1st Inf. Div. RVN (Ponce).

NAVY-MARINE CORPS

(b)   *GARCIA, Fernando L., Pfc., 1st Marine Div. USMC (San Juan).

AHEAM, Michael, Paymaster's Steward, USN (France).
AHERN, William, WT, USN (Ireland).
ALBANESE, Lewis, Pfc., 1st Cav. Div. (Italy).
ALBER, Frederick, Pvt., 17th Mich. Inf. (Germany).
ALLEN, Edward, BM1c, USN (Holland).
ALLEN, James, Pvt., 16th N.Y. Inf. (Ireland).
ALLEX, Jake, Cpl., 131st Inf. (Serbia, now Yugoslavia).
ANDERSON, Bruce, Pvt., 142d N.Y. Inf. (Mexico).
ANDERSON, James, Pvt., 6th U.S. Cav. (Canada East).
ANDERSON, Johannes S., 1st Sgt., 33d Div. (Finland).
ANDERSON, Robert, QM, USN (Ireland).
ANDERSON, William, Coxs., USN (Sweden).
ARCHINAL, William, Cpl., 30th Ohio Inf. (Germany).
ARTHER, Matthew, Signal QM, USN (Scotland).
ASTEN, Charles, QG, USN (Nova Scotia).
AVERY, James, Seaman, USN (Scotland).
BAKER, John, Musician, 5th U.S. Inf. (Germany).
BALLEN, Frederick, Pvt., 47th Ohio Inf. (Germany).
BARRETT, Richard, 1st Sgt., 1st U.S. Cav. (Ireland).
BARRY, Augustus, Sgt. Maj., 16th U.S. Inf. (Ireland).
BASS, David L., Seaman, USN (Ireland).
BATES, Richard, Seaman, USN (Wales).
BAYBUTT, Philip, Pvt., 2d Mass. Cav. (England).
BAZAAR, Philip, Ordinary Seaman, USN (Chile).
BEAUFORT, Jean J., Cpl., 2d La. Inf. (France).
BEDDOWS, Richard, Pvt., 34th N.Y. Btry. (England).
BEECH, John P., Sgt., 4th N.J. Inf. (England).
BEGLEY, Terrence, Sgt., 7th N.Y. Heavy Arty. (Ireland).
BEHNE, Frederick, FM1c, USN (Germany).
BEHNKE, Heinrich, Seaman 1c, USN (Germany).
BELL, George H., Captain of the Afterguard (England).
BELL, James, Pvt., 7th U.S. Inf. (Ireland).
BELPITT, W. H., Captain of the Afterguard, USN (Australia).
BENSON, James, Seaman, USN (Denmark).
BERGERNDAHL, Frederick, Pvt., 4th U.S. Cav. (Sweden).
BERTRAM, Heinrich, Cpl., 8th U.S. Cav. (Germany).
BEYER, Albert, Coxswain, USN (Germany).
BIEGER, Charles, Pvt., 4th Mo. Cav. (Germany).
BINDER, Richard, Sgt., USMC (Germany).
BJORKMAN, Ernest H., Ordinary Seaman, USN (Sweden).
BLACKWOOD, William R. D., Surg., 48th Pa. Inf. **(Ireland).**
BLAGHEEN, William, S.C., USN (England).
BLUCHER, Charles, Cpl., 188th Pa. Inf. (Germany).
BOEHLER, Otto, Pvt., 1st Md. Vol. Inf. (Germany).
BOIS, Frank, QM, USN (Canada).
BOQUET, Nicholas, Pvt., 1st Iowa Inf. (Germany).
BOURNE, Thomas, Seaman, USN (England).
BRADLEY, Charles, BM, USN (Ireland).
BRADLEY, Thomas W., Sgt., 124th N.Y. Inf. (England).
BRADY, George F., CGM, USN (Ireland).
BRANAGAN, Edward, Pvt., 4th U.S. Cav. (Ireland).
BRANNIGAN, Felix, Pvt., 74th N.Y. Inf. (Ireland).
BRATLING, Frank, Cpl., 8th U.S. Cav. (Germany).
BRENNAN, Christopher, Seaman, USN (Ireland).
BRINN, Andrew, Seaman, USN (Scotland).
BROGAN, James, Sgt., 6th U.S. Cav. (Ireland).

Continued

BRONNER, August F., Pvt., 1st N.Y. Arty. (Germany).
BROPHY, James, Pvt., 8th U.S. Cav. (Ireland).
BROSNAN, John, Sgt., 164th N.Y. Inf. (Ireland).
BROWN, Edward, Jr., Cpl., 62d N.Y. Inf. (Ireland).
BROWN, James, Sgt., 5th U.S. Cav. (Ireland).
BROWN, John, Captain of Forecastle, USN (Scotland).
BROWN, John, Captain of the Afterguard, USN (Denmark).
BROWN, John H., Captain, 12th Ky. Inf. (Canada).
BROWN, Robert, Captain of Top, USN (Norway).
BUCKLEY, Denis, Pvt., 136th N.Y. Inf. (Canada).
BURBANK, James H., Sgt., 4th R.I. Inf. (Holland).
BURGER, Joseph, Pvt., 2d Minn. Inf. (Austria).
BURK, Michael, Pvt., 125th N.Y. Inf. (Ireland).
BURKARD, Oscar, Pvt., Hosp. Corps, U.S. Army (Germany).
BURKE, Patrick J., Farrier, 8th U.S. Cav. (Ireland).
BURKE, Richard, Pvt., 5th U.S. Inf. (Ireland).
BURKE, Thomas, Pvt., 5th N.Y. Cav. (Ireland).
BURKE, Thomas, Seaman, USN (Ireland).
BURTON, Albert, Seaman USN (England).
BUTLER, Edmond, Capt., 5th U.S. Inf. (Ireland).
BYRNE, Denis, Sgt., 5th U.S. Inf. (Ireland).
BYRNES, James, BM, USN (Ireland).
CAHEY, Thomas, Seaman, USN (Ireland).
CALLEN, Thomas J., Pvt., 7th U.S. Cav. (Ireland).
CALUGAS, Jose, Sgt., 88th F.A., Philippine Scouts (Philippine Islands).
CAMPBELL, Daniel, Pvt., USMC (Canada).
CAMPBELL, William, Pvt., 30th Ohio Inf. (Ireland).
CAREY, Hugh, Sgt., 82d N.Y. Inf. (Ireland).
CAREY, James, Seaman, USN (Ireland).
CARROLL, Thomas, Pvt., 8th U.S. Cav. (Ireland).
CARTER, George, Pvt., 8th U.S. Cav. (Ireland).
CARTER, Joseph E., Blacksmith, USN (England).
CARUANA, Orlando E., Pvt., 51st N.Y. Inf. (Malta).
CASEY, David, Pvt., 25th Mass. Inf. (Ireland).
CASSIDY, Michael, Landsman, USN (Ireland).
CASTLE, Frederick, Brig. Gen., USAAC (Philippines).
CAVANAUGH, Thomas, FM1c, USN (Ireland).
CAVAIANI, Jon R., S/Sgt., U.S. Army Vietnam Tr. Adv. Gp. (England).
CAYER, Ovila, Sgt., 14th U.S. Volunteers (Canada).
CHANDRON, August, Seaman Apprentice 2c, USN (France).
CHAPMAN, John, Pvt., 1st Maine Heavy Arty. (Canada).
CHAPUT, Louis G., Landsman, USN (Canada).
CLAUSEN, Claus Kristian, Coxs., USN (Denmark).
COFFEY, Robert J., Sgt., 4th Vt. Inf. (Canada).
COHN, Abraham, Sgt. Maj., 6th N.H. Inf. (Prussia).
COLBERT, Patrick, Coxs., USN (Ireland).
COLEMAN, John, Pvt., USMC (Ireland).
COLLIS, Charles H.T., Col., 114th Pa. Inf. (Ireland).
CONNOR, John, Cpl., 6th U.S. Cav. (Ireland).
CONNOR, Thomas, Ordinary Seaman, USN (Ireland).
CONNORS, James, Pvt., 43d N.Y. Inf. (Ireland).
COOK, John H., Sgt., 119th Ill. Inf. (England).
COONEY, James, Pvt., USMC (Ireland).
COONEY, Thomas C., Chief Machinist, USN (Canada).
COOPER, John, Coxs., USN (Ireland).
CORAHORGI, Demetri, FM1c, USN (Austria).
CORCORAN, Thomas E., Landsman, USN (Ireland).
COSGROVE, Thomas, Pvt., 40th Mass. Inf. (Ireland).
CRAIG, Robert, 2d Lt., USA (Scotland).
CRAMEN, Thomas, BM, USN (Ireland).
CREED, John, Pvt., 23d Ill. Inf. (Ireland).
CROFT, James E., Pvt., Wis. Light Arty. (England).
CUKELA, Louis, Sgt., USMC (Austria).
CULLEN, Thomas, Cpl., 82d N.Y. Inf. (Ireland).

CURRAN, Richard, Asst. Surg., 33d N.Y. Inf. (Ireland).
DAHLGREN, John Olof, Cpl., USMC (Sweden).
DAILY, Charles, Pvt., 8th U.S. Cav. (Ireland).
DAVIDSON, Andrew, 1st Lt., 30th U.S. Colored Troops (Scotland).
DAVIS, George Fleming, Comdr., USN (Philippine Islands).
DAVIS, John, Ordinary Seaman, USN (Jamaica).
DAVIS, John, GM3c, USN (Germany).
DAVIS, Joseph, Cpl., 104th Ohio Inf. (Wales).
DAVIS, Thomas, Pvt., 2d N.Y. Heavy Arty. (Wales).
DEETLINE, Frederick, Pvt., 7th U.S. Cav. (Germany).
DELANEY, John C., Sgt., 107th Pa. Inf. (Ireland).
DEMPSEY, John, Seaman, USN (Ireland).
DEMPSTER, John, Coxs., USN (Scotland).
DENHAM, Austin, Seaman, USN (England).
DI CESNOLA, Louis P., Col., 4th N.Y. Cav. (Italy).
DICKENS, Charles H., Cpl., 8th U.S. Cav. (Ireland).
DICKIE, David, Sgt., 97th Ill. Inf. (Scotland).
DILBOY, George, Pfc., 103d Infantry (Greece).
DILGER, Hubert, Capt., 1st Ohio Light Arty. (Germany).
DODD, Robert F., Pvt., 27th Mich. Inf. (Canada).
DODDS, Edward E., Sgt., 21st N.Y. Cav. (Canada).
DOHERTY, Thomas M., Cpl., 21st U.S. Inf. (Ireland).
DONAVAN, Cornelius, Sgt., 8th U.S. Cav. (Ireland).
DONELLY, John S., Pvt., 5th U.S. Inf. (Ireland).
DONNELLY, John, Ordinary Seaman, USN (England).
DONOGHUE, Timothy, Pvt., 69th N.Y. Inf. (Ireland).
DOODY, Patrick, Cpl., 164th N.Y. Inf. (Ireland).
DOOLEN, William, Coal Heaver, USN (Ireland).
DORE, George H., Sgt., 126th N.Y. Inf. (England).
DORLEY, August, Pvt., 1st La. Cav. (Germany).
DOUGALL, Allan H., 1st Lt. and Adj., 88th Ind. Inf. (Scotland).
DOUGHERTY, James, Pvt., USMC (Ireland).
DOUGHERTY, Michael, Pvt., 13th Pa. Cav. (Ireland).
DOUGHERTY, Patrick, Landsman, USN (Ireland).
DOW, Henry, BM, USN (Scotland).
DOWLING, James, Cpl., 8th U.S. Cav. (Ireland).
DOWNEY, William, Pvt., 4th Mass. Cav. (Ireland).
DRURY, James, Sgt., 4th Vt. Inf. (Ireland).
DRUSTRUP, Niels, Lt., USN (Denmark).
DUNPHY, Richard D., Coal Heaver, USN (Ireland).
EADIE, Thomas, Chief GM, USN (Scotland).
EDWARDS, David, Pvt., 146th N.Y. Inf. (Wales, England).
EGLIT, John, Seaman, USN (Finland).
ELLIS, William, 1st Sgt., 3d Wis. Cav. (England).
ELMORE, Walter, Landsman, USN (England).
ENDERLIN, Richard, Musician, 73d Ohio Inf. (Germany).
ENGLISH, Edmund, 1st Sgt., 2d N.J. Inf. (Ireland).
ERICKSON, John P., Captain of Forecastle, USN (England).
ERICKSON, Nick, Coxs., USN (Finland).
EVANS, Thomas, Pvt., 54th Pa. Inf. (Wales).
EVANS, William, Pvt., 7th U.S. Inf. (Ireland).
EVERETTS, John, GM1c, USN (Canada).
FALCOTT, Henry, Sgt., 8th U.S. Cav. (France).
FALLON, Thomas T., Pvt., 37th N.Y. Inf. (Ireland).
FARQUHAR, John M., Sgt. Maj., 89th Ill. Inf. (Scotland).
FARREN, Daniel, Pvt., 8th U.S. Cav. (Ireland).
FASSEUR, Isaac L., Ordinary Seaman, USN (Holland).
FEGAN, James, Sgt., 3d U.S. Inf. (Ireland).
FESQ, Frank, Pvt., 40th N.J. Inf. (Germany).
FICHTER, Hermann, Pvt., 3d U.S. Cav. (Germany).
FISHER, Frederick Thomas, GM1c, USN (England).
FITZ, Joseph, Ordinary Seaman, USN (Austria).
FITZGERALD, John, Pvt., USMC (Ireland).
FITZPATRICK, Thomas, Coxs., USN (Canada).

FLANNAGAN, John, BM, USN (Ireland).
FLOOD, Thomas, Boy, USN (Ireland).
FLOYD, Edward, BM, USN (Ireland).
FLYNN, Christopher, Cpl., 14th Conn. Inf. (Ireland).
FOLEY, John H., Sgt., 3d U.S. Cav. (Ireland).
FORAN, Nicholas, Pvt., 8th U.S. Cav. (Ireland).
FORD, George W., 1st Lt., 88th N.Y. Inf. (Ireland).
FORSTERER, Bruno Albert, Sgt., USMC (Germany).
FOSTER, William, Sgt., 4th U.S. Cav. (England).
FOUT, Frederick W., 2d Lt., Ind. Light Arty. (Germany).
FOX, Henry, Sgt., 106th Ill. Inf. (Germany).
FRANTZ, Joseph, Pvt., 83d Ind. Inf. (France).
FRASER (FRAZIER), William W., Pvt., 97th Ill. Inf. (Scotland).
FREEMAN, Martin, Pilot, USN (Germany).
FREEMEYER, Christopher, Pvt., 5th U.S. Inf. (Germany).
FREY, Franz, Cpl., 37th Ohio Inf. (Switzerland).
FUGER, Frederick, Sgt., 4th U.S. Arty. (Germany).
GARCIA, Marcario, S/Sgt., USA (Mexico).
GARDNER, Charles, Pvt., 8th U.S. Cav. (Germany).
GARDNER, William, Seaman, USN (Ireland).
GARRETT, William, Sgt., 41st Ohio Inf. (England).
GASSON, Richard, Sgt., 47th N.Y. Inf. (Ireland).
GAUGHAN, Philip, Sgt., USMC (Ireland).
GAY, Thomas H., Pvt., 8th U.S. Cav. (Canada).
GEORGIAN, John, Pvt., 8th U.S. Cav. (Germany).
GERBER, Frederick W., Sgt Maj., U.S. Engr. (Germany).
GESCHWIND, Nicholas, Capt., 116th Ill. Inf. (France).
GIBBONS, Michael, Oiler, USN (Ireland).
GIBSON, Eric G., T/5, USA (Sweden).
GILMORE, John C., Maj., 16th N.Y. Inf. (Canada).
GINLEY, Patrick, Pvt., 1st N.Y. Light Arty. (Ireland).
GIRANDY, Alphonse, Seaman, USN (West Indies).
GLAVINSKI, Albert, Blacksmith, 3d U.S. Cav. (Germany).
GLYNN, Michael, Pvt., 5th U.S. Cav. (Ireland).
GOLDEN, Patrick, Sgt., 8th U.S. Cav. (Ireland).
GRACE, H. Patrick, Chief QM, USN (Ireland).
GRADY, John, Lt., USN (Canada).
GRAHAM, Robert, Landsman, USN (England).
GRAY, John, Pvt., 5th Ohio Inf. (Scotland).
GRBITCH, Rade, Seaman, USN (Austria).
GREBE, M. R. William, Capt., 4th Mo. Cav. (Germany).
GREEN, George, Cpl., 11th Ohio Inf. (England).
GREEN, John, Major, 1st U.S. Cav. (Germany).
GRESSER, Ignatz, Cpl., 128th Pa. Inf. (Germany).
GRIBBEN, James H., Lt., 2d N.Y. Cav. (Ireland).
GRIFFITHS, John, Captain of Forecastle, USN (Wales).
GRUEB, George, Pvt., 158th N.Y. Inf. (Germany).
HACK, John, Pvt., 47th Ohio Inf. (Germany).
HAGERTY, Asel, Pvt., 61st N.Y. Inf. (Canada).
HALEY, James, Captain of Forecastle, USN (Ireland).
HALFORD, William, Coxswain, USN (England).
HALLING, Luovi, BM1c, USN (Sweden).
HAMILTON, Frank, Pvt., 8th U.S. Cav. (Ireland).
HAMILTON, Mathew H., Pvt., 7th U.S. Cav. (Australia).
HAMILTON, Thomas W., QM, USN (Scotland).
HAMMEL, Henry A., Sgt., 1st Mo. Light Arty. (Germany).
HANSEN, Hans A., Seaman, USN (Germany).
HANSON, Robert Murray, 1st Lt., USMCR (India).
HARBOURNE, John H., Pvt., 29th Mass. Inf. (England).
HARDING, Mosher A., Blacksmith, 8th U.S. Cav. (Canada).
HARRINGTON, Daniel, Landsman, USN (Ireland).
HARRIS, John, Captain of Forecastle, USN (Scotland).
HART, John W., Sgt., 6th Pa. Res. (Germany).
HARVEY, Harry, Cpl., 22d N.Y. Cav. (England).

HAUPT, Paul, Cpl., 8th U.S. Cav. (Prussia).
HAURON, John H., Sgt., 1st R.I. Light Inf. (Ireland).
HAWKINS, Charles, Seaman, USN (Scotland).
HAY, Fred S., Sgt., 5th U.S. Inf. (Scotland).
HAYS, George P., 1st Lt., USA (China).
HEARTERY, Richard, Pvt., 6th U.S. Cav. (Ireland).
HEISCH, Henry William, Pvt., USMC (Germany).
HEISE, Clamor, Pvt., 8th U.S. Cav. (Germany).
HENDRICKSON, Henry, Seaman, USN (Germany).
HIBSON, Joseph C., Pvt., 48th N.Y. Inf. (England).
HIGGINS, Thomas J., Sgt., 99th Ill. Inf. (Canada).
HIGGINS, Thomas P., Pvt., 8th U.S. Cav. (Ireland).
HIGHLAND, Patrick, Cpl., 23d Ill. Inf. (Ireland).
HILL, George, Chief Quarter Gunner, USN (England).
HILL, James, 1st Lt., 21st Iowa Inf. (England).
HINEMANN, Lehmann, Sgt., 1st U.S. Cav. (Germany).
HINNEGAN, William FM2c., USN (Ireland).
HOFFMAN, Henry, Cpl., 2d Ohio Cav. (Germany).
HOGAN, Henry, 1st Sgt., 5th U.S. Inf. (Ireland).
HOLDEN, Henry, Pvt., 7th U.S. Cav. (England).
HOLEHOUSE, James (John), Pvt., 7th Mass. Inf. (England).
HORNE, Samuel B., Capt., 11th Conn. Inf. (Ireland).
HOUGHTON, George L., Pvt., 104th Ill. Inf. (Canada).
HOWARD, James H., Lt. Col., A.C. (China).
HOWARD, Martin, Landsman, USN (Ireland).
HOWARD, Peter, BM, USN (France).
HUDSON, Michael, Sgt., USMC (Ireland).
HULBERT, Henry Lewis, Pvt., USMC (England).
HUNT, Martin, Pvt., USMC (Ireland).
HYDE, Thomas W., Maj., 7th Maine Inf. (Italy).
HYLAND, John, Seaman, USN (Ireland).
IRLAM, Joseph, Seaman, USN (England).
IRVING, Thomas, Coxs., USN (England).
IRWIN, Bernard J., Assist. Surg., U.S. Army (Ireland).
IRWIN, Nicholas, Seaman, USN (Denmark).
IRWIN, Patrick, 1st Sgt., 14th Mich. Inf. (Ireland).
ITRICH, Franz Anton, Chief Carpenter's Mate, USN (Germany).
JACHMAN, Isadore S., S/Sgt., U.S. Army (Germany).
JAMES, John, Cpl., 5th U.S. Inf. (England).
JAMIESON, Walter, 1st Sgt., 139th N.Y. Inf. (France).
JARDINE, Alexander, FM1c, USN (Scotland).
JARDINE, James, Sgt., 54th Ohio Inf. (Scotland).
JENNINGS, James T., Pvt., 56th Pa. Inf. (England).
JENSEN, Gotfred, Pvt., 1st N. Dak. Vol. Inf. (Denmark).
JETTER, Bernhard, Sgt., 7th U.S. Cav. (Germany).
JIMENEZ, Jose Francisco, L/Cpl., USMC (Mexico).
JOHANNESSEN, Johannes J., Chief Watertender, USN (Norway).
JOHANSON, John P., Seaman, USN (Sweden).
JOHANSSON, Johan J., Ordinary Seaman (Sweden).
JOHN, William, Pvt., 37th Ohio Inf. (Germany).
JOHNSEN, Hans, Chief Machinist, USN (Norway).
JOHNSON, Henry, Seaman, USN (Norway).
JOHNSON, John, Pvt., 2d Wis. Inf. (Norway).
JOHNSON, Peter, FM1c, USN (England).
JOHNSON, William, Cooper, USN (West Indies).
JONES, Andrew, Chief BM, USN (Ireland).
JONES, William, 1st Sgt., 73d N.Y. Inf. (Ireland).
JUDGE, Francis W., 1st Sgt., 79th N.Y. Inf. (England).
KAISER, John, Sgt., 2d U.S. Arty. (Germany).
KALTENBACH, Luther, Cpl., 12th Iowa Inf. (Germany).
KANE, John, Cpl., 100th N.Y. Inf. (Ireland).
KAPPESSER, Peter, Pvt., 149th N.Y. Inf. (Germany).
KARPLES, Leopold, Sgt., 57th Mass. Inf. (Hungary).
KAUSS (KAUTZ), August, Cpl., 15th N.Y. Hvy. Arty. (Germany).

KAY, John, Pvt., 8th U.S. Cav. (England).
KEARNEY, Michael, Pvt., USMC (Ireland).
KEATING, Daniel, Cpl., 6th U.S. Cav. (Ireland).
KEELE, Joseph, Sgt. Maj., 182d N.Y. Inf. (Ireland).
KEEN, Joseph S., Sgt., 13th Mich. Inf. (England).
KEENAN, John, Pvt., 8th U.S. Cav. (Ireland).
KEENE, Joseph, Pvt., 26th N.Y. Inf. (England).
KELLEY, Charles, Pvt., 1st U.S. Cav. (Ireland).
KELLEY, John, FM2c., USN (Ireland).
KELLY, Thomas, Pvt., 6th N.Y. Cav. (Ireland).
KELLY, Thomas, Pvt., 5th U.S. Inf. (Ireland).
KELLY, Thomas, Pvt., 21st U.S. Inf. (Ireland).
KENNA, Barnett, QM, USN (England).
KENNEDY, John, Pvt., 2d U.S. Arty. (Ireland).
KENNEDY, Philip, Pvt., 5th U.S. Inf. (Ireland).
KEOUGH, John, Cpl., 67th Pa. Inf. (Ireland).
KERR, Thomas A., Capt., 14th Pa. Cav. (Ireland).
KERRIGAN, Thomas, Sgt., 6th U.S. Cav. (Ireland).
KERSEY, Thomas, Ordinary Seaman, USN (Canada).
KILLACKEY, Joseph, Landsman, USN (Ireland).
KILMARTIN, John, Pvt., 3d U.S. Cav. (Canada).
KING, Hugh, Ordinary Seaman, USN (Ireland).
KING, John, Chief Watertender, USN (Ireland).
KLEIN, Robert, Chief Carpenter's Mate, USN (Germany).
KLINE, Harry, Pvt., 40th N.Y. Inf. (Germany).
KLOTH, Charles H., Pvt., Ill. Light Arty. (Europe).
KNAAK, Albert, Pvt., 8th U.S. Cav. (Switzerland).
KOCAK, Matej, Sgt., USMC (Austria).
KOELPIN, William, Sgt., 5th U.S. Inf. (Prussia).
KOELSCH, John K., Lt. (jg.), USN (England).
KRAMER, Franz, Seaman, USN (Germany).
KRAUSE, Ernest, Coxs., USN (Germany).
KREHER, Wendelin, 1st Sgt., 5th U.S. Inf. (Prussia).
KUCHNEISTER, Hermann William, Pvt., USMC (Germany).
KYLE, Patrick J., Landsman, USN (Ireland).
LABILL, Joseph S., Pvt., 6th Mo. Inf. (France).
LAFFEY, Bartlett, Seaman, USN (Ireland).
LANGBEIN, J. C. Julius, Musician, 9th N.Y. Inf. (Germany).
LARKIN, David, Farrier, 4th U.S. Cav. (Ireland).
LATHAM, John Cridland, Sgt., U.S. Army (England).
LAVERTY, John, FM1c, USN (Ireland).
LAWRENCE, James, Pvt., 8th U.S. Cav. (Scotland).
LEAHY, Cornelius J., Pvt., 36th Inf. U.S., Vol. (Ireland).
LEJEUNE, Emile, Seaman, USN (France).
LEMON, Peter C., Sgt., USMC (Canada).
LENIHAN, James, Pvt., 5th U.S. Cav. (Ireland).
LEONARD, Patrick, Cpl., 23d U.S. Inf. (Ireland).
LEONARD, Patrick, Sgt., 2d U.S. Cav. (Ireland).
LESLIE, Frank, Pvt., 4th N.Y. Cav. (England).
LITTLE, Thomas, Bugler, 8th U.S. Cav. (West Indies).
LLOYD, Benjamin, Coal Heaver, USN (England).
LOGAN, Hugh, Captain of Afterguard, USN (Ireland).
LOMAN, Berger, Pvt., U.S. Army (Norway).
LONERGAN, John, Capt., 13th Vt. Inf. (Ireland).
LORD, William, Musician, 40th Mass. Inf. (England).
LOW, George, Seaman, USN (Canada).
LOYD, George, Sgt., 7th U.S. Cav. (Ireland).
LOZADA, Carlos James, Pfc., U.S. Inf. (Puerto Rico).
LUDGATE, William, Capt., 59th N.Y. Veteran Inf. (England).
LUDWIG, Carl, Pvt., 34th N.Y. Btry. (France).
LUKES, William F., Landsman, USN (Bohemia).
LUTY, Gotlieb, Cpl., 74th N.Y. Inf. (Switzerland).
MacGILLIVARY, Charles A., Sgt., 44th Inf. Div. (Canada).
MACHON, James, Boy, USN (England).

—FOREIGN BORN MEDAL OF HONOR RECIPIENTS—
Continued

MACK, Alexander, Captain of Top, USN (Holland).
MADDEN, Michael, Pvt., 42d N.Y. Inf. (Ireland).
MADDEN, William, Coal Heaver, USN (England).
MADDIN, Edward, Ordinary Seaman, USN (Canada).
MAHERS, Herbert, Pvt., 8th U.S. Cav. (Canada).
MAHONEY, Gregory, Pvt., 4th U.S. Cav. (Wales).
MANDY, Harry J., 1st Sgt., 4th N.Y. Cav. (England).
MANGAM, Richard C., Pvt., 148th N.Y. Inf. (Ireland).
MARTIN, Edward S., QM, USN (Ireland).
MARTIN, George, Sgt., 6th U.S. Cav. (Germany).
MARTIN, James, Sgt., USMC (Ireland)
MARTIN, Patrick, Sgt., 5th U.S. Cav. (Ireland).
MARTIN, William, Seaman, USN (Ireland).
MARTIN, William, BM, USN (Prussia).
MATHEWS, William H., 1st Sgt., 2d Md. Vet. Inf. (England).
MATHIES, Archibald, Sgt., USAAC (Scotland).
MATTHEWS, Joseph, Captain of Top, USN (Malta).
MAXWELL, John, FM2c, USN (Ireland).
MAY, John, Sgt., 6th U.S. Cav. (Germany).
McADAMS, Peter, Cpl., 98th Pa. Inf. (Ireland).
McALLISTER, Samuel, Ordinary Seaman, USN (Ireland).
McANALLY, Charles, Lt., 69th Pa. Inf. (Ireland).
McCABE, William, Pvt., 4th U.S. Cav. (Ireland).
McCANN, Bernard, Pvt., 22d U.S. Inf. (Ireland).
McCARREN, Bernard, Pvt., 1st Del. Inf. (Ireland).
McCARTHY, Michael, 1st Sgt., 1st U.S. Cav. (Canada).
McCORMICK, Michael, BM, USN (Ireland).
McDONALD, James, Cpl., 8th U.S. Cav. (Scotland).
McDONALD, James Harper, Chief Metalsmith, USN (Scotland).
McDONALD, John, BM, USN (Scotland).
McENROE, Patrick H., Sgt., 6th N.Y. Cav. (Ireland).
McGANN, Michael A., 1st Sgt., 3d U.S. Cav. (Ireland).
McGOUGH, Owen, Cpl., 5th U.S. Arty. (Ireland).
McGOWAN, John, QM, USN (Ireland).
McGRAW, Thomas, Sgt., 23d Ill. Inf. (Ireland).
McGUIRE, Patrick, Pvt., Ill. Light Arty. (Ireland).
McHALE, Alexander, U., Cpl., 26th Mich. Inf. (Ireland).
McINTOSH, James, Captain of Top, USN (Canada).
McKEE, George, Color Sgt., 89th N.Y. Inf. (Ireland).
McKEEVER, Michael, Pvt., 5th Pa. Cav. (Ireland).
McKENZIE, Alexander, BM, USN (Scotland).
McLEOD, James, Captain of Foretop, USN (Scotland).
McLOUGHLIN, Michael, Sgt., 5th U.S. Inf. (Ireland).
McMAHON, Martin T., Capt., U.S. Vol. (Canada).
McNALLY, James, 1st Sgt., 8th U.S. Cav. (Ireland).
McNAMARA, Michael, Pvt., USMC (Ireland).
McNAMARA, William, 1st Sgt., 4th U.S. Cav. (Ireland).
McPHELAN, Robert, Sgt., 5th U.S. Inf. (Ireland).
McVEANE, John P., Cpl., 49th N.Y. Inf. (Canada).
MEAGHER, Thomas, 1st Sgt., 158th N.Y. Inf. (Scotland).
MERTON, James F., Landsman, USN (England).
MESTROVITCH, James I., Sgt., Company C, 111th Inf. (Montenegro).
MEYER, William, CM, USN (Germany).
MILLER, Andrew, Sgt., USMC (Germany).
MILLER, Harry Herbert, Seaman, USN (Canada).
MILLER, Henry A., Capt., 8th Ill. Inf. (Germany).
MILLER, James, QM, USN (Denmark).
MILLER, John, Cpl., 8th Ohio Inf. (Germany).
MILLER, John, Pvt., 8th N.Y. Cav. (Germany).
MILLER, Willard, Seaman, USN (Canada).
MINDIL, George W., Capt., 61st Pa. Inf. (Germany).
MINUE, Nicholas, Pvt., 1st Armd. Div. (Poland).
MITCHELL, John, 1st Sgt., 5th U.S. Inf. (Ireland).
MITCHELL, John J., Cpl., 8th U.S. Cav. (Ireland).

MOLLOY, Hugh, Ord. Seaman, USN (Ireland).
MONAGHAN, Patrick, Cpl., 48th Pa. Inf. (Ireland).
MONSSEN, Mons, Chief GM, USN (Norway).
MONTAGUE, Daniel, Chief Master-at-Arms, USN (Ireland).
MONTGOMERY, Robert William, Captain of Afterguard, USN (Ireland).
MOORE, Charles, Landsman, USN (Ireland).
MOORE, Charles, Seaman, USN (England).
MOORE, Philip, Seaman, USN (Canada).
MORAN, John, Pvt., 8th U.S. Cav. (Ireland).
MORGAN, George H., 2d Lt., 3d U.S. Cav. (Canada).
MORIARTY, John, Sgt., 8th U.S. Cav. (England).
MORIN, William H., BM2c, USN (England).
MORRIS, James L., 1st Sgt., 8th U.S. Cav. (Ireland).
MORRISON, John G., Coxswain, USN (Ireland).
MORSE, Charles E., Sgt., 62d N.Y. Inf. (France).
MORSE, William, Seaman, USN (Germany).
MORTON, Charles W., BM, USN (Ireland).
MOTT, John, Sgt., 3d U.S. Cav. (Scotland).
MOYLAN, Myles, Capt., 7th U.S. Cav. (Ireland).
MULHOLLAND, St. Clair A., Maj., 116th Pa. Inf. (Ireland).
MULLER, Frederick, Mate, USN (Denmark).
MUNROE, Douglas A., Signalman 1c, USCG (Canada).
MURPHY, Charles J., 1st Lt., 38th N.Y. Inf. (England).
MURPHY, Dennis J. F., Sgt., 14th Wis. Inf. (Ireland).
MURPHY, Edward, Pvt., 1st U.S. Cav. (Ireland).
MURPHY, James T., Pvt., 1st Conn. Arty. (Canada).
MURPHY, Jeremiah, Pvt., 3d U.S. Cav. (Ireland).
MURPHY, John Edward, Coxs., USN (Ireland).
MURPHY, John P., Pvt., 5th Ohio Inf. (Ireland).
MURPHY, Michael C., Lt. Col., 170th N.Y. Inf. (Ireland).
MURPHY, Patrick, BM, USN (Ireland)
MURPHY, Philip, Cpl., 8th U.S. Cav. (Ireland).
MURPHY, Thomas, Cpl., 8th U.S. Cav. (Ireland).
MURPHY, Thomas C., Cpl., 31st Ill. Inf. (Ireland).
MURPHY, Thomas J., 1st Sgt., 146th N.Y. Inf. (Ireland).
MURRAY, Thomas, Sgt., 7th U.S. Cav. (Ireland).
MYERS, Fred, Sgt., 6th U.S. Cav. (Germany).
NEDER, Adam, Pvt., 7th U.S. Cav. (Germany).
NEIL, John, QG, USN (Canada).
NELSON, Lauritz, Sailmaker's Mater, USN (Norway).
NEWMAN, Henry, 1st Sgt., 5th U.S. Cav. (Germany).
NIBBE, John H., QM, USN (Germany).
NIHILL, John, Pvt., 5th U.S. Cav. (Ireland).
NISPEROS, Jose B., Pvt., Philippine Scouts (Philippine Islands).
NOIL, Joseph B., Seaman, USN (Canada).
NOLAN, John J., Sgt., 8th N.H. Inf. (Ireland).
NOLAN, Richard J., Farrier, 7th U.S. Cav. (Ireland).
NOLL, Conrad, Sgt., 20th Mich. Inf. (Germany).
NORDSTROM, Isidor, Chief BM, USN (Sweden).
NORRIS, J. W., Landsman, USN (England).
NUGENT, Christopher, Orderly Sgt., USMC (Ireland).
OAKLEY, William, GM2c, USN (England).
O'BEIRNE, James R., Capt., 37th N.Y. Inf. (Ireland).
O'BRIEN, Peter, Pvt., 1st N.Y. Cav. (Lincoln) (Ireland).
O'CONNELL, Thomas, Coal Heaver, USN (Ireland).
O'CONNOR, Albert, Sgt., 7th Wis. Inf. (Canada).
O'CONNOR, Timothy, Pvt., 1st U.S. Cav. (Ireland).
O'DEA, John, Pvt., 8th Mo. Inf. (Ireland).
O'DONNELL, Menomen, 1st Lt., 11 Mo. Inf. (Ireland).
OHMSEN, August, MA, USN (Germany).
OLSEN, Anton, Ordinary Seaman, USN (Norway).
O'NEAL, John, BM, USN (Ireland).
O'NEILL, Stephen, Cpl., 7th U.S. Inf. (Canada).
ORBANSKY, David, Pvt., 58th Ohio Inf. (Prussia).

ORR, Moses, Pvt., 1st U.S. Cav. (Ireland).
ORTEGA, John, Seaman, USN (Spain).
OSEPINS, Christian, Seaman, USN (Holland).
OSS, Albert, Pvt., 11th N.J. Inf. (Belgium).
O'SULLIVAN, John, Pvt., 4th U.S. Cav. (Ireland).
PAGE, John U. D., Lt. Col., X Corps Arty. (Philippine Islands).
PARKER, Thomas, Cpl., 2d R.I. Inf. (England).
PARNELL, William R., 1st Lt., 1st U.S. Cav. (Ireland).
PAYNE, Isaac, Trumpeter, Indian Scouts (Mexico).
PELHAM, William, Landsman, USN (Canada).
PENGALLY, Edward, Pvt., 8th U.S. Cav. (England).
PESCH, Joseph, Pvt., 1st Mo. Light Arty. (Germany).
PETERS, Alexander, BM1c, USN (Russia).
PETERSEN, Carl Emil, CMM, USN (Germany).
PETERSON, Alfred, Seaman, USN (Sweden).
PETTY, Philip, Sgt., 136th Pa. Inf. (England).
PHILIPSEN, Wilhelm, O., Blacksmith, 5th U.S. Cav. (Germany).
PHISTERER, Frederick, 1st Lt., 18th U.S. Inf. (Germany).
PHINNEY, William, BM, USN (Norway).
PICKLE, Alonzo H., Sgt., 1st Minn. Inf. (Canada).
PILE, Richard, Ordinary Seaman, USN (West Indies).
PLATT, George C., Pvt., 6th U.S. Cav. (Ireland).
PLATTEN, Frederick, Sgt., 6th U.S. Cav. (Ireland).
PLOWMAN, George H., Sgt. Maj., 3d Md. Inf. (England).
PLUNKETT, Thomas, Sgt., 21st Mass. Inf. (Ireland).
POWELL, William H., Maj., 2d W. Va. Cav. (Wales).
POWERS, Wesley J., Cpl., 147th Ill. Inf. (Canada).
PRANCE, George, Captain of Maintop, USN (France).
PRENDERGAST, Thomas Francis, Cpl., USMC (Ireland).
PRESTON, John, Landsman, USN (Ireland).
PYM, James, Pvt., 7th U.S. Cav. (England).
PYNE, George, Seaman, USN (England).
QUINLAN, James, Maj., 88th N.Y. Inf. (Ireland).
RABEL, Laszlo, S/Sgt., 173 ABN Bgde. (Hungary).
RAERICK, John, Pvt., 8th U.S. Cav. (Germany).
RAFFERTY, Peter, Pvt., 69th N.Y. Inf. (Ireland).
RAGNAR, Theodore, 1st Sgt., 7th U.S. Cav. (Sweden).
RANNAHAN, John, Cpl., USMC (Ireland).
READ, Charles A., Coxs., USN (Sweden).
REED, James C., Pvt., 8th U.S. Cav. (Ireland).
REGAN, Patrick, Ordinary Seaman, USN (Ireland).
REID, Patrick, Chief Watertender, USN (Ireland).
REID, Robert, Pvt., 48th Pa. Inf. (Scotland).
REYNOLDS, George, Pvt., 9th N.Y. Cav. (Ireland).
RICH, Carlos H., 1st Sgt., 4th Vt. Inf. (Canada).
RICE, Charles, Coal Heaver, USN (Russia).
RILEY, Thomas, Pvt., 1st La. Cav. (Ireland).
ROANTREE, James S., Sgt., USMC (Ireland).
ROBERTS, James, Seaman, USN (England).
ROBINSON, Alexander, BM1c, USN (England).
ROBINSON, Charles, BM, USN (Scotland).
ROBINSON, John, Captain of the Hold, USN (Cuba).
ROBINSON, John H., Pvt., 19th Mass. Inf. (Ireland).
ROBINSON, Joseph, 1st Sgt., 3d U.S. Cav. (Ireland).
ROBINSON, Thomas, Captain of Afterguard, USN (Norway).
ROBINSON, Thomas, Pvt., 81st Pa. Inf. (Ireland).
ROCHE, David, 1st Sgt., 5th U.S. Inf. (Ireland).
ROCK, Frederick, Pvt., 37th Ohio Inf. (Germany).
RODENBURG, Henry, Pvt., 5th U.S. Inf. (Germany).
ROGAN, Patrick, Sgt., 7th U.S. Inf. (Ireland).
ROSSBACH, Valentine, Sgt., 34th N.Y. Btry. (Germany).
ROTH, Peter, Pvt., 6th U.S. Cav. (Germany).
ROY, Stanislaus, Sgt., 7th U.S. Cav. (France).
RUBIO, Euripides, Capt., U.S. Inf. (Puerto Rico).

—FOREIGN BORN MEDAL OF HONOR RECIPIENTS—
Continued

RUSSELL, Henry P., Landsman, USN (Canada).
RYAN, David, Pvt., 5th U.S. Inf. (Ireland).
RYAN, Dennis, 1st Sgt., 6th U.S. Cav. (Ireland).
RYAN, Peter J., Pvt., 11th Ind. Inf. (Ireland).
SANTIAGO-COLON, Hector, Spec. 4, U.S. Cav. (Puerto Rico).
SCANLAN, Patrick, Pvt., 4th Mass. Cav. (Ireland).
SCHEIBNER, Martin E., Pvt., 90th Pa. Inf. (Russia).
SCHILLER, John, Pvt., 158th N.Y. Inf. (Germany).
SCHLACHTER, Philipp, Pvt., 73d N.Y. Inf. (Germany).
SCHMAL, George W., Blacksmith, 24th N.Y. Cav. (Germany).
SCHMAUCH, Andrew, Pvt., 30th Ohio Inf. (Germany).
SCHMIDT, Conrad, 1st Sgt., 2d U.S. Cav. (Germany).
SCHNITZER, John, Wagoner, 4th U.S. Cav. (Germany).
SCHORN, Charles, Chief Bugler, 1st W. VA. Cav. (Germany).
SCHOU, Julius, Cpl., 22d U.S. Inf. (Denmark).
SCHROETER, Charles, Pvt., 8th U.S. Cav. (Germany).
SCHUBERT, Martin, Pvt., 26th N.Y. Inf. (Germany).
SCHUTT, George, Coxs., USN (Ireland).
SCHWAN, Theodore, 1st Lt., 10th U.S. Inf. (Germany).
SCHWENK, Martin, Sgt., 6th U.S. Cav. (Germany).
SCOTT, Alexander, Cpl., 10th Vt. Inf. (Canada).
SEACH, William, Ordinary Seaman, USN (England).
SEITZINGER, James M., Pvt., 116th Pa. Inf. (Germany).
SEWELL, William, J., Col., 5th N.J. Inf. (Ireland).
SHAFFER, William, Pvt., 8th U.S. Cav. (Germany).
SHAMBAUGH, Charles, Cpl., 11th Pa. Res. (Prussia).
SHANAHAN, Patrick, Chief BM, USN (Ireland).
SHAPLAND, John, Pvt., 104th Ill. Inf. (England).
SHARP, Hendrick, Seaman, USN (Spain).
SHIELDS, Bernard, Pvt., 2d W. Va. Cav. (Ireland).
SHILLING, John, 1st Sgt., 3d Del. Inf. (England).
SHIVERS, John, Pvt., USMC (Canada).
SHUBERT, Frank, Sgt. 43d N.Y. Inf. (Germany).
SIMONS, Charles J., Sgt., 9th N.H. Inf. (India).
SIMPSON, Henry, FM1c, USN (England).
SIVEL, Henry, 1st Sgt., 2d Md. Vet. Inf. (England).
SLADEN, Joseph A., Pvt., 33d Mass. Inf. (England).
SLETTELAND, Thomas, Pvt., 1st N. Dak. Inf. (Norway).
SMITH, Henry I., 1st Lt., 7th Iowa Inf. (England).
SMITH, James, Seaman, USN (Sandwich Islands).
SMITH, John, Seaman, USN (Bermuda).
SMITH, Oloff, Coxs., USN (Sweden).
SMITH, Thomas, Seaman, USN (England).
SMITH, Thomas, Seaman USN (Ireland).
SMITH, Thomas J., Pvt., 1st U.S. Cav. (England).
SMITH, Wilhelm, GM1c, USN (Germany).
SMITH, William, QM, USN (Ireland).
SNEDDEN, James, Musician, 54th Pa. Inf. (Scotland).
SPICER, William, GM1c, USN (England).
SPILLANE, Timothy, Pvt., 16th Pa. Cav. (Ireland).
STACEY, Charles, Pvt., 55th Ohio Inf. (England).
STAHEL, Julius, Maj. Gen., U.S. Vol. (Hungary).
STANTON, Thomas, Chief MM, USN (Ireland).
STAUFFER, Rudolph, 1st Sgt., 5th U.S. Cav. (Switzerland).
STEINER, Christian, Saddler, 8th U.S. Cav. (Germany).
STEWART, George E., 2d Lt., 19th U.S. Inf. (New South Wales).
STEWART, Joseph, Pvt., 1st Md. Inf. (Ireland).
STEWART, Peter, Gunnery Sgt., USMC (Scotland).
STICKOFFER, Julius H., Saddler, 8th U.S. Cav. (Switzerland).
STOCKMAN, George H., 1st Lt., 6th Mo. Inf. (Germany).
STOKES, George, Pvt., 122d Ill. Inf. (England).
STOLTENBERG, Andrew V., GM2c, USN (Norway).
STRAUB, Paul F., Surgeon, 36th Inf. (Germany).
STREILE, Christian, Pvt., 1st N.J. Cav. (Germany).

SULLIVAN, Edward, Pvt., USMC (Ireland).
SULLIVAN, Thomas, Pvt., 7th U.S. Cav. (Ireland).
SULLIVAN, Timothy, Coxs., USN (Ireland).
SUMMERS, Robert, Chief QM, USN (Prussia).
SUMNER, James, Pvt., 1st U.S. Cav. (England).
SUNDQUIST, Axel, Chief CM, USN (Russia).
SUNDQUIST, Gustav A., Ordinary Seaman, USN (Sweden).
SWANSON, John, Seaman, USN (Sweden).
SWEENEY, James, Pvt., 1st Vt. Cav. (England).
SWEENEY, Robert, Ordinary Seaman, USN (Canada).
SWEGHEIMER, Jacob, Pvt., 54th Ohio Inf. (Germany).
TALLENTINE, James, QG, USN (England).
TAYLOR, Joseph, Pvt., 7th R.I. Inf. (England).
TEYTAND, August P., QM3c, USN (West Indies).
THACKRAH, Benjamin, Pvt., 115th N.Y. Inf. (Scotland).
THAYER, James, Ship's Cpl., USN (Ireland).
THIELBERG, Henry, Seaman, USN (Germany).
THOMASS, Karl, Cox., USN (Germany).
THOMPSON, Henry A., Pvt., USMC (England).
THOMPSON, J. (James) Harry, Surg., U.S. Vol. (England).
THOMPSON, John, Cpl., 1st Md. Inf. (Denmark).
THOMPSON, John, Sgt., 1st U.S. Cav. (Scotland).
THOMPSON, Joseph H., Maj., U.S. Army (Ireland).
THOMPSON, Peter, Pvt., 7th U.S. Cav. (Scotland).
THORDSEN, William George, Coxs., USN (Germany).
THORNTON, Michael, Seaman, USN (Ireland).
TOBIN, John M., 1st Lt. and Adj., 9th Mass. Inf. (Ireland).
TOBIN, Paul, Landsman, USN (France).
TOMICH, Peter, Chief Watertender, USN (Austria).
TOOMER, William, Sgt., 127th Ill. Inf. (Ireland).
TORGERSON, Martin T., GM3c, USN (Norway).
TORGLER, Ernst, Sgt., 37th Ohio Inf. (Germany).
TRACY, John, Pvt., 8th U.S. Cav. (Ireland).
TRAUTMAN, Jacob, 1st Sgt., 7th U.S. Cav. (Germany).
TRINIDAD, Telesforo, FM2c, USN (Philippine Islands).
TURVELIN, Alexander, Seaman, USN (Russia).
TYRRELL, George William, Cpl., 5th Ohio Inf. (Ireland).
UHRL, George, Sgt., 5th U.S. Arty. (Germany).
URELL, M. Emmet, Pvt., 82d N.Y. Inf. (Ireland).
VADAS, Albert, Seaman, USN (Austria-Hungary).
VALE, John, Pvt., 2d Minn. Inf. (England).
VALENTE, Michael, Pvt., U.S. Army (Italy).
VAN IERSEL, Ludovicus M.M., Sgt., U.S. Army (Holland).
VEUVE, Ernest, Farrier, 4th U.S. Cav. (Switzerland).
VIFQUAIN, Victor, Lt. Col., 97th Ill. Inf. (Belgium).
VOIT, Otto, Saddler, 7th U.S. Cav. (Germany).
VON MEDEM, Rudolph, Sgt., 5th U.S. Cav. (Germany).
VON SCHLICK, Robert H., Pvt., 9th U.S. Inf. (Germany).
VON VEGESACK, Ernest, Major aide-de-camp, U.S. Vol. (Sweden).
WAALER, Reidar, Sgt., U.S. Army (Norway).
WAGG, Maurice, Cox., USN (England).
WALKER, Edward Alexander, Sgt., USMC (Scotland).
WALKER, John, Pvt., 8th U.S. Cav. (France).
WALLACE, William, Sgt., 5th U.S. Inf. (Ireland).
WALSH, John, Cpl., 5th N.Y. Cav. (Ireland).
WAMBSGAN, Martin, Pvt., 90th N.Y. Inf. (Germany).
WARD, Charles H., Pvt., 1st U.S. Cav. (England).
WARREN, David, Coxs., USN (Scotland).
WEINERT, Paul H., Cpl., 1st U.S. Arty. (Germany).
WEISSEL, Adam, SC, USN (Germany).
WELCH, Richard, Cpl., 37th Mass. Inf. (Ireland).
WELLS, Thomas M., Chief Bugler, 6th N.Y. Cav. (Ireland).
WELLS, William, QM, USN (Germany).
WELSH, Edward, Pvt., 54th Ohio Inf. (Ireland).

WELSH, James, Pvt. 4th R.I. Inf. (Ireland).
WENDE, Bruno, Pvt., 17th U.S. Inf. (Germany).
WESTA, Karl, Chief MM, USN (Norway).
WESTERHOLD, William, Sgt., 52d N.Y. Inf. (Prussia).
WESTERMARK, Axel, Seaman, USN (Finland).
WHITE, Adam, Cpl., 11th W. Va. Inf. (Switzerland).
WHITE, Patrick H., Capt., Chicago Mercantile Btry., Ill. Light Arty. (Ireland).
WIDMER, Jacob, 1st Sgt., 5th U.S. Cav. (Germany).
WILKE, Julius A. R., BM1c, USN (Germany).
WILKENS, Henry, 1st Sgt., 2d U.S. Cav. (Germany).
WILLIAMS, Antonio, Seaman, USN (Malta).
WILLIAMS, Augustus, Seaman, USN (Norway).
WILLIAMS, Frank, Seaman, USN (Germany).
WILLIAMS, George C., Qm. Sgt., 14th U.S. Inf. (England).
WILLIAMS, Henry, CM, USN (Canada).
WILLIAMS, Louis, Captain of Hold, USN (Norway).
WILLIAMS, Peter, Seaman, USN (Norway).
WILLIAMS, William, Landsman, USN (Ireland).
WILLIS, Richard, Coxs., USN (England).
WILSON, August, BM, USN (Germany).
WILSON, Christopher W., Pvt., 73d N.Y. Inf. (Ireland).
WILSON, John, Sgt., 1st N.J. Cav. (England).
WINDOLPH, Charles, Pvt., 7th U.S. Cav. (Germany).
WINTERBOTTOM, William, Sgt., 6th U.S. Cav. (England).
WOOD, Mark, Pvt., 21st Ohio Inf. (England).
WOON, John, BM, USN (England).
WORTMAN, George G., Sgt., 8th U.S. Cav. (Moncton, New Brunswick).
WRIGHT, Robert, Pvt., 14th U.S. Inf. (Ireland).
WRIGHT, William, Yeoman, USN (England).
YOUNG, Benjamin F., Cpl., 1st Mich. Sharpshooters (Canada).
YOUNKER, John L., Pvt., 12th U.S. Inf. (Germany).
ZIEGNER, Hermann, Pvt., 7th U.S. Cav. (Germany).

ORDERING INFORMATION

If you are using a borrowed copy of *Spirit of America,* and wish to have a copy of your own, send $16.95 per copy direct to:

ETC Publications
Department Z
Palm Springs
California 92263-1608

Your copy will be promptly sent. California residents please add 6% sales tax.